TURIM

Studies in
Jewish History and Literature

Presented to
DR. BERNARD LANDER

Volume One

TURIM

Studies in
Jewish History and Literature

Presented to
DR. BERNARD LANDER

Volume One

Edited by
Michael A. Shmidman

Touro College Press
New York
2007

ISBN-13: 978-0-88125-959-9
ISBN-10: 0-88125-959-4

Distributed by
KTAV Publishing House, Inc.
930 Newark Avenue
Jersey City, NJ 07306
bernie@ktav.com
www.ktav.com

Typeset Design and Layout by:
HaDaF Typesetting
HaDaF.Dovid@Gmail.com

CONTENTS

CONTRIBUTORS

JUDITH BLEICH
Professor of Judaic Studies, Touro Graduate School of Jewish Studies
and Lander College for Women

NACHUM M. BRONZNICK
Professor of Hebraic Studies, Emeritus, Rutgers University

LEON A. FELDMAN
Professor of Jewish History, Touro Graduate School of Jewish Studies
Professor of Hebraic Studies, Emeritus, Rutgers University

SAMUEL N. HOENIG
Associate Professor of Judaic Studies, Touro Graduate School of Jewish Studies
and Lander College for Women

NAHEM ILAN
Senior Lecturer in Jewish History and Literature, Lander Institute, Jerusalem

EPHRAIM KANARFOGEL
E. Billi Ivry Professor of Jewish History, Yeshiva University

DAVID KRANZLER
Former Professor of Library Science, City University of New York

MONTY NOAM PENKOWER
Senior Professor of Modern Jewish History, Lander Institute, Jerusalem

BEZALEL SAFRAN
Formerly Associate Professor of Jewish Studies, Harvard University
and Visiting Professor of Jewish Philosophy,
Bernard Revel Graduate School, Yeshiva University

LAWRENCE H. SCHIFFMAN
Ethel and Irvin Engel Professor of Hebrew and Judaic Studies and Chair,
Skirball Department of Hebrew and Judaic Studies, New York University

MICHAEL A. SHMIDMAN
Dean and Victor J. Selmanowitz Professor of Jewish History,
Touro Graduate School of Jewish Studies

MOSHE SOKOL
Dean, Lander College for Men
Professor of Philosophy, Touro Graduate School of Jewish Studies
and Lander College for Men

RONNIE WARBURG
Research Scholar, Institute of Jewish Law, Boston University School of Law
Editor, Jewish Law Annual

PREFACE

"Rabbi Yehudah stated in the name of Rav: 'Adam, the first man, [originally] extended from one end of the world to the other.'" This talmudic statement (*Hagigah* 12a) was interpreted allegorically by some medieval Jewish philosophic commentators, as a concrete expression of abstract ideas concerning the unique nature of the human intellect. Whereas any other physical faculty is able to perform only a particular action, not a universal one – e.g., the sense of sight sees only a particular object in a particular place, at a specific time and in specific circumstances – the intellect is capable of cognizing universals; it apprehends the essence of existing phenomena. When, for instance, the intellect discerns that fire burns, it can accurately evaluate the nature of fire both in one specific place and anywhere in the physical world. Since, therefore, the man who exercises the intellect implanted within him by his Creator is capable of comprehending the essence of different created phenomena wherever they exist, he may be said to "extend from one end of the world to the other."

Rabbi Dr. Bernard Lander, to whom the volumes of this Festschrift are admiringly and affectionately presented, is the living embodiment of a literal interpretation of the above passage. As a visionary leader in the field of higher education, Dr. Lander's reach is uniquely and dazzlingly global; his pioneering educational programs literally extend throughout the world.

In 1970, at the age of fifty-five and at the peak of an already illustrious career in the rabbinate, academia and government service, Dr. Lander began to implement his grand vision of a national and international Jewish university. In a venture viewed as quixotic by many, he founded Touro College. Touro was chartered by the State of New York in June of 1970 and formally enrolled its first class of thirty-five freshmen in September of 1971. The phenomenal growth of the College to its current enrollment of more than 23,000 students in campuses in New York, California, Florida, Nevada, Jerusalem, Berlin and Moscow is a story that no doubt will be chronicled by scholars of Jewish history and the history of higher education for generations to come.

The central focus of that story is one individual, Dr. Bernard Lander, president of Touro College for the past thirty-six years and one of the longest-serving college presidents in the United States. His irrepressible creative genius continues to animate all of Touro's programs; his wisdom and experience guide and inspire Touro's faculty and staff; his personal warmth infuses his institutions with a keen sense of concern and compassion for all members of the Touro family; and his love of and commitment to Torah and scholarship mold the institution's mission.

This volume is the first of two volumes that together comprise this Festschrift. The second volume, expected to appear in the fall of 2007, will similarly include essays in Jewish history and literature by distinguished scholars from both Touro College and other academic institutions.

I take this opportunity to thank the contributors to these volumes for their masterful scholarship and gracious cooperation. I also acknowledge with gratitude: my colleagues, professors Leon Feldman, Carmi Horowitz and Moshe Sherman for their invaluable assistance at various stages of the planning and production of this Festschrift; my assistant, Suzannah Gordon, for her characteristically dedicated and tireless efforts;

David Shabtai and Meira Mintz for skillful editorial work on various articles included in these volumes; and, especially, Dovid Feinberg, not only for his superb typesetting of the entire manuscript, but also for his perceptive editorial observations and his willingness to meet at literally any hour.

Although a measure of uniformity of style and format was imposed upon the essays of this volume, stylistic variation was granted in some areas – notably in transliteration – as long as each essay retained internal consistency.

מוגש בברכה ובהוקרה

27 Tevet 5767   Michael A. Shmidman
January 17, 2007   New York City

DR. BERNARD LANDER

Dr. Bernard Lander, founder and president of Touro College, is a social scientist and educator, a preeminent leader in the Jewish community and a pioneer in Jewish and general higher education. As associate director of former New York City Mayor Fiorello LaGuardia's Committee on Unity, a precursor to the city's first Commission on Human Rights, Dr. Lander promoted key fair employment legislation and attacked discriminatory quotas in higher education. An ordained rabbi, he holds a doctorate in sociology from Columbia University.

Dr. Lander's record of achievement in building and creating new educational institutions is unparalleled. In 1943, he founded the Queens Jewish Center and two years later co-founded a major day school in Queens, Yeshiva Dov Revel. In 1955 he was a co-founder of Bar-Ilan University. Prior to establishing Touro College in 1971, he served as a professor of sociology for over two decades at City University of New York and at Yeshiva University, where he established the university's graduate schools of education, psychology and social work and served as dean of its Bernard Revel Graduate School. Today, Touro College/Touro University is a multi-campus, international institution with more than 23,000 students at campus locations in New York, California, Florida, Nevada, Israel, Russia and Germany.

Dr. Lander has served as a consultant to three United States Presidents and was part of the seven-member commission that established the historic "War on Poverty" program in the U.S. He served as a consultant to the White House Conference on Children and Youth; on an advisory council on public assistance established by Congress; and was a member of the President's Advisory Committee on Juvenile Delinquency and Youth Crime under the Johnson and Kennedy administrations. For eight years he served as a senior director of a national study for the University of Notre Dame of South Bend, Indiana on the problems of youth. He is the author of "Towards an Understanding of Juvenile Delinquency," published by Columbia University Press, and numerous articles in the field of sociology. He also served as a consultant to the Maryland State Commission on Juvenile Delinquency. Dr. Lander has been honored by the Council of New York State College Presidents for his lifetime contributions to higher education. A former Rabbi of Beth Jacob Congregation of Baltimore, Dr. Lander is also an Honorary Vice President of the Union of Orthodox Jewish Congregations of America.

Milestones in the History of Touro College

1970 Touro College is formally chartered by the State of New York.

1971 Touro College opens in September with a freshman class of 35 men.

1972 Division of Health Sciences is established, offering studies leading to a B.S. in health sciences and qualifying graduates as physician assistants.

1974 Women's division is established as part of the College of Liberal Arts and Sciences.

School of General Studies is established to serve the city's diverse ethnic communities.

1975 First annual commencement exercises host 59 degree candidates.

Total College enrollment reaches 1,000.

1976 Touro College receives accreditation from the Middle States Association of Colleges and Schools.

Physician assistant program is accredited by the American Medical Association.

1977 Flatbush men's division is established to serve the educational needs and career aspirations of full-time yeshiva students.

1978 Touro Israel Option organized to enable undergraduates to complete a year of intensive Judaic studies.

1979 Flatbush women's division opens in Brooklyn, N.Y.

1980 Touro College School of Law – Jacob D. Fuchsberg Law Center – admits its first class.

1981 The Graduate School of Jewish Studies admits its first class.

1982 New center opens in Midwood section of Brooklyn to accommodate growth of Flatbush division.

Jacob D. Fuchsberg Law Center relocates to Huntington, N.Y.

1983 Jacob D. Fuchsberg Law Center graduates its first class.

The Graduate School of Jewish Studies awards its first master's degrees.

The Center for Biomedical Education opens, initiating a bi-national cooperative effort between Touro College and the Technion medical school in Israel, leading to M.S.-M.D. degrees.

1984 Yeshivas Ohr HaChaim, a full-time yeshiva affiliate, opens in Kew Gardens Hills, N.Y.

Graduate program in physical therapy is established.

1985 Division of New Americans, serving immigrants from the Soviet Union, enrolls its first class. A decade later, it would become the School of Career and Applied Studies.

1986 The Graduate School of Jewish Studies establishes branch campus in Jerusalem, which in 2004 becomes Machon Lander (Lander Institute), an independent Israeli academic institution.

1988 First class of Touro College biomedical students receives their M.D. degrees from the Technion in Israel.

School for Lifelong Education opens for Chasidic and other non-traditional students.

1989 The Jacob D. Fuchsberg Law Center receives full accreditation from the American Bar Association.

1991 Touro College School of International Business Management opens its Moscow campus, the first American-sponsored business college in Russia.

Touro School of Jewish Studies opens in Moscow, enrolling some 300 students.

1992 New Manhattan women's division campus opens on Lexington Avenue.

1993 The Graduate School of Education and Psychology is organized.

1994 The new Manhattan women's division dormitory opens.

Mesivta Yesodei Yeshurun High School, an affiliate of Touro, opens in Forest Hills, N.Y.

1995 The modern Flatbush campus in the Midwood section of Brooklyn, N.Y. opens.

Touro opens a school of business, offering baccalaureate degrees, in the Talpiot section of Jerusalem.

1996 The School of Health Sciences establishes a center for M.A. studies in occupational and physical therapy in Manhattan.

Yeshivas Ohr HaChaim moves to new facilities in Kew Gardens Hills, N.Y.

1997 The College of Osteopathic Medicine (TUCOM) opens in San Francisco as the first division of Touro University California.

1998 The New York State Education Department authorizes Touro College to offer a master of science in international business finance.

1999 Touro University International, offering undergraduate and graduate degrees in business on the Internet, opens in Los Alamitos, California.

Touro establishes Machon L'Parnassa, or Institute for Professional Studies, offering undergraduate degree programs for Chasidic men and women.

2000 New Lander College for Men in Kew Gardens Hills, N.Y. admits its charter class.

Graduate program leading to a master's degree in speech language pathology is inaugurated in Flatbush.

2001 TUCOM holds its first commencement exercises for 63 doctor of osteopathic medicine degree candidates at its new campus in Vallejo, California.

2002 The master's program in speech language pathology graduates its first degree candidates.

2003 Touro College Berlin branch campus opens with a charter class of 19 students.

2004 Touro University College of Osteopathic Medicine, in Henderson, Nevada, opens as a branch of TUCOM California.

2005 Touro College Los Angeles accepts its first class of students.

Touro University Nevada's College of Health and Human Services launches three new schools, each with graduate-level offerings: a School of Nursing, the first private nursing program in Nevada; a School of Occupational Therapy (OT), the first and only OT program in Nevada; and a School of Education.

Touro College signs historic agreement with Province of Rome and Municipality of Zagarolo to open a branch campus subject to approval of American education agencies, in Italy.

Touro offers MBA and welcomes first class of MBA students.

2006 Touro College prepares to celebrate its 36th anniversary with special events and ceremonies, as the school continues to undergo significant growth.

Touro College receives unanimous preliminary approval from the New Jersey Board of Medical Examiners to initiate the process to open the state's first and only private medical school, to be known as Touro University College of Medicine. The new school will be the second Jewish-sponsored medical school in the country.

Touro College South opens in Miami Beach, Florida.

The Graduate School of Social Work is established to train clinical social work practitioners.

Touro College establishes a new Graduate School of Technology, offering a new master of science degree in Information Systems to prepare students for careers in IT leadership and management of information systems.

Lander College for Women moves into a new, ultra-modern facility in Manhattan, near Lincoln Center.

Touro's Jacob D. Fuchsberg Law Center relocates to its new campus in Central Islip, New York, adjacent to federal and state courthouses, becoming the first law school in the country to be located on a judicial "campus."

2007 Touro announces fall 2007 opening of Touro College of Osteopathic Medicine (TOUROCOM). Located in Harlem, TOUROCOM is Touro's third college of osteopathic medicine and the first such college with a special emphasis on training minority doctors.

The Circumcision Controversy in Classical Reform in Historical Context

Judith Bleich

Toward the close of the nineteenth century, a gathering of rabbinic leaders took place in the city of St. Petersburg. The primary issue on the agenda was the official stance to be taken vis-à-vis Jewish children who had not been circumcised, i.e., whether such children were to be officially registered as Jews in the communal records. The virtually unanimous response of the assembled rabbis was absolutely to forbid registration of uncircumcised boys as Jews. Clearly, their intent was to adopt this measure as a strategy designed to induce assimilated parents to acquiesce in the circumcision of their sons. The sole dissenting voice was that of R. Hayyim Soloveitchik of Brisk. R. Hayyim duly noted that an uncircumcised male is forbidden to partake either of *terumah* or of sacrificial offerings and that, if he does not undergo circumcision upon reaching the age of majority, he incurs the punishment of *karet*. He then proceeded to protest vigorously that there is no halakhic provision that would serve to support the view that an uncircumcised male be treated differently from other transgressors who are not excluded from the Jewish community.

Relating this incident, his grandson, the late Rabbi Joseph B. Soloveitchik commented that both from a pragmatic and socio-political standpoint as well as religiously, as a *hora'at sha'ah* (a temporary emergency ruling), the decision of R. Hayyim's colleagues was entirely justified. However, from the vantage point of pure Halakhah, R. Hayyim was entirely correct in his ruling; as the *Ish ha-Halakhah*, the champion of pristine halakhic purity, he was not willing to sacrifice truth even for a noble purpose.[1]

Culturally, Russian society was fifty years behind Western Europe. It took Russia fifty years to catch up to the social upheavals and assimilationist trends of the West. The problem confronting the rabbis in St. Petersburg was one with which their colleagues in Germany, France and Hungary grappled a half century earlier and which led to the eruption of one of the most searing controversies between adherents of Orthodoxy and Reform — a controversy that has been aptly described as "the classic modern instance of ritual ambivalence."[2] The ambivalences and strong emotions reflected in the controversy did not abate with the passage of time and their lingering echoes are still audible in current literature.

The Frankfurt Controversy

The controversy between exponents of Orthodoxy and Reform centered on the actual rite of circumcision. Concurrently, another debate raged primarily within the internal Orthodox community itself regarding the practice of *metzitzah* — a debate that is still very much alive and contentious to this very day.[3]

---

[1] R. Joseph B. Soloveitchik, "Ish ha-Halakhah," [Hebrew] *Talpiyot* 1 (*Nissan-Tishrei* 1944): 707.

[2] Lawrence A. Hoffman, *Covenant of Blood: Circumcision and Gender in Rabbinic Judaism* (Chicago and London: University of Chicago Press, 1996), 2.

[3] Traditionally, as explicitly recorded in the Mishnah *Shabbat* 133a, the circumcision ritual consists of three distinct acts: (1) *milah*, excision

In recent years, extensive discussions of the circumcision controversy and the numerous published rabbinic opinions it spawned have been authored by Jacob Katz (in Hebrew and translated into English)[4] and by Andreas Gotzmann (in German),[5] and for that reason only the briefest summary of the salient facts will be presented here. At the time of the controversy, the various governmental jurisdictions in Germany required every national to profess a religion. Baptism was required for Christian children; circumcision was required for Jewish males. Functionaries of the religious communities, priests, ministers and rabbis, were responsible for registration of children born to their respective communicants. The controversy erupted in 1843 in Frankfurt am Main when a member of the Frankfurt Jewish community, a banker named E. Flörsheim, declined to circumcise his son, but nevertheless presented the virtually unprecedented request that the child be registered as a Jew in the communal records.[6]

(hittukh) of the thick foreskin; (2) peri'ah, retraction and removal of the underlying mucous membrane covering the glans in order to uncover the corona; and (3) metzitzah, suction of blood from the wound and from the blood vessels flowing into the wound. In conjunction with this controversy, objections were also raised regarding the customary method of performing peri'ah with the fingernails. However, the issue of peri'ah did not engender as much furor as did the debate concerning metzitzah. Regarding peri'ah, see Moses Bunim Pirutinsky, Sefer ha-Berit (New York, 1972), 183-84, 206-13.

[4] Jacob Katz, Ha-Halakhah be-Meitzar: Mikhsholim al Derekh ha-Ortodoksiyah be-Hithavatah (Jerusalem: Magnes Press, 1992), 123-83; idem, Divine Law in Human Hands: Case Studies in Halakhic Flexibility (Jerusalem: Magnes Press, 1998), 320-402.

[5] Andreas Gotzmann, Jüdisches Recht im kulturellen Prozess: Die Wahrnehmung der Halacha im Deutschland des 19. Jahrhunderts (Tübingen: Mohr Siebeck, 1997), 251-302. See also Robert Liberles, Religious Conflict in Social Context: The Resurgence of Orthodox Judaism in Frankfurt am Main, 1838-1877 (Westport, Conn: Greenwood Press, 1985), 52-61.

[6] The exact form of the banker's surname is unclear. The Allgemeine Zeitung des Judenthums (hereafter AZdJ) 8 (1844): 405, spells the name "Floisheim." Josef Meisl, "Zur Geschichte der jüdischen Reformbewegung," Monatsschrift für Geschichte und Wissenschaft des Judentums 69 (1925):

The event occurred after the Frankfurt public health authorities had, on February 8, 1843, promulgated an ordinance requiring that circumcision performed by a *mohel* (religious functionary) must be conducted under medical supervision. The wording of the regulation, "Jewish citizens and residents, insofar as they wish to have their children circumcised" (*"Israelitische Bürger und Einwohner, insofern sie ihre Kinder beschneiden lassen wollen"*) implied that the decision to circumcise a child might be but an option to be exercised at the parents' discretion and not a necessary prerequisite for membership in the community. Despite the efforts of Rabbi Salomon Trier, the elderly rabbi of Frankfurt, to persuade the city Senate to declare that an uncircumcised child not be recognized as a Jew, the Senate refused to intervene and the ensuing internal Jewish debate developed into a heated controversy that engulfed the entire Jewish community in Germany.[7]

The issue was exacerbated because it was perceived not as a matter limited to a single rebellious individual but as part of a radical Reform agenda. Prior to this incident, a number of Jewish laymen had founded the Frankfurt Society

---

42, refers to the banker as "Flersheim." Katz, *Divine Law*, 322, employs the spelling "Flörsheim."

The press of the day intimated that Flörsheim was motivated by a desire for acceptance in non-Jewish society. An ironic Frankfurt news item reported that Flörsheim, whose request instigated the circumcision controversy, sought admission to the "Casino," a club which generally excluded Jews. A Christian banker's contemptuous response was *"Wir wollen keine Juden, keine beschnittene und keine unbeschnittene* – We want no Jews, neither circumcised ones, nor uncircumcised ones" and Flörsheim's candidacy for membership was unanimously rejected. See *AZdJ* 8 (1844): 405. Liberles, 239 n. 17, on the basis of an item in *Orient* 1 (1840): 7, reports that, in point of fact, members of the Rothschild Family who were Orthodox had been admitted to the Casino in 1838 and that later references in *Orient* 5 (1844): 178, 207, confused Flörsheim with the Rothschilds.

[7] See Liberles, 52-61. For Rabbi Trier's own account see Salomon A. Trier, ed., *Rabbinische Gutachten über die Beschneidung* (Frankfurt am Main: 1944), vii-xii.

for the Friends of Reform (*Verein der Reformfreunde*) and by September 1842 (before the promulgation of the public health ordinance and the Flörsheim incident), their agenda had become a matter of public knowledge. The initial unpublished statement of the *Reformfreunde* platform consisted of five principles, amongst them an explicit declaration that they did not consider circumcision binding, either as a religious obligation or as a symbolic act. Although the subsequent publication of the founding principles reduced those principles to three in number and omitted the reference to circumcision, the *Reformfreunde* were perceived as spearheading a concerted attack on the rite of circumcision.[8]

The covenant of circumcision is not only endowed with religious meaning but also serves as a symbol of identification with the community of Israel. Unique among *mitzvot*, circumcision — the mark of the covenant — is so powerful a symbol, that Spinoza, in his *Tractatus Theologico-Politicus*, although by

---

[8] For an incisive analysis of the *Reformfreunde*, see Michael A. Meyer, "Alienated Intellectuals in the Camp of Religious Reform: The Frankfurt Reformfreunde, 1842-1945," *AJS Review* 6 (1981): 61-86. See also the detailed account in David Philipson, *The Reform Movement in Judaism*, 2nd ed. (New York: MacMillan, 1931), 107-39 and cf. Liberles, 43-52. Meyer notes that although the three-year history of the *Reformfreunde* appears to be of but limited historical interest, this small group gave rise to a significant body of literature and "reflects currents and tendencies of considerably broader measure and of larger duration" (61). Zunz predicted correctly, in a letter of October 5, 1843, that "... the Frankfurt Reform requires no violent Petichat Ha-Arez in order for it to perish" but he was not quite right in his assertion that "in a year people will not be talking about it any more." See Nahum N. Glatzer, ed., *Leopold Zunz: Jude-Deutscher-Europäer* (Tübingen, 1964), 224, cited in Meyer, "Alienated," 65 n. 7.

Liberles, 54-55, 57, hypothesizes that the impetus for the 1843 Frankfurt circumcision ordinance can be traced to the *Reformfreunde* and points out that one of their prominent members, the influential physician Dr. Heinrich Schwarzschild, was later appointed a member of the Health Department Board itself. If Schwarzschild influenced the Board to promulgate the ordinance, the wording "*insofern sie ihre Kinder beschneiden lassen wollen*" was intentionally precise. Cf. Gotzmann, *Jüdisches Recht*, 256 nn. 9, 10.

no means did he endorse such particularity, acknowledged that "the sign of circumcision is, as I think, so important, that I could persuade myself that it alone would preserve the nation forever."[9] Little wonder that the controversy over circumcision within the Reform movement in the mid-nineteenth century was fierce and pitted advocates of Reform against one another — as well as against those outside that nascent movement. The bitterness of the debate was fueled at least as much by the need for expression of ethnic identity as by religious ideology.

Yet vehement opposition to circumcision persisted despite its pivotal role in forging a sense of Jewish identity. The opposition did not arise in a vacuum. Perceived by outsiders as tangible evidence of otherness, circumcision was viewed with a strange fascination — at one and the same time both barbaric and mysterious. It may be demonstrated that much of the then vocal criticism of circumcision among both Jews and non-Jews can be traced to the vicious attack on circumcision in the writings of the French intellectual elite of the eighteenth century. During the period before the French Revolution and in its aftermath, the ritual came under ever increasing attack from outside the Jewish community.

Perception of the teachings and religious observances of Judaism as outmoded and primitive was rooted in the currents of anti-Semitism that permeated intellectual circles of that era. During the eighteenth century, "the century of Voltaire," France developed an intelligentsia that unabashedly expressed pronounced anti-Jewish sentiments. By the end of the century, their influence had spread throughout Europe. In Germany,

---

[9] *The Chief Works of Benedict de Spinoza*, vol. 1, trans. R.H.M. Elwes (New York: Dover Publications, 1951), 56. *Sefer ha-Hinnukh*, no. 2, states that circumcision is designed "to separate [Israel] from the nations in the form of their bodies as in their souls." Both Ramban, *Commentary on the Bible*, Genesis 15:18 and R. Jacob Emden, *Migdal Oz, Bereikhah Elyonah* 2:20, assert that Israel is preserved from extinction in the Diaspora by virtue of the covenant of circumcision.

Immanuel Kant's hostility to Judaism and his characterization of the Jewish religion as obsolete and lacking in morality was emblematic of the thinking of his time. The only possibility for social rehabilitation of the Jews, according to Kant, lay in their rejection of unedifying rituals and acceptance of "purified" religious concepts. Nor was Kant's younger friend and some-time student, Johann Gottfried von Herder, commonly regarded as a liberal and philosemite, incapable of expressing anti-Jewish comments. Herder disparaged what he termed "pharasaism" and disdained halakhic distinctions as ponder-ous hairsplitting.[10] Deprecatory attitudes such as these were internalized by acculturated Jewish intellectuals in their desperate quest for acceptance in a society that had always rejected them as alien.

To be sure, opposition to the ritual of circumcision was often rooted in anti-Semitic bias and prejudice. However, that opposition was also an outgrowth of newly developing attitudes toward the body, together with scientific and medical advances, as well as anthropological studies of myths and rituals of primitive societies.

The Assault upon Circumcision

During this era, circumcision in general did indeed become the focus of strident negative attention. It is important to understand the extent to which anti-circumcision feelings permeated the cultural and intellectual milieu of Western Europe in order to ascertain the extent to which those senti-ments influenced Reform ideologues. A wide range of meanings were imputed to the practice and numerous analyses of its

---

[10] The ambiguities and ambivalences surrounding Emancipation in France are described in Arthur Hertzberg, *The French Enlightenment and the Jews* (New York and London: Columbia University Press and Philadelphia: Jewish Publication Society, 1968). An excellent portrayal of the German climate of thought is found in Paul Lawrence Rose, *German Question/Jewish Question: Revolutionary Antisemitism from Kant to Wagner* (Princeton, NJ: Princeton University Press, 1992); see especially, 90-132.

social implications as a marker of differentness were advanced.
The full-scale virulent cultural assault on the rite in nineteenth
century Germany may be assessed in terms of five distinct
factors: (1) medical, (2) anthropological, (3) socio-political,
(4) demonic and (5) aesthetic.

1. Medical

In the latter part of the nineteenth century, as governmental
authorities began to supervise various aspects of public health,
circumcision came under increasing medical scrutiny. It was
often Jewish physicians themselves who brought the subject of
the ritual and its attendant dangers to the attention of the
authorities. A ubiquitous argument against circumcision was
that it constitutes an unnecessary surgical procedure that
endangers the health of the infant. The incidence of tragic
complications and even deaths associated with circumcision
was publicized and exaggerated.[11] A manual for *mohalim*
prepared by Dr. Ph. Wolfers of Lemforde, Westphalia, championed retention of circumcision but nonetheless, noting the
medical dangers, recommended governmental supervision of
circumcision and the banning of *metzitzah* upon pain of a
fine.[12]

With the emergence of bacteriology as a science, concerns
regarding the practice of *metzitzah* became increasingly vocal.
Between 1805 and 1865 outbreaks of syphilis and tuberculosis
in several European cities were attributed to infected
mohalim.[13] Following allegations that the practice of *metzitzah*

---

[11] See Liberles, 55, 245 n. 116. See also Katz, *Divine Law*, 323 and the
references to the polemical literature, in particular, J. Bergson, *Die
Beschneidung von historischen kritischen und medizinischen Standpunkt*
(Berlin, 1844) and M.G. Salomon, *Die Beschneidung, historisch und
medizinisch Beleuchtet* (Braunschweig, 1844). See also Samuel Kohn, *Ot
Berit* (Cracow, 1903), 147-56.

[12] See Katz, *Divine Law*, 358.

[13] David L. Gollaher, *Circumcision: A History of the World's Most Contro-
versial Surgery* (New York: Basic Books, 2000), 28-29. Cf. allegations

led to infant fatalities, civil authorities in a number of cities, including Vienna, Cracow and London, banned the act.[14] In some instances the charges were disputed. Thus, in the celebrated case of a Viennese *mohel* accused of infecting children upon whom he had performed *metzitzah*, upon examination, the *mohel* showed no sign of the illness contracted by the children and consequently he was completely exonerated.[15] Similarly, the Orthodox periodical *Der treue Zionswächter* publicized views of medical experts defending *metzitzah* as medically harmful neither to the patient nor to the practitioner and, to the contrary, as having a positive therapeutic value.[16] Be that as it may, the possibility of danger could not be ruled out and the need for constant vigilance and supervision of *mohalim* (optimally self-regulatory rather than governmental) was acknowledged.

Ironically, in the United States, in the later decades of the nineteenth century, physicians outside the Jewish community became convinced of the medical benefits of circumcision and circumcision of neonates was routinely recommended.[17] Since then, scientific opinion has vacillated and the pendulum continues to shift to and fro with regard to the therapeutic value of circumcision.[18]

---

regarding *metzitzah*-related deaths in London reported in Alexander Tertis, *Dam Berit* (London, 1901), 1 and ibid., 3-9, reports of infections associated with circumcision in several European cities.

[14] See Aaron Friedenwald, "Circumcision – in Medicine," *Jewish Encyclopedia*, vol. 4 (New York: Funk & Wagnalls, 1906), 100 and Immanuel Jakobovits, *Jewish Medical Ethics* (New York: Bloch Publishing Company, 1967), 338 nn. 36, 37.

[15] See Katz, *Divine Law*, 360.

[16] *Der treue Zionswächter* 3 (1847): 417-18.

[17] See Gollaher, 73-108.

[18] Ibid., 161-76 and J. David Bleich, "Circumcision: The Current Crisis," *Tradition* 33 (Summer, 1979): 46-49, 61-63.

2. Anthropological

Further erosion in the perceived sanctity of circumcision resulted from the claim that circumcision was a borrowed rite that did not originate among Jews.

With increased knowledge of distant parts of the globe and exotic cultures beginning in the Age of Discovery during the late fifteenth and sixteenth centuries, Europeans became aware that various primitive tribes in Africa, the Americas and Australia practiced circumcision-like rituals. At first, some writers speculated that these primitive peoples were linked to ancient Israel, perhaps by virtue of being members of the lost tribes. Others later turned the theory around in claiming that circumcision originated in ancient and primitive civilizations and that Jews, in adopting the ritual, had merely imitated the practices of ancient Egypt.[19]

The English Deists, followed by Voltaire popularized the notion that the Jewish custom stemmed from Egypt.[20] Indeed, Greek and Roman writers had voiced the same argument in bygone days. Voltaire, quoting classical sources, repeatedly asserted that the Jews, an "ignorant crude people," were plagiarizers who borrowed everything in their culture from others and adopted all their religious rites from the Egyptians.[21] This view was reiterated in the writings of the influential orientalist Johann David Michaelis.[22]

J.H.F. Autenrieth, Chancellor of the University of Tübingen, published an influential work on circumcision in 1829 in which he advanced the thesis that circumcision represents a primitive act performed as a surrogate for human sacrifice.[23]

---

[19] See Gollaher, 53-54.

[20] S. Ettinger, "Yahadut ve-Yehudim be-Einei ha-De'istim ha-Angliyim be-Me'ah ha-18," [Hebrew] *Zion* 29 (1964): 184-88; L. Tonney, *Voltaire and the English Deists* (New Haven: Yale University Press, 1930), 170-71, 173.

[21] Hertzberg, 303, citing Voltaire, *Philosophical Dictionary*, vol. 1, ed. and trans. Peter Gay (New York: Harcourt, Brace & World, 1962), 62, 201, 499.

[22] See Gotzmann, 255.

[23] *Abhandlung über den Ursprung der Beschneidung* (Tübingen: Heinrich Laupp, 1829).

Subsequently, anthropologists formulated an evolutionary hypothesis positing that society passed through three stages: magic, religion and science. Religious circumcision, they maintained, retained magical elements and was essentially an initiation rite, a primitive people's sacrificial act, *viz.*, the sacrificing of a part of the body to divine powers in order to redeem the community.[24] If circumcision was merely a borrowed practice, objections to its abolition lost their cogency.

3. Socio-Political

The medical and anthropological arguments were seized upon and embellished by anti-Semitic French intellectuals in their campaign of social ridicule and mockery of Jewish practices, an endeavor for which circumcision provided a ready target. In references to Jews, those writers invariably included the adjective "circumcised" to accentuate their differentness. Circumcision was the distinctive mark of otherness. Spinoza was quite correct in observing that the laws that caused Jews to separate themselves from other nations drew down upon them "universal hate."[25]

Classical sources — a literature in which Voltaire was steeped — attacked circumcision viciously and accused Jews of hatred of others. Tacitus charged that Jews, obstinately devoted to one another, harbored an implacable hatred for the

---

[24] See Gollaher, 54-55, citing, for example, James Frazer, "The Origin of Circumcision," *Independent Review* 4 (1904-1905): 204-18. Cf. Howard Eilberg-Schwartz, *The Savage in Judaism: An Anthropology of Israelite Religion and Ancient Judaism* (Bloomington, Ind.: Indiana University Press, 1990), 141-76, who notes a current diminishing interest in ethnographic data on circumcision but himself argues in favor of the comparative perspective. He focuses on what he terms the "priestly" understanding of circumcision in presenting a highly conjectural theory based on a symbolic exegesis of biblical passages rooted in his acceptance of the documentary hypothesis. For recent anthropological literature see Sander L. Gilman, *Jews in Today's German Culture* (Bloomington and Indianapolis, Ind.: Indiana University Press, 1995), 121 n. 14.

[25] *Chief Works*, 1, 55.

rest of mankind.[26] The animus of Jews toward others was believed to be rooted in the latter's uncircumcised state. Juvenal, describing the repugnance Jews felt toward Roman laws, claimed specifically that they had been taught by Moses in a secret book not to lead an uncircumcised man to water. This categorization of Jews was repeatedly echoed by Voltaire in his portrayal of Jews as people who hate all other men and are fanatically intolerant. That they themselves are, in turn, universally detested, Voltaire averred, is the direct result of their peculiar laws and was reinforced because of their animosity "toward the uncircumcised Romans."[27]

The tone of such remarks is remarkably akin to the comments of a district procurator (in November 1793) denouncing the Jews of Lorraine and their alien practices. He noted: "It is the inhumane law of these people that the new-born male infant is to be bloodily operated upon as if nature herself were imperfect" and then proceeded to scoff at their long beards, devotion to a dead language and mischievous laws that commit them to make usurious loans.[28]

The extent to which circumcision became a theme of ridicule and a symbol of all that was backward and constricting to the spirit of political freedom and enlightenment may be seen in the words of a poem that achieved a popular currency. The author of the poem, *"Déclaration des Droits de l'Homme et du Citoyen"* (1789), wrote:

---

[26] *Histories*, 5.5.8-9. See also, M. Whittaker, "Jews and Christians: Graeco-Roman Views," *Cambridge Commentaries on Writings of the Jewish and Christian World: 200 B.C. to A.D. 200* (Cambridge: University Press, 1984), 22-23, 83.

[27] Hertzberg, 302-3, citing Voltaire, *Oeuvres complètes*, vol. 12, ed. Louis Moland (Paris: Garnier, 1870), 159-63. Hertzberg, 10, quite correctly observes that, "An analysis of everything that Voltaire wrote about Jews throughout his life establishes the proposition that he is the major link in Western intellectual history between the anti-Semitism of classic paganism and the modern age."

[28] Cited in Robert Anchel, *Napoléon et les Juifs* (Paris: Les Presses Universitaires de France, 1928), 18.

"Rien ô ma chère liberté
Ne peut te circoncire."

(Nothing, oh my dear liberty,
Is able to circumcise you).[29]

Precisely at a time when German Jews wished to emphasize their similarities to their countrymen rather than their differences from them, the spotlight on circumcision as a sign of inalienable otherness was experienced by them as a painful embarrassment. Moreover, the social critique of circumcision was often expressed in the context of political objectives. Johann David Michaelis maintained that circumcision originated as a formal prerequisite for citizenship in the Israelite nation, not as a practice of religious significance. If Jews desire to become integrated as citizens of Western nations, it was argued, distinctive physical marks were no longer appropriate.[30] This attitude found its most articulate exponent in the radical Reform spokesman Samuel Holdheim whose evolving view of circumcision became increasingly negative. In an answer to questions addressed to him by a Reform society in Arad in 1848, Holdheim emphatically advised abrogation of the ritual in stating:

> ... protest must be lodged against circumcision, the expression of an outlived idea. It testifies to something which is not true – yes, something which is, in fact, denied by all Israelites who have become self-conscious. The Jew today believes by no manner of means that he, through the accident of his descent from Abraham stands in a close special relationship to God and that he is obligated to give physical evidence of this closer relationship by a sign in the flesh. I am opposed to circumcision on principle and declare every Jew who confides in my religious insight and conscientiousness absolved from all obligation in this

---

[29] Zosa Szajkowski, "Jewish Religious Observance, during the French Revolution of 1789," *YIVO Annual* 12 (1958-9): 221.

[30] Cf. Liberles, 55.

matter. Yes, I declare every Jew who neglects to have his son circumcised because of his larger belief to be a true and complete Jew.[31]

4. Demonic

Perhaps the most bizarre of the anti-Semitic canards associated with circumcision was the demonic allegation that Jews, if empowered, would forcibly circumcise others.

As with most of the common anti-Semitic myths regarding Jewish ritual, the accusations bore no relationship whatsoever to the truth of Jewish practice. Blood ritual accusations run counter to strict prescriptions of Jewish law forbidding the admixture of any liquid other than water in preparation of matzot,[32] not to speak of the prohibition against ingesting blood.[33] So too did this accusation fly in the face of halakhic rulings that discourage the circumcision of non-Jews.[34]

But mythic fears feed on other fodder. Perhaps, in the case of circumcision, this fairly widespread misapprehension traces its roots to the biblical narrative (Genesis 34) concerning Simeon and Levi and the circumcision and subsequent annihilation of Shechem son of Hamor, his father and his people. The statement of Hamor and Shechem, "Only herein will the men consent unto us to be one people, if every male

---

[31] Cited in Philipson, 280.

[32] Blood is one of the seven liquids enumerated by the Mishnah, *Makhshirin* 6:4. The admixture of any one of those liquids or of fruit juice with water renders dough *hametz*. See *Shulhan Arukh, Orah Hayyim* 462:1 and commentaries, *ad locum*.

[33] *Keritut* 22a and Maimonides, *Mishneh Torah, Hilkhot Ma'akhalot Assurot* 6:2.

[34] See *Beit Yosef, Yoreh De'ah* 266; *Levush, Yoreh De'ah* 363:5; *Taz, Yoreh De'ah* 363:3. Cf., *Shakh, Yoreh De'ah* 363:8. Cf., however, *Shulhan Arukh, Yoreh De'ah* 268:9 and *Teshuvot ha-Rambam*, vol. 1, ed. R. Joshua Blau (Jerusalem: Mekitzei Nirdamim, 1958), no. 148, reprinted *in Iggerot ha-Rambam*, ed. R. Isaac Shilat (Ma'aleh Adumim, Israel: Ma'aliyot, 1987), 212-14.

among us be circumcised as they are circumcised" (34:22), may have been perceived as an ongoing demand which, if in power, Jews would insist be fulfilled as a precondition for peaceful coexistence with those not of their faith.

Whatever their provenance may have been, in the Middle Ages when blood libel accusations proliferated, the tales often included accounts of how Jews first circumcised the Christian children whom they later killed to utilize their blood for ritual purposes. For example, accounts of the martyred "Little Hugh of Lincoln," found murdered in 1255, related that he had been beaten, his nose had been broken and he had been circumcised before his death. The child, Simon, later beatified as Saint Simon of Trent, was found dead in Trento, Italy in 1475. Engravings and woodcuts celebrating Simon's martyrdom graphically depict Jews circumcising the lad — focusing on the cutting of his genitals with a large knife — while ghoulishly inflicting other wounds on his body and bleeding him to death.[35]

Despite the passage of time, these accusations continued to be given credence. In seventeenth-century England, one Samuel Purchas wrote that:

> One cruell and (to speak the properest phrase) *Jewish crime* was usuall amongst them, every yeere towards Easter ... to steale a young boy, *circumcise him*, and after solemn judgment, making one of their own Nation a Pilate, to crucifie him out of their divellish malice to Christ and Christians.[36]

Another English source, an account of the trial of Jacob of Norwich, accused him and his accomplices of "Stealing away, and Circumcising, a Christian child."[37]

---

[35] Gollaher, 38-39. In 1965, the Roman Catholic Church withdrew the cult of Saint Simon. Regarding Simon of Trent see R. Po-Chia Hsia, *Trent 1475: Stories of a Ritual Murder Trial* (New Haven, Conn.: Yale University Press, 1992).

[36] Cited in Gollaher, 40.

[37] *Loc. cit.*

Hateful stories of this genre, which served to exacerbate
xenophobic fears of mysterious Jewish rituals, resurfaced with
a renewed vigor during the tumultuous years preceding and
following the French Revolution. Prominent among eighteenth
century French clerical intellectuals who repeated medieval
calumnies against the Jews was Abbé Charles Louis Richard.
When a Parisian Jewish banker by the name of Liefman
Calmer bought a barony in 1774 and attempted to appoint
priests to two benefices on that land, Richard denounced
Calmer and asserted that no Jew had a right to make
appointments to Church offices. In Richard's essays he
denounced the Jew as "A born and sworn enemy of all
Christians," but in anonymous pamphlets he went much
further. Richard composed a letter purportedly authored by
"the rabbi of the synagogue of the Jews of Metz" addressed to
Mordecai Venture whom he described as "the rabbi of the
synagogue of Paris" in which the rabbi of Metz related that he
planned to convene a Sanhedrin to "instruct" Calmer not to
appoint any priest to a benefice unless that priest had been
circumcised. In his pose as a rabbi, Richard also imaginatively
put into the mouth of Voltaire the recommendation that Abbé
Guénée, a defender of the Jews, be circumcised and further
expounded on why the holder of a benefice conferred by a Jew
required circumcision.[38]

After the Revolution, the Catholic Church conducted a
well-organized campaign designed to persuade the legislature
to abandon proposals for Jewish emancipation and to provoke
uprisings against the new regime. Jews were blamed for the
new regime's decrees against the Church. Counter-
revolutionaries argued that Protestants and Jews supported
the new regime and together they would discriminate against
Catholics. In popular pamphlets the strongest warnings were

---

[38] See Hertzberg, 250-52.

issued against Jewish usurers who would compel Christians to forsake their faith. In this context, one newspaper writer went so far as to write that it was quite possible that within thirty years all Christians would be forced to undergo circumcision: "*Qui peut nous assurer, que nous ne serons pas forcés de nous faire tous circoncire avant trente ans.*"[39]

Similarly, in the course of the debates on the question of admitting Jews to citizenship, Camille Desmoulins ironically ventured to suggest that, in the event the Jews were to become citizens, circumcision might well become a condition of admission of any gentile to that status.[40] Desmoulins may have made his remarks in jest, but Jean François Rewbell of Alsace, a bitter opponent of emancipation of the Jews, was pleased to seize on this remark and wrote to Desmoulins that the remarks concerning circumcision had given him pleasure.[41]

Whether or not Rewbell took literally the canard that Jews would force circumcision on non-Jews, it was evident that he deemed the threat a useful and powerful symbol, demonstrating what he considered to be at the heart of the insidious danger of accepting Jews as equal citizens. He proclaimed that the teachings of the Jewish religion were incompatible with non-Jewish society: "You'll see it is not I who excludes the Jews; they exclude themselves." Only when Jews

---

[39] See Szajkowski, "Religious Propaganda against Jews during the French Revolution of 1789," *Proceedings of the American Academy for Jewish Research* 38 (1959): 105. Cf. idem, "Jewish Religious Observance," *YIVO Annual* 12: 221, who describes the strange report of one newspaper that the deputy Jean-Sylvain Bailly (1736-93) had felt prompted to go to the synagogue and have himself circumcised. He notes that during the Reign of Terror the district attorney of Strasbourg publicly attacked the practice of circumcision and a Jacobin publication urged a general prohibition of the rite.

[40] Hertzberg, 331, citing Léon Kahn, *Les Juifs de Paris pendant la révolution* (Paris: P. Ollendorff, 1898), 44-45.

[41] Hertzberg, 355.

would be prepared to leave the synagogue, renounce their particularistic practices and follow the customs of their neighbors, he argued, should their acceptance as citizens be considered.[42]

In all likelihood, intelligent individuals did not take these calumnies seriously but they were effective weapons in the arsenal of anti-Semites, useful in fanning the flames of enmity, stirring the primitive fears of the masses and whipping up a frenzy of hostility toward Jews. As the historian Arthur Hertzberg points out in the case of Richard, these writers took not only the "high roads" of theological anti-Semitism but also the "low roads of traditional anti-Semitism" in pandering to the crude ethnic hatreds of the masses.[43]

5. Aesthetic

The combination and culmination of the varied medical, anthropological, social and demonic arguments against circumcision brought into play and strengthened another fundamental element — the aesthetic. In Hellenistic society, antagonism to circumcision was rooted in an abhorrence of mutilating the body; the circumcised male was an affront to Greek aesthetics. Circumcised men were not permitted to participate in Greek athletic games. To avoid embarrassment at gymnasia and public baths, some Jews even underwent painful surgical procedures designed to disguise or reverse their circumcision.[44] During the eighteenth and nineteenth centuries, the Greek idealization of the "natural" male form reappeared in Germany and Austria in the writings of

---

[42] *Loc. cit.*

[43] Ibid., 252.

[44] See *Book of Jubilees*, 15:33-34. Attempts at reversal of circumcision by "drawing in" the foreskin — a technique the Greeks called *epispasmos* — is expressly forbidden in the Jerusalem Talmud, *Pe'ah* 1:1. For a description of this process and other methods of decircumcision see Gollaher, 16.

anatomists. Decircumcision came to be viewed as signifying the return to the beautiful and the healthy.[45]

The barrage of strident criticism created an atmosphere of distaste toward circumcision and the result was a visceral recoil from the ritual on the part of many Jews. Yearning to be accepted and desperate for integration within the general society, assimilated German Jews were quick to gauge social and religious practices by the reaction of their non-Jewish peers and to view their own lives through the prism of non-Jewish eyes. However, it was not only their desire for acceptance and wish to curry favor with the non-Jewish citizenry that influenced their self-perception; they themselves had internalized a new set of values. Educated in Western schools, steeped in Western culture, influenced as that culture was by both classical and Christian values and teachings, assimilated Jews developed an aesthetic temperament attuned to Western society. To the extent that they thought of religion, they tended to emphasize its rational, spiritual and aesthetic aspects in which they could see no place for an "irrational" physical rite.[46] Thus, it was not simply that Christians found the ritual of circumcision strange; German Jews themselves began to express revulsion toward it.

The language used during this era by *Jewish* critics of circumcision is revealing in the sheer vehemence of its rhetoric. Gabriel Riesser said of circumcision: "This repugnant ceremony, insofar as it is to be regarded as religious, must

---

[45] Sander L. Gilman, "Decircumcision: The First Aesthetic Surgery," *Modern Judaism* 17 (1997): 202. Noteworthy is also Gilman's published lecture, *The Visibility of the Jew in the Diaspora: Body Imagery and Its Cultural Context* (Syracuse: Syracuse University Press, 1991). Commenting on nineteenth century anti-Semitic stereotyping, Gilman notes that in *fin-de-siècle* Berlin there were self-conscious Jews who resorted to cosmetic rhinoplasty and he comments as well on Freudian interpretations that explore the relationship between the nose and the genitalia.

[46] See Michael A. Meyer, "*Berit Milah* within the History of Reform Judaism," *Berit Milah in the Reform Context*, ed. Lewis M. Barth (New York: Central Conference of American Rabbis, 1990), 143-44.

thoroughly disgust every cultured sensibility...."[47] Felix Adler
in the United States described the ritual as "simply barbarous
in itself and certainly barbarous and contemptible in its
origin."[48] And, in what has come to be a well-known passage in
his private correspondence to Zunz, Abraham Geiger wrote:

> The fact remains that it is a barbaric, gory rite which
> fills the infant's father with fear and subjects the new
> mother to harmful emotional strain. The sense of
> sacrifice, which in days long past lent an aura of
> consecration to this ceremony, has long since vanished
> from our midst; nor is so brutal a thought deserving of
> perpetuation. True, in the olden days religious
> sentiment may have clung to it; at present, however, its
> only foundations are habit and fear, and we surely
> have no desire to dedicate temples to either.[49]

The practice of *metzitzah*, in particular, aroused the most
forceful expressions of aesthetic repugnance. One word
reappears over and over again in the recorded medical reports:
the German word "*ekelhaft*" — a word connoting repulsiveness
to the point of nausea. The aesthetic recoil is often more
emphatic than the medical concern. Thus, Dr. Wolfers of
Lemforde, in his 1831 study of circumcision, declared that
metzitzah had no therapeutic value and was an "*ekelhaft*"
practice.[50] The same expression is found in a report of
Viennese medical experts who investigated *metzitzah* and
concluded that *metzitzah* "is superfluous, of no utility or

---

[47] Meyer, "Alienated," 77, citing, in translation, Riesser's comments as
found in M.A. Stern, "Briefe von und an Gabriel Riesser," *Zeitschrift für die
Geschichte der Juden in Deutschland,* o.s. 2 (1888): 55.

[48] Cited in Salo W. Baron, "The Modern Age," *Great Ages and Ideas of the
Jewish People* (New York: Random House, 1956), 366.

[49] Abraham Geiger, *Nachgelassene Schriften*, vol. 5, ed. L. Geiger (Berlin:
Gerschel, 1875), 181-82. For the English translation see *Abraham Geiger
and Liberal Judaism: The Challenge of the Nineteenth Century*, ed. Max
Wiener and trans. Ernst J. Schlochauer (Philadelphia: Jewish Publication
Society, 1962), 113-14.

[50] Cited in Katz, *Divine Law*, 359.

purpose, disgusting (*ekelhaft*) and to some extent even detrimental."[51] Again, the same word was utilized in the corroborating testimony by Dr. Wertheim, chief physician in the Jewish Hospital in Vienna. Wertheim stated that *metzitzah* is "disgusting" (*ekelhaft*) and added that "its roots are in unclean soil (*auf schmutzigen Boden wurzelndes Herkommen*)."[52] Although virtually all assimilated German Jews had long since abjured the practice of oral *metzitzah*, the frequent and numerous derogatory references to *metzitzah* as primitive and repulsive carried over to other aspects of circumcision as well. This contributed to an aura of distaste and to a nimbus of negativity that hovered over the practice of circumcision.

Alternative Rituals

Traditionalist rabbis did not succeed in harnessing the aid of the secular state and hence registry of uncircumcised children in Jewish community records was permitted. But the number of Jews who, in fact, took advantage of that option was not large. Astonishingly, despite continuing and pervasive negative propaganda, the overwhelming majority of even assimilated German Jews continued to practice circumcision. In this one area, the radicals lost the battle. Despite the initial Frankfurt challenge, the overwhelming majority of liberal rabbis opposed the *Reformfreunde* platform and supported retention of circumcision.[53]

---

[51] Ibid., 362, citing documents published by Menahem Mendel Stern in the periodical *Kokhvei Yitzhak* (Vienna, 1845), 38-43.

[52] *Loc. cit.*

[53] At the Reform rabbinic conferences of 1844-46, there was great reluctance to place an open discussion of the matter on the agenda. Although Rabbi Mendel Hess of Saxe-Weimar introduced a resolution declaring that, although circumcision is "universally considered sacred," there should be no "external coercion and exclusion" and those who do not choose to practice the rite "are to be considered members of the Jewish community," the motion was tabled and the subject removed from consideration lest the topic arouse too impassioned a debate.

As early as 1821, Olry Terquem, a French proponent of Jewish religious reform, writing under the pseudonym Tsarphati, expounded on the dangers of circumcision and proposed that the ritual of circumcision be replaced by a purely symbolic ceremony.[54] At the height of the Frankfurt controversy, a teacher of religion at the Frankfurt Philanthropin school, Josef Johlson, under the *nom de plume* Bar Amithai, published a pamphlet, *Über die Beschneidung in historischer und dogmatischer Hinsicht: Ein Wort zu seiner Zeit. Den Denkenden in Israel zur Prüfung vorgelegt* (Frankfurt am Main, 1843), in which he advocated abolition of circumcision and substitution of another ceremony. Johlson prepared a rubric for such a ceremony, prospectively termed "The Sanctification of the Eighth Day," designed as an egalitarian ritual suitable for both male and female infants.[55] Abraham Geiger also privately expressed the hope that a new ritual might be found to replace circumcision in the religious life of the Jew.[56] In more recent times, the idea of devising a new

---

See Philipson, 154. A physician's rather strange suggestion that circumcision caused venereal disease and impotence and that the ritual therefore be abandoned or fundamentally altered was briefly discussed at a closed session at the 1845 Frankfurt conference and summarily rejected. Again, at the Breslau conference in 1846, the role of circumcision was not disputed. The practice was taken as a given and a series of regulations designed merely to enhance the safety and hygienic aspects of the ritual was adopted. See Philipson, 216-17 and Meyer, *Response to Modernity*, 138-39.

[54] Olry, Terquem, *Deuxième Lettre d'un Israélite français. Projet de réglementation concernant la circoncision* (Paris, 1821), 8, cited in Philippe-Éfraim Landau, "Olry Terquem (1782-1862), Régénérer les Juifs et Réformer le Judaïsme," *Revue des Études Juives*, 160 (January-June 2001): 179. Although Terquem did not convert, he married a Catholic and his five children were all baptized. See Landau, 175.

[55] See Michael A. Meyer, *Response to Modernity: A History of the Reform Movement in Judaism* (New York and Oxford: Oxford University Press, 1988), 123, 423 n. 86. See also idem, "The First Identical Ceremony for Giving a Hebrew Name to Girls and Boys," *Journal of Reform Judaism* 32 (Winter 1985): 84-87.

[56] *Nachgelassene Schriften*, vol. 5, 202-3.

ritual of initiation into the Jewish community was advanced by Mordecai M. Kaplan.[57] Nevertheless, no novel rite of covenant was ever formally adopted and the ancient ritual of circumcision remains the only universally accepted Jewish sign of initiation.

In concluding remarks in his responsum regarding circumcision included in Rabbi Trier's volume of published responsa concerning the Frankfurt controversy, the eminent halakhic authority, Rabbi Jacob Ettlinger, emphasized that ultimately it is history that testifies to the abiding validity of the commandments: "Judaism itself, as it has endured in uniformity for thousands of years in all ends of the civilized world, bears witness to the inviolability of its content and structure."[58] Currently, more than a century and a half later, despite renewed protestations of a vocal minority,[59] circumcision remains the most practiced Jewish ritual worldwide, with the possible exception of burial rites.

---

[57] "Toward the Formulation of Guiding Principles for the Conservative Movement," *Tradition and Change*, ed. Mordecai M. Waxman (New York: Burning Bush Press, 1958), 304-6.

[58] *Rabbinische Gutachten*, 37.

[59] The renewed challenge to circumcision focuses once again on the medical argument that circumcision is possibly dangerous and, at best, medically neutral. However, emphasis is now placed on the pain caused to the helpless infant and the procedure is decried as an unwarranted genital mutilation and physical abuse which, as is claimed by some, results in harmful behavioral and psychological consequences. Moreover, among advocates of an egalitarian Judaism, the perception of circumcision as inherently sexist has led to further denigration of the practice. See, for example, Hoffman, 213-20; Ronald Goldman, "Circumcision: A Source of Jewish Pain," *Jewish Spectator* (Summer 1997): 16-20; Lisa Braver Moss, "Circumcision: A Jewish Inquiry," *Midstream* 38 (1992): 20-23; and, more recently, the various essays and discussions included in *The Covenant of Circumcision: New Perspectives on an Ancient Jewish Rite,* ed. Elizabeth Wyner Mark (Hanover, NH: Brandeis University Press/University Press of New England, 2003), 157-203. In sharp contrast, one should note the recent development of a Reform program to train and certify ritual circumcisers. See Lewis M. Barth, "Introducing the Reform Mohel," *Reform Judaism* 13 (Fall 1984): 18-19, 32.

It is evident that for many Jews there remains an un-
articulated, almost unconscious, deep religious attachment
to circumcision as the quintessence of identity as a Jew.
Lawrence Hoffman, in a sensitive discussion of current controversy concerning circumcision, acknowledges the tenacious
hold the ritual continues to have even over those with only
marginal association with the Jewish community. To his mind,
the response of early Reform to attempts to abolish the ritual
was remarkable in that, "Nowhere else, to the best of
my knowledge, were the reformers so adamantly tied to their
past as in the case of circumcision."[60] Similarly, in the contemporary world, he regards the persistent practice of the
ritual even by its ambivalent critics as no less remarkable.
Hoffman attributes this phenomenon to the perception of some
individuals that circumcision is a "manifest assertion of Jewish
continuity with the past." But he concedes that for others,
including many who find the ritual distasteful, it is retained
"out of a sense of obligation to Jewish tradition and a sign of
their belief that the covenant with God continues."[61]

Jacob Katz has described the persistence of the practice
of circumcision as "a collective reaction, a form of 'ritual
instinct,' which was not accompanied by a well thought-out
intellectual process."[62] Other thinkers, informed by kabbalistic
teachings, might attribute the phenomenon to the presence in
Jews, even if faint, of a divine spark (*nitzotz Eloki*) and argue
that in their innermost hearts many Jews continue to
acknowledge that circumcision is an inalienable part of Jewish
identity, or what a modern writer has called "the cut that
binds."[63] Traveling in Russia in the 1970's, this writer learned

---

[60] Hoffman, 9.

[61] Ibid., 220.

[62] Katz, *Divine Law*, 355.

[63] Barbara Kirshenblatt-Gimblett, "The Cut that Binds: The Western
Ashkenazi Torah Binder as Nexus Between Circumcision and Torah,"
Celebration: Studies in Festivity and Ritual, ed. Victor Turner (Washington,

how simple, untutored Jews relate to circumcision when a Russian Jew, with tears in his eyes, told her, "My grandsons have not yet been *'geyiddished.'*" In colloquial Yiddish, the term *"zu yiddishen"* (to make into a Jew) means "to circumcise."[64]

The practice retains a historical, almost mystical, hold over the Jewish people that is perhaps best expressed in the liturgy accompanying the circumcision ritual itself. The ritual is described as an eternal symbol to the Jew of sanctification unto the Lord who "has set His statute in his flesh and sealed his offspring with the sign of the holy covenant ... And it is said: 'He has remembered His covenant for ever, the word which He commanded to a thousand generations ... unto Israel for an everlasting covenant.'"

Enduring Literary Stereotypes

Current literature reflects lingering echoes of the ambivalences and strong emotions engendered by the conflicts over circumcision. Two striking examples from contemporary popular fiction may serve as illustration.

Philip Roth's 1986 novel, *The Counterlife*,[65] garnered almost universal acclaim on the part of literary critics.[66] Writing in *The New Yorker*, the author and critic John Updike, in a nuanced but generally favorable review, pointed to what he personally found to be a jarring and discordant note and wrote, "I wished I had liked the ending better."[67] In the concluding section of the novel, the protagonist, in an imaginative exchange of correspondence with his estranged wife, now

---

D.C.: Smithsonian, 1982), cited in Jonathan D. Sarna, *American Judaism: A History* (New Haven and London: Yale University Press, 2004), 26.

[64] Cf. Gilman, *Jews in Today's German Culture*, 74, 120 n. 7.

[65] New York: Farrar Straus & Giroux, 1986.

[66] See, for example, the remark of Robert Alter, "Defenders of the Faith," *Commentary* 84 (July 1987): 54, "It is, I believe, Roth's best book to date."

[67] John Updike, "Wrestling to Be Born," *The New Yorker*, 2 March 1987, 109.

pregnant with their child, writes that, if the child to be born is male, he will insist that she accede to his wish that the child be circumcised. The non-Jewish British wife, whose family are genteel anti-Semites, is portrayed as remonstrating that her estranged husband, totally atheistic and non-observant, merely wishes to harass and torment her. But the protagonist, Nathan Zuckerman — Roth's alter ego — is vigorous in his advocacy of the ritual. To Updike, the white Anglo-Saxon Protestant reviewer, the circumcision argument is overwrought and such a request on the part of "a narrator so scornful of church and synagogue" is indeed "a strange twist."[68] What Updike fails to grasp, but what a knowledgeable Jewish reviewer would have understood, is that, although Roth has no progeny, Roth — a Jew whose grandparents were Eastern European immigrants and whose mother lit Sabbath candles — if he did have a child, would, in all likelihood, not feel that the child was "his" were the child not to be circumcised.[69]

---

[68] Loc. cit.

[69] In his novel, Roth underscores the role of circumcision in reinforcing a sense of identity for an ambivalent Jew living in an unwelcoming environment through the blunt words of Nathan Zuckerman:

> Circumcision makes it clear as can be that you are here and not there, that you are out and not in — also that you're mine and not theirs.... Circumcision confirms that there is an us and an us that isn't solely him and me. England's made a Jew of me.... A Jew without Jews, without Judaism, without Zionism, without Jewishness, without a temple or an army or even a pistol, a Jew clearly without a home, just the object itself, like a glass or an apple (323-4).

Cf. the much later correspondence published in "An Exchange," *The New Yorker*, 28 December 1998 - 4 January 1999, 98-99. Mary McCarthy — as does Updike — finds the circumcision motif to be much ado about nothing. She comments:

> Then all that circumcision business. Why so excited about making a child a Jew by taking a knife to him? I have nothing against circumcision; the men of my generation were all circumcised — a *de-rigueur* pediatric procedure — and my son's generation, too ... And if Nathan Zuckerman *isn't* a believing Jew, why is he so hung up on this issue?

"The Circumcision," a German short story written in an entirely different tenor, is authored by a German jurist and fiction writer, Bernhard Schlink.[70] Schlink, whose best-selling novel *The Reader*,[71] is a Holocaust-related narrative, has also written several short stories which reveal a remarkable fascination with Jewish themes. "The Circumcision" describes a love affair between a non-Jewish young German student and his New York Jewish paramour. The German youth feels impelled to undergo circumcision although the Jewish woman has made no such request, nor, to his distress, does she even notice that he has undergone the surgical procedure. To the reader, it is evident that Schlink is presenting a fictionalized portrayal of lingering feelings of foreignness and differentness that come to the foreground in non-Jewish perceptions of the mystique that surrounds circumcision.[72] In his discussion of circumcision as

---

Noteworthy is the reply of Roth:

> I think you also fail to see how serious this circumcision business is to Jews. I am still hypnotized by uncircumcised men when I see them at my swimming pool locker room. The damn thing never goes unregistered. Most Jewish men I know have similar reactions, and when I was writing the book, I asked several of my equally secular Jewish male friends if they could have an uncircumcised son, and they all said no, sometimes without having to think about it and sometimes after the nice long pause that any rationalist takes before opting for the irrational.

[70] In Bernhard Schlink, *Flights of Love: Stories*, trans. John E. Woods (New York: Pantheon, 2001), 197-255. The original German is "Die Beschneidung," in *Liebesfluchten: Geschichten* (Zürich: Diogenes, 2000), 199-255.

[71] Trans. Carol Brown Janeway (New York: Random House, 1997). The original German is *Der Vorleser* (Zürich: Diogenes, 1995).

[72] Cf., Sander L. Gilman's detailed discussion, *Today's German Jews*, 71-108, of the current German literary interest in Jewish topics and, in particular, the numerous ambivalent references to circumcision. An earlier version of Gilman's discussion was published in Sander L. Gilman, "Male Sexuality and Contemporary Jewish Literature in German: The Damaged Body as the Image of the Damaged Soul," *Reemerging Jewish Culture in Germany: Life and Literature Since 1989*, eds. Sander L. Gilman and Karen Remmler (New York and London: New York University Press, 1994), 210-49. In that volume, see also the following: Jack Zipes, "The Contemporary German Fascination for Things Jewish: Toward a Jewish

both a physical and metaphoric sign of Jewish identity, Sander Gilman notes that "In German popular culture of the 1980's, the sign of circumcision marked the group fantasy about the hidden nature of the male Jew's body.... And for German Jews, the internalization of the sense of their body's difference cannot be underestimated."[73] Schlink's story does indeed reflect a phenomenon that is characteristic of the German experience.

At the close of the nineteenth century, the French historian Anatole Leroy-Beaulieu commented that the Jew is seen throughout Europe as "the circumcised pariah."[74] At the beginning of the twenty-first century, even when pariah status is eschewed, the idea of circumcision as a barrier separating the alien from the indigenous remains. Spinoza's observations regarding the importance of circumcision — both its distancing effect on strangers and its salutary effect on preservation of the Jewish people — have been amply confirmed by modern history.

Minor Culture," 15-17; Marion Kaplan, "What is 'Religious' among Jews in Contemporary Germany?" 83-84 ("In Germany most books about Jewish life are bought by non-Jews"); and Katharina Ochse, "'What Could Be More Fruitful, More Healing, More Purifying?' Representations of Jews in the German Media after 1989," 118-20.

[73] Gilman, 75-76.

[74] *Israel Among the Nations: A Study of the Jews and Antisemitism*, trans. Frances Hellman (New York: GP Putnam's Sons, 1895), 229.

Rabbi Samson R. Hirsch
as Bible Commentator

Nachum M. Bronznick

R. Hirsch's Approach to Bible Commentary

The critical scientific exegesis of the Bible that emerged in the nineteenth century professed anti-traditionalist ideas that had a decisive, alienating effect on many thinking Jews. In response to the exponents of this method, there arose three outstanding commentators who successfully took up the cudgels in defense of traditional Judaism. These three commentators were R. Ya'akov Mecklenburg, R. Meir Leibush ben Yehiel Michel (known by the acronym Malbim), and R. Samson Raphael Hirsch.

Common to all three commentators is their avowed endeavor to show, each in his own way, the essential and inseparable unity between the Written and Oral Law. R. Mecklenburg and R. Meir Leibush Malbim made this the main aim of their commentaries by highlighting it in the title of their respective works. R. Mecklenburg entitled his commentary הכתב והקבלה, Scripture and Tradition, and Malbim entitled his commentary התורה והמצוה, with תורה referring to Scriptures and מצוה designating

the Oral Law as defined in the Talmud.[1] To this end, Malbim
adduced and formulated a set of grammatical and syntactic
rules (613 in number, to be precise), which he skillfully
employed with resounding effect. R. Mecklenburg, in addition
to the use of various grammatical and syntactic rules,
frequently employed semantic analysis to demonstrate the
veracity of tradition by showing that its teachings were embed-
ded in the very words of Scripture.

R. Hirsch, by contrast, did not rely exclusively on such
devices to counter the anti-traditionalists, who carped and
caviled at the rabbinic interpretations of the Bible. In response
to those who viewed the rabbinic interpretations as forced and
flimsy or, at best, as clever and ingenious, R. Hirsch offered a
rather novel explanation through the use of an instructive
analogy. He compared the Written Law to short notes that
students take of a full-length lecture, which is the Oral Law. To
quote:

> For the student who has heard the whole lecture, short
> notes are quite sufficient to bring back afresh to his
> mind, at any time, the entire subject of the lecture.
> For him, an added mark of interrogation, or exclama-
> tion, a dot, the underlining of a word etc. etc. is
> often quite sufficient to recall to his mind a whole
> series of thoughts. For those who had not heard the
> lecture from the master such notes would be
> completely useless.... The wisdom, the truths, which
> the initiate reproduces from them are sneered at by the
> uninitiated.[2]

Following the implication of this model, Hirsch comes to
the startling conclusion that the Oral Law preceded the Written
Law and is, in a sense, of superior importance.[3] In his words:

---

[1] *Berakhot* 5a and employed by Maimonides at the opening of his introduction to *Mishneh Torah.*

[2] *Commentary* to Ex. 21:2.

[3] Hirsch was probably influenced by R. Yehudah ha-Levi's claim that

> The whole Torah with the full explanation had been
> virtually taught to the people before they were
> entrusted with the written Torah as notes with which
> to refresh their memories.[4]

What needs to be added is that the written Torah served as
authorized short notes not only to the Jews of Moses' generation, who were personally present at his lectures, but also to
all Jews of subsequent generations to whom these original
lectures were transmitted in full by word of mouth by each
previous generation. To such people, the Scriptures have
far-reaching implications as they serve to bring to mind the
entire range of the Oral Law, whereas to those who reject
Tradition out of hand, there is little coherent meaning to the
Scriptures, and most of the rabbinic interpretations tend to
appear to them as contrived fabrications.[5]

> oral communication is superior to written communication as con-
> tained in the well-known dictum מפי סופרים ולא מפי ספרים.... For in oral
> communication one is assisted by pauses ... by raising or lower-
> ing one's voice, by various gestures ... (*Kuzari* 2:72).

As to the source of the Hebrew dictum, see Even Shmuel in his translation
of the *Kuzari*. As to the meaning of סופרים, some render it as authors while
others as teachers. Cf. the commentary of the Gra to Isaiah, 6:10.

[4] *Commentary* to Gen. 9:18. R. Hirsch bases his view on the phrase
נעשה ונשמע, which he interprets to mean that the verb נעשה refers to the
performance of the Written Law, whereas ונשמע refers to the Oral Law. To
quote: "The Written Law contained the Law in the short basic formula,
[while] ... detailed meaning and explanation remained for verbal teaching
that entails applying one's mind by listening" (*Commentary* to Ex. 24:7).

[5] This construction lends new meaning to the technical term "*asmakhta*"
applied in the Talmud as a rationalization for the tenuous use of a biblical
verse to support an oral law (*Pesahim* 81b). This term is generally taken to
mean that the Rabbis made use of a biblical word, phrase, or verse as a
technical mnemonic device to facilitate the remembering of a particular
oral law. (See *Encyclopedia Talmudit* vol. 2, 106, for sources.)

Viewed, however, from the Hirschian perspective, the *asmakhta* is not to be
regarded as an invention of the Rabbis, but as an original note from Sinai
for those who heard orally the particular law and who handed it down to
the Sages of subsequent generations. Thus, while to those who are not in
reception of the Oral Law, such a note may appear vacuous, to those who
heard the Oral Law personally, or by way of direct transmission, such a
scriptural note has great meaning.

However, while it is sufficient for one to have been an auditor of the Oral Law to gain the proper understanding of all the connotations of the Written Law, there is an added requirement for qualifying as a valid would-be commentator of the Bible. There is a widely accepted assertion that to properly interpret an author, one must share some common ground with him, i.e., author and interpreter must be on a similar mental wave length. An inspired text requires an inspired interpreter, one who is imbued with similar religious thoughts and experiences, to explicate its deeper meanings. Hence, to qualify as a commentator of a divine work such as the Bible, one must possess a modicum of divine inspiration.

This truth is contained in R. Hirsch's perceptive comment on the verse, "Behold, there is a place with Me and thou shalt stand on the rock" (Ex. 33:21), which came in answer to Moses' request, "Show me Thy glory" (ibid., 18). Taking the words "with Me" as the key phrase in the verse, Hirsch expounds as follows:

> If we understand these words rightly ... [they mean that] Moses is not to see God, but to see the earthly and human condition from God's point of view ... not to try to obtain a glimpse of God, but, elevated by God, [Moses is] to look at man and the human condition from the height next to God ... from God's point of view.

Simply put, one cannot understand God's ways or His message that is embodied in the Torah unless he is uplifted to the divine plane, which enables him to view the world from the divine perspective.[6]

---

[6] This comment may have influenced A. J. Heschel in the formulation of his elaborate theory of pathos. The prophet, according to Heschel, possesses the knowledge and emotional ability to identify with the divine pathos vis-à-vis the people of Israel. To quote: "The prophet focused his emotions directly on the given pathos of God ... and is moved by the pathos of God [and] ... his declarations are made from the view of God," *The Prophets* (Philadelphia, 1967), 314. Mordechai Breuer must have had this point in mind when making, in passing, the remark "the characteristic

This is probably what R. Hirsch meant by the statement in the preface to his *Commentary* that one of his aims is to explain the biblical text organically, "out of itself." In its simple sense, this phrase means that one cannot bring external categories and concepts to bear on the biblical text.[7] That is why, for example, R. Hirsch ignores the terms for categorizing the commandments devised by various Jewish medieval thinkers and, instead, makes creative use of the terms he found in the Bible itself. In a deeper sense, however, what is meant by the concept of interpreting the Bible "out of itself" is that one must first feed his mind on the Bible and become thoroughly imbued with its nourishing message before beginning to interpret it. This will enable him to view everything from the lofty heights of the holy spirit contained in the Torah. Only then may one venture to explicate the biblical text.[8]

---

idea as divine anthropology, subsequently borrowed by Heschel, though without acknowledging his source...." *Tradition* (Summer, 1977): 144.

[7] It has been shown that there were some external influences on R. Hirsch's writings, such as Kant (I. Grunfeld in his introduction to the English version of *Horeb* [London, 1962], 24,42,75,82), Hegel (N. Rosenbloom, "Nineteen Letters ... A Hegelian Exposition" *Historia Judaica* 2 [1960]: 23-60), and Fichte (H. Levine, *Tradition* [Spring, 1963]: 294). R. Yechiel Weinberg indirectly responds to this concern in his assertion that

> according to the view of R. Samson R. Hirsch, it is within the power of the Torah not only to adapt to itself all the contents of the world's culture, but it also has the ability to shape their form that will change them and turn them into Torah. The principle is thus to activate the power of the Torah in all the activities of a person. (In the collection *Ha-Rav Shimshon R. Hirsch – Mishnato ve-Shitato*, Yonah Emanuel ed. [Jerusalem and New York, 1988], 192.)

This idea is reminiscent of Unamuno's organic thinking, according to which the organic thinker breaks down, digests, and assimilates all outside ideas to his own uniqueness. Unamuno demonstrates this concept by an example from nature. A piece of meat when consumed by a dog becomes dog flesh, but when the same piece is consumed by a human being it becomes human flesh.

[8] This may be part of the reason for the sense of certitude evinced by R. Hirsch in his interpretations. Interestingly, even when both Rashi and Ramban treat the interpretation of the Rabbis on the verse in Ex. 12:2 as a departure from the verse's plain meaning, R. Hirsch treats this interpretation

This is clearly implied in R. Hirsch's claim:

> My *Commentary* does have a connection to what I
> learned from [R. Isaac] Bernays inasmuch as he en-
> couraged me, and served as a paragon for me to enter
> into the Temple of the Torah in order to draw from it an
> awareness and an outlook.[9]

Under the spell of the Bible, R. Hirsch formulates his
comments in language that is charged with force and fervor.
While many of his comments are couched in suggestive and
provocative language, he does not wax unduly poetic. His
comments are always closely reasoned and clearly presented.
As a result, his interpretations and explanations are intellectu-
ally rational as well as perceptively illuminating, appealing to
heart and mind alike.

Salient Features of the *Commentary*

R. Hirsch's *Commentary* could thus be characterized as
representing the synergistic fusion of rational and illuminating
elements. However, these rational elements are not of
the abstract philosophical type, nor are the illuminating
elements of the kabbalistic mystic sort. They are of the
ordinary religious variety, raised to a higher level. In interpreting the phrase, "God is one" (Deut. 6:4), Hirsch ignores the
abstruse interpretations of the medieval Jewish philosophers
that explain that this phrase refers to the ultimate unity of the
various divine attributes. He also avoids the kabbalistic view
that the pantheistic or panentheistic concept (God is in
everything and everything is in God) is proclaimed in
this phrase. According to the deeply religious R. Hirsch, this

---

as being fully in accord with the plain meaning of the verse, stating, "I have
shown in my *Commentary* by clear proofs that, on the contrary, the *derash*
represents the plain meaning of the verse" (from ms., published in *The
Living Hirschian Legacy* [Hebrew] [New York, 1988], 3).

[9] Quoted by Mordechai Breuer in *Ha-Rav Shimshon R. Hirsch*, 40.

phrase refers to the all-pervasiveness of Providence. "God is one" means that nothing takes place outside God's active providential management of nature and history.

Similarly, knowledge of God is not obtained by abstract or negative definitions of His attributes, as conceived by medieval Jewish philosophers.[10] It is the product of the realization that His providence permeates the entire universe. This follows from R. Hirsch's comment on the following two consecutive verses: "Know this day and reflect in your heart that the Lord alone is God in heaven above and in the earth below.... Observe His laws and commandments, which I command you today" (Deut. 4:39-40). In his comment Hirsch states:

> This will be the only result of your knowledge of God ...
> in this world that is filled with His glory, and His will
> rules throughout...you shall acknowledge one task, the
> faithful observance of His laws....

The inclusion of the idea "and His will rules throughout," which is not explicitly stated in these verses, clearly indicates that, according to R. Hirsch, divine providence is an integral component in his definition of the concept of the knowledge of God.

This explains the deeply felt convictions and unfailing optimism that radiate from R. Hirsch's works. These are not due to the buoyant optimism that reigned supreme in the aftermath of the Emancipation, but are the result of his deep faith in Providence. This becomes clear from R. Hirsch's comment on the recurrent verse "and God saw that it was good" in the creation story.

It is this faith in Providence, and not faith in the Emancipation, that underlies R. Hirsch's conviction that there will come a time when anti-Semitism will wane and ultimately

---

[10] For an exposition of this view, see Harry A. Wolfson, "Maimonides on Negative Attributes," in *Louis Ginzberg Jubilee Volume*, American Academy for Jewish Research (New York, 1945), 411-46.

disappear, as alluded to in his comment on the verse, "And Esau ran to meet him, and embraced him, and fell on his neck and kissed him and they wept" (Gen. 33:4).

> A kiss can be false, but not tears that flow at such moments. Tears are drops from one's innermost soul. This kiss and these tears show us that Esau was also a descendant of Abraham.... Esau, more and more, gradually lays the sword aside, turns gradually more and more toward humaneness, and it is particularly Jacob on whom Esau has most opportunity to show that the principle of humaneness begins to affect him.... It is when the strong, as here, Esau, fall round the neck of the weak and cast the sword of violence away only then does it show that right and humaneness have made a conquest.

Whether Hirsch had in mind the times in which he lived, as suggested by Nehama Leibowitz,[11] or whether he had in mind future times is immaterial. One may suggest that he was not motivated in this comment by the rash promises of the Emancipation but rather by his abiding faith in the guiding hand of a beneficent Providence.

In fact, it can be shown that Hirsch was not at all blinded by the dazzling lights of the Emancipation into believing that anti-Semitism was about to disappear. Interpreting Jacob's castigation of Simeon and Levi, "cursed be their anger, for it is fierce, and their wrath for it is harsh, I will divide them in Jacob, and scatter them in Israel" (Gen. 49:7) rather startlingly as a blessing in disguise, R. Hirsch states:

> When the nation is in exile ... suffering from persecution and reviled by others, then the Jew peddling his wares from house to house stands in need of that element of zeal and passion to be able to cherish his self respect and look down on his tormentors.... By scattering the tribes of Simeon and Levi among the rest of the

---

[11] *Studies in Bereshit* (Jerusalem, 1966), 375.

house of Israel, all its members will share some of the badly needed courage and zeal.

Since the verse upon which the above comment is based refers to all exilic times, including those of the Emancipation, the claim that R. Hirsch was deluded into thinking that Esau's kisses and tears foreshadowed the improved condition of the Jew during the period of Emancipation is extremely questionable.

An important feature of R. Hirsch's commentary is his psychological insights in connection with biblical heroes and villains. Disregarding all apologetics, he explains Isaac's love for Esau and Rebekah's love for Jacob by means of the popular psychological observation that opposites attract. Hence, Isaac, having been raised in the spiritual environment that pervaded the house of his parents, was drawn to Esau the hunter, the man of the world. Rebekah, having grown up in the shadow of her brother Laban, a mundane man, was attracted to Jacob the Torah student. Jacob's obtaining of the blessings, an act that appears to have been accomplished by devious means and outright deception, is explained not by tortuous apologetics, but insightfully through a startling psychological approach. Rebekah never intended to deceive her husband. She merely wanted to demonstrate to him how easily he can be duped in order to make him aware of the possibility that his fondness for Esau might have been gained by trickery, by Esau's posing as a righteous person. When Jacob came close to making his father believe that he was Esau merely by putting on some hairy goatskins, Isaac became suddenly and painfully aware of his own gullible nature. In R. Hirsch's words:

> If a simple man can so easily pose as a master hunter, how much more can Esau masquerade as a simple man. In this – Isaac's undeception through Jacob's deception – Rebekah succeeded perfectly.... As soon as he realized this, he immediately added his confirmatory

and fully consciously expressed blessing "And indeed he shall be blessed."[12]

Another important feature of his commentary is R. Hirsch's distinctive use of symbolism as an exegetical tool. While symbolism has been part and parcel of biblical exegesis throughout all ages, R. Hirsch made particularly effective use of this method. Shunning the esoteric and mystic, he developed sets of appealing and engaging symbols not only for the purpose of giving meaning to the various commandments, but also to render all ritual realia esthetically attractive and spiritually meaningful to the modern mind. Discounting the Kabbalists, Hirsch is unique in his comprehensiveness and thoroughness in this area. When explaining anything symbolically, every single detail of the commandment or the ritual object is invested with a specific symbolic meaning. All of these elements are then coordinated to form an integrated symbolic mosaic structure.

As one example of his virtuosity in this area, reference ought to be made to his brilliant symbolic representation of the

---

[12] *Commentary* to Gen. 27:1. Another example of this approach is R. Hirsch's explanation of Sarah's seemingly abominable behavior toward Hagar during the latter's pregnancy. The critical verb ותענה (Gen. 16:6), which is ordinarily rendered "and she afflicted her," is rendered by R. Hirsch as "and she humbled her." However, even this act requires justification. R. Hirsch goes on to explain that Sarah's actions were not taken in anger as punishment for Hagar's overbearing attitude toward her. Rather, they were taken for psychological reasons, for the sake of the child to be born. Sarah desired that the child come under her guiding influence, not Hagar's. She, therefore, tried to make Hagar responsive (a meaning that the verb in question contains) to Sarah and dependent on her by humbling Hagar and ridding her of her undue arrogance.

One more example: Rachel's stealing of her father Laban's household gods (ibid., 31:19) was not done, as it appears, to keep her father from discovering through the power of these gods the escape of Jacob and his family. On the contrary, Rachel wanted to prove to her father the worthlessness of these gods. In R. Hirsch's words: "If they can be stolen, and cannot even protect themselves, how much less can one put any trust in them to protect his home!"

menorah, in which every minute part of the *menorah* is infused
with its own particular symbolic importance.

Basing himself on the verse, "not by might nor by power,
but by My spirit, saith the Lord" (Zech. 4:6), referring to the
prophet's vision of the *menorah*, R. Hirsch concludes that the
menorah is symbolically representative of the divine spirit.
Since elsewhere the divine spirit is defined as consisting of six
qualities, "wisdom and understanding, counsel and strength,
knowledge and the fear of the Lord" (Isaiah 11:2), we are led to
the logical conclusion that the *menorah* symbolizes these
qualities. In order to establish this connection, R. Hirsch
shows that these six qualities are comprised in reality of three
parallel pairs. Each pair represents two aspects of one particular quality, the theoretical and the applied. Thus, the first set,
comprised of wisdom and understanding, represents the
quality of intellectual wisdom in its theoretical and applied
form. Similarly, the second set represents the quality of
mundane knowledge in its theoretical and applied form, and
the third set represents spiritual knowledge in both forms. All
six qualities combine synergistically to form the quality of the
divine spirit.[13]

All of this is symbolically represented by the *menorah*.
The right branches represent the theoretical aspects of these
qualities while the left branches represent the applied aspects.
In ascending order of importance, the outer set represents the
first set of qualities, the one next to it, the second set, and the
inner branches represent the third set. The middle stem, which
forms the base of the *menorah*, represents the combined force

---

[13] This construction also may be employed to explain the symbolism
represented by the hexagram, known as *Magen David*. As prophesied by
Isaiah, the scion that will arise from the house of David will be endowed
with these six qualities, which, according to R. Hirsch, are in reality three
in number, each of which is composed of two aspects, a theoretical and an
applied. We may thus view the hexagram, which is formed by two equilat-
eral triangles, as symbolizing the three characteristic qualities – in their
double capacity – that the future scion of the house of David will represent.

of all six branches, thus symbolizing the divine spirit. This is why the wicks of all six candles must turn and face the middle candle when the *menorah* is lit – to symbolize their merged unity as represented by the central candle.[14]

R. Hirsch makes extensive use of symbolism in explaining the meanings represented by the various furnishings of the Tabernacle, and he attaches supreme importance to these symbols. He goes so far as to claim that

> both the making as well as the delivering, and finally, at the assembling and erecting, the holy and symbolic meaning and purpose of each and every part which made up the whole edifice was present and vivid in the mind of the workers and Moses.... No object can stand as a symbol if it is not intended and made to be that symbol.[15]

R. Hirsch thereby rationalizes the prohibition of gazing at the holy objects when they are being covered for transit, stating:

> The holy objects must remain to their bearers as symbolic objects, subjects for the mind ... to fill the mind with thoughts of their meaning.... Gazing at them being wrapped up ... could very well have a disturbing effect.[16]

---

[14] See *Commentary* to Ex. 25:32.

[15] See *Commentary* to Ex. 36:8.

[16] *Commentary* to Num. 4:20. Another example of R. Hirsch's symbolic interpretation is his explanation of why the erection of a pillar (*matzevah*) was acceptable during the period of the Patriarchs, but was outlawed with the giving of the Torah. In his words:

> A pillar consists of a single stone whereas an altar is an elevation built by many stones. Thus, the pillar is presented by nature whereas an altar is made by man. Before the giving of the Torah, God's rule was manifest primarily only in ways of nature and the fate of man ... in what man receives from the hand of God. This is characterized by a pillar, a stone taken from God's creation, as a memorial for something which He has done. But with the giving of the Torah, God wishes to be revealed not so much in what man receives from Him as in what man does with what he receives from Him, not with God's gifts but with man's deeds is God to be

R. Hirsch's attention to minor details leads him to the discovery of major ideas. In the account of the creation of man, in contrast to that of the creation of animals, the verb וייצר is spelled with a double "*yod*" (Gen. 2:7). Most commentaries are quite satisfied with the famous interpretation, based on the Midrash, that the double "*yod*" represents the two inclinations, the good and the bad, within man. The fact that only one "*yod*" is sounded while the other one remains quiescent is ignored by all standard commentaries, but this point attracted R. Hirsch's inquisitive attention and produced the following illuminating comment:

> One inclination is always predominant, yet it does not do away with the other. The other is always there. The highest man still belongs to earth and there is always in every man a glimmering of humanity shining through.[17]

In other words, it all depends on man as to which of his inclinations will become dominant, the good one or the bad one, and which will be suppressed.

R. Hirsch does not generally cite other commentaries, whether in support of his views or for the purpose of criticizing their views. This might appear to be a negative feature of his commentary but, upon closer examination, proves to be a positive one. R. Hirsch was certainly aware of the Bible critics, whether of the higher or lower variety, but he does not engage them in confrontational argumentation. This is not because, as some surmise, R. Hirsch did not want to pollute his work with heretically repugnant views;[18] the Bible itself often cites directly heretical views for the purpose of negating

---

glorified (*Commentary* to Gen. 28:18, and Cf. *Commentary* to Gen. 33:20 and Deut. 16:22).

[17] *Commentary* to Gen. 2:7.

[18] See I. Grunfeld in his introduction to Isaac Levy's translation of Hirsch's *Commentary* (New York, 1945), xxiii.

them.[19] R. Hirsch refrains from doing likewise primarily for methodological reasons. By leaving out the views of others, he not only avoids needless displays of ostentatious scholarship, he also thereby shields the reader from becoming distracted and confused by intrusive cumbersome material. Instead, he presents his own interpretation in such a way that it obviates the need for other interpretations. And in the case of the Bible critics, he neatly removes, by his well aimed elucidations of the relevant passages, the textual grounds upon which their critical views are based.

Thus, by widening and deepening the traditional explanation for the change of God's name *Elokim* in the first section of the creation story to *Ha-Shem Elokim* in the second section, R. Hirsch effectively removes the underpinnings of the well-known Documentary theory. In the first section, before man was created, nature was following unswervingly on the course set for it by God; thus the name *Elokim*, signifying pure justice and strict regularity, is used. However, following the creation of man, who was endowed with the power of free choice, including the ability to deviate from God's path, the world could no longer survive if it were to be governed by pure justice alone. Now, in addition to justice, the world was in need of compassionate love, represented by the name *Ha-Shem*, hence the appearance of the combined form *Ha-Shem Elokim*.

R. Hirsch notes with perceptive insight that this idea is intimated in the change of the order of creation recorded in the Bible. When referring to the original creation, the order is given as "heaven and earth" (Gen. 1:1; 2:4) because at that point everything was guided strictly by the rules of Heaven. In the second creation story, following the appearance of man, the order is reversed, "earth and heaven" (ibid., 2:4) because now, given man's power of free will, a concession had to be made to

---

[19] For example, "The fool says in his heart, there is no God" (Psalms 14:1); "How long shall the wicked speak arrogantly ... and they say, the Lord does not see, the God of Jacob does not observe" (ibid. 94:3,7).

the earthly nature of man by introducing the quality of compassionate love. In R. Hirsch's words:

> As *Elokim*, God created heaven and earth and fixed its development on law and order. As *Ha-Shem*, He interferes with this development ... in accordance with its purpose, the education of mankind. There, in the physical arrangement of the world, earth is dependent on heaven; here in the moral and spiritual considerations for ruling the world ... the heaven is swayed by the contemporary behavior of mankind on earth.

However, not all attacks against the traditional concept of the Bible lend themselves to indirect responses. The bold denial of the divine origin of the Bible on the part of many Bible critics, for example, called for a direct response. And R. Hirsch unhesitatingly took up the challenge in a direct and forthright manner. In a comment on the verse, "And Moses hearkened to the voice of his father-in-law, and did all that he said" (Ex. 18:24), R. Hirsch observes:

> So little was Moses in himself a legislative genius, he had so little talent for organizing, that he had to learn the very first element of state organization from his father-in-law.... [Such] a man could never have given the people a constitution and laws out of his own head. Indeed just because of this, he was the best and the most faithful instrument of God.

The lack of certain innate talents on the part of Moses is also apparent, according to R. Hirsch, in Moses' requesting his father-in-law to serve as a guide for the Israelites in their journey in the desert.[20]

R. Hirsch finds additional proof for his contention in the fact that Moses hesitated in accepting the charge, asking God to send someone else instead. This leads him to conclude: "The utter lack of confidence in himself is in itself the most vivid

---

[20] *Commentary* to Num. 10:31.

proof of the divine origin of all which was done and spoken by Moses."[21]

In another context, R. Hirsch argues similarly that we should view Moses simply as a faithful instrument of God and not as a superman in his own right. He claims that the "absolutely ordinary human nature" of Moses is firmly established by the Bible right at the outset of his activity. He bases his claim on the fact that the genealogy of Moses and Aaron is recorded in the Bible in the middle of the narrative of their mission to Pharaoh. This genealogy appears in the section following their initial failure and immediately preceding the account of their successes. The reason for inserting their genealogy precisely at this point in the story is to indicate to us that, despite the extraordinary miracles that Moses and Aaron were about to perform, they should not be viewed as angels or supermen; they are to be treated as normal human beings, as demonstrated by their parentage and family relations. In R. Hirsch's words:

> From the earliest times ... men who have shown themselves as striking benefactors by their "godlike" deeds, have been invested, after their passing away, with "godlike" origins.... By this citation of origin, [the Bible] opposes all erroneous deification, every illusion of a Divine incarnation in human form.... Moses, the greatest man of all time was nothing but an ordinary human being and did not transcend the sphere of mortal beings.[22]

In dealing with the Temple, R. Hirsch similarly eschews the miraculous and supernatural and, instead, takes a spiritually rational approach. In his comment on the verse regarding the pilgrimage to the Temple three times a year (Ex. 23:17), he offers a thoughtful explanation as to why the lame and the

---

[21] *Commentary* to Ex. 4:13.

[22] *Commentary* to Ex. 6:14.

blind are excluded from the obligation of making the pilgrimage. To quote:

> Only the mature, free, healthy, young and strong are
> bound to appear in the Temple on the three pilgrim fes-
> tivals. People of weak intellect ... deaf or dumb, lame,
> blind, ill, are free from this duty (*Hagigah* 2a).... The
> Jewish Temple is no place of "wonder working grace" to
> which it is, above all, the diseased, the suffering, the
> aged, the blind, the lame ... who make the pilgrimage ...
> to seek miraculous healing.... It is the elite who must
> come there to seek spiritual enlightenment.

Here, as in numerous other instances, R. Hirsch demonstrates his remarkable ability to take an apparently simple verse and deduce from it lofty morals and edifying concepts that are of importance for all times.

Timelessness and Timeliness

To R. Hirsch, the timelessness of the Torah does not at all preclude the quality of timeliness. On the contrary, true timelessness is nothing but the sum total of an endless succession of timely messages. By a careful and searching examination of the biblical text, R. Hirsch found answers to many of the problems facing his generation while yielding at the same time keen and subtle explanations for textual difficulties. He made this one of his avowed tasks in his capacity as commentator, stating in his preface, "that the Torah is permeated with ideas that have a vital bearing on the problems and endeavors of each period in history."

One of the most vexing problems that R. Hirsch faced was whether proponents of traditional Judaism should stay within the general organized communal structure or should, instead, secede and form their own independent community. It seems that he found a strong intimation in favor of secession in Jacob's introductory words to the blessing of his sons before his death. When Jacob called his sons together to come and hearken to his final words, he uses the verbs האספו and הקבצו

(Gen. 49:1-2). The first verb generally denotes to withdraw from somewhere, whereas the second one denotes to join together and form a united group. Thus, Jacob's message, according to R. Hirsch, was "Break away from everything to which you really do not belong, and find yourself all united in the one common purpose. Be all taken up with that which is common to you all." Without explicitly applying this interpretation to the particular problem of his day, it is nonetheless clear from the wording that the issue of secession must have been present in his mind in formulating his interpretation.

R. Hirsch also addresses the more encompassing problem of the Jewish exile in his *Commentary*. In his commentary on the verse "And the Lord rooted them out of their land ... and cast them into another land" (Deut. 29:27), which describes the process of exile, R. Hirsch considers why the letter *lamed* of the word וישלכם ("and cast them") is written large. R. Hirsch writes that while exile is meted out as a punishment, it is to be conceived as serving a higher purpose, i.e., to enable the Jewish people to act as a teacher to all the nations by spreading them throughout the world. Basing himself on the fact that the denotation of the letter *lamed* is "to teach," R. Hirsch propounds as follows:

> Wherever they are that is not their original homeland, and wherever they may find themselves, they are not there just by chance. God has cast them there, as a great *lamed*, as a great instructive sign for the history of the development of the nations ... to serve among the nations His purpose for mankind.

Apparently troubled by the negative connotation of the phrase "He cast them," R. Hirsch finds an added function for the large *lamed* in the verse under discussion. He suggests that the largeness of the *lamed* overshadows the letter *shin* that is next to the *lamed* in the verb וישלכם; the *shin*'s importance is thus minimized, leaving the verb to be read alternatively as וילכם, "He led them." If we act as a light unto the nations, exile can be viewed not as a casting away by God, but as a purposeful instrument of God's leading hand.[23] This conceptualization of the Jewish exile enjoyed wide currency in R. Hirsch's day.

In keeping with the tenor of this idea, R. Hirsch shows elsewhere that it is the task of the Jew to be concerned with the needs of the rest of humanity. He proves this point through the hermeneutic tool of juxtaposition in the context of the accounts of Abraham's hospitality to three strangers and the previous performance of his own circumcision. Circumcision, which is a sign denoting Jewish separateness, should not to be construed as indicating selfish isolationism; on the contrary, this separateness is for the purpose of dedicating the Jew to the service of humanity at large. To quote in part:

> [It has been said that] this segregating sign is supposed to strip them of all cosmopolitan feelings and thoughts for mankind in general, [but] ... for fostering such humaneness, they were set apart.[24]

---

[23] In this connection, it is worth noting that, according to R. Hirsch, the mission of Israel is one of the fundamental causes of anti-Semitism and the persecution of the Jewish people. In commenting on the verse, "When the Ark was set out, Moses would say, Arise O Lord, and let Thy enemies be scattered and Thy foes flee" (Num. 10:35), R. Hirsch, basing himself on the interpretation of the *Sifrei* that the term משנאיך in this verse refers to those who persecute the Jews, elaborates:

> This Torah from its very entry into the world would have to expect opponents.... Its demands for self control and sanctification of morals are so much in contrast to the allures of ignoble passions that one finds in the breasts of ignoble masses in all classes, not only the hatred but persecution....

Cf. Nehama Leibowitz, *Studies in Bamidbar*, 91.

[24] *Commentary* to Gen. 18:1. This comment may perhaps serve as additional justification for R. Hirsch's formation of his secessionist community. The segregation was meant not only to fortify his own community but also for the purpose of more effectively serving the general community. Cf. P. Rosenblit in *Torah im Derekh Eretz*, M. Breuer ed. (Ramat-Gan, 1987), 39.

In commenting on the legal and ritual portions of the Torah, R. Hirsch first offers a detailed review of the particulars of each law in question, followed by an elaborate conceptual rationale of the law. It is therefore quite puzzling that in commenting on the verse concerning the law of *niddah*, R. Hirsch dismisses its conceptualization with a brief remark, stating that is for the purpose of raising sexual relations from their base level to a higher level of purity and holiness.[25] Elsewhere, he makes use of R. Meir's explanation – without mentioning his name – that the prohibition of conjugal relations during the *niddah* period serves to refresh the love between husband and wife.[26] What is even more enigmatic in this context is the total omission of a rationale for the laws of *niddah* from R. Hirsch's book *Horeb*, especially considering that the conceptualization and explanation of *mitzvot* is characteristic of this work.

Heinemann, grappling with this problem, suggests that it was for reasons of prudery that Hirsch was constrained in dealing with this issue.[27] Rosenbloom rejects this suggestion as "unacceptable," but fails to offer an explanation of his own.[28]

If conjecture we must, I would proffer the following possibility. R. Hirsch undoubtedly entertained in his fertile mind various thoughts regarding the laws of *niddah*. However, because of the supreme importance of these laws, as well as the way they irritate the sensibilities of the modern Jew, he was not sure whether his theorizations were satisfying enough.

---

[25] *Commentary* to Lev. 18:19.

[26] See *Niddah* 3lb. R. Hirsch thereby explains the juxtaposition of the punishments for cohabitation between brother and sister and that of the cohabitation with a *niddah*, "to tell that there are periods...in which husband and wife live as sister and brother...such a condition has the capacity to deepen the intimacy, raising it constantly" (*Commentary* to Lev. 20:18).

[27] *Ta'amei ha-Mitzvot be-Sifrut Yisra'el* (Jerusalem, 1956), v. 2, p. 133.

[28] Noah Rosenbloom, *Tradition in an Age of Reform* (Philadelphia, 1976), 435.

He therefore postponed to a later date their sorting out and final formulation. Most probably, he meant to include the conceptualization of these laws in his projected work *Moriah*, which, as we know, was not realized.

R. Hirsch was not averse to forced interpretations of the text when he felt that they were necessary, especially when the result yields a valid idea. For example: The well-known phrase "a land flowing with milk and honey" (Ex. 3:8) is rendered by R. Hirsch as "a land that can flow with milk and honey." Since the land of *Eretz Yisrael* is often afflicted with droughts and famine, R. Hirsch introduced the qualifying word "can," which he interpreted to imply that this abundance is conditional, depending on Israel's performance of the commandments. To support his rendition, a rather questionable definition of the verb זוב is proposed. Since this verb occurs in the Bible either in a pathological context (e.g., Lev. 15:2) or in a miraculous one (e.g., Ps. 78:20), it is to be defined as having reference only to an unnatural flow. Hence, the land's flowing with milk and honey is not affected by natural causes, but only through divine intervention.

Philological Analysis

A preponderant element of R. Hirsch's commentary is the mining of the Hebrew language for ideological nuggets. According to R. Hirsch,

> the study of Hebrew etymology is the most instructive way of gaining an insight into the concepts and ideologies which the Hebrew language means to convey.... Every word down to the very smallest connecting article represents an idea in its own right.[29]

---

[29] *Samson R. Hirsch – The Collected Writings* (New York and Jerusalem, 1992), v. 7, pp. 71, 74. While R. Hirsch makes a persuasive argument for the importance of the knowledge of Hebrew to the outside world (63-80), he also included its instruction as part of the Jewish religious education in the curriculum of the school he founded in Frankfurt (67).

Faithful to tradition, according to which Hebrew was the original language of mankind,[30] and in keeping with his axiomatic principle that the Torah must be interpreted from within, R. Hirsch denies the validity of comparative linguistics for exegetical purposes.[31]

In his interpretations, R. Hirsch makes creative use of the extended meanings of many Hebrew lexemes. His philological system is known by the term "speculative etymology,"[32] with "speculative" to be taken in its primary sense, the intellectual examination of a subject. However, since, in its secondary sense, it is used to describe conjectural or undemonstrable reasoning, thus carrying pejorative overtones, R. Hirsch's philological system should have been called "philosophical etymology."

This undoubtedly indicates that to R. Hirsch the study of the Hebrew language is in the category of studying Torah. There are halakhic sources to support such a view. Thus, e.g., it is forbidden to read secular material on Shabbat, but if it is written in Hebrew, it is permitted to do so (*Shulhan Arukh, Orah Hayyim* 307:16). This is because "the Hebrew language itself has holiness in it, and one may learn from it words of Torah" (*Mishnah Berurah, ad loc.*). Cf. ibid. 85:1. Similarly, R. Yoseph Hayyim Sonnenfeld maintains that the study of Hebrew grammar is treated as part of studying Torah (*Salmat Hayyim*, part 4, responsum 62).

Mordechai Breuer's contention that R. Hirsch did not distinguish curricularly between religious and secular subjects (*Ha-Rav Shimshon R. Hirsch*, 37) is correct only insofar as the ultimate goal of both studies was concerned; according to R. Hirsch, the aim of both religious and secular study is the creation of the unified Jewish person. As to the educational means for achieving this ideal, however, R. Hirsch distinguished in his school curriculum between Jewish and secular subjects of study.

30 *Targum Yonatan* to Gen. 11:1; *Tanhuma*, Noah 9.

31 Aramaic is the only exception (e.g., *Commentary* to Gen. 4:1; 6:14), most likely because it is considered a language close to Hebrew (*Pesahim* 87b). It is worth noting that R. Moshe Isserles in his responsa makes use of this assertion to resolve the following question. According to Maimonides, a *get* written partly in one language and partly in another language is invalid (*Gerushin* 4:8), and yet every *get* has Hebrew words mixed in with the Aramaic. According to Rema, Hebrew and Aramaic are not regarded as two separate languages (Responsum no. 126).

32 See I. Heinemann, *Ta'amei ha-Mitzvot*, v. 2, p. 109. For the background of this system, see idem in *Zion* 16: 61-67.

In truth, "philosophical semantics" is an even better description of R. Hirsch's philological analyses. Unlike general semantic studies, however, which, on the whole, are prosaic in nature, Hirsch semanticized the Hebrew vocabulary in order to extract spiritual and ideological messages. Accordingly, his philological scheme would best be named "ideological semantics."

Although R. Hirsch does not offer a fully elaborated presentation of the philological principles of his etymological system – hoping to do so at a later date, as stated in the preface to his *Commentary* – two important principles emerge from his many interpretations. One is the thesis held by many linguists that although the Hebrew stem consists of three letters, it is essentially biliteral, composed of two root letters that represent its basic meaning with the third letter merely serving as a further refinement of the basic meaning. It is frequently difficult to prove which two letters are to be taken as the basic root letters that signify the primary meaning of the stem since, according to the biliterality theory, any two letters may serve this purpose. Only in a limited number of cases, such as in the following example, does the determination seem to be rather self-evident: פרש, פרק, פרך, פרץ, פרע, פרס, פרם, פרט, פרז, פרד. In this set, the first two letters evidently represent the basic concept of "breaking apart," with the added third letters representing a particular refined variation on the basic theme.[33]

The second principle widely employed by R. Hirsch is that of phonetic similarity; that is, words that are similar in sound are also related in meaning. This assumption is in consonance with R. Hirsch's view of the precedence of the Oral Law over the Written Law as discussed above. This explains the

---

[33] For further examples, see S. Moscati, *Biblica* 28 (1947): 113-35. For a review of the problem, see G. J. Botterweck, *Der Triliterismus im Semitischen* (Bonn, 1952). Also see, M. Seidel, *Hiqrei Lashon* (Jerusalem, 1986), 29,30.

importance of the sounds of spoken words, allowing for the connection in meaning between words with related sounds. This importance is reflected in the Hebrew noun משמע, used to refer to the plain sense of a word; the root meaning of משמע is the act of hearing.[34] In interpreting the Torah, R. Hirsch was not only attentive to the letters of the text through close reading, but also by close listening to the sound of the words.

This principle, however, if not critically defined in accordance with a scientific study of Hebrew phonetics, can easily be misapplied and lead to unsound connections and wrong conclusions. It would be a worthwhile enterprise to review all phonetically based interpretations made by R. Hirsch with an eye towards reconstructing the phonetic theories that underlie these interpretations, but this would require a separate study.

It is important to stress here that R. Hirsch as a commentator was ideologically driven to analyze the vocabulary of the Torah semantically with a view to derive from it lofty ideas and instructive messages. His ingenious semanticizations, adorningly interspersed throughout his *Commentary*, are legion.

For the sake of illustration, two short examples should suffice, one of which will be strictly religious in nature while the other will contain humanistic elements as well. R. Hirsch sees the word אדם, the term for "man," as being etymologically related to the verb דמה, "to be similar," and the noun הדום, "a footstool," which leads him to the following observation: "Man must try to be similar to God by emulating His ways and becoming a footstool of the Divine Presence on earth as a transmitter and bearer of the glory of God on earth."[35]

The noun אשר, "happiness," is etymologically related, according to R. Hirsch, to the verb אשר, meaning "to step" or "to

---

[34] For Talmudic citations, see W. Bacher, *Exegetische Terminologie* V.1, s.v.; Jastrow, *Dictionary*, 856. The overriding importance of the hearing faculty is reflected in the halakhic ruling that whoever causes deafness to a person is liable to such payment as if he caused total incapacitation (*Bava Kamma* 85b).

[35] *Commentary* to Gen. 1:26.

step forward." He thus reaches the conclusion that happiness is not to be conceived as a static state to be attained once and for all, but rather as something dynamic and ongoing. Accordingly, true happiness expresses itself in forward movement, in going ahead, and reflects itself in continuous progress.[36]

Additional Factors

In any evaluation of the *Commentary*, due account must be taken of two factors. First, the *Commentary* is based on drafts recorded by auditors of the weekly lectures on *humash* given by R. Hirsch in the community synagogue.[37] Second, Hirsch's main motivation in his *Commentary* was not so much to illuminate the text as to edify and illuminate the reader. The first factor will explain in part, as conceded by R. Hirsch himself in his preface, the style of the *Commentary*, which retains some of the oratorical echoes of the original lectures. Both factors serve to explain the presence of many digressive disquisitions in the *Commentary*.[38] Lectures by nature are given to such excursions. And because, as said, his aim was to

---

[36] *Commentary* to Gen. 30:13 and Ps. 1:1. It must be noted that R. Hirsch all too often overloads his semantic derivations by imposing upon them far-fetched ideological implications. For example, the noun *nasi* has two meanings, a prince and a cloud. The semantic nexus between these two meanings according to R. Hirsch is resolved as follows:

> The function of a prince represents that of a cloud ... the cloud receives its substance from the earth below ... for the purpose of sending it back to earth in the form of rain to make it yield fruit. Similarly, the prince derives his power from the people below, and must use these powers ... to advance the welfare of his subjects (Samson R. Hirsch, *Collected Writings*, v. 7, p. 73).

For this reason, the editors of the Hebrew version of his *Commentary* are to be commended for having the semantic interpretations set off, appearing in a different typeface.

[37] Cf. R. Hirsch's Preface to Genesis, which was published first. For the rest of the *Commentary*, see M. Breuer in *Ha-Rav Shimshon R. Hirsch*, 40.

[38] For examples, see comments on Ex. 12:2, 21:37; Lev. 7:18, 16:23; Num. 9:2, 15:18; Deut. 6:4-9, 11:19, 19:15, 24:16.

educate the reader, R. Hirsch turned the *Commentary* into a
source of instruction in the basic laws and concepts of Judaism for the intelligent layman.

These factors may also help explain the difference between the *Commentary* and *Horeb* in the order of presentation
of the subject matter. In the former, R. Hirsch presents first
the law in its details followed by their conceptualization,
whereas in the latter the order is reversed. *Horeb* was intended
for the uninitiated Jew,[39] and R. Hirsch felt that such a Jew
must first become convinced of the intrinsic value of this law
through the presentation of a persuasive rationale in order for
him to become interested in studying its various details. On
the other hand, the *Commentary* was mainly intended for the
initiated and committed Jew. Such a Jew will observe the laws
whether he is aware of their rationale or not. Consequently,
R. Hirsch's primary interest was in teaching the various
requirements for the proper observance of the commandments,
and only subsequently to grant a conceptual appreciation of
their value. In this regard, R. Hirsch follows in the footsteps of
his teacher R. Ya'akov Ettlinger, who, in commenting on the
phrase "נעשה ונשמע", states: "Following the fulfillment of the
commandments, a person is obligated to study, investigate and
search out ... the reasons of the Torah."[40]

There is one final concern in this area that needs to be
resolved. In sketching the details of the ritual and civil laws,
R. Hirsch supplies the sources on which these are based,
whereas in the presentation of their rationalizations and in his
exegetical explanations he does not provide any sources. Three
possible reasons suggest themselves in resolving this question.
First, cut and dried laws easily lend themselves to citation of
sources. The character of a concept, however, even one with
antecedents in earlier sources, is to a large extent transformed
by its particular formulation. Thus, R. Hirsch considered his

---

[39] I. Grunfeld, introduction to his English version of *Horeb*, 144.

[40] *Minhat Ani, Parshat Va-Yetzei*; beginning of *Parshat Yitro*. Cf. *supra*, n. 4.

conceptualizations his own creations. Second, every law listed in the *Commentary* is taken directly from the sources. With regard to the conceptualizations, on the other hand, only some have their origin in the sources, whereas others are wholly or partly R. Hirsch's own. Because of his desire that the reader treat all the offered explanations equally, R. Hirsch decided not to offer any sources, even for those concepts on which he relied on other opinions. Finally, R. Hirsch considered his conceptualizations sufficient for the intellectual needs of the initiated layman, for whom the *Commentary* was intended, and there was thus no need to provide sources for further study. Regarding his halakhic sketches, however, R. Hirsch was aware that they were incomplete, and he therefore provided sources for the purpose of further study.

That R. Hirsch considered the above emerges from his response to R. Bamberger's criticism that the laws concerning *mikveh* given in R. Hirsch's *Commentary* were inadequate. Making use of Hillel's words to the would-be proselyte who wanted to have the entire Torah taught to him while standing on one foot,[41] R. Hirsch replied that his aim was "to set before the student the main elements of every commandment, 'and as for the rest, go on and study.'"[42]

Conclusion

Due to its multifaceted exegesis, the *Commentary*, in its English and Hebrew versions, enjoys a modicum of popularity in many circles of modern orthodox Judaism. It has a strong appeal for the so-called right-wing segments of modern orthodoxy because of its novel exegetical extrapolations and because of its charged spiritualization of the commandments in their full halakhic strength. For the so-called liberal elements in

---

[41] *Shabbat* 31a.

[42] Correspondence in Hebrew, published from manuscript by Yonah Emanuel in *Hama'ayan* 29:1 (1988): 47.

modern orthodoxy, the *Commentary* serves them as a source for their moralization of Judaism and for their views of a moderated Zionism.

However, to arrive at a judicious evaluation of the *Commentary*, due consideration must be given to the overall aim of its author. True, R. Hirsch lists in his preface five aims. These serve, however, in an ancillary capacity to the ultimate goal, which, as it emerges from the overall effect of his *Commentary*, seems to be to persuade the student of the transcendent worth of the observance of all the commandments and induce him to engage in further study of all the particular details that are required for their proper performance. To what extent R. Hirsch succeeded in reaching this goal is the task of investigative research in the history of the Hirschian community, which is outside the confines of this study.

Haftarah – Sidrah:
Mirror Images

Samuel N. Hoenig

The ancient synagogue practice of reading from the Prophets on the Sabbath, Festivals and Fast Days – commonly referred to as *haftarah* reading, is shrouded in mystery. Despite the centrality of the *haftarah* in the synagogue service – especially on bar mitzvah and *aufruf* celebrations and *yahrtzeit* commemorations – the origin of the *haftarah* reading is a matter of controversy. Even the meaning of the word *haftarah* has puzzled scholars through the ages.[1]

The institution of the *haftarah* was already known in Tannaitic times.[2] Although the *Tosefta*[3] lists only the *haftarah* texts for special occasions and festivals, nevertheless, it is clear

---

[1] See *Sefer Abudarham ha-Shalem* (Jerusalem, 1963), 173; *Sefer ha-Manhig, Hilkhot Shabbat* (Jerusalem, 1961), sec. 35; *Mahzor Vitry* (Jerusalem, 1963), 98; *Arukh ha-Shulhan, Orah Hayyim* (New York, 1961), 284:1.

[2] See Mishnah *Megillah*, ch. 4 and *Tosefta Megillah*, ch. 3.

[3] *Tosefta*, ibid. and *Megillah* 23a.

that the *haftarah* was read as well on every Sabbath morning;[4] the exact texts however, unfixed and possibly varying from place to place.[5]

The origin of the reading of the *haftarah* is unknown and is the subject of various hypotheses, ranging chronologically from medieval to modern times.

According to R. Tam, as quoted by R. Isaiah of Trani (c. 1200),[6] the reading of the *haftarah* dates back to the days of Ezra. Ezra is responsible for instituting the reading of the Torah on Sabbath afternoons (*minhah*) and for the reading of the *aliyot* totaling a minimum of ten verses on Mondays and Thursdays.[7] According to R. Tam, Ezra also enacted that a portion from the Prophets (*haftarah*) be read each Sabbath morning. While R. Tam does not mention Ezra's intentions in establishing the *haftarah* reading, perhaps Ezra wished to emphasize the unity of the Torah and Prophets and therefore juxtaposed various prophetic readings and the Torah portion. According to R. Tam's hypothesis, it would follow that the reading of the *haftarah* served as an extension of *keri'at ha-Torah* and thus was of an obligatory (*hovah*) nature.[8]

---

[4] Mishnah *Megillah* 4:2: "*be-Shabbat shiv'ah ... u-maftirin be-Navi*," and comments of R. Isaiah of Trani, *Sefer ha-Makhri'a* (Jerusalem, 1998), sec. 31. Regarding the reading of the *haftarah* at *minhah* on Shabbat, see Mishnah *Megillah* 4:1; *Shabbat* 24a; *Tosafot Megillah* 21a, s.v. *ha-Koreh*; *Sefer ha-Ittim* (Berlin, 1903), 271; *Teshuvot ha-Ge'onim, Hemdah Genuzah* (Jerusalem, 1967), sec. 95; and R. Nissim (Ran), *Megillah*, ibid.

[5] *Sefer ha-Eshkol*, part 1, ed. Albeck (Jerusalem, 1935), 171; R. Yosef Karo, *Kesef Mishneh, Hilkhot Tefillah* 12:12; Shlomo Yehuda Rapoport, *Sefer Erekh Millin*, vol. 1 (Jerusalem, 1970), 330. However, see *Megillah* 30b and *Yerushalmi Nedarim* 6:8, which seem to indicate that there were fixed *haftarot* in Talmudic times.

[6] *Sefer ha-Makhri'a*, ibid. Cf. *Sefer ha-Yashar* [*Hiddushim*] (Jerusalem, 1959), p. 140. See also *She'eiltot*, no. 161 and Eliezer Levi, *Yesodot ha-Tefillah* (Tel Aviv, 1958), 319.

[7] *Yerushalmi Megillah* 4:1; *Bava Kamma* 82a.

[8] See *She'eiltot*, ibid. However, according to R. Hai Gaon, as quoted in *Sefer ha-Ittim* (Cracow, 1903), 275, the reading of the *haftarah* is not a mitzvah. "*She-haftarah gufah einah mitzvah, she-hayavin le-hizaher bah*." See also

A most intriguing theory is advanced by R. David Abudarham (14th century).[9] Abudarham sees the reading of the *haftarah* as a substitute or replacement for the Torah portion. Due to persecutions forbidding the public reading of the Torah, the rabbis enacted that in its stead, a portion of the Prophets, thematically similar to the censored Torah portion, be read. This also, writes Abudarham, explains the meaning of the word *haftarah*. The word *haftarah* comes from the root "*p-t-r*" (to exempt), meaning that with the reading of the *haftarah*, one exempts himself from *keri'at ha-Torah*. It is for this reason that a *haftarah* should consist of a minimum of twenty-one verses, corresponding to the minimum three verses read from the Torah for each of the seven *aliyot*.[10] Although the persecutionary decree was repealed, the *takanah* of the rabbis was retained.

Abudarham does not pinpoint the date of this *takanah*. It is the opinion of R. Elijah Bahur (1469-1549), that Abudarham undoubtedly refers to the religious persecutions of Antiochus Epiphanes (168-165 BCE).[11] Indeed, the author of *Book of Maccabees*, when delineating the Epiphanic decrees, states:

> And wherever they found the Books of the Law, they tore them up and burned them. And if anyone was

---

R. Joseph B. Soloveitchik, *Shi'urim le-Zekher Abba Mari ZL*, vol. 2 (Jerusalem, 1985), 212.

[9] Ibid., 172.

[10] Ibid. According to *Sofrim* 14:1, the *haftarah* consists of 22 verses, the additional verse corresponding to the *Hazan ha-Keneset*. *Sefer ha-Ma'asim le-Benei Eretz Yisrael* (Tel Aviv, 1971), 49, sets the minimum number of verses for a *haftarah* at 24. See D. Sperber, *Minhagei Yisrael*, vol. 1 (Jerusalem, 1990), 158-59.

[11] *Sefer Tishbi* (Isny, 1541), "*patar*." See also *Tosafot Yom Tov, Megillah*, 3:4; R. Mordechai Jaffe, *Levush OH* 284:1. As to why the ban did not extend to the *haftarot*, see Rapoport, 329; and J. D. Eisenstein, *Otzar Dinim u-Minhagim* (New York, 1917), 102. For other examples of liturgical *takanot* as a result of persecution, see Jacob Mann, "Change in the Divine Service of the Synagogue Due to Religious Persecutions," *HUCA* 4 (1927): 241-302.

found to possess a Book of the Agreement or respected the Law, the king's decree condemned him to death.[12]

According to Abudarham, inasmuch as the *haftarah* is a substitute for the Torah reading, it is now clear why the various *halakhot* of the *haftarah* reading are patterned after those of *keri'at ha-Torah*. As mentioned above, the *haftarah* portion must contain a minimum of twenty-one verses, corresponding to the seven Torah *aliyot*, and be thematically connected to the *sidrah*. Similar to *keri'at ha-Torah*, the reading of the *haftarah* must be carried out in the presence of a quorum of ten (*minyan*).[13] The five blessings recited before and after the *haftarah* (one before and four after) correspond to the five books of the Torah (Pentateuch).[14] Just as the Torah reading in Talmudic times was translated into Aramaic by a *meturgaman*, so too, the *haftarah* portion was translated into Aramaic.[15] Furthermore, according to some opinions, the scroll from which the *haftarah* is read must be written in accordance with the *halakhot* governing the writing of a *sefer Torah*.[16] In these ways, the institutors of the *haftarah* were highlighting the fact that the *haftarah* was to serve as a substitute for the banned weekly Torah reading.

A third possible origin of the *haftarah* reading is found in *Sefer ha-Pardes* (11th century).[17] This view maintains that the

---

[12] *1 Maccabees* 1:56-57. Cf. Josephus, *Antiquities*, book 12, 5:4.

[13] Mishnah, *Megillah* 4:3. As to whether the requirement of a *minyan* for *keri'at ha-Torah* and *haftarah* is based on *davar she-bi-kedushah*, see *Me'iri, Beit ha-Behirah, Megillah* (Jerusalem, 1962), 23b; and R. Nissim (Ran) on R. Alfasi (Rif), *Megillah*, 13b.

[14] Abudarham, 172.

[15] Mishnah, *Megillah* 4:4, *Yerushalmi Megillah* 4:3.

[16] *Levush*, ibid. Cf. *Magen Avraham, Turei Zahav, Orah Hayyim* 284:1; *Shulhan Arukh ha-Rav, OH* 284:2; and *Mishnah Berurah,* 284:1.

[17] *Sefer Pardes ha-Gadol* (reprint of 1870 edition), 14-15. Cf. *Sefer Shibbolei ha-Leket* (Jerusalem, 1962), 37-38; *Teshuvot ha-Ge'onim*, ed. J. Musafia (Lyck, 1863), 29; and *Teshuvot ha-Ge'onim Sha'arei Tzedek* (Jerusalem, 1966), sec. 55.

haftarah readings on Sabbaths and Festivals are a relic of an old practice. The custom was that one completes the weekday morning service with the study of *mikra*, i.e., Torah and *Nevi'im* (Prophets). Following the Talmudic dictum "one should always divide his days into three: a third to *mikra*, a third to Mishnah and a third to Talmud," the practice was to study daily these three disciplines.[18] As part of this curriculum, at the end of *shaharit*, portions of the Prophets were read (studied). In later times, when people were pressed to earn a livelihood and could not afford the additional time for study, the practice was partially abandoned. Instead of reading a whole section of Prophets connected with the weekly Torah reading, two verses from the Book of Isaiah (59:20-21), which speak about the Torah in general, were recited.[19] However, on the Sabbath and Festivals when one does not work, the original practice was retained, to read after the Torah portion a full section from the Prophets, i.e., the *haftarah*.

An altogether different approach to the origin of the *haftarah* is offered by Shlomo Yehuda Rapoport (*Shir*) (1790-1867).[20] Rapoport is of the opinion that the *haftarah* did not become a fixed part of the Sabbath service until Amoraic times. When it was formally introduced, it was in conjunction with the *derashah* (sermon) delivered at the Sabbath service. A section of the Prophets, relevant to the weekly Torah reading,

---

[18] *Kiddushin* 30a.

[19] It is interesting to note that the prayer *u-vah le-Tziyyon*, recited at the conclusion of the daily *shaharit* service, consists of a conglomeration of verses from *Nevi'im* and *Ketuvim*. Although the author of *Sefer ha-Pardes* cites only the first two verses of *u-vah le-Tziyyon* as a substitute for the study of *Nevi'im*, it is possible that the entire prayer was to satisfy the daily requirement of the study of *mikra* (*Torah*, *Nevi'im*, and *Ketuvim*). It is especially interesting, that according to the Sephardic ritual, on Mondays and Thursdays, *u-vah le-Tziyyon* is recited before the return of the Torah to the ark. This also explains why on Sabbaths and Festivals *u-vah le-Tziyyon* is not recited during the morning service; since the *haftarah* is read, there is no reason to recite its "substitute."

[20] Rapoport, 328-30.

was selected and expounded upon to the congregation. The purpose of the *derashah* was to inspire and rebuke. The passionate and fiery messages of the prophets were most suitable for this purpose. According to Rapoport, when the Talmud speaks of *sefer aftarata* (*Gittin* 60a), it refers to these *derashot haftarah*, i.e., *targum* (Aramaic rendition) of the *haftarah* together with relevant *aggadot* and *midrashim.* Remnants of the *derashot* are found in parts of the *Targumim* to *Nevi'im* and in various midrashic collections, especially the *Pesikta midrashim.*[21]

According to all of the above theories, the choice of a particular *haftarah* was based on its connection to the portion of the Torah reading.[22] The exact nature of these connections is not elaborated upon.

Careful study shows that the connection between *haftarah* and *sidrah* varies from *haftarah* to *haftarah.* Sometimes the connection is obvious while other times it is obscure and elusive.[23] Especially in light of Abudarham's view, that the *haftarah* was chosen as a substitute for the Torah portion, it is important to establish the exact connection between the two.

The relationship of the Torah to the Books of the Prophets in itself is an interesting area of research, deserving a study of its own. Throughout the Talmud and Midrash, the books of the Prophets are used to explicate the Torah. A scanning of *Midrash Rabbah, Yelamdenu* (*Tanhuma*) and other *midrashim*

---

[21] See Rimon Kasher, *Toseftot Targum la-Nevi'im* [Hebrew] (Jerusalem, 1996), 16-18. Of further interest is the view of R. Joseph B. Soloveitchik, *Divrei Hashkafah* (Jerusalem, 1994), 77. R. Soloveitchik maintains that while the Torah reading was instituted to teach "*da'at Torah, mitzvoteha ve-hukehah,*" the *haftarah* was established to strengthen belief in the forthcoming redemption and the return of the Jewish people to their homeland: "*Matarat ha-haftarah hayetah le-hazek be-kerev ha-am et ha-emunah ba-ge'ulah she-tavo be-shivatah shel Keneset Yisrael el Eretz ha-Avot u-be-vi'at ha-Mashi'ah.*"

[22] The idea that the *haftarah* should be analogous to the Torah reading is enunciated in *Megillah* 29b, s.v. *de-dami lah.*

[23] R. Joseph B. Soloveitchik, 73.

will show that the rabbis consistently stressed the unity of the
Tanakh, demonstrating that there is nothing in the Torah that
cannot be found in the Prophets and Hagiographa. Conversely,
the medieval philosopher and exegete R. Yosef ibn Kaspi (1279-
1340), succinctly notes that promises about the future contained in the Prophets and Hagiographa were already alluded
to in the text of the Torah:[24]

כי אחד משלמות תורתנו הוא כי כל מה שהתנבאו הנביאים
מיעודים עתידים, הוא כתוב בתורה במין אחד מובן אצל הבקיאים
בעברי ובהגיון עד שאין ספרי הנביאים רק פרושים לספר התורה.
וזה ענין יקר וזכרהו.

Similarly, R. David b. Zimra (Radvaz) (1479-1573), commenting on the Talmudic statement that in messianic times
the books of the Prophets and Hagiographa will become null
and void,[25] explains that in the messianic era the meaning of
the Torah will be as clear as it was in the days of Moses and
there will be no need to turn to the prophetic writings (*Nevi'im*)
and Hagiographa (*Ketuvim*) for interpretation.[26] Thus, according to Radvaz, in pre-messianic days, the importance of the
books of the Prophets and Hagiographa lies in their serving as
biblical exegesis.[27] When attempting to understand the exact
relationship between the *haftarah* and its respective *sidrah*, the
views of R. Yosef ibn Kaspi and R. David b. Zimra should be
kept in mind.

A study of the *haftarah* will reveal that its relationship to
the *sidrah* is multifarious. There seem to be two general
categories: thematic resemblances and textual connections. In
many cases, both categories guided the rabbis in selecting the
haftarah, while in others it was one or the other.

---

[24] *Mishnat Kesef*, ed. Yitzhak Last (Cracow, 1906), 53.

[25] *Yerushalmi Megillah* 1:5.

[26] *She'eilot u-Teshuvot ha-Radvaz*, no. 666.

[27] It is unclear, according to Radvaz, how this exegetical process unfolds,
especially in the halakhic realm. This and other *haftarah* related issues are
discussed in my forthcoming book on *haftarot*.

Thematic resemblances between the *sidrah* and *haftarah* fall into two sub-categories: analogous and contrasting themes. Analogous themes exist when the *haftarah* and *sidrah* share similar subject matter – where the *haftarah* echoes the ideas and thoughts previously read in the *sidrah*. In some instances, the *haftarah* is almost a continuation of the *sidrah* narrative.[28]

Some examples of analogous themes are: *Va-Yera* (Genesis 18-22), where the beginning of the *sidrah* extols Abraham's virtue of kindness (*hakhnasat orhim*), followed by the birth of Isaac to the hitherto barren Sarah, and finally concluding with the *akedah*. Thus, the *sidrah* contains three basic themes – the importance of *hakhnasat orhim*, that God keeps His promise and rewards the righteous, and the idea of sacrifice. These three themes are likewise contained in the *haftarah* for that *sidrah* (2 Kings 4:1-37). Similar to the *sidrah*, the *haftarah* describes the woman of Shunam's hospitality towards Elisha, being rewarded in her old age with a child, and the child's untimely death and subsequent resurrection. The *sidrah* of *Toledot* (Genesis 25:19-28:9) and its *haftarah* (Malachi 1) are thematically analogous. Both the *sidrah* and *haftarah* speak of God's love for Jacob and His animosity for Esau. Very often, analogous themes are not obvious and become clear only on the basis of midrashic interpretation. Thus, the choice of Amos 2:6-3:8 as the *haftarah* for the *sidrah* of *Va-Yeshev* (Genesis 37:1-40:23) is obviously rooted in the midrashic view that the brothers sold Joseph for a "pair of shoes" – corresponding to the opening verse of the *haftarah*: "So said God, for three rebellious sins of Israel – but should I not exact retribution for the fourth – for their having sold a righteous man for silver, and a destitute one for the sake of a pair of shoes."[29]

---

[28] Fievel Meltzer, *Parashat ha-Shavu'a ve-Haftaratah* (Jerusalem, 1974), 37.

[29] See *Midrash Eleh Ezkerah* in *Otzar ha-Midrashim*, vol. 2 (New York, 1915), 440-43. For other examples of this phenomenon, see *Lekh Lekha* and *Bereshit Rabbah*, 43:44; *Be-Shalah* and *Mekhilta*, 14:24; *Va-Yakhel* and *Yalkut Shimoni*, 1 Kings, sec. 185.

At other times, the linkage between *haftarah* and *sidrah* is rooted in contrasting themes. The point of the contrast is generally to demonstrate how, in time, the generations have become spiritually inferior. R. Mendel Hirsch (1833-1900), in his commentary to the *haftarot*, has noted many contrasting themes. On the opening section of the *haftarah* to *Va-Yera* (2 Kings 4:1-7) R. Hirsch states:

> We see a widow, the wife of a prophet, left with her two orphaned children in the direst poverty – a creditor who, as there is nothing more to be found, is about to take the children into debtor's slavery – a society in which nobody in better circumstances is to be found to take the case in hand and give relief – can there be a greater contrast to the acts of kindness and love of the ancestor which the words of the *sidrah* present to us?[30]

Another such example, from the *haftarah* for *Va-Yeshev* (Amos 2:7), contrasts Joseph's drawing strength from the image and thoughts of his father, thus enabling him to resist temptation,[31] with the *haftarah*'s "son's" inability to gain moral strength from his father – "and a man and his son go unto the same maid, to profane my holy name."[32]

Indeed, more can be written concerning analogous and contrasting *sidrah-haftarah* themes. However, at this time, I wish to turn to the area of textual similarities. The *Rishonim*, when discussing the *haftarah* and its relationship to the *sidrah*, always emphasize the thematic connection. Thus, Maimonides writes, "*u-maftirin be-khol Shabbat ve-Shabbat be-Navi me'ein she-kara ba-Torah.*"[33] Similarly, R. Abraham b. Nathan *ha-Yarhi* (c. 1155-1215), the author of *Sefer ha-Manhig*, states: "*Ve-ahar kakh maftir lefi inyan parashat ha-yom.*"[34]

---

[30] R. Mendel Hirsch, *The Haphtoroth* (London, 1966), 34.

[31] *Sotah* 36b.

[32] Hirsch, 96-97.

[33] *Mishneh Torah, Hilkhot Tefillah* 13:3.

[34] *Sefer ha-Manhig, Hilkhot Shabbat* (Jerusalem, 1961), sec. 33.

However, close scrutiny of the weekly *haftarot* reveals that the *haftarot* contain words and/or phrases almost identical to those found in their respective *sidrot*. In all the forty-one *haftarot* from *Bereishit* through *Pinhas* (the *haftarot* from *Matot* through *Ve-Zot ha-Berakhah* are unrelated to their respective *sidrot*) are found numerous textual parallels.[35]

These analogous texts range from single words to complete phrases. No doubt, it was these "parallel" expressions that played a significant role in the matching of a *haftarah* with its respective *sidrah*. Analogous phrases often appear in the opening verse of the *haftarah*.[36] Examples include: *Parshat Hayei Sarah* with 1 Kings 1:1 – "*Ve-hamelekh David ba ba-yamim*," which parallels "*Ve-Avraham zaken ba ba-yamim*" (Genesis 24:1). *Parshat Shemot* with Isaiah 27:6 – "*Ha-ba'im yashresh Ya'akov*" with "*Ve-eleh shemot Benei Yisrael ha-ba'im Mitzraymah*" (Exodus 1:1). *Parshat Miketz* with 1 Kings 3:15 – "*Va-yikatz Shelomoh*" with "*va-yikatz Par'oh*" (Genesis 41:7). *Parshat Tzav* with Jeremiah 7:21 – "*oloteikhem*" with "*Zot torat ha-olah*" (Leviticus 6:2). *Parshat Bamidbar* with Hoseah 2:1 – "*Ve-hayah mispar Benei Yisrael ... ve-lo yissafer*" with "*be-mispar shemot*" (Numbers 1:2). *Parshat Shelah* with Joshua 2:1 – "*Va-yishlah Yehoshu'a bin Nun*" with "*Shelah lekha anashim*" (Numbers 13:2).

---

[35] Ibid.

[36] See Jacob Mann, *The Bible as Preached in the Old Synagogue*, vol. 2 (Cincinnati, 1966); and Daniel Patte, *Early Jewish Hermeneutic in Palestine* (Missoula, 1975), 39-42. Mann, in his attempt to reconstruct the *haftarot* for the triennial cycle of the reading of the Torah, came up with the principle of "tallying." Mann claims that the *sidrah* and *haftarah* were connected "by mere linguistic affinity" (Patte, 41) and not by a common theme. The linguistic "artificial" connection was always between the first verse of the *sidrah* and the first or second verses of the *haftarah*. Furthermore, Mann maintains that it was the principle of tallying which determined the choice of halakhah in the *Midrash Yelamdenu, petihah*. On the basis of a particular word found in the *haftarah*, the homilist would select a particular halakhah to begin his sermon. In this way, the *haftarah* is the bridge between the halakhah on the one hand and the *sidrah* on the other hand; see Patte, 46.

Of particular interest are those *haftarot* where parallel words/phrases are not limited to one or two verses, but are interspersed throughout the portion. An example of this phenomenon is *Va-Yera* (2 Kings 4:1-37), where throughout the prophetic narrative concerning the Shunamite woman and Elisha, a series of analogous expressions, corresponding to the *sidrah* (Genesis 18-22) are found:

Haftarah	Sidrah
1. ואישה זקן (4:14)	1. ואדני זקן (18:12)
2. למועד ... כעת חיה (4:16)	2. למועד ... כעת חיה (18:14)
3. ותעמוד בפתח (4:15)	3. שומעת פתח האהל (18:10)
4. ותהר האשה ותלד בן למועד אשר דבר אליה אלישע (4:17)	4. ותהר ותלד שרה ... למועד אשר דבר אותו אלקים (21:2)
5. ותחבוש האתון (4:24)	5. ויחבוש את חמורו (22:3)
6. ותאמר אל נערה (4:24)	6. ויאמר אברהם אל נעריו (22:5)

In addition, the following semi-parallel phrases are also found in this *haftarah*:

Haftarah	Sidrah
1. אל תכזב בשפחתך (4:16)	1. ותצחק שרה בקרבה (18:12)
2. ותחזק בו לאכל לחם (4:8)	2. ואקחה פת לחם (18:3)
3. ותלך ותבא אל איש האלקים אל הר כרמל (4:25)	3. ולך לך אל ארץ המוריה ... על אחד ההרים (22:5)

The *haftarah* for *Be-Shalah* (Judges 4:4-5:31) contains numerous analogous expressions, as shown below:

Haftarah	Sidrah (Exodus 13:17-17:16)
1. ויגד לסיסרא (4:12)	1. ויוגד למלך מצרים (14:2)
2. ואת כל העם אשר אתו (4:13)	2. ויאסר רכבו ואת עמו לקח עמו (14:6)
3. תשע מאות רכב ברזל (4:13)	3. ויקח שש מאות רכב בחור (14:7)
4. ותאמר דבורה אל ברק, קום כי זה היום אשר נתן ה' את סיסרא, הלא ה' יצא לפניך (4:14)	4. התיצבו וראו את ישועת ה' אשר יעשה לכם היום (14:13)
5. ויהם ה' את סיסרא (4:15)	5. ויהם את מחנה מצרים (14:24)
6. לא נשאר עד אחד (4:16)	6. ולא נשאר בהם עד אחד (14:28)
7. ותצא יעל (4:18,22)	7. ותצאן כל הנשים (15:20)
8. ויאמר אליה השקיני נא מעט מים כי צמתי (4:19)	8. תנו לנו מים ונשתה (17:2)
9. ויכנע אלקים ביום ההוא (4:23)	9. ויושע ה' ביום ההוא (14:30)
10. ותשר דבורה וברק בן אבינעם ביום ההוא לאמר (5:1)	10. אז ישיר משה ובני ישראל את השירה הזאת לאמר (15:1)
11. הלא ימצאו יחלקו שלל ... שלל צבעים (5:30)	11. אמר אויב ארדף אשיג אחלק שלל (15:9)

These parallel, word for word, expressions in the *haftarah* and *sidrah* are yet another reason why the rabbis designated this portion (Judges 4 and 5) rather than the "Song of David" (2 Samuel 22) as the *haftarah* for *Be-Shalah*.[37]

Similar "ongoing" analogous expressions are found in the *haftarot* for *Terumah* (1 Kings 5:26-6:13), *Pekudei* (1 Kings 7:51-8:21), *Kedoshim* (Ezekiel 22:1-16), and *Naso* (Judges 13:2-25).

This emphasis on textual similarities supports the thesis of Abudarham, that the *haftarah* was instituted as a substitute for the reading of the weekly portion in times of religious persecution. The choice of a *haftarah* with analogous words and phrases immediately reminded one of the respective banned *sidrah*. These textual similarities were to serve as instant memory aids. The analogous terms created a textual as well as thematic substitute for the banned Torah portion.

It is unlikely, however, that the analogous expressions alone were the determining factor in the selection of *haftarot*. No doubt, common themes, as well, serve as *sidrah-haftarah* connections.

---

[37] 2 Samuel 22 is the *haftarah* for the seventh day of Passover when the *shirah* in *Be-Shalah* is read; see *Megillah* 31a. As to the connection between 2 Samuel 22 and *Be-Shalah*, see Rashi, *Megillah* 31a, s.v. *u-mafterin* and Y. Jacobson, *Hazon ha-Mikra*, vol. 2 (Tel Aviv, n.d.), 278-79.

Returning to the Jewish Community
in Medieval Ashkenaz:
History and Halakhah[*]

Ephraim Kanarfogel

In his pioneering study of Rashi's halakhic attitudes and posture toward Jews who had accepted Christianity either willingly or under duress, Jacob Katz argued that Rashi's interpretive expansion of the talmudic principle, *'af 'al pi she-hata Yisra'el hu*, had a decisive impact on subsequent halakhic policy in medieval Ashkenaz. On the basis of his understanding of this principle, Rashi ruled, for example, that it was forbidden to take interest from a *meshummad* (except for extreme situations in which the apostate had resorted to

---

[*] The following is an expanded and annotated version of a paper presented at a conference, "Conversion and Reversion in Judaism, From the Crusades to the Enlightenment," sponsored by the Touro College Graduate School of Jewish Studies, and held at the Center for Jewish History in New York in March, 2006. I hope to return to this theme, together with several related ones, in a larger study. Thanks are due to Prof. Michael Shmidman for his collegiality and forbearance.

trickery in order to hurt a Jewish lender). Similarly, Rashi ruled (as did Rabbenu Gershom, against the regnant geonic position), that a *kohen* who had accepted Christianity but later recanted and returned to the Jewish community could resume his participation in the priestly blessing.[1]

Rashi's rulings in instances such as these were not always novel, nor were his rulings or those of his Tosafist successors perfectly consistent.[2] Nonetheless, Rashi had two overall aims. First, he wished to dispel the notion that apostasy to Christianity constituted an irrevocable dislocation or separation of the individual from Judaism and the Jewish community. Baptism did not vitiate the individual's halakhic status as a Jew, even in cases where the apostate had accepted Christianity willingly. Second, many Jewish converts to Christianity in this period vacillated in their new religious commitment. In accordance with the status of a *mumar* in talmudic parlance (whose rejection of Judaism was perhaps only partial or temporary, and whose return to observance was always deemed possible if not imminent), Rashi and many leading halakhists in Ashkenaz during the twelfth and thirteenth centuries wished to encourage and ease the way for the apostate's return.

Nonetheless, on the popular level, members of Ashkenazic society intuitively felt that anyone who had undergone baptism should no longer be considered part of the community. Thus, despite the smooth and immediate process of return advocated by Rashi, Katz maintains that

---

[1] J. Katz, "Even Though He Has Sinned He Remains a Jew," [Hebrew] *Tarbiz* 27 (1958): 203-17 [=idem., *Halakhah ve-Qabbalah* (Jerusalem, 1986), 255-69]. See also idem., *Exclusiveness and Tolerance* (Oxford, 1961), 67-81.

[2] See, e.g., E. Fram, "Perception and Reception of Repentant Apostates in Medieval Ashkenaz and Premodern Poland," *AJS Review* 21 (1996): 300-04, and S. Emanuel, "Teshuvot ha-Geonim ha-Qezarot," *Atarah le-Hayyim: Mehqarim be-Sifrut ha-Talmudit veha-Rabbanit Likhvod Professor Haim Zalman Dimitrovsky*, ed. D. Boyarin et al. (Jerusalem, 2000), 447-49.

> the popular view did not ... accept the view [of Rashi] that baptism did not affect the Jew's character *qua* Jew. Indeed, in contrast to the geonic period, the practice won acceptance that the repentant apostate must undergo a ceremony of purification in the ritual bath in the same way as a proselyte.[3]

Katz notes that this popular practice was occasionally referred to and recognized within rabbinic circles of the thirteenth century, by sources and authorities such as *Sefer Hasidim* and R. Meir of Rothenburg.[4]

Katz' characterization of the origins and status of ritual immersion for the returning apostate was adopted by several historians who came across other kinds of evidence for this immersion ceremony within medieval Europe. Yosef Yerushalmi, in his study of the French Inquisition in the time of Bernard Gui (c. 1320),[5] presented several examples of otherwise unattested information on Jewish practices that surfaced in confessions obtained by the inquisitor Bernard from Jewish converts to Christianity who had subsequently lapsed. In reporting "on the manner in which apostates were received back into the Jewish community," Bernard offers a description of a ritual allegedly employed to rejudaize them. The returning apostate was stripped of his garments and sometimes bathed in warm water. The Jews would energetically rub him with sand over his entire body (but especially on his forehead, chest and arms, which were the places that received the holy anointments during baptism). The nails of his hands and feet would be cut (until they bled), and his head was shaved.

---

[3] See Katz, *Exclusiveness and Tolerance*, 73.

[4] See below, nn. 17, 41. Katz also refers (ibid., n. 3) to *Nimmuqei Yosef*, a fourteenth-century Spanish commentary on *Hilkhot ha-Rif* by R. Yosef Haviva (which in turn cites a formulation of Ritva), that records this practice in the name of *Tosafot Aharonot*. Cf. below, nn. 10, 44.

[5] Y. H. Yerushalmi, "The Inquisition and the Jews of France in the Time of Bernard Gui," *Harvard Theological Review* 63 (1970): 317-76. Cf. the formulation in the *Sifra* commentary attributed (incorrectly) to R. Samson of Sens, below, n. 34.

He was then immersed three times in the waters of a flowing stream, and a blessing over this immersion was recited.[6]

Yerushalmi searched for Jewish legal sources that might confirm these practices. He writes that there is no such requirement found in "the standard medieval codes," although he does point to the small number of medieval rabbinic passages that seem to acknowledge these practices (which had been noted by Katz).[7] At the same time, Yerushalmi found that quite a few leading sixteenth and seventeenth century halakhists in eastern Europe did refer to the need for immersion, including R. Moses Isserles (Rema), R. Solomon Luria (Maharshal), R. Yo'el Sirkes (*Bah*), and R. Shabbetai b. Meir ha-Kohen (*Shakh*), among others. Yerushalmi concludes that

> from the sources available to us, we cannot prove with finality that the rejudaizing rite as described by Bernard Gui is authentic. We can assert, however, that most of the elements appear highly plausible. The custom of requiring a ritual bath of the penitent apostate definitely existed.[8]

Like Katz, however, Yerushalmi regards this act of "debaptism" as a popular custom that perhaps had some measure of rabbinic approbation in the medieval period, rather than as a rabbinically mandated act, as it seems to have become in the early modern period. In the words of William Chester Jordan (characterizing the situation in northern France during the twelfth and thirteenth centuries), "whatever elitist rabbinic views might have been, an "unbaptizing" ritual was being practiced."[9]

Writing a decade after Yerushalmi, Joseph Shatzmiller returned to the question of whether one who had decided to

---

[6] Yerushalmi, 363-67.

[7] See above, n. 4.

[8] Yerushalmi, 371-73 .

[9] W. C. Jordan, *The French Monarchy and the Jews* (Philadelphia, 1989), 140-41.

abandon Christianity and return to Judaism was required to undergo immersion. Shatzmiller notes that R. Solomon b. Abraham ibn Adret of Barcelona (Rashba, d.c. 1310), an older contemporary of Bernard Gui, ruled (in accordance with the geonic view) that such an immersion ceremony or ritual was not required, although public admonition or even flagellation might be indicated instead. Shatzmiller highlights two other rabbinic sources in this regard: Maharshal's *Yam shel Shelomoh*, and the talmudic commentary of Rashba's student, R. Yom Tov b. Abraham ibn Ishvilli (Ritva), to tractate *Yevamot*. Ritva asserts that while there is no requirement according to the letter of the law to undergo immersion, there is a rabbinic requirement to do so (*ve-'af 'al pi khen hu tovel mi-derabbanan mishum ma'alah*, which Shatzmiller translates as "for the sake of perfection"). After citing an additional inquisitorial account of such an immersion, Shatzmiller concludes that Rashba's formulation (which dismisses the need for immersion) was essentially a prescriptive legal instruction that should not be considered as evidence for what was actually being done in Spain in his day. Even if this immersion was being imposed only "for the sake of perfection" (as his younger contemporary Ritva put it), Rashba regarded this custom as unnecessary and even inappropriate, since it implied a recognition of the efficacy of the Christian sacrament of baptism. By stating unequivocally that no such immersion was required, Rashba, who was also an effective communal leader, meant to stress that no such recognition ought to be extended or implied in any way, against the prevailing popular practice.[10]

Basing herself in part on the studies of Yerushalmi and Shatzmiller, Elisheva Carlebach concluded that despite the vigorous efforts of R. Meir of Rothenburg in the late thirteenth century, following those of Rabbenu Gershom in the eleventh

---

[10] J. Shatzmiller, "Converts and Judaizers in the Early Fourteenth Century," *HTR* 74 (1981): 63-77. Cf. above, n. 4.

and Rashi in the twelfth, to sustain the Jewish status of repentant apostates,

> Jewish folk beliefs and traditions concerning the efficacy of baptism endured. Returning apostates or forced converts were required to undergo various purification rites in order to rejoin the Jewish community. The persistence of these rituals reinforces the notion that medieval Jews in Ashkenaz attributed potency to baptism despite the fact that Jewish law did not recognize it.[11]

Among the responsa cited by Carlebach to show that these ritual forms of counter-baptism survived over time is one by R. Israel Isserlein, from the fifteenth century. The questioner asked whether an apostate who had come forward to be purified on the intermediate days of the festival (hol ha-mo'ed) could be shaved in order to be immersed and thereby (re-)enter the true faith. In his response, Isserlein permits this to be done on hol ha-mo'ed. Without this shaving and subsequent immersion, the penitent

> cannot be included in a quorum or any holy matter (davar shebi-qedushah). Although [the absence of] this [requirement of immersion] surely does not prevent him from doing so (ve-'af 'al gav de-vadai 'eino me-'akkev), the custom of our forefathers is akin to the law of the Torah (minhag 'avoteinu Torah hi).[12]

Commenting on the historical implications of this responsum, Edward Fram has called attention to the fact that rather than trying to eliminate this "folk custom", Isserlein manages to adduce a biblical interpretation (of Rashi, following R. Mosheh ha-Darshan) that supported it.[13]

According to all of the studies discussed to this point, it would appear that ritual immersion for a returning apostate

---

[11] E. Carlebach, Divided Souls (New Haven, 2001), 28-29.

[12] Isserlein, Terumat ha-Deshen, Responsa, no. 86.

[13] See Fram, "Perception and Reception of Repentant Apostates," 318.

was not mandated by Jewish law. Moreover, such immersions were hardly mentioned in medieval rabbinic texts and were not required or promoted in any way by Ashkenazic rabbinic authorities during the high Middle Ages, in accordance with the halakhic posture of Rashi that the rejudaization of an apostate who wished to return to the Jewish community should be relatively easy and unencumbered. These rituals did emerge, however, as a kind of folk custom or popular tradition, one that rabbinic decisors began to countenance and even to embrace by the late Middle Ages and beyond.[14]

We can point to two additional twelfth-century Tosafist texts that support this assessment. The early German Tosafist R. Isaac b. Asher (Riva) ha-Levi of Speyer (d. 1133) asserts that

> ritual immersion [as an act of conversion or reversion] can never be required of a Jew who had already been circumcised [i.e., one who had been born a Jew], even according to [or, on the level of] rabbinic law.[15]

Moreover, R. Isaac b. Abraham (Rizba, d. 1210), a student of Rabbenu Tam (d. 1171) and Ri of Dampierre (d. 1189), ruled that an apostate who had repented did not have to appear before a *beit din* tribunal of three (either to verify his sincerity or to formally supervise his re-inclusion within the community), since

> it can easily be ascertained that he has returned to his Creator.... And even according to those who might be more stringent in this matter, his wine is no longer considered to be that of an idolater once he [again] practices the Jewish faith, even if he did not immerse

---

[14] Cf. E. Carlebach, "Early Modern Ashkenaz in the Writings of Jacob Katz," *The Pride of Jacob: Essays on Jacob Katz and His Work*, ed. J. M. Harris (Cambridge, Mass., 2002), 77.

[15] See the standard *Tosafot* to *Pesahim* 92a, s.v. *'aval 'arel Yisra'el*, and *Tosafot ha-Rashba mi-Rabbenu Shimshon b. Avraham mi-Sens 'al Massekhet Pesahim*, ed. M. Y. From (Jerusalem, 1956), 221. On the role of Riva in the formation of *Tosafot*, see I. Ta-Shma, *Ha-Sifrut ha-Parshanit la-Talmud*, vol. 1 (Jerusalem, 1999), 66-70.

himself (va-afilu lo taval), or even if he lent money at interest to a Jew and has not yet returned the interest.... An apostate who has repented is considered a penitent (ba'al teshuvah) in every respect, and is a bit comparable (domeh qezat) to a convert. All he needs to do is to return to his Creator and to correct his misdeeds.[16]

This formulation of Rizba is quite similar to one found in *Sefer Hasidim*, the bulk of which was composed in Germany no later than 1225:

An apostate who returned to being a Jew (lihyot yehudi), and accepted upon himself to repent (la'asot teshuvah) according to the directives of the rabbinic authorities (ka'asher yoruhu hakhamim), from the time that he has accepted to do this they may drink wine with him and he may be included in a quorum, provided that he does as all other Jews do. For on the festivals, an 'am ha-'arez is believed with respect to ritual impurity.[17]

Like Rizba, *Sefer Hasidim* permitted wine that was touched by an apostate immediately after his return, provided that he appears to be observing Jewish practices generally. As Katz

---

[16] See Urbach, *Ba'alei ha-Tosafot* (Jerusalem, 1980), 1:268-269, citing R. Moses of Zurich's *Semaq mi-Zurikh*, ed. Y. Har-Shoshanim, vol. 2 (Jerusalem, 1977), 49 (mizvah 156), and *Teshuvot ha-Rashba ha-Meyuhasot la-Ramban*, no. 180. See also S. Goldin, *Ha-Yihud veha-Yahad* (Tel Aviv, 1997), 94-95. Note also the similar position of Ri mi-Corbeil (ostensibly the little-known Tosafist, R. Judah of Corbeil), also cited by the *Semaq mi-Zurikh*, that the penitent apostate (whom Ri mi-Corbeil characterizes as a Yisra'el ba'al teshuvah) does not need a (court) document verifying that he has repented, since he conducts himself according to Jewish law. On the identity of Ri mi-Corbeil, cf. my "Rabbinic Figures in Castilian Kabbalistic Pseudepigraphy: R. Yehudah he-Hasid and R. Elhanan of Corbeil," *Journal of Jewish Thought and Philosophy* 3 (1993): 88-99.

[17] *Sefer Hasidim* (Parma), ed. Y. Wistinetzki (Jerusalem, 1924), sec. 209 [=*Sefer Hasidim* (Bologna), ed. R. Margoliot (Jerusalem, 1957), sec. 206]. Cf. R. Moses Isserles' gloss to *Shulhan 'Arukh, Hoshen Mishpat*, 34:22 (based on *Teshuvot Mahariq*, no. 85).

had noted,[18] this passage suggests that *Sefer Hasidim* was perhaps aware of the popular practice (as was Rizba) that required the former apostate to immerse himself and therefore maintains, at least by implication (that which Rizba had stated explicitly), that no such act is required according to Jewish law. *Sefer Hasidim* finds support for this position in a talmudic source (*Hagigah* 26a), according to which an *'am ha-'arez* present in Jerusalem during a festival period may be entrusted to come in contact with *terumah* and other consecrated foods and utensils, which is not typically the case. On the basis of a verse in the book of Judges, the Talmud derives that *'ammei ha-'arez*, who are in close quarters during the festival with the *haverim* and who are committed to proper observance of ritual purity at that time, immediately acquire the status of a *haver* for this purpose.[19]

Against the view held by Rizba and *Sefer Hasidim*, however, there are several manuscript passages which suggest that a number of *Ba'alei ha-Tosafot* and other leading Ashkenazic rabbinic authorities clearly recognized the need for ritual immersion by an apostate who wished to return to the community. Although we shall see that no Ashkenazic rabbinic figures regarded ritual immersion as an absolute halakhic obligation on the level of Torah law (*mide-Oraita*), this practice was rabbinically mandated and supported to a significant degree, and was not viewed simply as a popular custom or folk tradition. Although I believe that Professor Katz' overarching thesis concerning the impact of Rashi's approach to reversion on subsequent generations in Ashkenaz remains largely intact, these manuscript passages also suggest the need for an adjustment in our understanding of Ashkenazic rabbinic views on conversion to Christianity.

---

[18] See above, n. 3.

[19] Cf. *Tosafot ha-Rosh 'al Massekhet Hagigah*, ed. A. Shoshana (Jerusalem, 2002), 251.

Let us begin with a passage that involves Rizba's major teacher, R. Isaac b. Samuel (Ri) of Dampierre. A rich collection of marginal glosses to *Sefer Mordekhai* includes the case of an apostate who had returned to Judaism in Troyes.[20] The central issue in this case was akin to the one taken up by Rizba and *Sefer Hasidim*. Two Jews in Troyes had questioned a penitent former apostate about the sincerity of his repentance. Affirming that he had repented but still wary, the penitent withdrew from his questioners. Subsequently, he became a servant or waiter (*shamash*), which brought him into contact with Jewish wine. The question put to Ri concerned the status of the wine.

Ri responded that the wine was certainly kosher. Only with respect to the designation of a (newly careful) *'am ha-'arez* as a fully qualified *haver* (who could now handle ritually pure foods) does the Talmud require a religious tribunal of three to confirm or to ratify this change in status.[21] In the case of this apostate, however,

> he knows that as long as he has not immersed himself and accepted upon himself the dicta of the rabbinic authorities (*she-kol zeman she-'eino toveil u-meqabbel 'alav divrei hakhamim*), his status is considered to be that of a non-Jew (*muhzaq ke-goi*). Thus, it is not necessary to have [a tribunal of] three before whom he must accept [Judaism once again], since it is easy for us to verify that he has returned to his Creator (*debe-qal yesh lanu lomar she-shav 'el bor'o*), for he now conducts himself in accordance with the Jewish religion (*keivan she-noheg 'azmo ke-dat yehudit*).

Despite the similarities in both phrasing and content, Ri, unlike his student Rizba, clearly acknowledges that the penitent should undergo ritual immersion. Indeed, for Ri, this

---

[20] See ms. Vercelli (Bishop's Seminary) C 235/4, fol. 291v.

[21] Ri alludes to his discussion of this matter in tractate *Bekhorot*. See *Tosafot Bekhorot* 31a, s.v. *ve-kulan she-hazru*, and *Tosafot Shanz 'al Massekhet Bekhorot*, ed. Y. D. Ilan, 61-62; and *Shitat ha-Qadmonim 'al Massekhet 'Avodah Zarah*, ed. M. J. Blau (New York, 1969), 45 (*A.Z.* 7a).

act is crucial in establishing the fact that the apostate is no longer to be regarded by the Jewish community as having the status of a non-Jew (with respect to touching Jewish wine and the like). The immersion does not have to be undertaken by the penitent in the presence of a rabbinic body or public tribunal, but it does serve to alert the penitent to his (renewed) status and his responsibilities. For Ri, ritual immersion was seen as a means of indicating and ensuring the compliance of the penitent with the requirements of Judaism (in addition to his acceptance of the words and dictates of the rabbis), if not as a means of "undoing" his baptism.[22]

Just prior to this passage, the marginal glosses to *Sefer Mordekhai* record that Ri was asked about a convert who had undergone circumcision (improperly) at night, in front of a tribunal of three that was also not properly constituted. In this case, Ri ruled that most of the conversion procedures had to be redone, in light of the requirement that a (new) convert must be initiated into Judaism by a properly constituted legal body. The formal differences between this case and that of the former apostate in Troyes are clear, but so is the basic expectation or requirement for a returning apostate to undergo immersion on his own. Unlike *Sefer Hasidim* (and on the basis of different talmudic *sugyot*), Ri noted that an *'am ha-'arez* who wished to be accorded the status of a *haver* (for the long term, and not

---

[22] *Sefer Yosef ha-Maqqane*, ed. J. Rosenthal (Jerusalem, 1970), 79, records an anecdote that involved R. Yosef Bekhor Shor of Orleans (who, like Ri, was a student of Rabbenu Tam) and an apostate, who was so thoroughly convinced or mortified by R. Yosef's refutation of his claims with respect to Isaiah 53 that "he immediately tore his garments, rolled in the dust, and returned [to the Jewish community] in repentance." Cf. M. A. Signer, "God's Love for Israel: Apologetic and Hermeneutical Strategies in Twelfth-Century Biblical Exegesis," *Jews and Christians in Twelfth-Century Europe*, ed. Signer and J. Von Engen (Notre Dame, 2001), 124-25. Presuming the facticity of the anecdote itself, the omission of halakhic details (such as ritual immersion) in a polemical text such as this would not be surprising. Moreover, these actions appear to have represented an initial, public demonstration of repentance by the apostate that could easily have been followed later by immersion.

just during a festival) must present himself to a rabbinic tribunal for its approbation. Although the returning apostate does not have this particular requirement, he cannot rejoin the community simply by henceforth observing the law under their watchful eyes. He must undergo ritual immersion as well.

It is also instructive to compare Ri's formulation with Rashi's response to a similar question:

> With regard to forced converts ('anusim) [who have repented], must one abstain from their wine until they have maintained their repentance for a lengthy period ('ad she-ya'amdu bi-teshuvatan yamim rabbim), so that their repentance is confirmed and well-known to all (ve-tihyeh teshuvatan mefursemet u-geluyah)?

Rashi offers a multi-faceted response that permitted the wine to be consumed immediately. Part of his response relates to the fact that these were forced converts, who had never really intended to embrace idolatry. But Rashi also adds (in accordance with his broad halakhic policy of 'af 'al pi she-hata Yisra'el hu) that "as soon as they accept upon themselves to return to fear our God (le-yir'at Zurenu), their wine is kosher (as are they; harei hen be-kashrutan)."[23] Ri agrees with Rashi that no public procedure or lengthy waiting period is necessary to verify the sincerity of the apostate's return, even in a case where the apostasy had been undertaken willingly. But for Ri, immersion was nonetheless incumbent upon the penitent. This private act served to seal his return to the Jewish community. For Rashi, however, this practice does not appear to have been required or even to have existed.[24]

---

[23] See Teshuvot Rashi, ed. I. Elfenbein (New York, 1942), 188-89, no. 168, and A. Grossman, Rashi (Jerusalem, 2006), 257-58.

[24] Urbach, Ba'alei ha-Tosafot, 1:244-45, maintains that Ri took the more lenient stance toward a returning apostate, and was a model in this regard for his student Rizba (above, n. 16, who did not require immersion). Urbach bases his assessment of Ri primarily on the responsum about the wine of the 'anusim (in the above note), which is attributed by modern scholarship to Rashi. For reasons that are not fully clear, Urbach instead

A number of rabbinic texts (both published and in manu-script) cite a ruling of the German Tosafist and halakhist, R. Simhah of Speyer (d. c. 1225), that all penitents (ba'alei teshuvah) are required to undergo tevilah (ritual immersion).[25] R. Simhah bases his position on a case found in Avot de-R. Natan, in which a young woman was held captive by Gentiles. During the period of her captivity, she ate from their (non-kosher) food. Although partaking of non-kosher food and drink does not create or engender ritual impurity of the body (that must be nullified or removed according to statute), an immersion was required upon her release in order to purify her from this sinful act or perhaps from her state of sinfulness (ke-dei le-taher min ha-'aveirah).

R. Simhah's student, R. Isaac b. Moses Or Zarua', adds that although this immersion is required (ve-khen qibbalti mi-mori ha-rav Rabbenu Simhah she-kol ba'alei teshuvah zerikhin tevilah), its absence or delay does not withhold or compromise the state of repentance ('einah me-'akkevet 'et ha-teshuvah). Rather, as soon as a person who has trans-gressed a sin of any magnitude (willingly or unwillingly) decides to repent, he (or she) is immediately considered to be fully righteous. However, one must make himself uncomfort-able (le-za'er 'et 'azmo) and afflict his body (le-sagef 'et gufo) in order to achieve expiation (kapparah), and this is the role of the ritual immersion that was prescribed by R. Simhah.[26]

---

believed this to be a responsum of Ri. The suggestive (and more stringent) responsa of Ri found in ms. Vercelli were apparently not yet available to Urbach.

[25] The references to both published and manuscript versions are conven-iently collected in S. Emanuel, "Sifrei Halakhah Avudim shel Ba'alei ha-Tosafot," (Ph.D. diss., The Hebrew University of Jerusalem, 1993), 213-14. As Emanuel notes, one of the manuscript texts (ms. Vatican 183, fol. 186r) identifies R. Simhah's (no longer extant) halakhic tome, Seder 'Olam, as the literary source of this ruling. Cf. ms. Bodl. 1210, fol. 83v (katav Rabbenu Simhah b"R. Shmu'el); ms. Bodl. 784, fol. 99v; and J. Elbaum, Teshuvat ha-Lev ve-Qabbalat Yissurim (Jerusalem, 1993), 225-26.

[26] See R. Isaac b. Moses, Sefer Or Zarua' (Zhitomir, 1862), part 1, fol. 20b (responsa), no. 112. R. Isaac Or Zarua' resided for a time in R. Simhah's

R. Isaac Or Zarua's son, R. Hayyim Eliezer, and the Italian halakhist R. Zedekiah b. Abraham ha-Rofe, based the Ashkenazic custom for (all) Jewish males to immerse themselves on the eve of Rosh HaShanah and/or Yom Kippur on R. Simhah's ruling.[27]

One of the manuscript versions of R. Simhah's ruling, which contains some additional information and discussion, was published by Efraim Kupfer more than thirty years ago.[28] A case had arisen concerning a Jewish woman who had been "submerged" (nitme'ah, with an 'ayin, signifying conversion) among non-Jews, and who had given birth as a non-Jew (yaldah be-goyut). She then returned to Jewish practice and life together with her young sons, who were immersed in the mikvah prior to their (delayed) circumcisions. These immersions were not considered, however, to be part of a halakhically mandated conversion process (since the mother was Jewish) and as such, these immersions did not require the presence of three rabbinic scholars (sitting as a Jewish court). Nonetheless, the immersion itself was considered to be necessary in accordance with the case in Avot de-R. Natan (mentioned above), of the young woman who had been immersed after her experiences in captivity. It was further noted, however, that these young boys would not have rendered any wine that they touched as yayn nesekh prior to their immersion, for even an adult who had been an apostate does not render wine as such

---

home in Speyer. See Sefer Or Zarua', pt. 4, pisqei 'avodah zarah, sec. 271 (fol. 36a); Urbach, Ba'alei ha-Tosafot, 1:413-14; and cf. my Jewish Education and Society in the High Middle Ages (Detroit, 1992), 66-67.

[27] See Pisqei Halakhah shel R. Hayyim Or Zarua' (Derashot Maharah), ed. Y. S. Lange (Jerusalem, 1993), 153; Shibbolei ha-Leqet, ed. S. Buber (Vilna, 1887), 266, sec. 283; and cf. 'Arugat ha-Bosem le-R. Avraham b. 'Azri'el, ed. E. E. Urbach, 2:110.

[28] Teshuvot u-Pesaqim, ed. E. Kupfer (Jerusalem, 1973), 290-91 (sec. 171). The manuscript from which Kupfer published this volume, Bodl. 692, is a significant repository of material from R. Simhah's lost Seder 'Olam. See Kupfer's introduction, 11-12, and the index (343); and Emanuel, "Sifrei Halakhah Avudim," 211-13.

from the moment that he renounces his actions and begins his return. "A Jew who announces that he has sinned but wishes to return is still a Jew, and he can immerse himself privately (*ve-tovel beino le-vein azmo*)."

At this point, the text cites R. Bonfant (perhaps Bonenfant, a sobriquet for the German halakhist R. Samuel b. Abraham ha-Levi of Worms), in the name of [his teacher] *SaR* (=Rabbenu Simhah),[29] that the purpose of the immersion here was to purify the penitent from sin. Although non-Jewish food did not defile the body of the young captive woman more than other things (*yoter mi-she'ar devarim*), these penitents (who returned to Judaism with their mother) had to undergo immersion (as she did) in order to be purified from sin, so that they could repent and return in purity. This passage continues by noting that a *sugya* in tractate *Pesahim*[30] may also have mandated immersion for a penitent. Moreover, partial proof (*qezat yesh re'ayah*) can be brought from the case of Queen Esther, who immersed herself upon returning from Ahashverosh to live with Mordekhai. Since that immersion was

---

[29] Kupfer also published several rulings by R. Samuel, along with some additional comments. See *Teshuvot u-Pesaqim*, 129-32 (for a ruling issued jointly by R. Samuel and his teacher, R. Simhah); 218-20 (*seder halizah me-nimmuqei R. Shmu'el ha-Levi*) 282-89; and the index. See also I. A. Agus, *Teshuvot Ba'alei ha-Tosafot* (New York, 1954), 206-15, and S. Emanuel, "Teshuvot Maharam mi-Rothenburg she'Einan shel Maharam," *Shenaton ha-Mishpat ha-'Ivri* 21 (1998-2000): 173-76. I discuss R. Samuel's contributions to Ashkenazic *piyyut* in my forthcoming *The Intellectual History of Medieval Ashkenazic Jewry: New Perspectives* (Wayne State University Press, Detroit, 2008), chapter three. On R. Bonfant's close tutorial relationship with R. Simhah, see Kupfer's introduction, ibid.; I. Ta-Shma, *Knesset Mehqarim*, vol. 1 (Jerusalem, 2004), 161-62. On the name Bon(en)fant, cf. S. Schwarzfuchs, *Yehudei Zarefat Bimei ha-Benayim* (Tel Aviv, 2001), 319, n. 27. R. Samuel's son was the German *dayyan* and *payyetan*, R. Yaqar ha-Levi of Cologne. See Kupfer's introduction, 12-13, and 122-23, 264, 287; Ta-Shma, vol. 1, 168-74; and my "Religious Leadership During the Tosafist Period: Between the Academy and the Rabbinic Court," *Jewish Religious Leadership*, ed. J. Wertheimer (New York, 2004), vol. 1, 277-79, 292.

[30] 92a; cf. above, n. 15.

seen as a means of ridding Esther of the impurity (perhaps, the filth) imparted by the wicked king (*mishum zuhamato shel 'oto rasha*), penitent apostates (*ba'alei teshuvah*) must also immerse themselves in order to eliminate the residue transmitted by the impurity of idolatry (*mipnei zihum tum'at 'avodah zarah*).[31] Further support may be derived from a passage in the Jerusalem Talmud that requires immersion whenever one passes from a profane to a holy state. Indeed, it is for this reason, according to the *Talmud Yerushalmi*, that a utensil purchased by a Jew from a non-Jew must be immersed prior to its use.

Although we cannot be certain that this entire passage was composed by R. Simhah or by his student R. Samuel ha-Levi of Worms, it does raise the possibility that the initial formulation of R. Simhah's ruling, that immersion should be undertaken as part of the overall process of repentance, was expressed in the case of a Jewish apostate who had returned to the community (and was then broadened to include other sins).[32] The circumstances of apostasy reflect precisely the situation of the young women who had been held captive as described in *Avot de-R. Nathan*. Whether or not apostates to Christianity lived with non-Jews in sexual arrangements, they (like the young women) had ample opportunity to sin, through the partaking of non-Jewish food and other acts. Although the additional proof suggested on the basis of Esther's return to

---

[31] On Esther's immersion in this way, see *Megillah* 13b, and see also *Tosafot*, ad loc., s.v. *ve-tovelet*.

[32] See the formulation in I. Z. Kahana, "She'elot u-Teshuvot R. Yizhaq Or Zarua' u-Maharam b. Barukh," *Sinai* 24 (1949), 312, sec. 109, and cf. R. David Ibn Zimra (Radvaz), *Responsa*, pt. 3, no. 858. Radvaz, a leading sixteenth-century Sefardic authority, begins (and concludes) his responsum on the status of forced converts to Islam by citing the position of R. Simhah of Speyer, that while a *ba'al teshuvah* from any sin (including apostasy) should immerse himself (and thereby afflict himself), the absence of such an immersion does not inherently compromise or deny his repentance. The only other (named) position cited by Radvaz in this responsum is that of Riva ha-Levi of Speyer (above, at n. 15).

Mordekhai does bespeak a sexual context, the phrase *mipnei zihum tum'at 'avodah zarah* can also refer to other forbidden activities that one might encounter while living within an enclosed non-Jewish setting.

For R. Simhah of Speyer and his student R. Bonfant, the immersion of a returning apostate was necessary primarily as an act of penance, and not simply as a sign or indicator of the apostate's return to the fold, as it was for Ri. Although this immersion was not technically required by Jewish law, it was mandated as a penitential act. R. Simhah displays several affinities with the German Pietists, although the presence of various penitential acts (*tiqqunei teshuvah*) in the writings of a number of German Tosafists and rabbinic authorities from the late twelfth and early thirteenth centuries reflects the currency of these practices even outside the narrowly constructed circle of *Hasidei Ashkenaz*.[33] Moreover, the comparison to Esther here suggests a kind of un-baptism. In any case, for R. Simhah of Speyer and for R. Samuel ha-Levi of Worms, as for Ri, ritual immersion for a returning apostate was not merely a matter of popular custom or tradition. It had their overt approbation and support.

A formulation attributed by the early fourteenth-century compendium, *Semaq mi-Zurikh*, to R. Simhah's German contemporary, R. Eliezer b. Yo'el ha-Levi (Rabiah), goes even further. According to Rabiah, an apostate who wished to return

---

[33] On the affinities between R. Simhah and the *Hasidei Ashkenaz*, see my *"Peering through the Lattices": Mystical, Magical and Pietistic Dimensions in the Tosafist Period* (Detroit, 2000), 102-11, 255-28. Among those Ashkenazic rabbinic scholars who preserve and apply R. Simhah's ruling (above, nn. 27-28), R. Isaac Or Zarua' and R. Abraham b. 'Azri'el were also direct students of the leading German Pietists, R. Judah he-Hasid and/or R. Eleazar of Worms. For the influence of *Hasidei Ashkenaz* on *Shibbolei ha-Leqet*, see my "Mysticism and Asceticism in Italian Rabbinic Literature of the Thirteenth Century," *Kabbalah* 6 (2001): 135-49. On *tiqqunei teshuvah* in the writings and thought of the Tosafist R. Ephraim b. Isaac and his rabbinic colleagues in Regensburg, see my "R. Judah he-Hasid and the Rabbinic Scholars of Regensburg: Interactions, Influences, and Implications," *Jewish Quarterly Review* 96 (2006): 17-37. See also below, n. 39.

must shave and immerse himself just as a convert does
(ka-ger). The apostate's immersion does not have to take place
during the daytime (as does the immersion of a ger), but the
apostate's (re-)acceptance of Judaism (ha-qabbalah) must be
accomplished before three people.[34] Unlike R. Simhah (or Ri),

---

[34] Cited in *Semaq mi-Zurikh*, above. n. 16. Despite the gap in time of about
a century, E. E. Urbach, as noted, presumed that the attributions to Rizba
(and others) found in this wide-ranging passage are reliable although, to be
sure, the names of Rizba and R. Eleazar of Worms also appear in the
parallel passages found in *Teshuvot ha-Ramban*, and in ms. Vercelli; see
also below, n. 36. S. Goldin, *Ha-Yihud veha-Yahad*, 200, n. 46, specifically
accepts the authenticity of the Rabiah passage (which is not found in his
name in any other source) as well. Indeed, I have had occasion to show
that a highly significant position of Rabiah (*Avi ha-'Ezri*) on Jewish
martyrdom, which was found initially only in *Semaq mi-Zurikh*, can be
confirmed by its appearance (in somewhat tighter form) in several
manuscripts of R. Abraham b. Ephraim's *Sefer Simmanei Taryag Mizvot*, a
northern French halakhic digest based on R. Moses of Coucy's *Sefer
Mizvot*, that was completed c. 1265. See my "Halakhah and *Mezi'ut* (Realia)
in Medieval Ashkenaz: Surveying the Parameters and Defining the Limits,"
Jewish Law Annual 14 (2003): 211-16. Moreover, the recent publication of
this work, under the title *Qizzur Sefer Mizvot Gadol le-R. Avraham b.
Ephraim*, ed. Y. Horowitz (Jerusalem, 2005), reveals that this work
contains a number of passages cited in the name of *Avi ha-Ezri* (see, e.g.,
29, 32, 69, 94, 102, 129, 178-80, 204, 225), some of which can be found
in Rabiah's extant *Sefer Avi ha-'Ezri/Sefer Rabiah*, and others that cannot,
but which seem nonetheless to be authentic. (In one instance, p. 206, a
position attributed to R. Eliezer b. R. Yo'el by name cannot be found in his
extant writings.) It should also be noted that most of Rabiah's commentary
to tractate *Yevamot* (which, as the present study confirms, is a common
locus in medieval rabbinic literature for discussion of the status of
returning apostates), was part of Rabiah's later (and now lost) halakhic
work, *Sefer Avi'asaf*; cf. S. Emanuel, "Sifrei Halakhah Avudim," 103-08.
Interestingly, the Rabiah passage in *Semaq mi-Zurikh* on the treatment of a
returning apostate is also found, essentially verbatim, in *Qizzur Sefer
Mizvot Gadol*, 194, as a directive put forward by (unidentified) *'omrim*. Note
also that a passage in the Sifra commentary attributed to R. Samson of
Sens, *parashat Emor, parsheta* 14, n. 1 (Jerusalem, 1959), fol. 110b,
maintains that the custom in vogue for a penitent apostate was to shave
his head and cut his nails prior to his immersion, and that he was indeed
referred to as a *ger*. It has been shown that the author of this commentary
was not R. Samson (or any other French rabbinic figure), but rather
a German contemporary of Rabiah, who refers to R. David b. Qalonymus
of Muenzberg as his teacher. R. David asked a halakhic question of
Rabiah's father R. Yo'el, and both answered and asked queries of Rabiah.

Rabiah appears to be focused on formalizing the return of the apostate in a rather public way. Interestingly, Rabiah characterizes the custom of men immersing before *Yom Kippur* as an act of general piety (*perishut*), and not as a *tiqqun teshuvah* that was associated with the ruling of R. Simhah.[35]

The position of R. Eleazar b. Judah of Worms, a prominent German halakhist and a leading figure among the German Pietists, and a contemporary of both R. Simhah of Speyer and Rabiah, requires some clarification. In a text found in several rabbinic collections,[36] R. Eleazar is noted as being relatively lenient, similar to Rizba, with a returning apostate. R. Eleazar does not require the returnee to accept upon himself any acts of physical suffering or self-abnegation, even though these kinds of physical *tiqqunei teshuvah* were typically prescribed by R. Eleazar for those who had sinned in various other ways.[37] R. Eleazar also does not make any reference in this passage to the need for ritual immersion. When the one returning

> rejoins the exile of his brethren, and recites the *Shema* twice daily, and is careful once again with what is permitted and prohibited to every other Jew, he is vouchsafed that he will not sin (grievously) again as a Jew,

See, e.g., Urbach, *Ba'alei ha-Tosafot*, 1:366: S. Emanuel, "Biographical Data on R. Barukh b. Isaac," [Hebrew] *Tarbiz* 69 (2000), 436-37; Y. Sussman, "Rabad on Shekalim? A Bibliographical and Historical Riddle," [Hebrew] *Me'ah She'arim: Studies in Medieval Jewish Spirituality in Memory of Isadore Twersky*, ed. E. Fleischer et al. (Jerusalem, 2001), 147-48, n. 64.

[35] See *Sefer Rabiah*, ed. V. Aptowitzer, vol. 2, 185; my *Peering through the Lattices*, 45; and *Pisqei Rabbenu Yosef Talmid Rabbenu Shmu'el ha-Ro'eh mi-Bamberg* in *Shitat ha-Qadmonim*, ed. M. J. Blau (New York, 1992), 372, sec. 271. Cf. R. Eleazar b. Judah of Worms, *Sefer Roqeah* (repr. Jerusalem, 1967), secs. 214, 218.

[36] See Urbach, *Ba'alei ha-Tosafot*, 1:407 (and above, n. 16), and ms. Vercelli, fol. 291v (upper margin).

[37] See e.g., I. Marcus, "Hasidei Ashkenaz Private Penitentials: An Introduction and Descriptive Catalogue," *Studies in Jewish Mysticism*, ed. J. Dan and F. Talmage (Cambridge, Mass., 1982), 57-83.

and we should not be so strict with him, by requiring him to undergo afflictions in order to achieve expiation.

On the other hand, R. Eleazar, in his penitential treatises, explicitly mandates immersion (as well as a series of more arduous *tiqqunei teshuvah*) for an apostate who wished to return.[38] In the fullest version of these works, R. Eleazar puts forward the paradigm of Menasheh son of Hezekiah, who denied the Almighty for some thirty-three years and yet was able to return, from the moment that he repented fully in his heart and pledged to correct his actions. According to R. Eleazar, the returning apostate must similarly remove all signs of splendor or glory from himself and feel remorse, and fast regularly over a period of several years. He should not eat meat or drink wine, he should not bathe except a bit prior to the festivals, he should wash his head only once or twice a month and so on. In addition, he should not sit together with clergymen and priests, or where people are discussing the "impure idolatry". He must keep away from all idolators and derive no pleasure from them, and he may not come near to their homes or to the courtyard of a church. From the moment that he regrets what he has done *and immerses himself*, he is considered to be as a Jew. He must return to his Creator from all the sins that he has done and regret the pleasures that he had.[39]

---

[38] On this apparent contradiction within texts by and about R. Eleazar, see Y. Dinari, *Hakhmei Ashkenaz be-Shilhei Yemei ha-Benayim* (Jerusalem, 1984), 86, n. 74. Cf. Y. Elbaum, *Teshuvat ha-Lev*, 28, n. 22, and the next note.

[39] See ms. Vatican 183/3, fols. 165v-166v. This *seder ha-teshuvah* (which ends on fol. 188v) begins (on fol. 162r) with a penitential responsum ascribed to R. Judah he-Hasid. The long penitential text that follows, however, corresponds to the style and teachings of Eleazar's other penitentials. See Marcus, "Hasidei Ashkenaz Private Penitentials," 74, and cf. idem., "Hibburei ha-Teshuvah shel Hasidei Ashkenaz," *Mehqarim be-Qabbalah, be-Filosofiyah ube-Sifrut ha-Musar vehe-Hagut Mugashim le-Yeshayah Tishby*, ed. J. Dan and J. Hacker (Jerusalem, 1986), 369-79. See also Eleazar's *Sefer Roqeah* (repr. Jerusalem, 1967), *Hilkhot Teshuvah*, 31, sec. 24 (and Marcus, "Private Penitentials," 62-63); *Sefer Kol Bo*, sec.

Although the specific physical afflictions prescribed by R. Eleazar vary a bit within his different penitential treatises, the need for ritual immersion in all of these works is unequivocal. That act, together with the former apostate's good intentions, re-establishes his presence within the Jewish community. Moreover, while the passage attributed to R. Eleazar in the medieval rabbinic sources which downplays the need for *tikkunei teshuvah* does not specifically mention *tevilah*, positing the need for ritual immersion does not contradict anything else found in that passage. The immersion of the penitent for R. Eleazar of Worms can be understood, as it was for R. Simhah of Speyer, as a painless, yet necessary *tiqqun teshuvah*. It can also reflect the more basic kind of commitment that the apostate must make, as had been suggested by Rabiah (together with other, more public manifestations), or by Ri (as a private act).

These findings take us beyond the first quarter of the thirteenth century, in both northern France and Germany.[40] We are now in a better position to understand the historical

---

66 [*sefer niqra Moreh Hatta'im ve-niqra Sefer ha-Kapparot, hibbero ha-R. Eleazar mi-Germaiza*] (Tel Aviv, 1997), fol. 26a (and Marcus, 69-70); and *Darkhei Teshuvah* [appended to *Responsa* of R. Meir of Rothenburg (Prague, 1608), ed. M. A. Bloch (Budapest, 1895)], fol. 160c (and Marcus, 69). R. Simhah of Speyer's ruling that repentant sinners should immerse themselves, as derived from the case in *Avot de-R. Nathan* of the young woman who returned from captivity, appears toward the end of Eleazar's *seder ha-teshuvah* in ms. Vatican 183; see above, n. 26. R. Judah he-Hasid's responsum in this manuscript (along with two others found in ms. Bodl. 682) was published by S. Spitzer, "She'elot u-Teshuvot Rabbenu Yehudah he-Hasid be-'Inyanei Teshuvah," *Sefer ha-Zikkaron le-R. Shmu'el Barukh Verner*, ed. Y. Buksboim (Jerusalem, 1996), 199-205. Cf. Marcus, "Hibburei ha-Teshuvah," 380-82.

40 Although there was something of a separation in terms of literary sources as well as the movement of students between the Tosafist centers in northern France and Germany during the fifty-year period between 1175 and 1225, both centers have been amply represented in the discussion to this point. As in many other instances, the various positions begin to come together in the halakhic writings and thought of R. Meir of Rothenburg and his teachers. See, e.g., my "Religious Leadership During the Tosafist Period," 281-305.

and halakhic underpinnings of the rather striking responsum
penned in the second half of the thirteenth century by R. Meir
of Rothenburg (d. 1293), concerning the testimony of a former
apostate in the case of a missing husband. R. Meir writes that
he was loathe to accept the testimony of this individual whom
he describes as "one who had become an apostate (*mumar*) and
then repented, albeit not with a full heart (*shav ve-lo bekhol
libbo*), but just enough to be deceitful (*teshuvah shel remiyyah*)."
At the end of his responsum, R. Meir again remarks that the
testimony of this individual is unacceptable,

> since this abominable one and others like him immerse
> themselves while holding a *sherez* in their hands
> (*tovlim ve-sherez be-yadam*). And it is well known that
> they do not consider themselves to be Jews except in
> order to have other [Jews] give them food, and in order
> to steal and to fulfill their every desire.[41]

Maharam was undoubtedly referring to a rabbinically
endorsed or required immersion when he says that the apostate in question was *tovel ve-sherez be-yado*, no matter which
reason for this immersion he might have favored. For R. Meir,
(genuine) *teshuvah* and *tevilah* were both needed. Having
studied with Tosafists in northern France and Germany
(including students of both Ri and Rabiah), in addition to

---

[41] See *Teshuvot Maimuniyyot le-Nashim*, no. 10; [*Haggahot*] *Mordekhai*
to *Ketubot*, sec. 306. Rabbenu Yonah of Gerona (d. 1263), who had studied
in his youth at the Tosafist academy of Evreux (in Normandy; cf. below,
n. 48), is cited by his student Rashba as having heard from *Hakhmei
Zarefat* that an apostate who moved from city to city, professing allegiance
to Christianity in one place and to Judaism in the next, is to be treated, in
the absence of other information, as a Jew (who does not render wine *yayn
nesekh*). The underlying assumption is that his sincere commitment is to
Judaism and that his other claims are fundamentally false, and are being
made only in order to derive pleasure or benefit. See Rashba, *Responsa*,
vol. 6, no. 179. Irrespective of any precise comparisons between this ruling
and that of Maharam, both these passages suggest that the phenomena of
those who assumed dual or mixed religious allegiances was not as
uncommon in medieval Jewish society as might have been imagined.
See also Urbach, *Ba'alei ha-Tosafot*, 1:245.

having numerous affinities with *Hasidei Ashkenaz* and R. Eleazar of Worms in particular, R. Meir had easy access to this evolving (and by now dominant) trend in Ashkenazic rabbinic thinking.[42] Indeed, another of his teachers and senior colleagues, R. Avigdor b. Elijah Kohen Zedeq (Katz) of Vienna, assumed without question (and so noted) that a married couple who were both returning apostates must be immersed prior to their re-acceptance into the community. The matter before R. Avigdor for his consideration was whether they also had to be separated for a period of three months (*havhanah*), as was required of a couple who were converting anew to Judaism.[43]

Moreover, there is an additional *Tosafot* text which originated in northern France in the mid-thirteenth century, that may have also informed the responsum of R. Meir of Rothenburg. As noted above, Ritva in his talmudic commentary to tractate *Yevamot* (followed by *Nimmuqei Yosef*) cited the view that ritual immersion was required for a returning apostate according to rabbinic law or policy (*mi-derabbanan, mishum ma'alah*), from an Ashkenazic source that he called *Tosafot Aharonot*.[44] According to these *Tosafot Aharonot*, the immersion for an apostate was akin to or an extension of the talmudic (rabbinic) requirement that an *'eved kena'ani* had to undergo ritual immersion twice, once at the beginning of his servitude when he was initiated into the Jewish faith (and the partial

---

[42] See Urbach, *Ba'alei ha-Tosafot*, 2:523-28, and my *Peering through the Lattices*, 115-24, 234-38.

[43] See *Perushim u-Pesaqim le-Rabbenu Avigdor (Zarefati) mi-Ba'alei ha-Tosafot*, ed. Makhon Harerei Qedem (Jerusalem, 1996), 410-11. R. Avigdor ruled that *havhanah* was not required in this case. On the provenance and literary output of (this) R. Avigdor, see my *Peering through the Lattices*, 107-10, 225-27, and my "Mysticism and Asceticism in Italian Rabbinic Literature," above, n. 33.

[44] See *Hiddushei ha-Ritva le-Massekhet Yevamot*, ed. R. A. Jofen, 330-32 (*Yevamot* 47b); *Nimmuqei Yosef*, ad loc. (at the top of fol. 16b in the standard pagination of *Hilkhot ha-Rif*); and above, nn. 4,10.

observance of *mizvot*), and again at his release, when he
became a full-fledged member of the Jewish community.

Several *Tosafot* texts maintain that this second immersion of the *'eved kena'ani* was required (only) by rabbinic law,
and both Nahmanides and Rashba attribute this position to
rabbotenu ha-Zarefatim.[45] A more recently published *Tosafot*
variant to *Yevamot* characterizes this rabbinic requirement as
a means of distinguishing formally between the states of
slavery and freedom (*le-hakkir bein 'avdut le-herut*).[46] But none
of these *Tosafot* passages refer to the case of a returning
apostate.

In the manuscript glosses to *Sefer Mordekhai* discussed
above, however, there is a passage marked *Tosafot Shitah* that
explicitly extends the requirement of immersion to an apostate
who had repented, for the same reason as the *'eved kena'ani*
who had been freed. Although the refrain of Rashi, *'af 'al pi
she-hata Yisra'el hu,* is specifically mentioned by this *Tosafot
Shitah* passage as well, the passage asserts that the penitent
apostate must undergo an immersion, *la'asot hekkera,* in order
to make a distinction or demarcation.[47] This is the rabbinic
requirement (and *Tosafot* source) for immersion referred to by
Ritva and *Nimmuqei Yosef,* which they characterized as
mishum ma'alah. The apostate is not going from a state of
slavery to one of freedom, but he is returning to a different or

---

[45] See *Tosafot* and *Tosafot ha-Rosh* to Yevamot 47b, s. v. *sham ger
ve-'eved (meshuhrar) tovlim; Hiddushei ha-Ramban* and *Hiddushei
ha-Rashba* to the end of Yevamot 47b; and cf. *Tosafot Qiddushin* 62b, s.v.
'ela me-'attah. Nahmanides' own position is that this immersion is required
according to Torah law (and is akin to the immersion of a *ger*). This
possibility is implicit in some of the *Tosafot* texts as well. See, e.g., the
discussion in *Ritva li-Yevamot,* ed. Jofen, 332, n. 263, and 348-49, n. 294.

[46] See *Tosafot Maharam ve-Rabbenu Perez 'al Massekhet Yevamot,* ed. H.
Porush (Jerusalem, 1991), 129-130 (48a), s.v. *ki tanya ha-hi le-'inyan
tevilah 'itmar.* This passage (and explanation) is not found, however, in a
parallel collection, *Tosafot Yeshanim ha-Shalem 'al Massekhet Yevamot,* ed.
A. Shoshana (Jerusalem, 1994), 283-86.

[47] See ms. Vercelli, fol. 291v.

higher status, as a fully recognized and religiously obligated member of the Jewish community. The comparison to an *'eved kena'ani* is thus particularly apt.

The term *Tosafot Shitah* in this text refers, in all likelihood, to a type or genre of *Tosafot* that were produced in the Tosafist *beit midrash* at Evreux (led by the brothers R. Moses, R. Samuel and R. Isaac b. Shene'ur) during the mid-thirteenth century.[48] According to this text, the ritual immersion serves as an indication or as a sign for the penitent of his new status, and for the community as well, rather than as a personal act of penance (as had been suggested by R. Simhah of Speyer). It would seem to be a way of further formalizing what Ri of Dampierre had assumed from the private or personal perspective, although there is no indication that this immersion had to be undertaken more publicly, in front of a rabbinic tribunal.[49] At the same time, however, the talmudic paradigm for this immersion, the newly released *'eved kena'ani*, might well have had to undergo his second immersion in the presence of a

---

[48] On *Tosafot/Shitat Evreux*, see Urbach, *Ba'alei ha-Tosafot*, 1:479-84, esp. 480, n. 11 and 484, n. 26* [the responsum of Maharam (ed. Prague) listed in 480, n. 11, should be corrected to no. 608 = *Mordekhai Shavu'ot*, sec. 771; cf. S. Emanuel, "Teshuvot Maharam mi-Rothenburg she'-Einan shel Maharam," 181-84]; I. Ta-Shma, *Ha-Sifrut ha-Parshanit la-Talmud*, vol. 2, 108-10; idem., *Knesset Mehqarim*, vol. 2 (Jerusalem, 2004), 111-14; my *Jewish Education and Society in the High Middle Ages*, 74-76; and *Tosafot Yeshanim ha-Shalem 'al Massekhet Yevamot*, editor's introduction, 24-26. On Ritva's awareness and use of additional sources of northern French *Tosafot* (as compared to Ramban and Rashba), see my "Between Ashkenaz and Sefarad: Tosafist Teachings in the Talmudic Commentaries of Ritva," *Between Rashi and Maimonides: Studies in Medieval Jewish Law, Thought and Culture*, ed. E. Kanarfogel (forthcoming).

[49] Indeed, *Tosafot ha-Rosh* (above, n. 45, which does not discuss a returning apostate) argues that the requirement of *tevilah de-rabbanan* means that the freed slave does not have to be immersed in the presence of a rabbinic court, since he is technically able to give *qiddushin* from the moment that he is freed. If a court of three was yet required to oversee his immersion, he would not be able to give *qiddushin* at that point, according to talmudic law. This is ostensibly the position of the *Tosafot Shitah* as well. Cf. R. Isaac of Corbeil (a student of *Hakhmei Evreux*) in his *Sefer Mizvot Qatan*, sec. 159.

rabbinic tribunal, at least according to some leading medieval halakhists.[50] If this was also the case for a returning apostate, the *Tosafot Shitah* text would support the somewhat unusual view attributed above to Rabiah, that a form of public ratification was required, even as the *Tosafot Shitah* passage invokes the (more lenient) principle of *'af 'al pi she-hata Yisra'el hu* as well. In any event, when Maharam mi-Rothenburg characterizes the shortcomings of the former apostate in question as one who was *tovel ve-sherez be-yado*, he is not merely referring to a popular custom that had been ineffective in ensuring the returnee's sincerity. Rather, his ire was directed toward the flouting of a solemn rabbinic requirement by someone who had undergone the required ritual immersion without the co-requisites of proper repentance and subsequent Jewish practice.[51] In terms of access to the *Tosafot Shitah* passage, it should be noted that R. Samuel of Evreux was also a direct teacher of R. Meir of Rothenburg, during Meir's student days in Chateau-Thierry.[52]

How are we to understand the changing attitudes of Ashkenazic rabbinic authorities during the twelfth and thirteenth centuries with respect to the requirement of ritual immersion for an apostate who wished to return to the Jewish community, as reflected in the texts that have been presented here? This rite might have begun initially in Ashkenaz as a local custom, and it may also have been embellished along the way by popular practice. If so, the main goal or intent of the Tosafists was to provide more formal legal grounding for this rite, as was their wont with regard to other bona fide customs that preceded them.[53] On the other hand, it is entirely possible

---

[50] See e.g., Rambam, *Mishneh Torah, Hilkhot Issurei Bi'ah* 13:12; the comment of the *Maggid Mishnah* ad loc.; and above, n. 45.

[51] Cf. I. Z. Kahana, *Maharam mi-Rothenburg: Teshuvot, Pesaqim u-Minhagim*, vol. 1 (Jerusalem, 1957), 157 (secs. 90-92).

[52] See Urbach, *Ba'alei ha-Tosafot*, 2: 528.

[53] See, e.g., my "Halakhah and Realia in Medieval Ashkenaz," 193-201.

that the practice of ritual immersion for a returning apostate was initiated by talmudists and halakhists who were part of the rabbinic elite. In either case, was the change in the rabbinic view on the need for this immersion, which can be traced from the late twelfth century onward, solely the result of talmudic or other rabbinic considerations, or were there temporal factors that impacted the rabbinic view as well?

Several such factors can be suggested. Robert Chazan has drawn attention to the list presented by the rabbinic author and chronicler, R. Ephraim b. Jacob of Bonn, of no fewer than eleven anti-Jewish incidents that occurred between 1171 and 1196 (the year before Ephraim's death): five in Rhineland Germany (including one in Speyer), one in Austria, two in northern France, and two in England. These incidents, which occurred nearly a hundred years after the First Crusade, were precipitated, according to Chazan, by the deepening Christian perception of the Jews as enemies.[54] It stands to reason that an apostate who joined the Christian community in the late twelfth or early thirteenth centuries was seen by rabbinic authorities, as well as by the Jewish community at large, in an increasingly unfavorable light. The growing rabbinic demand for a demonstrative act of contrition, which indicated in a more graphic way that a significant line had been crossed, may also be understood in light of this series of events and the worsening perceptions that accompanied them.[55]

---

[54] R. Chazan, *Medieval Stereotypes and Modern Antisemitism* (Berkeley, 1997), 53-78.

[55] For additional dimensions of the deterioration of the status of the Jews in Christian society through the twelfth century, see, e.g., A. Funkenstein, "Changes in the Patterns of Christian Anti-Jewish Polemic," [Hebrew] *Zion* 33 (1968): 137-43; A. Sapir Abulafia, *Christians and Jews in the Twelfth-Century Renaissance* (London, 1995), chapter 6; and J. Cohen, *Living Letters of the Law: Ideas of the Jew in Medieval Christianity* (Berkeley, 1999), 147-66, 254-70. In an unpublished paper, Dr. Rami Reiner of Ben-Gurion University of the Negev has demonstrated that from the second half of the twelfth century and through the first half of the thirteenth, a

Perhaps even more significant in this regard is the formulation of Pope Innocent III in 1201 (in a letter to the Archbishop
of Arles), that effectively expanded the meaning of voluntary
conversion to Christianity to include even those who were
baptized only as a last-ditch means of avoiding death.[56]
Innocent's new interpretation (which addressed a problem that
had been raised several times during the twelfth century)
meant that virtually every Jewish apostate was considered
according to Christian dogma to be a full-fledged, willing
Christian.[57] As we have seen, thirteenth-century Ashkenazic
rabbinic formulations refer to ritual immersion as a means of
removing the impurity of Christianity (*zuhama*), or as a demonstrative sign of change in status (*la'asot hekkera*), which
might well mean that this requirement was seen on some level,
even by the rabbinic leadership, as a kind of un-baptism.[58]

We must also bear in mind, however, that unlike the
more demanding physical forms of *tiqqunei teshuvah* (which
were often accompanied by public humiliation), ritual immersion would not have been seen as much of an impediment to

---

number of leading northern French and German Tosafists embraced more
positive views toward Christian converts to Judaism than had been the
case in the prior period. He too sees this change in attitude as a function of
the worsening position of the Jews in medieval Europe, as expressed in
religious, political and cultural terms. Although the increasingly negative
perception of Jews led fewer Christians to convert to Judaism at this time,
it also caused Ashkenazic society and its rabbinic leadership to be
markedly more accepting of those who did.

[56] See S. Grayzel, *The Church and the Jews in the XIIIth Century*, vol. 1
(New York, 1966), 101-02.

[57] See E. Fram, "Perception and Reception of Repentant Apostates," 304-
05. Cf. J. M. Elukin, "The Discovery of Self: Jews and Conversion in the
Twelfth Century," *Jews and Christians in Twelfth-Century Europe*, ed.
Signer and Von Engen, 63-76, and A. Haverkamp, "Baptised Jews in
German Lands During the Twelfth Century," ibid., 260-67, 291-98.

[58] For references in Jewish polemical literature and *piyyut* during this
period to baptism as pollution (*tinnuf*) or defilement (*shemez*), see e.g., S. L.
Einbinder, *Beautiful Death* (Princeton, 2002), 34-35, and D. Berger, *The
Jewish-Christian Debate in the High Middle Ages* (Philadelphia, 1979), 94,
sec. 78.

re-entry into the Jewish community, especially if it could be undertaken privately by the penitent. This essential part of Jacob Katz' thesis, that medieval Ashkenazic rabbinic authorities (following Rashi) did not wish to unnecessarily encumber an apostate's return, remains, for the most part, intact. The other axiom of Rashi highlighted by Katz, that a Jew who had undergone baptism retains his status as a Jew, is also not directly contradicted (except perhaps by the *Tosafot Shitah* of Evreux, if we presume that a rabbinic *beit din* had to oversee the immersion that was required). Nonetheless, at least some of the Tosafists and Ashkenazic rabbinic figures who supported the need for ritual immersion were positing the existence of a gap between the apostate and the Jewish community that Rashi (and others) did not recognize.

As the texts presented here have shown, the practice of ritual immersion in northern France and Germany during the twelfth and thirteenth centuries for a returning apostate enjoyed a good deal of rabbinic approbation and even encouragement. In light of these new findings, a number of other suggestive and somewhat elusive issues, including the frustration of Maharam of Rothenburg with insincere returnees (and his invalidation of their testimony), the inquisitorial reports presented by Y. Yerushalmi and J. Shatzmiller, and R. Israel Isserlein's fifteenth-century characterization of this immersion as *minhag 'avotenu Torah hi*,[59] are now more readily understood. Moreover, the data and analysis presented here surely have implications for assessing more precisely the transition to the early modern period, specifically in terms of the rabbinic requirements for immersion in that period, as well as rabbinic attitudes more generally toward the return of apostates to the Jewish community.

---

[59] Above, n. 12. Isserlein also refers to Maharam's responsum concerning the testimony of the insincere apostate. See *Terumat ha-Deshen, Ketavim*, no. 220, and cf. no. 138.

Orthodox Rabbis Confront
the War Refugee Board

David Kranzler

Introduction

While historians have recently begun to recognize the contributions of the War Refugee Board (henceforth: WRB) on behalf of rescue efforts during World War II, they have largely ignored the pivotal role played by some Orthodox rabbis and community leaders in the United States and overseas.[1] Many of these

---

[1] See my chapter on the role of Orthodox Jews entitled, "Orthodox Ends, Unorthodox Means: The Role of the Vaad Hatzalah and Agudath Israel during the Holocaust," *American Jewry During the Holocaust*, ed. Max Finger (American Jewish Commission on The Holocaust, 1984), Appendix 4-3. This was the first attempt to present the role of Orthodox leaders in war-time rescue efforts. Cf. idem, *Thy Brother's Blood* (New York, 1987), a fully-documented, albeit popular presentation of the issues. My scholarly analysis of this issue is forthcoming.

For some related articles, see Efraim Zuroff, "Rabbis' Belief and Rescue: A Case Study of the Vaad ha-Hatzalah of the American Orthodox Rabbis, 1942-1943," *Simon Wiesenthal Center Annual* 3 (1986): 121-83; and idem,

Orthodox leaders were European-trained Talmudic scholars
and laymen who, in most cases, could not express themselves
well in English, nor did they have easy access to the President
of the United States.

In examining the role of American Orthodox leaders
within the context of the War Refugee Board, personality
differences among the members of the WRB appear to be
greatly significant. What emerges is a complex picture of
success, failure and frustration that sheds light on the larger
issues of rescue during the Holocaust.

The War Refugee Board and
Rescue Efforts During 1944-45

Orthodox leaders played a leading role in the formation of the
War Refugee Board. The rabbis' march on Washington the day
before Yom Kippur Eve 1943, inspired by Hillel Kook (alias
Peter Bergson), and their dealings with him which led to
Bergson-inspired Congressional Hearings on Rescue in the fall
of 1943, culminated in President Roosevelt creating the WRB
on January 22, 1944.[2] Orthodox leaders were responsible for
the Board's first rescue act: obtaining a license to send "free
currency," i.e., Swiss francs, directly into enemy-occupied
territory. John Pehle, the first director of the WRB, acknowledged that the "program [was] approved by this Government
on January 22, 1944, the very day that the late President

"Rescue Via the Far East: The Attempt to Save Rabbis and Yeshiva
Students 1939-1941," *Simon Wiesenthal Center Annual* 1 (1984): 153-83.

See also, more recently, E. Zuroff, *The Response of Orthodox Jewry in the
United States to the Holocaust: The Activities of the Vaad ha-Hatzala Rescue
Committee, 1939-1945* (Hoboken, NJ, 2000); my review-essay, "Orthodoxy's
Finest Hour: Rescue Efforts During the Holocaust" in *Jewish Action* 63:1
(2002); and our subsequent debate, entitled "Orthodox Rescue Revisited,"
in *Jewish Action* 63:3 (2003): 32-39.

[2] See *Thy Brother's Blood*, 100-101.

Roosevelt created the WRB."[3] Assistant Secretary of State Adolph A. Berle added that this "probably involved the direct renunciation of the no ransom policy ... a policy no longer suitable to the times."[4]

The act differed from previous license requests by the Joint Distribution Committee [Joint] and the World Jewish Congress [WJC] in that it not only facilitated the rescue of people in clear-cut danger, but also of those in places of "relative safety," i.e., from Poland to Hungary or Slovakia.[5] It enabled other Jewish relief organizations, especially the Joint, to legally send large sums of money to impoverished refugees in Europe, as well as Shanghai. This was accomplished primarily through the efforts of Rabbi Abraham Kalmanowitz, who courageously sent money overseas, often ignoring illegalities and FBI threats of arrest.[6]

While the creation of the Board came late in the war, its importance should not be minimized. Between 100,000 and 200,000 Jews owe their lives, in part, to efforts of the Board. For example, the WRB made the services of American embassies available to rescue activists, especially access to the diplomatic pouch and cables. While Orthodox leaders continued to use the confidential Polish diplomatic pouch to bypass American censorship, it was neither as reliable nor inexpensive. This valuable, but illegal, means of communication

---

[3] See John Pehle's speech at the Vaad Hatzalah Dinner, 17 December 1945, Abraham Kalmanowitz Papers [KP], p. 2.

[4] Memo by William Riegelman, 26 January 1944 to Rabbi Abraham Kalmanowitz NA/SDDF, 840.48 Refugees/5136. [Riegelman Memo 1/26/44, WRB Papers.]

[5] Riegelman Memo 1/26/44. Cf. Monty Noam Penkower, *The Jews Were Expendable: Free World Democracy and the Holocaust* (Urbana, Il., 1983), 130-36.

[6] Cf. David Kranzler, *Japanese, Nazis and Jews: the Jewish Refugee Community of Shanghai 1938-1945* (New York: Yeshiva University Press, 1976), 558, 573-74 nn. 57, 59.

was offered to all Jewish organizations, but only Orthodox leaders made use of it in the U.S., Switzerland, and Turkey.[7]

With the creation of the WRB, large sums of American dollars could be transmitted to various rescue activists. American ambassadors were recruited to work on behalf of the Board. The American government provided over a million dollars for administrative expenses, in addition to Jewish sources of funds.[8]

Rescue opportunities were utilized by other groups of Orthodox Jews interacting with the WRB, both in the U.S. and abroad. While the Jewish establishment in the U.S. and Switzerland frowned upon their approach involving bribes, ransom, and other illegalities, Orthodox leaders used these methods in several successful rescue operations. Frequently, the chances for success were in direct proportion to the sympathy and willingness of the particular representative of the WRB at that place and time. Orthodox rabbis and communal leaders made courageous attempts to fulfill the Torah's dicta of *pikuah nefesh* (rescuing endangered lives) and *pidyon shevuyim* (ransoming of prisoners).

The greatest impact of the WRB was on Treasury Secretary Henry Morgenthau Jr., a Jew and cabinet member most responsible for the WRB. Several members of Roosevelt's cabinet were technically part of the War Refugee Board, including the Secretaries of State, War and Treasury, but the first two only involved themselves in occasional decisions. In reality, Treasury Secretary Henry Morgenthau Jr. and his assistant John Pehle were in charge.[9] Morgenthau, Pehle, and

---

[7] Kranzler, "Orthodox Ends," 2. Regarding the price of using a Polish diplomatic pouch, I am indebted to Herman Landau. Mr. Landau was executive director of HIJEFS, the Vaad Hatzalah branch in Switzerland, headed by Recha and Isaac Sternbuch. See interview with author.

[8] See David Wyman, *Abandonment of the Jews* (New York: Pantheon Books, 1984), 213-14.

[9] See for example, the *Morgenthau Diaries* [*MD*], books 718-72, FDR Library. Over 800 brief volumes in the Franklin Delano Roosevelt Library

later William O'Dwyer, understood the persistence of Orthodox Jews, and however discomfited, frequently reacted favorably to their requests. On the other hand, there is little doubt that the negative reaction by other representatives of the WRB accounted directly or indirectly for countless deaths. All of these efforts provided a forum for the drama in which Orthodox leaders were at times on the periphery, at times partners with other groups, and at times the crucial factor in rescuing tens of thousands of Jews, up to the last moments of Hitler's *Gottesdammerung*.

WRB Personalities in the United States

Prior to World War II, Orthodox Jews did not constitute a powerful social, political or economic bloc. They also did not control any major Jewish organization, such as the Joint Distribution Committee, the American Jewish Committee, or the American Jewish Congress. Their leadership included a few highly motivated, charismatic European-trained rabbis, heads of *yeshivot*, and a fledgling Zeirei Agudath Israel organization comprised primarily of recently arrived refugees.

Among the most prominent of the immigrant rabbis and *roshei yeshivot* were Rabbis Abraham Kalmanowitz, Aaron Kotler, Eliezer Silver, and lay leaders such as Mike (Elimelech) Tress and Irving Bunim. Other rabbis included Shabse Frankel and Baruch Korff, who often took part in various rescue confrontations with the WRB.[10] Korff was particularly important for his political connections, his original rescue plans, and his audacious personal intercessions with government and WRB representatives.

---

contain documents as well as stenographic accounts of conversations. See details below, notes 14-30.

[10] Cf. *Thy Brother's Blood* for information about these and twenty-two other Orthodox rescue activists.

In early 1945, Pehle was replaced by William O'Dwyer, as director of the WRB. Pehle's assistants from the Treasury Department, including Randolph Paul and Josiah DuBois, had written a well-known report about the State Department's suppression of information on Nazi atrocities and were thus a factor in creating the WRB. While all of these men were humanitarians, their individual differences had practical consequences for the rescue board. Pehle, for example, was far more cautious in approving unusual rescue schemes by the Orthodox leaders than were DuBois or O'Dwyer.

Since almost any rescue measure required the co-operation of WRB representatives overseas as well as in Washington, these differences in policy perspective played a crucial role. Other examples of differing personalities included Roswell McClelland in Switzerland and Ira Hirschmann in Turkey, both vital centers for rescue during the last year and a half of the war. McClelland was a legalistic bureau-crat, unsympathetic to the rescue of Jews in Europe, while Hirschmann proved to be very helpful.

The Story of Vittel and
the "Bogus" Latin American Papers

The influence of Orthodox leaders and the obstacles they faced with members of the WRB in Washington and especially in Berne can be seen in a relatively unknown episode that took place in the winter and spring of 1943-44 in the Vittel detention camp in Occupied France. The inmates possessed "bogus" Latin American papers, originating in 1941 with Eli Sternbuch of Montreaux, and purchased from the Paraguayan and later other consuls in Switzerland at a cost of 500 to 3,000 Swiss francs. With the help of his sister-in-law, Recha Sternbuch and her husband Isaac, Eli Sternbuch was able to supply Paraguayan and other papers to Jews in Poland and other occupied countries. Recha and her husband Isaac had founded HIJEFS, a relief and rescue division of the Vaad Hatzalah in Switzerland. Because there were several hundred-thousand Germans residing in Latin America, the Nazis chose to recognize these papers and allowed their owners to stay out of the ghetto, while others were sent to detention camps such as Vittel, Tittmoning and the 'privileged' section of Bergen Belsen.[11] In the fall of 1943, the Nazis decided to no longer recognize the validity of these papers. The Swiss and Spanish Protecting Power for the Latin American countries in Nazi-occupied Europe refused to act on the Jews' behalf, thereby endangering not only those in Vittel and other such camps, but the thousands of bearers of such papers.

On December 1, 1943, a German commission arrived in Vittel, and confiscated all Latin American passports from Jewish inmates and sent the passports to Berlin for verification. The Jews assumed that all of these inmates would be killed. However, since they were able to communicate with Switzerland through the IRC, they immediately contacted the Sternbuchs, who had long been in touch with friends and relatives in Vittel. On December 15, four days after the visit of the German commission, the Sternbuchs sent an urgent cable to Jacob Rosenheim of the World Agudath Israel and the Vaad Hatzalah in New York, demanding immediate intercession with the State Department and the War Refugee Board to persuade the Latin American countries to officially recognize these papers.[12]

---

[11] Nathan Eck, "The Rescue of Jews with the Aid of Passports and Citizenship Papers of Latin American States," *Yad Vashem Studies* 1 (1957): 126-28.

[12] See Isaac Sternbuch to Jacob Rosenheim, 15 December 1943; January 1944; 13 April 1944. (Sternbuch Papers [SP]). See also undated Memo (probably 12/11/44) SMP, RG-25 Administration-5, JCCA. This document gives detailed information on the visit of the German Commission and pleads for help in the rescue of this endangered group of about 240 Jews with Latin American papers. It is likely that the memo came from Sternbuch to Saly Mayer. The Sternbuchs were the ones most directly involved in all

Vaad Hatzalah and Agudah representatives immediately met with State Department officials, who promised to send cables to this effect to the various Latin American countries. This communication might have been helpful, since the United States had great influence in the affairs of Central and South American states during those years. The Vaad Hatzalah discovered four months later that the State Department never sent the cables. On April 5, the Sternbuchs sent another urgent cable to the Vaad Hatzalah, informing them that, based on the information of recent appeals from Vittel inmates, the entire group would be sent to their deaths unless the United States took immediate action.

The following day, April 6, 1943, which was Passover, three rabbis from the Vaad Hatzalah traveled by train to Washington to meet with Treasury Secretary Henry Morgenthau Jr. In deference to them, he canceled other plans and spent the rest of the day in an heroic attempt to save the lives of the Vittel inmates.[13] Earlier, the rabbis had attempted to meet with Judge Samuel Rosenman, speechwriter and confidant of the President, but he agreed to receive only one of the three representatives, Rabbi Korff. American-born, politically sophisticated, and the youngest of the three, Korff refused to go into Rosenman's office unless the entire rabbinic delegation was allowed entry. John Pehle told Henry Morgenthau Jr. that, "Rosenman had to come out and see him [Korff] personally and beg him to come in alone."[14]

---

facets of rescue and potential rescue involving the inmates of Vittel detention camp. See also Sternbuch's cable to Rosenheim, 12/15/55, SP. Copies of all of these papers may be found in the author's personal archives. Although the documents were usually written and signed by either Mrs. Sternbuch's husband Isaac (Yitzchok) Sternbuch or Herman Landau ("*Hilfsverein fuer Juedische Fluchtlinge in Shanghai*" later changed to "*in usland*"), they were primarily inspired or instigated by her. Cf. Penkower, 250-53.

[13] See Moshe Prager, *Disaster and Salvation* [Vaad Hatzalah] (New York, 1957), 498.

[14] *MD*, 4/6/44, p. 86.

Although he promised to prod the State Department into action, as soon as the rabbis left, Rosenman phoned Morgenthau to tell him that the problem belonged to the WRB. He claimed that he was too busy to look after particularist Jewish concerns.[15] The fact that Rabbi Korff had close relations with John McCormack, Speaker of the House, and Senator Mead of New York, gave the rabbis ready entry to the Treasury Secretary.

After Morgenthau greeted the rabbis, Kalmanowitz, in his poor English, made the opening plea:

> Coming to you Mr. Secretary about saving the lives of the Jewish. We have a question from two-thousand two-hundred and thirty-eight interned people in the camps of Vittel and Tittmoning.

> We received yesterday [April 5] by cable that every inmate there is in danger of life and death. We come to the office of Mr. Pehle, and Mr. Pehle, I know very well, in the four or six weeks or less that he is working very hard to save the lives ... Mr. Lesser, Miss Hodel and Mr. DuBois, who are willing to work day and night for the saving – I know very well and I recognize – the saving has not come. I don't know about the blame. I think the blame is in the State Department. There is every danger not only for the lives of the two-thousand two-hundred and thirty-eight people, but for three and a half million people. We have not very much help.[16]

At this point, as Morgenthau later told Secretary of State Cordell Hull, "the rabbis broke down and cried here in my office, and we had quite a time." Morgenthau said, "Now, look, you get upset and you get me upset, and I can't do anything either."[17] But Rabbi Kalmanowitz continued:

> I know Mr. Lesser and [Miss] Hodel and [Mr.] DuBois have at hand three cables that must go yesterday, and

---

[15] Ibid., 93.

[16] Ibid., 87.

[17] Ibid.

the cables are not going; one cable to Spain, one
cable to the Swiss,. one cable to the South American
countries. You know very well, the less cables you have
to send throughout the State Department....[18]

Unlike Judge Rosenman, Morgenthau, under the prodding
of the audacious Rabbi Korff, decided immediately to goad
the State Department into sending those cables. He demanded
that "the Swiss Government, as the intervening power,
insist that the passports be recognized by the Germans."[19]
He telephoned Secretary of State Cordell Hull and reached
his secretary [Brown], who was unfamiliar with the issue.
When he assured Morgenthau that he would pass the message
along, Morgenthau replied, "Well, either you or Mr. Hull call me
back ... and I'll just sit here and wait until I hear from you."[20]

Within an hour, with the rabbis waiting outside, Morgenthau was on the phone with Hull. He explained the problem
and demanded that Hull's assistant, George Warren, come over
that night to settle the matter of the cables. Again, he added,
"I'll wait till he comes." That evening the matter was settled.[21]

The next morning, April 7, Morgenthau noted that:

> ... Nothing has pleased me more than being able to get
> the State Department to send out this cable in regard
> to Camp Vittel. *It just shows that if we put enough heat
> in the right place it can be done, and believe me, we
> have put plenty of heat on Mr. Hull proper....* When these
> things are out and nothing happens, they must ask
> themselves, "Well, after all, what is all this fighting
> for?" So the fact that the March 16 cable went – of
> course, in the room I can say it is a tragedy it didn't go
> on March 16 – most likely two hundred and fifty people

---

[18] Ibid. Regarding the last phrase, "the less cables you have to send throughout the State Department," perhaps, one should add, "the better."

[19] Ibid.

[20] *MD*, 7 April 1944, p. 221.

[21] Ibid.

[in Vittel] have been murdered because it didn't go out on the 16th of March.

I made up my mind last night, and I told these people [i.e., the rabbis] I would stay here until it did go. I did stay here with the help of you people, and with the result that people over there who were opposed to the thing – evidently Mr. Hull, although I haven't spoken to him since last night.... But the results were good. I just made up my mind I would stick it out... [emphasis added].[22]

Morgenthau not only pinpointed the culprit but pointed out:

Well, it turned out it wasn't the last word, and he most likely can say again as he did once before, "It is that damned Jew in the Treasury" who overruled him. He said it once before, and now most likely he will say, "God-damned Jew." It is a badge of honor.[23]

Revealing the same naive trust in the President as had Stephen Wise and most Jews, he preferred to lay the blame on the State Department instead:

It is unfortunate that such people exist in Mr. Roosevelt's administration, and they should be gotten rid of, but Mr. Hull doesn't seem to want to get rid of them.[24]

Concluding in a lighter vein, Morgenthau regaled his staff with the story of how

he called up, this Rabbi [i.e., Kalmanowitz] and [I] wanted to thank him. After all it was a nice Passover present. He said, "I want to wish you Mr. Morgenthau an Orthodox Passover." [laughter] So I wish you all a very Orthodox Passover.[25]

---

[22] Ibid.

[23] Ibid., 222.

[24] Ibid.

[25] Ibid. What Rabbi Kalmanowitz undoubtedly meant was the standard greeting of "Have a kosher Passover," which Morgenthau translated as an "Orthodox Passover."

That night, at 10 p.m., Morgenthau was awakened by George Warren of the State Department, still trying to procrastinate by telling Rabbi Korff one thing and Morgenthau another. Then, Morgenthau discovered that Korff had called Hull directly, causing Miss Klotz, Morgenthau's secretary, to exclaim, "They [i.e., the rabbis] won't stop at anything," adding on her own, "They're right."[26]

Korff did not hesitate to call Mr. Pehle at 2:00 a.m., saying, "[Pehle was] an angel to stand the pressure that we put on him." Nor did he hesitate to include the columnist Drew Pearson, who wrote about the State Department's procrastinating tactics in his syndicated column.[27] When Morgenthau asked Korff, "Did you talk as forcefully as that?" the young rabbi answered:

> ... Oh yes, Mr. Secretary ... When you feel in the heart and soul as I feel about it, there is no question about talking forcefully whether [it involves] Mr. Hull or Mr. Morgenthau or [even the President] Mr. Roosevelt – human life is at stake.[28]

Such determination had a profound effect on Morgenthau, as is evident from his response to Rabbi Korff:

> ... I got so upset the other day that I have been physically ill until last night. It is very unimportant, but I have been so moved by this thing. After all, I feel this thing very, very closely, and the tragedy is that these things don't happen in the same day. Maybe Mr. Hull will take more interest now.[29]

Still unwilling to accept the assurance that a cable to the Latin American countries and Spain was now authorized by

---

[26] *MD*, 719, 4/10/44, p. 169.

[27] Ibid., pp. 180, 182 as well as a taped interview with Rabbi Korff.

[28] *MD*, 719, 4/10/44.

[29] Ibid., p. 184.

the Secretary of State himself, Rabbi Korff asked whether it was possible to call directly to Ambassador Carleton Hayes in Spain. Morgenthau sympathized but suggested:

> ... Let [the sympathetic] Dubois write the cable in that manner [i.e., to act without delay]. You see it before it goes over. Write it that Mr. Hull is ordering Ambassador Hayes to see the proper authorities today – today is Monday – to the proper authorities on Tuesday and report back the same day....[30]

Despite the fact that all these efforts were too late to save the 238 inmates of Vittel, they were not in vain. The eventual recognition of these Latin American papers by their governments, and the guarantee of protection by Spain and Switzerland, meant that tens of thousands of Jews in Nazi-occupied countries were able to survive.

Clearly, both the WRB and State Department required constant pressure. While the American rabbis sought and even obtained allies among other Jewish organizations, such as the American Jewish Committee or the Jewish Labor Committee, the rabbis were practically the only ones to persist. Had a united American Jewry kept up the same pace throughout 1944, there is little doubt that tens of thousands more Jewish lives would have been saved.

Unfortunately, in Switzerland, a crucial location for rescue, Roswell McClelland, the individual sent for the purpose of promoting rescue, turned out to be an obstructionist of the worst kind. Not only did he fail to initiate any rescue efforts, as did Wallenberg in Hungary, he actually discouraged many, including those of George Mandel-Mantello, the Jewish First Secretary of the El Salvador Consulate in Switzerland.

Since his arrival in Switzerland in mid-1942, Mantello had issued gratis thousands of Salvador citizenship papers to

---

[30] Ibid., p. 182.

anyone with names of Jews in occupied Europe.[31] This was in stark contrast to the "sale" of passports of other Latin American countries, such as Cuba, Paraguay or Chile, by consuls seeking to make a fortune at the expense of Jewish victims, charging several thousand Swiss francs each. In February 1944, John Winant, the American Ambassador to Britain wrote to the State Department that, "The average price of a passport was approximately 700 Swiss francs. Only the consul of El Salvador has acted from purely humanitarian motives."[32]

McClelland obstructed Mantello's efforts at almost every step. While Sternbuch tried to utilize the help of Monsignor Bernadini, the sympathetic papal nuncio in Berne, and his connection to the Vaad Hatzalah in New York, Mantello called upon Maitre Muller and Rabbi Tuviah Lewenstein (formerly of Holland) who had influence with the Dutch Queen Wilhelmina, for the same end.[33] From August 1944, after the recognition of the papers by El Salvador and other Latin American countries through January 1945, McClelland subverted Mantello's efforts. From May 1 through May 16, 1944, Maitre Muller, who managed Mantello's "Salvador Paper Operation," made four urgent pleas for an audience with McClelland, all of which were ignored. Only on June 21, when the Czech Ambassador Jaromy Kopecky took up Muller's cause, did McClelland finally meet with him on the matter of the Salvador papers. Yet even the intervention by this sympathetic Czech Ambassador proved futile. As McClelland noted to Kopecky:

> ... Since I saw not less than five separate persons last week in connection with the same matter [i.e., Latin American papers], I frankly do not see the utility of

---

[31] See Kranzler, *The Man Who Stopped the Trains to Auschwitz: George Mantello, El Salvador and Switzerland's Finest Hour* (Syracuse: Syracuse U. Press, 2000), chap. 3 and see esp. "Salvadoran Papers" in the index.

[32] John Winant to the State Department, 6/17/43, WRB Papers.

[33] On Mantello and Queen Wilhelmina, see Jeno Levai, *Zsidosors Europaban* (Budapest, 1948), 26-27; also see George Mantello, recorded interview.

talking to Muller ... I personally doubt that the present Hungarian Government would accept Switzerland's role as protective power should the Swiss agree to undertake it at the request of the Salvadoran Government ... the *large increase of such illegal Latin American documents* ... may quite possibly jeopardize the precarious safety of those persons already in German internment camps... [emphasis added].[34]

When McClelland was informed on August 2, 1944 that the Swiss had agreed to represent the interests of the Salvadoran paper-holders in Budapest, the American representative of the WRB was not particularly pleased. Nor was he favorably disposed toward an idea approved by the Swiss that Mantello, at his personal cost, send two Swiss members of the Salvador Consulate to help with the Salvador paper holders at the Budapest Embassy.[35] He declared:

> ... It is difficult to see just what value these papers would have, since they do not entitle their holders to emigrate to El Salvador. At best, as I have always told you, I feel that these false documents offer only very slight protection, and that increasing the number of them only weakens the precarious position of the many other people already holding them at present.[36]

The very fact that holders of Salvador papers were not entitled to emigrate was a major advantage, since it meant that they could not be deported from Hungary. They were to be treated as citizens of a protected foreign country and were not required to relocate to the ghetto or wear a Yellow Star. Moreover, regarding the two men Mantello sought to send to

---

[34] Roswell McClelland to Jaromir Kopecky, 21 June 1944, and McClelland-Banyai 8/11/44, WRB Papers; also see Maitre Muller, interview.

[35] M. Banyai to Roswell McClelland, 2 Aug. 1944, WRB. Mr. Banyai headed the *Schweizerische Hilfskomitee Fuer die Juden in Ungarn* (The Swiss Committee of Assistance for the Jews of Hungary), organized by Mantelli in March 1944, after the German occupation of Hungary.

[36] McClelland to Banyai, 11 August 1944, WRB Papers.

Budapest to help Swiss Consul Lutz expedite the Salvador paper rescue project, McClelland answered, "I can only say that I remain somewhat skeptical."[37]

As late as September 1944, McClelland still referred to these papers as the "documents fraudulently issued by their Geneva Consular General [George Mantello],"[38] as if it were a criminal offense to issue false papers to save lives. Moreover, unlike the other Latin American papers, the Salvador papers were issued with the full knowledge of the Geneva Salvador Consulate with no thoughts of profit. Yet, McClelland still balked. On September 12, 1944, with complete approval by the government of El Salvador, McClelland did not alter his stance. A memo of that date prepared by the State Department explicitly stated, "The government of El Salvador recognizes and will recognize the validity of the documents of Salvadoran Nationality ... I request through your worthy medium that Your Excellency's Government transmit the foregoing to the Department of Foreign Relations of Switzerland.[39]

Several days after the Salvadoran memo, McClelland found reason once again, on a technicality, to question the validity of the Salvador papers.[40]

In a cable dated September 23, the Secretary of State responded to McClelland's use of a technicality as a means of obstruction.

> Your attention is drawn again to the general declaration which was reported in [the American] Legations [Cable No.] 3671 of June 17 ... The confirmation by the Salvadoran Government of specific persons whose names were submitted to it does not repeat nor accordingly imply either the need or desirability of forwarding

[37] Ibid.

[38] McClelland to WRB, 4 Sept. 1944, WRB Papers.

[39] Cf. Memo US Legation, 4 Sept. 1944, WRB Papers.

[40] McClelland to WRB, 16 Sept. 1944, WRB Papers.

to that government further specific names. You are therefore requested to proceed along lines of ... previous communications which reference is made in present telegram.[41]

In as diplomatic a way as possible, the Secretary of State, no doubt still chafing under the pressure of the rabbis, tried to persuade McClelland to facilitate, rather than obstruct rescue efforts.

The same consideration should guide you also in dealing with documents of other American republics which have notified the Swiss Government that persons in enemy territory who are subject to persecution to whom documents in their names have been issued must receive treatment as nationals of such republics from the enemy. *In this connection, your attention is drawn to Department No. 2490 July 21, sixth paragraph, in which there is set forth the desirability of placing the most liberal possible construction on any communication from any American republic with respect to the protection of persons from cruelty and persecution,* and in which it is stated that slowness in action arising from *unwavering attachment to technicalities,* which would be proper enough under ordinary circumstances, *merely results in these abnormal times in ruthless killing of further numbers of innocent people.* Even though this passage was intended primarily as a suggestion for Swiss officials, it is suggested that the attitude you adopt be governed by it [emphasis added].[42]

Yet, as late as January 11, 1945, when Sternbuch again requested that McClelland pressure the Swiss into taking a stronger stand on the Salvador papers, he remained just as cool, legalistic and unresponsive. He claimed that Salvador had not provided the proper recognition necessary in this instance, and that the U.S. was not represented by the Swiss for the

---

[41] Cordell Hull to McClelland, 23 Sept. 1944, WRB Papers.

[42] Ibid.

"papers issued by Mr. Mantello of the Consulate of El Salvador at Geneva." Sternbuch pointed out to him that as early as June 1944, Agudath Israel [of the U.S.] cabled him that Salvador had recognized the holders of its papers.[43]

Although McClelland still failed to see their value as life-savers in Hungary and all other occupied countries, the papers were, in fact, forged by the thousands by Boris Teichholtz, Chaim Roth, Samuel Frey and others working in the Jewish underground in Budapest.[44] Mr. Mantello confirmed McClelland's negative attitude toward rescue. At first McClelland had agreed to take up the question with the Swiss Political Department in Berne. Subsequently, he asked for the original documents, and later he ignored it all, losing a precious three months.[45]

While not fully aware of McClelland's negative role in rescue matters, the War Refugee Board found his position towards the Latin American papers less than satisfactory. In reports by WRB staffer Benjamin Akzin, of a conversation with Clattenberg of the State Department, among the more activist members of the War Refugee Board, Akzin noted the change in attitude of the Swiss concerning the papers and their demands for proof of legality before they would approach the Germans. This occurred in December 1944, after the full, shocking revelations of the Auschwitz Protocols, which detailed the mass murder of 1,765,000 Jews during the period of April 1942-April 1944. Instigated by Mantello's Swiss press campaign, these matters appeared in several Swiss newspapers. George Mantello, the Jewish First Secretary of El Salvador in Switzerland, had obtained copies of the Protocols as well as the Hungarian Report, which gave

---

[43] Hull to McClelland, 15 Jan. 1945, WRB Papers.

[44] Interview with Messrs. Chaim Roth, Samuel Frey and Boris (Bruce) Teichholtz.

[45] Mantello, interview.

information about the ghettoization and deportation of 335,000 Hungarian Jews to Auschwitz from April through the beginning of June 1944. By brilliantly orchestrating the Swiss press and churches into publishing large excerpts of the two reports in over 120 newspapers and almost every church – revealing the ghastly methods of the death camp in Auschwitz and the ongoing deportations in Hungary – and with the active help of the Swiss people, Mantello was able to break the curtain of silence over the Nazi and Hungarian role in the world's greatest crime. Within two weeks, this press campaign evoked, for the first time, a public response and warning to Admiral Horthy of Hungary, by the Pope, President Roosevelt, Britain's Anthony Eden, Sweden's King Gustav (who then dispatched Wallenberg to Budapest), the International Red Cross and the Swiss government. By July 7, 1944, Horthy halted deportations.[46] Clattenberg realized that on this matter of Latin American Papers, far too much red tape seemed to be emanating from the American Legation in Berne. The representative of the State Department expressed

> doubt whether McClelland [and the American Legation] ... isolated from the U.S. and very much overworked as they are, have themselves a sufficient grasp of the problem, and asked whether it would not be advisable for the Refugee Board to send [James] Mann [WRB representative in London] on a short mission to Berne in order to acquaint the Legation and McClelland with the situation, as well as to have a talk with appropriate officials at the Swiss Foreign Office.[47]

McClelland's continuing refusal to help is seen most clearly in an incident that took place in September 1944.

---

[46] See my *The Man Who Stopped the Trains to Auschwitz*, chaps. 7-9.

[47] Memo of talk by Benjamin Akzin with Mr. Clattenberg of the State Department, 11 Dec. 1944, WRB Papers. Historians of the Holocaust do not mention McClelland's obstructionist stance.

Sternbuch, the Vaad Hatzalah, and the International Red Cross (IRC) wanted to send packages of food and clothing into the camps at Birkenau, Bergen Belsen and Theresienstadt. The IRC had balked for so long at helping Jewish inmates of the camps, that not until Mantello's press campaign of June-July 1944 did they finally come forth. But even then, the IRC would not waive its usual bureaucratic delay of 3-4 weeks. Recha Sternbuch asked the American representative of the War Refugee Board to use his position to intervene with the IRC, "since the inmates were totally exhausted and every day's delay is injurious."[48]

It took McClelland over a week to respond. Then he said, "I do not feel that circumstances at Theresienstadt are so critical that it will not be possible for you to tolerate three to four weeks time required by the Joint Commission [of the IRC] to procure the supplies you wish to buy." Deftly, McClelland ignored Bergen Belsen and Birkenau, emphasizing instead Theresienstadt, the "model" camp with relatively better conditions.[49] But even in that camp, both McClelland and Sternbuch knew the inmates were on an extremely poor diet and most people always went hungry. Recha Sternbuch did not rest with McClelland's negative reply. Two days later she tried her best to deal directly with the IRC and succeeded at least partially in her goal of sending the packages.[50]

The next rescue opportunity which McClelland attempted to thwart involved what became known as the "Bergen Belsen Train," or the "Kastner Transport," named for Rudolph Kastner, the Hungarian Zionist leader (and representative of the Jewish Agency) involved in the negotiations with the Nazis and organizer of this "transport." In June 1944, following

---

[48] Sternbuch to McClelland, 26 Sept. 1944, WRB Papers.
[49] McClelland to Sternbuch, 4 Oct. 1944, WRB Papers.
[50] Sternbuch to McClelland, 6 Oct. 1944, WRB Papers.

the failure of the Joel Brand Mission to effect negotiations with Heinrich Himmler via Adolph Eichmann for the "ransoming" of Hungarian Jewry, Rudolph Kastner organized a transport of about 1200 select Jewish leaders (later "accidentally" increased to 1684) to go, presumably, to Palestine. These 1200 included 700 Zionist holders of Palestine Certificates, friends and relatives of Kastner, "paying" passengers able to finance their own "places" and those non-paying groups. Among those who paid was Philip Freudiger, head of the Orthodox *kehillah* in Budapest and a negotiating partner with Rabbi Michoel Ber Weissmandl and, for a short while, with Dieter Wisliceny, Eichmann's assistant, before Kastner pushed him out of the negotiations. Freudiger paid for 80 Orthodox rabbis, communal leaders and others, including Rabbi Joel Teitelbaum, the Hassidic *rebbe* of Satmar, Rabbi Jonathan Steiff and Rabbi Strasser (of Debrecen).[51]

To avoid an otherwise inevitable break of negotiations with the Gestapo because of the failure of the Brand negotiations, a desperate Rabbi Weissmandl sent a message to Eichmann's assistant, Dieter Wisliceny, via Philip Freudiger, that the Jews possessed 300 tractors available in Switzerland. This "tractor deal" was to be arranged by Sternbuch in Switzerland and to begin with a letter of credit of 150,000 SF for the first 10 tractors. As Kastner himself admitted to Nathan Schwalb in a letter of July 24, 1944, it was this tractor deal, originating with Weissmandl and organized by the Sternbuchs, that was the basis for the Gestapo permitting the departure of the train from Budapest on June 30, 1944.[52]

Since Sternbuch possessed only 150,000 SF, desperate negotiations transpired, for several weeks, between Freudiger

---

[51] See Kranzler, "Orthodox Ends," 14-15. Cf. Penkower, 210-12.

[52] Rudolph Kastner to Natan Schwalb, 28 July 1944, WRB Papers. Cf. Yehuda Bauer, "The Negotiations Between Saly Mayer and the SS," *Rescue Attempts During the Holocaust* (Jerusalem, 1977), 27, 34.

in Budapest, Weissmandl in Bratislava and Sternbuch in Montreaux, in an attempt to obtain the 750,000 SF necessary to forestall deportations to Auschwitz. A passionate attempt was made to raise the funds through Saly Mayer, Swiss representative of the American Joint Distribution Committee, and to convince McClelland to allow "ransom" to be paid to save the lives of the "Kastner Transport." It was the impression on all sides that the "transport" consisted of "1200 rabbis" and Orthodox leaders. Yet, both Mayer and McClelland refused to sanction such an "illegal" deal, particularly since it involved Orthodox rabbis. A desperate Rabbi Weissmandl, who feared for the lives of the 1200 cabled: "prima ware ["top-grade goods," i.e., the so-called 1200 rabbis] to enemy unless letter of credit to bank within 24 hours."[53]

McClelland scribbled on the plea, "Teleg from the Holy Men! Rec'd 7/2/44." Another plea was sent by Weissmandl on July 4, 1944:

> Deportations from Hungary to Poland [i.e., Auschwitz] irreversible unless your firm [i.e., Mayer] puts up one million Swiss franc letter of credit [for the tractors].

To which McClelland added on the margin, "typical."[54]

At the same time, under pressure by Orthodox leaders and the WRB, Moses A. Leavitt of the American Joint, cabled Dr. Joseph Schwartz, head of the European Joint:

> ... Sternbuch cabled Rabbinical group here [i.e., Vaad Hatzalah] that 1200 Hungarian Rabbis other leaders are now entrained Nicuna for deportation. He claims you refused help to save this group ... Orthodox groups here deeply disturbed by this situation and exerting great pressure on us....[55]

---

[53] Kranzler, "Orthodox Ends," 17.

[54] Ibid., 16.

[55] Ibid., 17. Cf. Penkower, 255.

Treasury Secretary Morgenthau cabled McClelland, saying, "The Rabbis put heavy pressure on us because Mayer won't help rescue 1200 rabbis."[56] In an "illegal" cable, utilizing the Polish diplomatic pouch made available to Sternbuch by Polish Ambassador Alexander Lados, Sternbuch cabled to Vaad Hatzalah that, "... part of the money is used for bribes in order to rescue people. It is impossible for us to discuss such things with McClelland."[57]

Tragically, the delays and procrastination by both McClelland and Mayer prevented the train from going straight to Switzerland instead of Bergen Belsen, and, it was Orthodox pressure on the War Refugee Board and the Joint to pay for the 40 tractors, that was the primary reason for the train's release to Switzerland in August and December 1944.[58]

Banyai Committee and the Auschwitz Protocol

In addition to Mantello's efforts to obtain Salvadoran papers, he was seeking other ways of lobbying for rescue and gathering first-hand information about conditions in Nazi-occupied countries, especially in Hungary, which the Germans had occupied since March 1944. To these ends, Mantello organized two organizations: the Rabbis' Committee, headed by Rabbi Zvi Taubes and the Swiss Committee of Assistance for the Jews in Hungary, headed by Michael Banyai, a Swiss Jew of Hungarian origin.[59] Soon after the ghettoization of Hungarian Jews on May 10, Banyai pleaded with McClelland in a series of letters and memos. Among other requests, he asked that McClelland, as representative of the WRB, convince the IRC to check into

---

[56] *MD*, 11 Aug. 1944, p. 3. Cf. also McClelland to Sternbuch, 18 Aug. 1944, SP.

[57] Confidential, Sternbuch to Vaad Hatzalah, 13 July 1944, SP.

[58] Contrary to the assertion of Yehuda Bauer; cf. Bauer, "Mayer," 34-38.

[59] M. Banyai to McClelland, 11 April 1944, WRB Papers.

conditions in the ghettos. Finally, on May 19, McClelland granted him an appointment for the 24th of that month. Banyai asked again five days later, with no apparent response.[60]

As conditions for Jews deteriorated and news about deportations began to arrive from several sources, the "Banyai Committee," as it became known, dispatched such information to McClelland, imploring him to take immediate action. Concerned for Hungarian Jewry, including his parents in Bistrice [Transylvania], Mantello sent 1,000 completed and stamped Salvador papers to be distributed by Moshe Krausz, head of the Palestine Certificate Office in Budapest. He sent these along with an unspecified sum of money, as well as medicine with his friend, Dr. Florian Manoliou, the Rumanian commercial *attache* in Geneva.[61] On June 21, Manoliou returned with two atrocity reports, the first known as the Auschwitz Protocol – detailing the mass murder of 1¾ million Jews in Auschwitz – dictated by two escapees, Alfred Wetzler and Rudolph Vrba, to the Jewish underground ("Working Group") headed by Gisi Fleischman and Rabbi Weissmandl. The second report by Freudiger detailed the deportation of over 300,000 Hungarian Jews. The day after Manoliou returned with the two reports, Banyai sent a more desperate letter imploring McClelland to give Manoliou an audience. At the same time, Banyai sent him the reports.[62]

McClelland declined to meet with Manoliou and two weeks later, on July 6, sent out a very brief summary to Washington of the two reports. While never doubting their

---

[60] Banyai to McClelland, 16 May 1944; May 19, 1944, WRB Papers.

[61] Banyai to McClelland, 22 June 1944, WRB Papers. Manoliou had arrived in Budapest on June 19, after his unsuccessful bid to find Mantello's parents in a now *Judenrein* Bistrice. See Kranzler, *The Man Who Stopped the Trains to Auschwitz*, chap. 5-6.

[62] Ibid.

authenticity, McClelland waited until October 12, almost five months, before sending the full reports, via regular mail, to the WRB, not reaching Washington until November 1, 1944. Adding a disclaimer, he remarked, "I personally feel that [while] the handling of such material as the enclosed reports cannot be considered as a positive contribution to real relief or rescue activities, it does constitute a tragic side to the whole problem."[63]

Fortunately, as soon as Mantello got hold of the reports, he created a flurry of rescue activities culminating in the now well-known Swiss press and church campaigns that publicized the Nazi mass murders and brought about a world-wide outcry, which in turn caused Admiral Horthy to stop the deportations to Auschwitz.[64]

Refoulement

A further dispute between McClelland and Recha Sternbuch, highlights the tragedy of having the wrong person in the wrong place at the wrong time. This involved the Swiss policy of refoulement, or returning Jewish ('racial' rather than political) refugees who had made it into Switzerland back across the border into Nazi hands. The few exceptions were children under sixteen and adults over sixty. Since March of 1944, even before McClelland came into his official position as representative of the WRB, Recha Sternbuch had tried several times to get the American Legation to take a strong stand vis-à-vis the Swiss refoulement policy on the French-Swiss border, just as the papal nuncio, Monsignor Bernadini, had accomplished on the Italian-Swiss border for Jews. This took place after

---

[63] McClelland to John Pehle 12 Oct. 1944, WRB Papers. It took another three weeks before this appeared on the front page of the *New York Times* on 26 Nov. 1944.

[64] *The Man Who Stopped the Trains to Auschwitz*, chaps. 7-9.

Mantello's press campaign highlighting the horrors of Auschwitz had been in full swing throughout Switzerland for almost three weeks.[65]

In a letter of July 13, 1944, following her meeting with McClelland on several issues, but particularly on refoulement, it is not difficult to perceive the deep disappointment and bitterness in her tone. One may also surmise that McClelland made no official overtures to the WRB on this matter. Based on Mrs. Sternbuch's response, we can reliably reconstruct his answer as, "If you don't like Swiss laws then why don't you settle in your beloved Sweden?" Mrs. Sternbuch responded:

> I do not believe that I should have to leave my mother country for the past 35 years for Sweden, just because I disagree with some aspects such as the laws of refoulement and believe that much more should be done for these unfortunate ones. All this involves neither personal ambitions nor any search for improving my lot elsewhere. It concerns a broader, general question. For this very reason I consider it my duty to remain there, where I could contribute to an improvement, however modest.

She then proceeded to lecture McClelland on more general aspects of humanitarian principles:

> However, as you are surely aware, my dear Mr. McClelland, that one is no better Swiss or American merely by total agreement with the actions of each and every department of the country. Nor is one, by the same virtue, a worse citizen for dissatisfaction with any one of these. The good Swiss foundation is based upon free and open criticism, as long as it remains within its constitutional limits and pursued by

---

[65] Sternbuch was obviously unaware that the day before, on July 12, the Swiss press campaign was already responsible for the abolishment of the racist regulations of refoulement. See Kranzler, *The Man Who Stopped the Trains to Auschwitz*, 134-35.

legal means. I can only assure you that my views coincide with those of Switzerland's greatest personalities. We frequently heard their voices in the national assembly and lately from private authoritative sources as well.

Sternbuch defended her opposition to many so-called Swiss patriots, including Saly Mayer who, under pressure of the Swiss, acted and probably even felt super-patriotic in reactions to the "Jewish question." She noted:

> I have much greater respect for the [true] Swiss mentality, than those who keep silent [under these circumstances] or [worse] demand the [imposition] of refoulement. That is why I raise my voice in opposition to actions that besmirch the good Swiss reputation. It is an embarrassment for civilization that in this day and age, tolerates such things. It is from such shame that I hope to see my fatherland cleared, let alone assist those, who out of want and despair gave them-selves up to the enemy.

> It is quite paradoxical, on the one hand to sacrifice large sums of American money to rescue individual families, while on the other, watch passively at what is occurring at the border. The number of those turned back (refoulees) is irrelevant. Surely the enemy has murdered most of these. Somewhere there are those still hidden who would brave the danger in enemy territory, if they did not have to contend with the additional danger at the Swiss border. It is through refoulement that the real danger accosts the refugees.

In simple terms, Recha Sternbuch criticized the myth propagated by Bauer that the number of refoulees amounted to about 5,000. She continued:

> There is no longer any time to prove this question. One cannot lose even a day. Enclosed please find a small list of refoulees for the months of May and June [1944] and these only insofar as we are aware of them.

Most are expedited at the border and nobody learns anything about them. For example, a Mrs. Schreiber, who was "returned" across the border six weeks ago, was not on the list. I similarly know of the case of a Mrs. Engel, on whose behalf Prof. R. of Geneva did so much to intervene. A few weeks ago these people were "returned" a second time, although they had been in Switzerland [and therefore, according to law, should have been permitted to remain, though in internment].

There is an abundance of proof. The Swiss authorities need no such proof, since they are fully aware of these objectionable facts. These are not actions that have to be proved, because they are not unjust according to the law. These actions conducted at the borders are performed in accordance with the regulations of the federal alien-office that we wanted to abolish.

After so many years of refoulement, it is high time to give thought [to abolishing such harsh laws]. Most people did not want to believe in the Hungarian deportations, and the daily figure of 12,000 people to Auschwitz when we received the cable after the first deportations. There were numerous individuals who did not believe in Hitler's determination to exterminate, despite his open declarations to this effect.

Recha then gets to the practical aspect. With diplomatic skill and a deep concern for her fellow human beings, she appealed to an obviously bureaucratic-minded official.

From within me springs the will to rescue what is still possible and it hurts deeply. You must understand me fully, dear Mr. McClelland, since you too desire to rescue. I believe that I would not fulfill my duty were I to leave such very tragic concerns as they are.

Appealing to the pacifist beliefs of McClelland's Quaker background, Recha Sternbuch argued:

There is still another voice, which must be heard – the voice of God, who asks, "Where is your brother?" Were one to ask this of John Fox or William Penn, they would surely find no means in the world sufficiently vigorous, to stand up for the rights of these unfortunate ones.

In conclusion, she pleaded:

I therefore repeat my request to you once again, dear Mr. McClelland, to interest yourself in these aforementioned matters in order to carry out the immediate abolition of the different regulations for crossing the border. Should you however not share my views – which I cannot assume – or, if you are of the opinion that one cannot expect any changes in these official regulations, I would be ever so much obliged to you if you notify me immediately. This way I can pursue other means without losing any more precious time. I felt it to be my duty to submit this matter to you first. Please accept my apologies for troubling you repeatedly. I remain with the best wishes. Your devoted servant.[66]

Saly Mayer, the "legalist" representative of Joint Distribution Committee, had no inclination to change his stance when he was so fully supported by his friend, the American representative whom Mayer dubbed "Hannukah."[67]

Ira Hirschmann

On the other hand, Ira Hirschmann, WRB representative in Turkey, was flexible, imaginative and daring. While McClelland

---

[66] For further analysis of McClelland's slow dispatching of vital rescue messages, see my, "Why Auschwitz Really Wasn't Bombed" (lecture, 10th World Congress of Jewish Studies, 17 August 1989). Cf. Yehuda Bauer, *American Jewry and the Holocaust* (Detroit, 1981), 432, 440.

[67] See Ira Hirshmann, *Caution to the Winds* (New York, 1962), ch. 11. Cf. Jacob Griffel, *Memoirs* (unpublished), 15-16.

disliked the Orthodox, Hirschmann accepted them as equals and assisted all rescue efforts, regardless of religious or political ideologies. He tried very hard, and to some extent succeeded, in unifying the splintered groups among the Jewish delegations working on rescue in Turkey. When Chief Rabbi Isaac Halevy Herzog came from Jerusalem to Ankara in February 1944, the rabbi persuaded Lawrence Steinhardt, America's Jewish Ambassador to Turkey, to take a much more proactive role in rescue efforts, thus greatly facilitating Hirschmann's rescue activity.[68]

Among Hirschmann's initiatives was his successful negotiations with the Rumanian Ambassador Cretzianu in obtaining Premier Antonescou's sanctioning of emigration of Jews from Rumania. As a result, the WRB asked Ambassador Steinhardt to follow suit with the Jews of Hungary by negotiating directly or indirectly with the Hungarian Mission in Turkey. While, for various reasons, this was not successful, it was not for lack of trying.[69] Nor did Hirschmann hesitate to disagree with the British when he felt that they were obstructing potential rescue efforts. This was particularly important in the case of Joel Brand, sent from Hungary to Turkey to secure the lives of 1,000,000 Hungarian Jews in return for 10,000 Allied trucks. Brand had been arrested in June 1944 by the British in Aleppo, Syria on his way to Palestine and incarcerated in Cairo. As Hirschmann observed, it took considerable American pressure on the resident British Minister, Sterndale Bennett, and later Lord Francis Moyne, the British Deputy Minister of State in the Middle East, to interrogate Brand personally and eventually effect his release.[70]

---

[68] Griffel, 39.

[69] *MD*, Report 5/29-6/3/44, p. 5.

[70] Hirschmann, *Caution*, ch. 13; Joel Brand, *Desperate Mission* (New York: Criterion Books, 1958), 153, 181; Griffel, *Memoirs*, 20.

The importance of Ira Hirschmann is evident when one reads the memoir of Dr. Jacob Griffel, a major Orthodox rescue activist:

> ... Mr. Ira Hirschmann arrived from the US with authorization by President Roosevelt permitting him to negotiate with the enemy territories regarding the rescue of Jews. A very energetic activity of rescue started ... Ira Hirschmann always emphatically stated that he would do everything possible for the rescue of Jews....[71]

In Turkey, the Vaad Ha-hatzalah of the Jewish Agency (not to be confused with the New York based Orthodox Vaad Hatzalah) was active in rescue matters. In this committee, or *Moetzah*, most political parties from Palestine, including Agudath Israel, were represented. Agudah's spokesmen were Dr. Jacob Griffel (a non-party, Orthodox individual), Ludwig Kastner (not to be confused with Rudolph Kastner, the left-wing anti-Orthodox representative of the Jewish Agency) from Budapest, and Dr. Joseph Klarman, a non-Orthodox Revisionist-Zionist who represented the Revisionists and worked closely with Dr. Griffel, and who later became the official WRB-recognized partner of Griffel to represent the Vaad Hatzalah in New York. Griffel was a major conduit of information from Hungary and the rest of the Balkans (mostly via Rabbi Michael Ber Weissmandl and Recha Sternbuch) to the *Moetzah*, headed by Chaim Barlas. The latter was the sole official recognized by the Turkish Government, at least until the WRB designated Griffel and Klarman to represent the WRB and Vaad Hatzalah. As a left-wing labor ideologue, Barlas and most of his *Moetzah* disliked the Orthodox and Revisionists alike, and they frequently clashed. The left-wing was not nearly as enthusiastic about rescue per se, as it was about *aliyah*. The emphasis was

---

[71] Griffel, *Memoirs*, 15.

on the selective process of *aliyah* – young, *halutzim*-trained, ideologically inspired, potential *kibbutzniks* which Barlas and the *Moetzah* sought to bring out of the Balkan inferno.[72]

On the other hand, while Griffel had great affinity for Orthodox Jews and Klarman for fellow Revisionists, both did all they could to help any Jew survive, whether an Agudist or an atheist member of Hashomer Hatzair. At one point, Griffel secretly loaned $25,000 of the Orthodox Vaad Hatzalah's funds to members of the *Moetzah*, which was never returned – and for which the Orthodox never pressed.[73]

Hirschmann became involved in intra-party conflicts and the Griffel rescue efforts in July 1944 in transporting refugees from Hungary to Turkey via Rumania by boat and from there to *Eretz* Israel. The problem was the highly discriminatory practice of *aliyah*. As bad as it had been during the 1920's, it was tragic during the Holocaust. Moshe Krausz, who had headed the *Palestina Amt* (Palestine Certificate Office) in Budapest for 15 years, admitted that he never gave out certificates other than to bona fide Zionist party members – regardless of how many lives were in danger. The one exception he admitted to was an old *melamed* (Hebrew teacher) with six children – all of whom spoke Hebrew.[74]

---

[72] Ibid., 48-49. See for example, Leon Kubowitzki to Lawrence Lesser, 6/8/44, WRB Papers. Sternbuch to VH, 7 August 1944, SP; VH-Sternbuch, 13 Sept. 1944, Sternbuch Papers. John Mendelsohn, ed., *Relief and Rescue of Jews from Nazi Oppression 1943-1945, The Holocaust*, vol. 14 (New York, 1982), 47-51. The fact that the first-hand primary passengers of the so-called Kastner train were the 600 Palestine Certificate holders can be seen from many sources and was admitted by Kastner himself. See *Der Kastener-Bericht*, ed. E. Landau (Kindler, 1961), 77, 85, 97, 130-32. It was only when Eichmann demanded two million dollars (in kind), that seats were opened up to anyone who paid about $2,000 per individual. It was then that Freudiger paid for 80 Orthodox Jewish leaders, including the *Admor* of Satmar, etc. to get on the train.

[73] Griffel, Memoir, 31-32. This is confirmed in Arye L. Avner, *From Velos to Taurus: The First Decade of Jewish "Illegal" Immigration to Mandatory Palestine* (Tel Aviv, 1985), 362.

[74] Interview with author.

During this time (mid-1944), when Polish and later Hungarian refugees were brought out of Rumania via boat, the *Moetzah*, ruled by the iron hand of Chaim Barlas, enforced the Jewish Agency's guidelines for *aliyah*. The fact is that at that particular moment, due to Griffel's extraordinary efforts to expedite the paperwork on Palestine Certificates, the majority of the refugees able to leave Rumania were Orthodox, some Agudists and many more non-affiliated. The *Moetzah* sought to limit their number of certificates to 6%, since all who made it to Turkey were by agreement permitted entry into *Eretz Israel*.[75]

After Ambassador Steinhardt arranged a meeting between Ira Hirschmann and the Rumanian Ambassador in Turkey, Hirschmann persuaded the ambassador to allow greater numbers of Jews to leave by boat instead of the old formula of nine certificate holders per month by train.[76] Additionally, to Griffel and Klarman who had worked so hard to help all potential immigrants, the Jewish Agency's "selective" process was unconscionable. Griffel, along with Rabbi Eliezer Hager, the *Admor* of Wysnitz, then in Bucharest, immediately cabled the New York Vaad Hatzalah via Sternbuch to protest that Chaim Barlas and the Jewish Agency "confuse rescue with *aliyah*." They demanded the money to hire a separate boat since over 1,000 Orthodox were ready and able to leave Rumania.[77]

The Jewish Agency, however, was not going to relinquish its monopoly on *aliyah* regardless of the circumstances, and when Griffel told Barlas that the Rumanian Jews had organized their own boat transport, Barlas responded that

---

[75] See for example, Memo of J.B. Friedman, 18 November 1944, WRB Papers.

[76] Griffel, *Memoirs*, 39.

[77] See for example, Sternbuch to VH, 12 July 1944; 7 August 1944, SP; Yaakov Griffel to VH and Jacob Rosenheim, 22 October 1944, KP.

he "would not let those Jews into Palestine."[78] The only recourse Griffel had was to ask Ira Hirschmann, as WRB representative, for help in preventing such gross discrimination. Hirschmann had earlier created an umbrella rescue organization called The Operating Group of Relief Organizations for the different factions including the *Moetzah*, the Joint (at first represented by Herbert Katzki) as well as the Orthodox HIJEFS, and a group associated with Peter Bergson in the U.S. This problem was discussed at meetings held from July through October 1944.

> [Zev Schind, a member of the *Mapai* in the *Moetzah*] raised the question of the chartering of Turkish boats by Mr. Griffel for the evacuation of refugees in whom the organizations which he represented are interested. In his opinion, the WRB had no right to authorize Mr. Griffel to send a telegram to Bucharest in the name of Mr. Hirschmann to the effect that all Jewish refugees arriving in Istanbul would be able to secure Palestine visas. In the first place, it is only the Jewish Agency which has the right to determine who shall and who shall not receive such certificates. In the second place, Mr. Griffel's entrance into the field of shipping complicates the market in Istanbul, and confuses issues in Bucharest, should more than one agency be involved in the embarkation of refugees from that point ... Essentially, Mr. Griffel wants to secure a larger percentage for Agudath Israel people in the allotment of places on those boats which sail from Constanza, and in fact, had proposed to Mr. Schind that he would want 'half a ship' for his protegees [sic].[79]

Hirschmann's response to Schind's "charges" illustrates not only his sense of fairness, but his fearless approach no matter whom he dealt with:

---

[78] Mendelsohn, 48.

[79] Ibid.

... The War Refugee Board policy at the time encouraged Mr. Griffel to undertake steps for separate ships. Mr. Griffel was informed that the Board had no objection if he was able to secure boats in an orderly way and that the Board, not being interested in the age, politics, or anything else of people to be rescued, would encourage any organization which puts forward a reasonable scheme. Before Mr. Griffel was thus advised, Mr. Hirschmann had discussed the matter with Dr. Joseph Schwartz [of the Joint] and Mr. Eliezer Kaplan [of the Jewish Agency] in Istanbul. Furthermore, this statement of policy had been reported to Washington, which had approved thereof. Consequently, there can be no question of withdrawing this statement of policy....[80]

Mr. Schind, in response, noted:

If it is Mr. Griffel's intention to send ships to Constanza, he would immediately telegraph to Bucharest to the effect that no Agudath Israel people were to be embarked on vessels sponsored by the Jewish Agency....[81]

Hirschmann was not taken in by any such threats and "reaffirmed the Board policy as he had stated it and advised Schind not to send the telegram he proposed."[82]

While it appeared that the Board was in control, it was actually Mr. Katzki of the Joint who replaced Ira Hirschmann. Neither as fair nor as forceful as Hirschmann, he arranged matters so that the Orthodox were unable to send the ship, sealing the fate of the potential immigrants in Rumania.[83] Mr. Schind quickly told Mr. Kazim, the ship dealer, "that he will have to make up his mind as to whom he wants to work for,

---

[80] Ibid.

[81] Ibid.

[82] Ibid.

[83] Griffel, *Memoirs*, 49; Cf. Penkower, 172-74.

[Eric] Jabotinsky or the Jewish Agency. If the latter, this would
have to be exclusive."[84]

Meanwhile, Mr. Abraham L. Zissu, the Jewish Agency's
representative in Bucharest "tried to send only members of
Zionist groups."[85] The minutes of a meeting of September 4,
1944 of the umbrella "Operating Group" refer to the obstructionist tactics of Mr. Zissu, which are said to have resulted in a
reduction of thousands in the numbers of persons evacuated
from Rumania by sea.[86] Hirschmann reiterated that

> the War Refugee Board will not condone any such atti-
> tudes, and that it will refuse its aid, financially or in
> any other way, to projects which reflect personality
> clashes, partisanship and rivalry to the detriment of
> the objective of rescue activities, and are not demo-
> cratic in their conception and execution.[87]

In response to the Jewish Agency's misuse of the WRB as
an instrument for its policy of *aliyah*, he added:

> ... The War Refugee Board could not be used as an in-
> strument to assist in the immigration of people into
> Palestine in response to a desire on the part of the Jew-
> ish Agency to build up that country for reasons of its
> own.[88]

Vaad Hatzalah vs. Joint

It is interesting to note the different approaches to rescue of
the Orthodox rabbis and a few laymen and other Jewish
leadership, especially in their dealings with government
officials. A brief description of the "Orthodox" method is found

---

[84] Ibid., 48-50.

[85] Bauer, *American Jewry*, 354.

[86] Mendelsohn, 79-80. Cf. Penkower, 255.

[87] Mendelsohn, 79-80.

[88] Ibid.

in an article in a rabbinical journal written during the
Hungarian crisis of 1944:

> On behalf of the rescue of Jews everywhere, the leaders
> of Vaad Hatzalah pound the doors of the government
> officials in Washington every day with every ounce of
> their strength. With bitter souls and unending streams
> of tears, they cry and plead before the government until
> the point where the government officials themselves cry
> with them, because they feel the pain and the tragedy.
> And all the information that comes to the government
> is immediately passed on to Vaad Hatzalah, helping
> them as much as possible.[89]

Contrast this with the "rational" appeal by Joseph C.
Hyman and Moses H. Leavitt, representatives of the Joint, who
asked the Treasury Department to approve the sending of
money to Shanghai to feed thousands of starving refugees,
despite the "Trading With the Enemy Act" which forbade such
transactions. As they noted in their memo of this unsuccessful
meeting that, "We pointed out that the JDC will accept any
decision of the Treasury with every good grace."[90] Contrasting
their style with "others," i.e., the rabbis who never gave up,
they added, "We are not a pressure organization and never
used any pressure methods in our work. They [the State Dept.]
said they realized this and appreciated it very much."[91]
In conclusion they wrote, "We left the conference with the
feeling that there was very little hope of securing permission to
arrange this transaction."[92]

Ironically, as we have seen, it was Rabbi Kalmanowitz,
who had never stopped transferring money to Shanghai despite
the "Trading With the Enemy Act," who was largely responsible

---

[89] *HaPardes* 18:3 (June 1944): 4.

[90] Memo, J.C. Hyman and M.A. Leavitt, 22 July 1942, Joint Distribution
Committee Archives (JDCA).

[91] Ibid.

[92] Ibid.

for the decision in early December 1943, almost two months prior to the establishment of the War Refugee Board, to send the money legally.[93]

As Dr. Joseph Schwartz of the Joint noted to this author, when asked why the American government finally approved sending money into enemy-occupied territory: "There was a rabbi with a long white beard [i.e., Kalmanowitz], who, when he cried, even the State Department listened."[94]

Rabbis Confront the War Refugee Board

As part of one of the most fascinating rescue efforts arranged by Recha Sternbuch in the winter of 1944-45 with the help of Dr. Jean-Marie Musy, the anti-Semitic, fascist former president of Switzerland, an agreement had been made with Heinrich Himmler to release all the surviving inmates of the concentration camps into Switzerland. Himmler was to obtain from the Vaad Hatzalah, or "The Union of Orthodox Rabbis of the U.S. and Canada" as the Orthodox presented themselves, a million dollars (US) in Swiss francs and most importantly, good press about the release of Jews. This was especially vital in view of the widespread devastating publicity engendered by the above-mentioned press campaign about the Auschwitz and Hungarian reports in June-July 1944. Keeping to his part of the "bargain," Himmler, through General Walter Schellenberg, arranged for the release of the first convoy of 1,210 inmates from Theresienstadt on February 7, 1945. It was now up to the Orthodox to produce both the press and the million dollars for further convoys to leave the camps.[95]

---

[93] See above, note 4; Kranzler, *Shanghai*, 559.

[94] Ibid., 573 n. 57.

[95] On the "Musy Affair," see *Thy Brother's Blood*, 109-115. Cf. Penkower, 257-64.

We will not dwell on the sad chapter of the "good press" following the release of the Theresienstadt train, but on the attempts by the Orthodox in the U.S. to obtain a license to send the million dollars to Switzerland. On February 7, 1945, 1,210 Jews in the first trainload from Theresienstadt arrived, dispelling skepticism about the Musy negotiations voiced by McClelland and other members of the WRB. As General William O'Dwyer, the last chairman of the War Refugee Board, noted at an important meeting on February 28, 1945:

> ... The Vaad Hahatzalah [sic] succeeded in getting twelve hundred and fifty [sic] people across the line [into Switzerland] about two weeks ago. They had a man in Switzerland named Sternbuch who had been saying right along that through his friendship and work with Musy, the Swiss, that he could arrange to have people taken out of the land [of Germany] in large numbers and frequently, and no one believed him, apparently, but the twelve hundred and fifty [sic] came.[96]

O'Dwyer continued to review the circumstances in order to make a final decision about sending the money to Switzerland.

> ... It so happened that between the time that they [i.e., the rabbis] got the money and came to us for the license that we had some official communications from Switzerland and also ... some information here and there that there was something about the arrangements between Musy and Himmler and the generals under Himmler that might indicate ransom....[97]

After much research, O'Dwyer concluded, "the Germans wanted to let these people out anyhow, and that it didn't look like ransom."

---

[96] *MD*, 28 February 1944, p. 239.

[97] Ibid.

He then came to the crux of the problem:

> ... Now the question of whether or not the money would
> be paid to Musy or how it would be paid to him was not
> the question before us. The question was would we say
> in a cable to Sternbuch, "You can't have any money," or
> would we say to him, "You can have the money, but it
> must be under our control until we tell you to let it go."[98]

O'Dwyer felt positively about the matter and

> recommended that the license be granted to send this
> money to Switzerland in the name of Sternbuch and
> McClelland ... if we were to say, "You can't have the
> money," without having all the facts, that ... might
> have the effect of stopping the passage of these people
> through the lines to safety. We might very well, by do-
> ing it that way, have defeated the purpose for which
> this organization was set up....[99]

Pehle, however, did not see things in quite the same way.
His influence on the Jewish Treasury Secretary was striking.
While ostensibly agreeing with O'Dwyer on sending the license,
Pehle argued that he wanted to play "the devil's advocate from
the Treasury's [i.e., Morgenthau's] point of view." In a clear
warning to the Treasury Secretary, who might be overly
sympathetic with the rabbis and his people, he told Morgenthau:

> I want to raise a question as to whether a sound case
> has been made out for issuing this license. The rabbis
> aren't going to be satisfied with this license at all. They
> are only satisfied because this gets the money in Switz-
> erland, one step nearer release.[100]

Expressing an obvious fear of the growing influence of the
rabbis, Pehle said, "I would guess that once the money is sent,

---

[98] Ibid., 240.

[99] Ibid.

[100] Ibid., 241.

there would be tremendous pressure [by the rabbis] for the actual release of the money so that issue will have to be faced."[101] Pehle informed Morgenthau of the criticism faced by the War Refugee Board by such negative forces as the State Department and the British government among others, when he noted, "This license and the sending of this money may be taken as a signal [sic] ... maybe all the critics of this thing are waiting for it to let loose a blast."[102]

Such critics argued against the U.S. dealing in any way with a Nazi such as Himmler and the Swiss fascist, Musy, particularly in view of McClelland's negative reaction. As Pehle noted:

> The sending of the money takes you in with the Musy-Himmler negotiations, because that is what this money and this whole thing is a part of. Now we are dealing with a guy – Musy – nobody trusts; we don't know what the deal is and we don't know why the money is being sent, and *I am raising a question whether as Secretary of the Treasury you ought to take the position that this money should be sent* [emphasis added].[103]

Pehle had little doubt about the potential of such negotiations. As he put it:

> I don't think much of a case has to be had to show this will actually save lives ... but the case is dubious to say the least ... I think it should be cleared. There will be criticism either way you act. If the money doesn't go, the rabbis are going to tear the town loose.[104]

Obviously, the rabbi Pehle and Morgenthau feared most was the young, public relations-wise, persistent Rabbi Baruch

---

[101] Ibid.

[102] Ibid., 242.

[103] Ibid.

[104] Ibid. An amazing commentary on the deep concern engendered among the WRB executives by the "rabbis."

Korff, supported by the powerful Speaker of the House. At one point in this discussion about the Musy negotiations, suspicions were aroused about the rabbis and their method of communications via the Polish cable. Morgenthau noted to his colleagues at WRB that, "It looks to me like one of the reasons we are in this trouble is because these rabbis have completely gone around us."[105]

Pehle characterized the rabbis very aptly when he said, "They are very persistent. As you know they have been driving Miss Hodell and General O'Dwyer crazy, and they certainly added some gray hairs to my bald head, but they do get around."[106] Referring to the secret Polish cable, he said that, "the idea is that can be stopped. We have never wanted to stop it because they get results."[107]

Highlighting the attitude of the skeptics, both secularists and Orthodox, who saw the old-fashioned Orthodox rabbi and especially the "*golus*-Jew," as nothing but *shlemiel*s, is an episode recorded more than 20 years after the Holocaust, by Rabbi Eliezer Silver, founder of Vaad Hatzalah. He described the following account of a conversation he had back then with a philanthropist who was being asked for a considerable sum to facilitate the rescue of thousands of Jews:

> He asked me ... "With all due respect ... it is difficult for me to understand why in ... saving Jews in Europe there is no one who can do anything ... not one of our famous help organizations ... and none of our political leaders – only a handful of Orthodox rabbis. Forgive my frankness, but will some old-fashioned rabbis and inepts succeed in such an undertaking?"
>
> I answered, "When it is a matter of rescuing Jewish lives, we, the rabbis, are forbidden to be inept ... By

---

[105] *MD*, WRB Meeting, 27 February 1945.

[106] *MD*, 27, February 1945, p. 90.

[107] Ibid., 107.

command of our Holy Torah we are prepared to violate many laws ... to save lives. We are ready to pay ransom for Jews and deliver them from concentration camps with ... forged passports. For this purpose, we do not hesitate to deal with counterfeiters and passport thieves. We are ready to smuggle Jewish children over the borders, and to engage expert smugglers for this purpose ... We are ready to smuggle money illegally into enemy territory ... to bribe ... the killers of the Jewish people, those dregs of humanity! We are even ready to send special emissaries to plead with the chief murderers ... and try to appease them at any cost!"

"Now I understand," said the man and handed me a fine gift.[108]

---

[108] Vaad Hatzalah, 38-39.

Rabbi Abraham Isaac Selmanovitz: Guardian of Tradition

Monty Noam Penkower

On December 30, 1920, the *SS Kroonland* steamed into New York City harbor. Its voyage from Antwerp, the other end of the ship's standard round-trip route, had taken fifteen days. First launched by the Red Star line in 1902, the double smoke-stacked vessel disgorged several hundred immigrants from across Central and Eastern Europe into the cavernous reception halls of Ellis Island. To the question, "length of time alien intends to remain in the United States," every individual in the classification "steerage passengers only" responded in identical fashion: "always."

Among the throng of arrivals that cold Thursday, was a Polish Jew who gave his name in English as "Abram Zelmanowicz." Registered on list number 6, line 12, of the *Kroonland*'s manifest, this passenger stood out from the rest. At 43, he was about 20 years older than the average age of those who alighted from the crammed holds. Moreover, while the query "calling or profession" elicited from fellow travelers such answers as "peasant," "workman," "tailor," "laborer," "hairdresser," "housewife," and "none," Zelmanowicz answered "*Rabin.*" The word was then rewritten as "Rabbi."

Several other details rounded out Zelmanowicz's replies to the U.S. immigration officer on duty that day. The married male in question could read and write Polish. "Polish" was also given for the two categories "nationality" and "race or people." Bielsk was entered as his last place of permanent residence, with Chana Zelmanowicz of that town his "nearest relative or friend" from Poland. Zelmanowicz paid his own passage, carried a total of $10 on his person, and had never before been to the United States. This alien resident intended to join his father, listed as "Wigdar Zelman" of 19 Benson St. in Paterson, New Jersey. Planning to become an American citizen, Zelmanowicz averred that he had never been in prison, an almshouse, or an institution for the insane, and had never been supported by charity. Neither a polygamist nor an anarchist, he also did not believe in the overthrow of the U.S. government. He had not come through any "offer, solicitation, promise, or agreement" to work in the United States.

Finally, there was the issue of Zelmanowicz's appearance. The inspector judged his condition of health, "mental and physical," to be "good." The rabbi was neither deformed nor crippled. He stood at 5 feet 6 inches, and his complexion was deemed "fair." "Brown" described the color of his hair, "fair" the color of the eyes. No specific marks of identification received mention. The journeyer's final entry supplied Lohrer, Poland, as his birthplace.[1]

His personal odyssey to what East European Jews then called "*di goldene medina*" (the golden land) had been a long one; some of its details would be forever shrouded in the mists of time. While Zelmanowicz, for the *Kroonland*'s manifest, had provided 1877 as the year of his birth in Lohrer, family recollection cites 1887 and the Polish town of Tomashov. (This error

---

[1] Microfilm T-715, #6664, reel no. 2901, p. 23, National Archives and Records Administration, North East Region (hereafter NARA-NE).

was to be repeated in later Jewish publications.) In Poland, the lad studied with one of the generation's most formidable Talmudic scholars, the Hasidic master Rabbi Abraham Bornstein of Sochaczew, known as the *"Avnei Nezer"* after his most famous work. Garnering plaudits as an *ilui* (genius in Torah) at the tender age of six, Zelmanowicz was encouraged to continue in his studies. The young man went on to earn *semikhah* (rabbinical ordination at the *yoreh yoreh* instructional level) at the age of seventeen from Lodz's chief rabbi, Elijah Hayim Meisel, who in 1873 had established the first *Talmud Torah* in Poland's central textile city. Zelmanowicz was later granted a higher degree, *yadin yadin*, which permitted him to serve as a judge on a *beit din* (rabbinical court) and to issue divorces.[2]

One year after receiving *semikhah*, Zelmanowicz married Chana Fuks of Opoczno, a town in central Poland. Like her groom, the young bride of sixteen could lay claim to a family of scholars who adhered to the formidable *Gur* (Yiddish: *Ger*) Hasidic dynasty. Founded in 1859 by Isaac Meir Alter (the *"Hiddushei ha-Rim"*) in Gora Kalwaria, nineteen miles southeast of Warsaw, this particular school emphasized Torah study, profundity of thought, and continuous striving after self-perfection. Judah Aryeh Leib Alter, a grandson who became the *admor* (head) of *Gur* in 1870, similarly distinguished himself as a scholar of modest demeanor who also concerned himself with issues affecting Jewry in general.

Abraham and Chana's first marital years were spent in her native hometown. Their union emerged from a *"shiddukh,"* an arranged marriage typical for their Hasidic Orthodox circle, which had initially been prompted because Chana's brother Berl was married to Abraham's aunt Zirel. Yet romance blossomed early. According to family lore, when the intended husband was to visit her home for the first time, beautiful Chana looked out the window. Viewing an elderly gentleman

---

[2] Victor Selmanowitz, interview with Idelle Rudman, 10 Sept. 1996, New York City.

approach, she cried. When Abraham came in, however, and she saw the slender, handsome young man, Chana fell in love; he did as well. The couple would remain in Opoczno, numbering 2,425 Jews in 1897, for a few years. Abraham devoted his waking hours to learning in the *beit midrash* (study hall), his well-to-do in-laws providing the newlyweds a roof over their heads during that idyllic period.

During the next two decades, Zelmanowicz served as a *rav* (rabbi) in Poland. According to one grandson, Abraham first went to Radom in Kielce province, with father-in-law Fuks providing the necessary means for livelihood. Commerce and industry, *yeshivot* and welfare institutions – all could be found aplenty in that city, whose 24,465 Jews would make up one-third of its population in 1921. Another document places Zelmanowicz later on in the Warszawa province city of Plock (*Plotsk* in Russian), whose 7,352 Jews in 1921 could boast of a yeshivah and a Jewish high school. The small town of Bielsk in northeast Poland, which Zelmanowicz gave for the *Kroonland*'s record as his last full-time residence on European soil, claimed under 2,400 Jews when the country's final, sovereign boundaries were determined in 1921.[3]

These were not encouraging years for Polish Jewry. The rise of nationalist fervor, accompanied by the development of a Polish middle class eager to oust Jewish *bourgeoisie* rivals, exacerbated Polish-Jewish relations. Jews constituted an overwhelmingly urban population in a country whose other major groups (Polish, Ukrainian, and Byelorussian) were primarily Catholic and rural. The founding of the National Democratic Party (Endecja) in 1897 was symptomatic of growing anti-Semitism, with extremist leader Roman Dmowski

---

[3] Victor Selmanowitz, interview; Esther (nee Selmanowitz) to Victor (Selmanowitz), 16 Oct. 1977, Victor Selmanowitz MSS., Touro College; *Encyclopedia Judaica*, 7:784-86, 12:1415. Family tradition also has the name of Selmanowitz dating to Schneur Zalman of Lyady in Russia, founder of Chabad (Lubavitch) Hasidism. Livia Straus, interview with author, 8 July 1998.

announcing a national boycott of Jewish businesses in 1912, when Jews actively supported a Socialist candidate for the Russian Duma. The masses of Jews, small shopkeepers and artisans who were Yiddish-speaking and Orthodox, drew constant assault as the cardinal enemy. The rebirth of Poland as a sovereign entity after World War I exacerbated matters. When Jews were caught between opposing armies – Poles versus Lithuanians in Vilna, Poles versus Ukrainians in Lvov, and Poles versus Bolsheviks during the War of 1920 – pogroms often would follow. Poles bitterly accused Jews of being pro-Ukrainian in eastern Galicia or of being allied with the Russian Bolsheviks. A falling birthrate and a more serious economic decline, the latter dictated by the policies of the new Polish state, would rapidly ensue for this Jewish community in the interwar years.[4]

Wisely, Zelmanowicz looked to emigrate. Mounting crises in Poland, where Jews numbered at least ten percent of the population, included the personal, vivid memory of Jewish families being shot down in cold blood during a local pogrom. Hearing the approach of stomping boots on that occasion, Chana quickly hid her sons in the house garret until danger passed. In addition, Abraham had to consider supporting a very large family. Eight children had been born to Chana and Abraham during these same years. Esther, the oldest, was followed by the boys Simha Bunim, Moshe, Aryeh Leib, and Yaakov, and then daughters Miriam, Brakha, and Ita.

America seemed the logical haven, since Abraham's father had moved to the States prior to World War I. There, with his wife Yehudis (Judith), their other son and five daughters, patriarch Avigdor (Victor in English) took up permanent residence in Paterson. Resuming work as a *shohet* (ritual

---

[4] Victor Selmanowitz, interview; *Encyclopedia Judaica*, 13:1500, 13:648, 4:981. When declaring his intention to become an American citizen (see below), the rabbi listed Plotz, Russia, as his last foreign residence, with Warsaw his birthplace.

slaughterer), which he had first practiced in Lodz, Avigdor listed his trade in the 1920 U.S. Federal Census as "rabbi." He had remarried by then, his first wife having died of influenza two years earlier during the great worldwide epidemic. To stave off local anti-Semitism, the 62-year-old *shohet* had decided to shorten his family name to "Selman"; the six other children retained this change thereafter. Understandably, New Jersey would be Abraham's first destination in America. First, however, he would make the arduous trek alone, leaving Chana and family in the care of her brother in Opoczno until they could be summoned to a new life.[5]

The Zelmanowicz clan proceeded with all necessary steps to become yet another story in "the great immigration" saga. Some 2,378,000 Jews, the great bulk from the Russian empire, arrived in the United States between 1880 and the end of free immigration in 1925; by then close to 25 percent of world Jewry called America home. As his immediate family's pioneer in this epoch-making movement, Abraham quickly filed a Declaration of Intention "in good faith to become a citizen of the United States of America and to permanently reside therein: SO HELP ME GOD." Before William F. Schneider, Clerk of the Supreme Court of New York County, "Abraham Isaac Zelmanovitz," giving his birthdate as April 30, 1877, his height as 5 feet 7 inches, his hair and eyes as brown, and his weight as 160 lbs., duly informed the U.S. Department of Labor's Naturalization Service on March 29, 1921, that he resided at 61 W. 115th St. in Manhattan. It was, the applicant

---

[5] Celia S. Heller, *On the Edge of Destruction: Jews of Poland between the Two World Wars* (New York, 1977), ch. 2-3; Yisrael Gutman, "Polish Antisemitism between the Wars: An Overview," in Y. Gutman, E. Mendelsohn, J. Reinharz, and C. Shmeruk, eds., *The Jews of Poland between Two World Wars* (Hanover, 1989), 97-108; George Castellan, "Remarks on the Social Structure of the Jewish Community in Poland between the Two World Wars," in B. Vago and G. Mosse, eds., *Jews and Non-Jews in Eastern Europe, 1918-1945* (New York, 1974), 187-201.

Livia Straus, interview; Victor Selmanowitz interview; Microfilm T-625, reel no. 1064, vol. 99, sheet 2, line 88, NARA-NE.

asserted, his true intention "to renounce forever all allegiance and fidelity to any foreign prince, potentate, state, or sovereignty, and particularly to 'The Republic of Poland' and Russia," of which he was a subject. His wife, noted here as "Anna" and currently living in "Russia," would now finalize preparations to follow her life's mate.[6]

Chana, along with "Lejb" (11), "Jakob" and "Marjam" (both listed as 9, though she was 8), and "Brucha" (7), set sail on the SS *Zeeland* from Antwerp on September 29, 1921. Tickets had also been purchased for Esther (declared 21, yet actually about to celebrate her 20th birthday) and Ita (2). Since, however, Ita's sudden attack of measles forced the two girls to remain in Poland, a line was drawn through their names on the ship's manifest. Arriving in New York City on October 9th, Chana indicated that her "calling or occupation" was "wife," that she possessed $87, could read Hebrew, and was a Polish citizen from Bielsk. Her "race or people" was registered as "Hebrew." She gave New York as the group's final destination, with husband "A. Zelmanowicz" residing at 61 W. 115th St. A doctor present certified that this new arrival (together with the four children) suffered from "malnutrition – special example." She was described as being 5 feet 3 inches tall, of "fair" complexion, with dark hair and eyes, and having no distinctive marks of identification.[7]

"Benjamin" and "Moszak" Zelmanowicz reached Ellis Island on October 11 aboard the SS *France*, six days after leaving Le Havre. "Benjamin" declared himself 16, although in fact he would soon be 19 according to his father's official registry of "Binen" (Simha Bunim – now Benjamin) in 1927;

---

[6] *Encyclopedia Judaica* 15:1608; Gerald Sorin, *A Time for Building: The Third Migration, 1880-1920* (Baltimore, Md., 1992), 12; *Naturalization Service, Record of Declaration of Intention, Mar. 16-April 1, 1921*, vol. 499, p. 320 (Surrogate's Court, Hall of Records, 31 Chambers St., New York, NY).

[7] Microfilm T-715, #6913, reel no. 3034, p. 41, NARA-NE.

the younger brother's age was properly inscribed (17). Each had $25, with "Moszak" listed as "workman" and Benjamin's trade given as "none." "Moszak" was headed for "father Abraham Zelmanowicz," while Benjamin's destination was written as "father Wigder Zelman." Esther and Ita followed on the *SS Gothland*, which departed Antwerp on October 23. Landing in New York two weeks later, Esther gave "housework" for her trade, and noted that she and Ita jointly owned $49 and that their father's name was "A. Selmanowitz." All of these four arrivals received the evaluation "good" for their condition of health.[8]

How long the reunited family stayed on Manhattan's upper West Side is uncertain, as are their subsequent peregrinations until the latter half of the decade. The apartment Abraham chose at 61 W. 115th St. appeared suitable at first. Located between Fifth and Lenox Avenues just north of Central Park, the building bordered upon a sizeable Jewish enclave in Harlem. But that distinctive ethnic presence, at its height 100,000-strong, peaked by 1925. A daughter recalls that the ten-member clan moved downtown for one year, to a residential hotel on East Broadway in the heart of the Lower East Side. That neighborhood, which in 1915 sheltered an estimated 350,000 Jews in less than two square miles, had long passed its prime as European Jewry's epicenter abroad. Many Jews left the teeming area for Brownsville, Flatbush, Crown Heights, and the Grand Concourse. Not Abraham and Chana, who first moved to 251 Division St. and then gave up their sojourner status for good in April 1926 with the purchase of a three-story house (20' x 100') on Rodney Street in Williamsburg.[9]

---

[8] Microfilm T-715, #6916, reel no. 3035, p. 36, NARA-NE; Microfilm T-715, #6942, reel no. 3046, p. 58, NARA-NE.

[9] Jeffrey S. Gurock, *When Harlem Was Jewish, 1870-1930* (New York, 1979); Bertha S. Machlis, interview with Idelle Rudman, 16 July 1996; Microfilm KC-2083, Liber 4666, pp. 500-501, conveyances – Kings County, City Register, Dept. of Finance. For the lower East Side, see Moses Rischin,

The first significant mention of 214 Rodney Street in the family biography surfaces on February 24, 1927, the day that its head became an American citizen. Abraham's petition for naturalization to the U.S. District Court for the Eastern District of New York, accompanied by the earlier Declaration of Intent and official confirmation of his arrival at Ellis Island, gave this home address and his occupation as "rabbi." Having supplied the birthdates of the entire family, the applicant renounced fealty to his former country of allegiance in particular, "The Republic of Poland & (or) The Present Government of Russia." He proceeded to sign his full name in a clear hand as "Abraham Isaac Selmanovitz" to an oath to "support and defend the Constitution and laws of the United States of America against all enemies, foreign and domestic." Two witnesses endorsed an affidavit attesting to Selmanovitz's *bona fides*, and certificate no. 2380356, approved by Judge Inch, became thereby an integral part of the country's history.[10]

With the move to Williamsburg, Abraham had arrived in his element. A choice location before World War I for wealthy industrialists and professionals, including some German-born Jews, the district in the 1920's became an Orthodox Jewish community of the moderate Ashkenazic Russian-Polish type. By 1930, two-thirds of the approximately 20,000 people who lived there were Jews of the lower and lower-middle class. Hasidic Galician and Polish Jews of Selmanovitz's background began to settle in great numbers. Synagogues, makeshift Hasidic *shteibels* for prayer and learning, Hebrew schools, and sundry Jewish organizations dotted the landscape. Yeshivah Torah Voda'ath, later to achieve national renown among Orthodox Jewry, was founded. Beards, *pe'ot* (earlocks), and

---

The Promised City: New York's Jews, 1870-1914 (New York, 1962); Irving Howe, *World of Our Fathers* (New York, 1976).

[10] *Naturalization Service, Petition and Record*, vol. 245, petition #67376, NARA-NE.

yarmulkas dominated; kosher stores could be found alongside dance halls, movie theatres, and poolrooms for the young.[11]

Selmanovitz quickly became the head of the small *Gerer* community there. His ties to the *rebbe* at that time, Abraham Mordecai Alter (the *"Imrei Emes"*), had begun when he had been a boy studying in the *Gur* yeshivah in Warsaw. Abraham's bed in the dormitory was next to that of the young Alter, eldest son of Judah Leib. Selmanovitz later remembered being awakened one night when he heard the prospective father-in-law of Abraham Alter come to view the boy as he slept. Once the latter became *rebbe*, he gave *Gur* Hasidim a dynamic, organized framework of schools and organizations, even while exploring the possibility of moving with his followers to Palestine. Like Torah chieftains Jacob Willowski (*Ridbaz*) and Israel Meir *ha-Kohen* (*Hafetz Hayyim*), Alter saw little hope for Orthodoxy in the United States. He requested Selmanovitz to care for the small contingent, perhaps 100, of *Gerer* Hasidim there; family members recall Selmanovitz refusing the role of *Gerer Rebbe* in America, saying that one must be born to the position rather than be appointed.[12]

Selmanovitz assumed leadership of two Williamsburg congregations, Talmud Torah Anshei Emes and Beth Aaron Anshei S'fard. In the former, at 326 Keap St., he was the recognized rabbi. As such, he received a small salary, sat near the Torah ark, and addressed those present at the times usually set aside for rabbinic homilies and speeches. In the second *shul*, known locally as *"der Poilisher Shteibel,"* he served as *rav* and the recognized leader of the *minyan* (quorum for prayer) of *Gerer* Hasidim, many of whom were among the original organizers in 1910.[13]

---

[11] George Kranzler, *Williamsburg: A Jewish Community in Transition* (New York, 1961), 16-19. For the changes wrought by the entry of the extremist Hungarian Jews to the area, beginning in the mid-1930's, see ibid., 250.

[12] Victor Selmanowitz, interview; *Encyclopedia Judaica*, 7:786, 15:518,1611.

[13] Victor Selmanowitz, interview.

The Poilisher Shteibel on Division Avenue became the true hub of Orthodox Jews in the neighborhood. The *mikvah* (ritual bath) in the basement, for a long time the only one available in Williamsburg, was built under Selmanovitz's supervision; he, Rav Yitzhak Bunim, and the *Novominsker Rebbe*, Yehuda Aryeh Perlow, certified its validity according to Halakhah (Jewish law). Upstairs, past a steep staircase leading to the first floor, the din of voices coming from a mix of voluntary instructors, young students, professionals, and everyday workers reflected the exhilaration of Torah study. *Sefarim*, religious volumes that were strewn across each table and stacked from floor to ceiling, were in use day and night. Eyeglasses, stored in several cigar boxes, and cups of tea were handed out by the impressive-looking Reb Chazkel Engelman to those in need. An air of passion and commitment to a deeper understanding of Torah, palpable and never forgotten by those witness to the scene, reigned in these lively quarters.[14]

Selmanovitz would join the Hasidim at the Poilisher Shteibel in the traditional *shalosh seudos* (or *shaleshudis*) held late Saturday afternoon between the *minhah* and *ma'ariv* services. On various other occasions, when not required to occupy his pulpit on Keap St., Selmanovitz would join the *minyan* of *Gerer* Hasidim. Every year at the close of Yom Kippur services, he would go to the Poilisher Shteibel for *ne'ilah* (closing) prayers, the final segment of this most solemn day in the Jewish calendar.[15]

In both Williamsburg *shuls*, Selmanovitz's tasks as leading cleric were many and varied. He answered questions of ritual, performed weddings, gave regular classes, and helped provide for the welfare of his charges. As a judge in a rabbinic

---

[14] Louis (Lipa) Brenner, "The Poilisher Shteibel: Reflections on Life in Williamsburg in the '30's and '40's," *Jewish Observer*, 22-28 Nov. 1992; Bernard Belsky, telephone conversation with author, 17 Feb. 1998.

[15] Bertha Machlis, interview.

court, he also granted divorces and ruled on cases brought before those assembled. In his capacity as the *rav* of these two congregations, he was subsequently elected to the first vice-presidency of the *Agudat ha-Rabbanim*, the Union of Orthodox Rabbis of the United States and Canada. The oldest organization of Orthodox rabbis in the country, established in 1902 by rabbis trained in Eastern Europe, this group would became increasingly involved in all matters affecting the Orthodox in America, who were still relatively weak.[16]

Selmanovitz is remembered as displaying keen judgment in the course of performing his communal tasks. One time, a couple asked him to officiate at their wedding. The young woman came with her parents; the young man was alone. The rabbi questioned the prospective groom as to his Hebrew name and antecedents, but was unhappy with the answers. Selmanovitz then asked the young man to accompany him upstairs. When the latter realized that he would be required to show physical proof that he was a member of the circumcised covenant of Abraham, he confessed that he was not Jewish. The marriage did not proceed.

On another occasion, a childless older couple came to Selmanovitz seeking to arrange a divorce. He proceeded, since according to Jewish law, a couple has the right to divorce if no children are born with the passage of ten years. In time, however, the rabbi realized that the couple cared deeply for each other and were unhappy apart. They returned to his study and he performed the remarriage.[17]

Selmanovitz was also called upon to answer queries as to the status of ritually slaughtered chickens. Housewives would come to his house with animals which they thought were of dubious *kashrut*. He frequently ruled that the chickens were kosher, using all the leniencies allowed by Jewish law.

[16] Bertha Machlis, interview; Aaron Rothkoff, *Bernard Revel: Builder of American Jewish Orthodoxy* (Philadelphia, 1972), 14-16.

[17] Bertha Machlis, interview.

When questioned about this tendency, the rabbi explained that when he would arrive at the *Beit Din shel Ma'alah* (the Court of Judgment on high), he did not want to answer for bearing the responsibility of preventing a poor woman from having a chicken to feed her family for the Sabbath.

In a related incident, a chicken of ambiguous *kashrut* was brought to him. Selmanovitz put it on the kitchen table, and then had to leave the room with the chicken lying unattended. Upon returning, he found the chicken not there. The ubiquitous cats of Williamsburg, kept for chasing mice, had dragged the chicken to the back yard, thereby rendering it non-kosher. Responded the rabbi: "The cat has *paskened* the *shaylah*" (ruled on the question).[18]

Understandably, Selmanovitz joined attempts to obtain effective *kashrut* supervision in New York City and beyond. His active involvement in getting out the Jewish vote for Fiorello LaGuardia's successful mayoralty campaigns aided in this regard. Earlier attempts at overseeing Jewish dietary practice in the metropolis had proven a resounding failure, given extensive fraud, competition between Orthodox rabbis and organizations for valuable endorsements, and the lack of a powerful enforcement agency. Selmanovitz threw his full support behind a *kashrut* campaign, spearheaded by Shimon Shain of the Poilisher Shteibel, aimed at Williamsburg and environs. He also labored for the creation, which took place in 1934, of a Kosher Law Enforcement Bureau incorporated within the New York State Department of Agriculture, as well as a *kashrut* advisory board representing the Jewish community. In time, his son Leib (Louis) would work as an inspector for that department's *kashrut* division and ultimately be named to head the division.[19]

---

[18] Victor Selmanowitz, interview.

[19] Harold P. Gastwirt, *Fraud, Corruption and Holiness: The Controversy Over the Supervision of the Jewish Dietary Practice in New York City, 1881-1940* (Port Washington, NY, 1974); Ruchama Shein, *All for the Boss* (New York,

Soon after moving to Rodney St., Selmanovitz began teaching at the Rabbi Isaac Elchanan Theological Seminary (RIETS) in New York. He had been recommended to that position by the Talmud luminary Rabbi Moshe ha-Levi Soloveitchik. The latter, a member of a brilliant dynasty of Torah masters from Lithuania with links to Rabbi Hayyim of Volozhin, the outstanding pupil of the 18th century's *Gaon* Elijah of Vilna, had earlier conferred *semikhah* on one of Selmanovitz's uncles. He and Abraham established close contact in Warsaw, where Soloveitchik headed the Talmud department of the Tahkemoni Rabbinical Seminary sponsored by the Mizrachi religious-Zionist movement. Soloveitchik recommended to Dr. Bernard Revel, president of RIETS, that his friend be invited to join the teaching staff of the Orthodox seminary that had been founded in 1897 on the Lower East Side.[20]

Revel, himself an acknowledged *talmid hakham* (Torah scholar) from Lithuania, had also, in 1911, received the first doctoral degree granted by Philadelphia's Dropsie College. After a stint with his wife's family in the Oklahoma oil refinery business, he began reorganizing RIETS in 1915, opening it to laymen and teachers as well as rabbinical students. In 1916, Revel founded Talmudical Academy, the first combined yeshivah-high school in the United States where a full program of Hebrew and English studies was taught. Yeshiva College, the first institution of higher learning to embrace Jewish religious and secular studies and thus integrate Orthodoxy with American life, would open twelve years later. To strengthen RIETS, Revel sought a scholar who could appeal both to young men of Polish Hasidic background and to the majority of students

---

1984); Victor Selmanowitz, interview; Vita and Nathan Friedman, telephone conversation with author, 17 Nov. 1998.

[20] Victor Selmanowitz, interview; *Encyclopedia Judaica*, 15:127-31; Shulamith Meiselman (sister of Joseph B. Soloveitchik), interview with Idelle Rudman, 15 Feb. 1996; Philip Reiss, interview with Idelle Rudman, 1 Sept. 1996.

from *Litvishe* (Lithuanian) roots. With Soloveitchik's warm support, he offered the post of *rosh yeshivah* (Talmud lecturer) and *mashgiah* (role model and guide) to Selmanovitz; in 1927, his employment began.[21]

The new appointee who moved about the *beit midrash* cut an impressive figure. His pleasant face wreathed in a full black beard, the well-groomed Selmanovitz appeared tall in stature. He always wore a substantial satin *yarmulke* atop his head and a Hasidic *kapote* (Prince Albert coat). Aside from teaching his own pupils, Selmanovitz advised students on matters of personality and character, an integral part of their religious training. His Galician-sounding Yiddish led to much joshing, in which he took part, since it differed markedly from the Lithuanian pronunciation common to the bulk of RIETS's student body. Yet the friendly and outgoing individual won much respect, exhibiting shrewdness in evaluating students and in establishing close relationships with the brightest among them. In turn, Selmanovitz received a gift from each graduating class as a token of its admiration.[22]

Some who came under his supervision at RIETS recall Selmanovitz's practical approach in helping them prepare for examinations. Review sessions were held to study those subjects most emphasized in rabbinic practice. These focused on questions and problems relating to dietary laws, ritual slaughter, marriage, and divorce. As one of the *roshei yeshivah* who conducted the reviews, he was always available to answer queries and to indulge in intensive discussions clarifying these matters. A former student graphically remembered Selmanowitz bringing in the lungs of a cow, and blowing them up to show the future clergymen the difference between a

---

[21] Rothkoff, *Bernard Revel*, ch. 2-3; Israel Schorr, interview with Idelle Rudman, 5 Aug. 1996.

[22] Melech Schechter, interview with Idelle Rudman, 23 July 1996; Maurice Wohlgelernter, interview with Idelle Rudman, 13 Feb. 1996; Israel Schorr, interview; Vita and Nathan Friedman, telephone conversation.

kosher animal and one that was *treif* (non-kosher) based upon abnormalities in the lungs.[23]

In addition to his academic duties in RIETS, located in Washington Heights as of 1928 along with the new Yeshiva College, Selmanovitz acted as an informal congregational rabbi to the students and to local residents. He would answer what were popularly referred to as *teppel* (pot) and *leffel* (spoon) questions. These queries dealt with daily life, the problems of religious practice that would arise in the everyday actions of fellow Jews. Local housewives would even bring their chickens into the *beit midrash*, in order to ascertain whether or not the chicken was kosher. Once secular college classes took over, usually around 3 P.M., Selmanovitz headed back on the long train ride home to Williamsburg.[24]

In 1929, the rabbi traveled to Palestine and Europe. While in *Eretz* Israel he also visited the Slobodka yeshivah branch in Hebron, where some fellows who had previously been enrolled in RIETS were studying. Shortly after his visit, two of them were among the sixty-seven Jews killed there on the Sabbath in a pogrom perpetrated by local Arabs. As a result of this trip, his attitude toward the secular Zionists who were dubbed the "*halutzim*" (pioneers) was positive. Subsequently, in discussing these youngsters who were building up the Land of Israel, Selmanovitz became angry when they were criticized for contravening Torah. In the end, he averred, the secularists would do *teshuvah* (repent) and comply with Torah law. Then and later, Selmanovitz was known as an *ohev Yisrael* (lover of the Jewish people).[25]

Traveling on across Europe, he met with several distinguished rabbis. In Paris, he visited with Rabbi Joel Herzog,

---

[23] Melech Schechter, interview; Julius Hyatt, interview with Idelle Rudman, 26 July 1996; Murray Grauer, interview with Idelle Rudman, 24 Nov. 1996.

[24] Israel Miller, interview with Idelle Rudman, 18 Sept. 1996.

[25] Rothkoff, *Bernard Revel*, 126; Bernard Belsky, interview with Idelle Rudman, 17 Feb. 1996.

father of the future first Ashkenazic chief rabbi of the State of Israel. Herzog expressed admiration for RIETS, and hoped that his son Isaac, currently chief rabbi of the Irish Free State, would have the opportunity to meet with this guest from across the Atlantic. Selmanovitz stopped off in Frankfurt-am-Main, Germany, for a Sabbath, where he was acknowledged from the pulpit by Rabbi Joseph Breuer, noted head of the local Orthodox Jewish community. In Warsaw, he visited with Rabbi Moses Soloveitchik, then ill and awaiting official permission to enter America with his family and assume the post of senior *rosh yeshiva* at RIETS. He also spent time with his own family and that of his daughter-in-law, Esther, who had married Benjamin in New York City three years earlier. Returning to the United States via the port city of Trieste, Selmanovitz was recognized in the synagogue, whose Sabbath service included a prayer for the welfare of the Yeshiva.[26]

Apprised of the trip, Revel had reason to value Selmanovitz's special contribution to RIETS's welfare. Aside from his own teaching, the Polish-born *rosh yeshivah* kept the institution's president informed about the progress of Soloveitchik's classes and the progress of the students in general. A 1935 letter indicates that, as *mashgiah*, he also felt compelled to acknowledge the absence of some dormitory residents from the daily morning *minyan*. Most significantly, as a member of the *Agudat ha-Rabbanim* presidium, Selmanovitz served as an important bridge to that European-oriented body. At the same time that the financially strapped Yeshiva reeled under the Great Depression, a harried Revel had to contend with attacks leveled by the *Agudat ha-Rabbanim* and other Yiddish-speaking Orthodox elements. This right-wing faction persistently frowned upon Revel's effort at synthesizing religious and secular studies; the *Agudat ha-Rabbanim* also resented the professional competition posed by RIETS's graduates to its membership. Buttressed by critiques against Yeshiva

---

[26] Rothkoff, *Bernard Revel*, 126; Victor Selmanowitz, interview.

from some Talmudic sages of Eastern Europe, the Union of Orthodox Rabbis regularly questioned the American institution's true commitment to strict Torah practice.[27]

Of his colleagues at RIETS, Selmanovitz maintained the closest friendship with Soloveitchik, one year his senior. Theirs was a unique bond, built upon mutual respect, as well as trust in and love for the same religious values. Soloveitchik's daughter later described seeing her father and Selmanovitz, framed by the large windows in the RIETS study hall, oblivious to all as they engaged in conversation. No matter that one typified the litvak (Lithuanian Jew) and the other the hasid, with their Yiddish accents most pointedly in contrast. Soloveitchik's youngest son later confirmed that they acted as brothers toward one another. When Soloveitchik's oldest son, Joseph Baer, was installed as chief rabbi of Boston in December 1932, Selmanovitz was invited to attend the ceremony along with such distinguished personages as Rabbi Ze'ev Gold, president of the American Mizrachi movement, and Rabbi Meir Berlin (later Bar-Ilan), president of the world Mizrachi movement.[28]

At the end of 1940, Revel became seriously ill, passing away on December 2. The board of directors immediately began a search for a new president. Rabbi Soloveitchik felt that his oldest son, an acknowledged Talmudic authority and a Ph.D. graduate in Philosophy from the University of Berlin, would be the best choice for Yeshiva College. He met an especially sympathetic ear in Selmanovitz, but Soloveitchik died suddenly on January 31, 1941, after being hospitalized for a relatively

---

[27] Selmanovitz to Revel, 4 Apr. 1935, folder 5/1-6, General Correspondence "S", 1928-1935, Bernard Revel MSS., Yeshiva University Archives, New York City; Bernard Lander, interview with author, 9 Mar. 1998; Rothkoff, *Bernard Revel*, ch. 7. For more on the *Agudat ha-Rabbanim*'s particular stance, see Louis Bernstein, "Generational Conflict in American Orthodoxy: The Early Years of the Rabbinical Council of America," *American Jewish History* 59 (Dec. 1979): 230-34.

[28] Shulamith Meiselman, interview; Aaron Soloveitchik, interview with Idelle Rudman, 19 Feb. 1996; Shulamith Soloveitchik Meiselman, *The Soloveitchik Heritage* (Hoboken, NJ: Ktav, 1995), 248.

minor ailment. Yeshiva now needed both a president and a senior *rosh yeshivah*. In Jewish tradition, a son who is capable of assuming the position held by his father is automatically thought suitable to succeed as heir. Rabbi Joseph B. Soloveitchik was eminently qualified to follow his father in the position of *rosh ha-yeshivah*, the argument advanced by Rabbi Herbert S. Goldstein of RIETS and leader of the West Side Institutional Synagogue. Many times the father expressed the wish that his oldest son should succeed him when the time came. That hour had now arrived.

Some of those involved in the Yeshiva College administration, however, thought that in the New World, a different model could be used. They frowned upon the automatic succession of Rabbi J. B. Soloveitchik to his father's place. Rabbi Leo Jung, a faculty member who also led the influential Jewish Center on Manhattan's West Side, nominated Talmudist and Bible scholar Dr. Chaim Heller of RIETS. From a separate quarter, *Agudat ha-Rabbanim* president Rabbi Eliezer Silver, while backing Joseph Baer, telegraphed Yeshiva that his colleagues were prepared to step in and reset the institution's priorities.[29]

Selmanovitz, active in RIETS and the *Agudat ha-Rabbanim*, participated in the deliberations concerning the two most important positions at Yeshiva. He strongly advocated insuring the proper place for his dear friend's son. The talents exhibited by Selmanovitz in negotiation and persuasion, coupled with his intelligent, friendly manner, made a positive impression. Rabbi Joseph B. Soloveitchik's son later remembered his parents speaking of Selmanovitz with warmth and affection, and referring to him as "a foreign minister." His quiet, diplomatic skills carried weight.

---

[29] Jeffrey S. Gurock, *The Men and Women of Yeshiva: Higher Education, Orthodoxy, and American Judaism* (New York, 1988), 128-32; Bernstein, 228; Shulamith Meiselman, interview; Philip Reiss, interview; Maurice Wohlgelernter, interview.

After considerable discussion, the Yeshiva board invited Joseph Baer to serve in his late father's stead for one-year, "during which time he was to prove his usefulness," but only if he agreed to waive his right of succession. A month later he accepted. Rabbi Samuel Belkin, another European-trained Torah scholar and Ph.D. (from Brown University), became Yeshiva's dean and (in 1943) president. Once in place and over the next four decades, Rabbi Joseph B. Soloveitchik ("the *Rov*," as thousands of disciples would later call him) came to personify Revel's credo for Yeshiva *par excellence*.[30]

The outbreak of World War II provided another chapter in Selmanovitz's life, probably the most dramatic. In September 1939, his beloved *rebbe* of *Gur*, along with his entire household, moved to Warsaw. Upon the entry of the German *Wehrmacht* forces into Poland's largest city, Abraham Mordecai Alter and family were hidden in order to evade the Gestapo. These secret state police of Hitler's Third Reich were specifically searching for the "*wunder rabbiner*" (wonder rabbi), by then head of 100,000 Hasidim, without success. The *Gur* entourage continued to elude capture while remaining underground. In fact, the last contact that the *Gerer Rebbe* had with his American adherents was the bar mitzvah gift which reached Selmanovitz's eldest grandchild, Benjamin's son Victor, in the Spring of 1940. The present consisted of a set of inscribed *humashim* (Pentateuch) and a set of *tefillin* (phylacteries).[31]

Some American Jewish circles quickly realized that this representative symbol of Orthodox Jewry should be saved

---

[30] Maurice Wohlgelernter, interview; Philip Reiss, interview; Chaim Soloveitchik, interview with Idelle Rudman, 17 Mar. 1996; Gurock, 132; *Encyclopedia Judaica*, 15:132-33.

[31] Uri Kaploun, *Rebbes of Ger* (New York, 1987), 263; Moshe Yehezkieli, *Nes ha-Hatzalah Shel ha-Rebbi mi-Gur* (Jerusalem, 1959), 17; Ruth Lichtenstein, telephone interview with author, 7 May 1999; Victor Selmanowitz, interview.

without delay. Selmanovitz was among the organizers of a committee that already set to work in October 1939 for the *rebbe*'s rescue. To facilitate the escape of the individual he termed "the *tzaddik* [righteous man] of the generation," they resorted to political pressure and raising funds across the United States. Selmanovitz put aside his daily pursuits and devoted himself fully to this mission. The members of the Poilisher Shtiebel proved natural allies in what was to follow.[32]

Rabbi Menahem Kasher, distinguished author of *Torah Sheleimah* and *de facto* head of the *Gerer* community in New York, went to Washington for help. Another active participant was Mordecai Goldman, who at Alter's suggestion had opened a store, *Otzar ha-Sefarim* (treasury of books), on the Lower East Side in 1919 to service the religious community's ritual needs. Two others on the committee were *Gerer* Hasidim Chaim Fisch and Benjamin Ze'ev Hendeles, an active member of Agudath Israel, the Orthodox party founded in 1912, which Alter had strongly advocated as an antidote to Zionism and secular influences in general. The Bienenfeld brothers (one an uncle of Benjamin Selmanowitz's wife), wholesale suppliers of glass for the East Coast and chief funders of the *Gur* yeshiva in Jerusalem, served as well.

This committee placed a small notice in the religious Yiddish press announcing its purpose; an immediate and positive reaction followed. The dynamic head of Yeshiva Torah VoDa'ath, Rabbi Shraga Feivel Mendlowitz, joined without delay. *Agudat ha-Rabbanim*'s Rabbi Eliezer Silver, instrumental soon after the war erupted in founding the Orthodox Va'ad Hatzalah rescue organization, maintained close contact in the matter with Selmanovitz. Silver became head of the fundraising committee and, as a prominent Cincinnati resident, contacted Senator Robert Taft of Ohio. The influential Republican

---

[32] Yehezkieli, 26; Selmanovitz to Mazaloff(?), 30 Jan. 1940, Selmanowitz MSS.

congressman in turn inquired of Secretary of State Cordell Hull as to the *Gerer Rebbe*'s current plight.[33]

In Washington, Kasher approached Congressman Sol Bloom of New York, head of the House Foreign Affairs Committee. Although a Jew, Bloom was not persuaded as to Alter's significance. Only with the intervention of former Supreme Court Justice Louis Dembitz Brandeis, who realized the importance of this personage for the future of Orthodox Jewry, did Bloom consent to intervene. Although the country maintained neutrality in the war at this point, its relations with Germany were strained. Accordingly, Bloom and the rescue committee concluded that it would be best to contact the U.S. ambassador to Italy in this regard. It was decided to resort to Italians in order to obtain transit visas through Italy (thence to Palestine), and to handle the bribe that would ultimately reach the Gestapo officials directly involved.

In the meantime, Dr. Chaim Shoshkes, a well-known journalist and community leader who had been a member of the *Judenrat* (German-appointed Jewish Council) in Warsaw, escaped Poland via forged papers and arrived in New York. He carried a concealed note with the address of Goldman's bookstore on Essex St. The note was signed by Rabbi Isaac Meir Levin, Alter's son-in-law, who had left the *Judenrat* to go into hiding once the Nazis showed an inordinate amount of interest in him and his family. Reading the note, "It is necessary to save the *Admor Shlita* (leader who should live to a good and long life) immediately because it is a truly life-threatening situation," the committee redoubled its efforts. Kasher took the train a number of times to the nation's capital, even camping

---

[33] Yehezkieli, 26; Eugene Goodman (grandchild of the Bienenfelds), interview with Idelle Rudman, 24 Oct. 1996; David Silver (son of Eliezer Silver), telephone interview with Idelle Rudman, 23 Apr. 1996; Aaron Rakeffet-Rothkoff, *The Silver Era* (New York, 1981), 194. For *Va'ad Hatzalah* activities during World War II, see Monty Noam Penkower, *The Jews Were Expendable: Free World Diplomacy and the Holocaust* (Urbana, Il: 1983), ch. 9.

out in Bloom's office on the Sabbath. This last gesture convinced the congressman of the seriousness of the situation, and he agreed to undertake sustained diplomatic initiatives.

While the Italian consul in Warsaw was notified, it also became necessary to assure an effective exit route for the *rebbe*. The representative of the Italian shipping line in Poland, a Polish count, had dealt with Alter a few years earlier when the latter had traveled to Palestine. This shipping line had been used on a regular basis by Polish Jews, since they could easily travel to Trieste and then embark on a ship to *Eretz* Israel. At the time of his last trip in 1935, every courtesy had been extended to Alter. He was remembered with great respect and veneration.[34]

At this crucial moment, a postcard to *"Ameryka"* reached "Rabbi A. Selmanowicz" at 214 Rodney St. The sender, "Mendel Alter," signing his name "M. Alter," added nothing more than a Warsaw address: Pawia 11a, m.13. Unwittingly, the Gestapo, in approving the mail by stamping a Nazi symbol on the recipient's address, had transmitted the *rebbe*'s hiding place in the Praga suburb of Warsaw. This precious information was then given to a representative in Warsaw of the American Jewish Joint Distribution Committee, who was able to visit the aged, ailing leader and tell him of the efforts being made in America on his behalf.

The Polish aristocrat enlisted the services of a young Italian engineer, who agreed to travel to Warsaw, deal with the Germans, and personally escort the *rebbe* and his entourage to safety. Not long thereafter, the anxious committee in New York received a telephone call from Rome: the engineer would contact them that same evening. At 2 a.m., the entire group, meeting in Selmanovitz's home, heard that the Gestapo had demanded an exorbitant amount in American dollars. And

---

[34] Yehezkieli, 25, 29; Chaim Shoskes, *"Ersht itst kehn mehn dertseilin di geshikhte vegen vunderbarer raytung fun velt-baremt Gerer Rebbe,"* Der Morgen Zhurnal, 22 Feb. 1948, p. 9.

unless his honorarium was doubled, the engineer would not return to Warsaw. Shoshkes urged those present not to yield to this ultimatum. Selmanovitz quickly rose from his chair, and motioned to Shoskes not to be so inflexible. The war of nerves lasted twenty minutes, when the engineer agreed to accept a much smaller remuneration than he had originally stipulated. Eventually, Alter and some members of his family, after considerable obstacles and danger, reached the safety of *Eretz* Israel.[35]

Selmanovitz's understandable joy, like that of his committee colleagues, was tempered by the horrific annihilation since termed the Holocaust. Rare, indeed, was this achievement of *pidyon shevuyim* (redeeming Jewish captives) in his people's most anguished years. The war prevented Benjamin and Esther from carrying out a planned visit to her parents in Poland. Nathan Fuks (Chana's brother) and wife Chaya were murdered by the Nazis in 1940, Nathan hanged in the town square for underground resistance activity. In March, 1941, Selmanovitz dispatched three $7 packages of food to Chana's family in Opoczno, officially listed as being in "German Poland," via the Agudath Israel relief campaign. Before long, all contact was lost; half of her kin would perish in the *Shoah*.[36]

The toll exacted on Abraham was considerable. Resolute faith precluded a questioning of his God. Yet a test in wartime of New York City's siren system frightened the rabbi so that he sought refuge in the house cellar. His predilection for Camels cigarettes intensified as well, singed fingertips turning yellow from nicotine in these same years. Poignantly, when about to escort his youngest child down the aisle to her wedding canopy, Selmanovitz explained why all the lights in Brooklyn's

---

[35] Alter to Selmanovitz (date unclear), Victor Selmanowitz MSS.; Yehezkieli, *passim*.

[36] Victor Selmanowitz, interview; Livia Straus, correspondence to author, 9 July 1998; receipts of Selmanovitz packages to Nissen, Cirel, and Szmul Fuks, 14 Mar. 1941. See Selmanowitz MSS.

Grand Paradise Hall ballroom should be put on: "The whole world is dark. Let there be light. My daughter is getting married!"[37]

Confronted by a deafening silence from Washington vis-à-vis the methodical murder of European Jewry, Selmanovitz joined 400 Orthodox rabbis in an unprecedented march on the Capitol on October 6, 1943. The date was chosen to coincide with the ten Days of Penitence preceding Yom Kippur. After presenting a petition to Vice President Henry Wallace on the steps of the Senate that called for rescue without delay, the bearded, gabardined assembly heard one of their number chant Hebrew prayers at the Lincoln Memorial (to the tune of the "Star-Spangled Banner") for Hitler's primary victims. From there the patriarchal-looking group silently proceeded to the White House for an expected interview with President Franklin D. Roosevelt, long venerated by the American Jewish community. Told that the chief executive had "other business," they trudged to Union Station for trains home. (FDR, in fact, left 1600 Pennsylvania Ave. to dedicate some bombers to the Yugoslav forces.) When the bells of victory pealed across the Allied world in May 1945, the Selmanovitz clan, like fellow Jews everywhere, had little cause for celebration. Among the victims of Adolf Hitler's "Final Solution" of "the Jewish question" was the vibrant *Gerer* community of Poland.[38]

---

[37] Bertha Machlis, interview with author; Vita and Nathan Friedman, interview.

[38] Penkower, *Expendable*, 136; Victor Selmanowitz, interview. A visit in 1999 to Poland by Stephen Straus, brother-in-law of Livia Straus, uncovered the last Jew of *Ger*, Felix Karpmann. A survivor of the Holocaust and waves of local postwar pogroms, Karpmann showed the Americans what remained of the quadrangle that housed the former *Gerer* residence, *shul* and rabbinic court: "Decaying buildings form an 'L' around a muddy courtyard. A few Poles came out in curiosity to see the new group of Jewish tourists and to have their palms greased with a few zlotys for allowing us into the building that once housed the *Rebbi's shul.* It is a large barn-like structure with poor fluorescent lighting and a 60 feet stretch of cheap pine tables and benches. The kids hauled in several boxes of provisions and made sandwiches for the road. I couldn't connect spiritually with the place

As in past decades, the couple's mutual love and regard evident to all, Chana stood by Abraham's side throughout the difficult times of the Great Depression and World War II. Raised in the East European *milieu* of Jews who especially valued the pious scholar, she always referred to the dignified-looking rabbi as "her *sefer Torah*." He, on the other hand, was devoted since their wedding to a woman who served as wife, mother, and custodian of tradition in this punctiliously Orthodox home. He frequently brought jewelry to the woman he adored, heartily fulfilling the precept of honoring a wife by buying her gifts. It was not beyond Abraham to clear the table and wash the dishes, or to prepare a glass of tea and some cake for Chana, so that his tired helpmate could sit and rest her legs, heavily wrapped in elasticized gauze due to severe edema. Their shared values permeated the two lives, best glimpsed in a lively table on Shabbat and religious holidays. Melodies, usually of *Gerer* origin, filled the dining room. The stories with which Selmanovitz, dressed especially in a black *kapote*, regaled his invitees contributed to the distinctive atmosphere.

Abraham always took the view that "his wife was the boss in the house and he was the boss outside." Chana was a good cook and usually could be found in the kitchen, preparing food for the large family and for many visitors. Fridays saw carp swimming in the bathtub, to be killed on site for fresh gefilte fish. Chicken soup with light, Polish-style *kneidlach*; pastries thin-crusted and sweet; *petcha* (calves-foot jelly) with hot prunes and raisins – all were served to the many Hasidim who came for Shabbat. The front parlor room had a long table at

---

at all. For me there were no echoes of brilliant *drashas* and joyous prayers in this building, but it came to life briefly when we sang for Felix." Straus diary, copy given to the author by Livia Straus, 5 June 1999. Today, there are an estimated 25,000 *Gerer* Hasidim in Israel, with another 1,000 families in Brooklyn's Borough Park. The current *Gerer Rebbe* is Yaakov Aryeh Alter, son of Simha Bunim Alter (d. 1992), one of the sons of the *Imrei Emes* (d. 1948). Ruth Lichtenstein, telephone conversation with author, 7 May 1999.

which the family and the many guests who came were seated for meals. It was also one of the two studies that Selmanovitz had in the house, both book lined. Their grandchildren remember coming to a home filled with volumes everywhere and papers loaded on a large roll-top desk, to grandparents who were always busy but able to express great love for their family. Sunday was the day they visited most often at 214 Rodney St., when children and grandchildren came together and got to know each other well.[39]

To his own children, Selmanovitz was a warm, gentle father. Duties in the local *beit din* (rabbinical court) from early morning to late evening left little time during the week for paternal attention. Fortunately, Shabbat and *yamim tovim* (religious holidays) offered welcome respite from this demanding schedule. With clan seated around the table, he then paid heed to their individual matters and would raise topics for discussion – usually in Yiddish, such as reasons for affirming that humanity has a higher nature than the beast. Any sneeze or sore throat prompted his devoted, nursing care. Requests were also made by telegram to the *Gerer Rebbe* for a blessing on special occasions. And though a number of the children eventually rejected their *heder* (elementary school), Rabbi Jacob Joseph Yeshiva, and Bais Ya'akov education, the rabbi chose neither to see imperfection nor to sit in judgment.[40]

A simple yet profound response on one occasion to his nephew, Jerry (Yehuda) Selman, reflected Selmanovitz's particular outlook. When the then six-year-old visited Rodney Street with his father, the rabbi interrupted a class, called over Selman, and asked about his Hebrew lessons. The youngster answered that they were pretty good, but that he did not like

---

[39] Victor Selmanowitz interview; Livia Straus to the author, July 9, 1998; Livia Straus conversation with the author, Nov. 26, 1997; Livia Straus memoir, given to the author, June 5, 1999.

[40] Bertha Machlis, interview with author.

the history of the Jews – kings and wars, and kings who ruled without belief. Commented Selmanovitz: "Beliefs change all the time, like the seasons. It gives you something to expect, to think about. But you, yourself, must shift your doubts and beliefs into knowing in your heart of hearts."[41]

In some ways, Selmanovitz maintained an independent streak that set him apart. There was one rabbinic task, common for his peers in the *Agudat ha-Rabbanim* and like organizations, that he refused to undertake. He did not give *hashgahot* (rabbinic certifications) on any food product, declaring that he would not approve as kosher anything "that his eyes do not see and his hands do not make." In another departure from his crowd, Selmanovitz refused to join Agudath Israel, perhaps because its anti-Zionism was at sharp odds with his favorable view of the secularist *halutzim*'s vital contribution to the development of *Eretz* Israel. His firm support of Rabbis Moshe and Joseph Baer Soloveitchik, who legitimized Revel's centrist Orthodox philosophy despite right-wing religious opposition, never wavered. Perhaps most remarkably, when his daughter Bertha (Brakha) asked her father for permission after graduating Hunter College to attend the Jewish Theological Seminary, explaining that that bastion of Conservatism could give her the best education in Hebrew for a teaching career, he consented.[42]

Still, Selmanovitz's world remained that of staunch Orthodoxy. Faced with the unremitting challenges of the New World to the rules and cohesion which marked Jewish life in the Old, he resolved not to follow his father's example entirely. He would keep the European name intact. (In RIETS circles, it would always be pronounced "Zalmanovitz.") The same held

---

[41] Jerry Selman to Yaelle Ehrenpreis, 7 Apr. 1999.

[42] Bertha Machlis, interview with Idelle Rudman; Victor Selmanowitz, interview. For Agudat Israel's stance on Zionism in the years before 1939, see Monty Noam Penkower, "A Lost Opportunity: Pre-World War II Efforts towards Mizrachi – Agudat Israel Cooperation," *Journal of Israeli History* 17 (Summer 1996): 221-61.

true for his *kapote*, his *yarmulke*, and the unmistakable Galician-Yiddish accent that permeated his speech.

This overall position governed family relations as well. Discovering that most of his siblings did not remain strictly Orthodox once in America, Selmanovitz chose to have very little involvement with them. The exception was Yutta Rachel (Ray), his older sister, who stayed within the Orthodox fold. The two were very close; she and her husband Elya (Alex) Cohen, prosperous residents of Washington Heights, helped Abraham financially when times were difficult. In related fashion, on a first visit to the apartment of son Louis's future in-laws, he was appalled by the bearskin rug that lay on the floor. Little wonder that Abraham kicked the rug aside, saying that it was inappropriate for a Jewish home; housewife Sarah Simon, herself very religious and in awe of this imposing figure, promptly threw the offending item down the incinerator chute.

His strict adherence to custom also explains why the oldest Selmanovitz child, Esther, married later in life. When her father discovered that the Hebrew name of her suitor Albert was identical with his own, he refused to allow the engagement to proceed. (This is based on the tradition that one should not have a spouse with the same name as a parent, so that no disrespectful mix-up can ensue.) Heartbroken, the obedient daughter delayed marriage to another man for some years. In another instance, the rabbi refused to officiate at or even attend a nephew's wedding because it took place in a non-Orthodox synagogue; estrangement within the clan inevitably followed.[43]

Selmanovitz's personal example exerted considerable influence on some of his children, but not on others. All kept to the name "Selmanovitz" or "Selmanowitz." Yet, his attempt to find suitable husbands for his daughters by inviting the more

---

[43] Victor Selmanowitz, interview; Livia Straus correspondence to author, 8 July 1998; Victor Pollock, interview with author, 18 Nov. 1998.

able Yeshiva students to 214 Rodney St. for a Shabbat on one occasion failed; the effort would not be repeated.[44] With America offering freedom from want and freedom of motion, his daughters and sons contended with seemingly endless possibilities that had never existed for Jews in Europe. Together with second-generation Americans of the twentieth century – Jew and Gentile – theirs was a world awaiting reinvention. Selmanovitz's universe of sacred text and custom was, therefore, on a definite collision course with secularism and change. Choices had to be made.

Esther became a very successful interior designer. She ultimately married Joseph Dubow, a *shohet* and Torah scholar, much in Selmanovitz's mold. Dubow, a good man, offered financial help to the widow and two teen-aged children of Esther's brother Leib (Louis) when the latter died at a young age. Esther and Joe, who had no children, visited Israel frequently, and bought an apartment in Jerusalem in the 1950's. After Joe's death, Esther married Abe Shulman, whom she met in that city's Central Hotel. They spent time both in her home in Riverdale, New York, and in her Jerusalem apartment before they retired to Israel's capital. In Riverdale, she maintained close ties with Rabbi Irving Greenberg, later head of CLAL, who was the executor of her estate.

Subsequently, Esther bought another, more modern apartment in a large Jerusalem building at 22 Pinsker Street, known for the large number of Americans living there. She became very active in charity work, especially on behalf of the Sha'arei Zedek Hospital and institutions that cared for orphans. A special fund was set up to underwrite their weddings, where she was a frequent guest. Esther was a good friend of *Rabbanit* Sarah Herzog, widow of the first Ashkenazi chief rabbi of the State of Israel, Rabbi Isaac (Yitzhak *ha-Levi*) Herzog. Esther eventually had a small volume of her father's

---

[44] Victor Selmanowitz, interview.

short essays collected and published, and donated her father's religious books to the *Gur* yeshivah and to *Yeshivat Merkaz ha-Rav Kook*, both in Jerusalem. She also purchased antique Torah scrolls from Italy for use in the synagogue maintained in the building at 22 Pinsker St., dedicating one to the memory of her father and another to the memory of her brother Louis. In her will, Esther left her apartment and its furnishings, which contained a number of art works, to the Sha'arei Zedek Hospital.[45]

Simha Bunim (Benjamin), called "Benny," once on these shores, married Esther Spiegel of Racaiz, Poland. Also from a family of *Gur* Hasidim, Esther had arrived in America aboard the *SS Mount Clay* in October 1922, coming alone at the invitation of an older brother already living here. The pair met in 1925 via a *shiddukh* (in the tradition of Benny's parents) and married one year later. Like his grandfather, with whom he lived when first coming to America, Benny became a *shohet*. He was active in the Jewish ritual slaughterer's union, going on strike and having his family march with him. Later on, his father laughingly told Benny that he had learned to go on strike from his son, since the *roshei ha-yeshivah* at RIETS later struck once when their salaries had not been paid for some time. Benny also received *semikhah* privately and would officiate at weddings. When this couple became naturalized in 1937, their occupations were given as "rabbi" and "housewife." Esther was an excellent cook, and for a time she and Benny entered the catering business. Rabbi Selmanovitz was known to be very fond of her, and to have admired her culinary abilities greatly. He also felt very close to Benny and Esther, since they, of all Abraham's children, most followed the *Gerer* Hasidic tradition.

---

[45] Victor Selmanowitz, interview; Abraham Selmanovitz, *Zekher Avraham Yitzhak*, compiled, Aaron Rakeffet-Rothkoff (Jerusalem, 1976). For a sense of the rabbi's Torah scholarship, see Avraham Yitshak Selmanowitz, *"Hasagot al Sefer Emek Halakhah,"* in *Sefer Yevul ha-Yovelot*, 102-110.

Their oldest child, Victor, spent much time in Williamsburg with his grandparents Abraham and Chana. He was an
exceptionally bright student, whose college career was cut
short because of a mastoid infection, which affected his sight
and left him with other health problems. Benny and Esther had
two other children, both daughters. Judith died at the age of 33,
leaving two young children, a son and a daughter, who were
raised by their father, Ted Rosenzweig. The other, Ruth (Rose),
married Julius Liebb; they had three daughters and one son.[46]

Benny and Esther's bungalow colony in the Catskill
Mountains reflected yet another key piece in the mosaic that
made up the immigrant Jewish experience in America. Eastern
European Jews who, at the turn of the century, tried to do
mixed farming in that inhospitable soil had found, like their
non-Jewish neighbors, that they had to take in boarders to
make ends meet. Initially, friends and kin arrived to escape the
heat and toil associated with New York City one hundred miles
away; they reveled in the fresh air, the sun, and the uplifting
power of nature. Rising demand, reinforced by refusal of
admission to "Hebrews" by Gentile-owned resorts in the area
and the Adirondacks, created in turn hundreds of Jewish
bungalow colonies and boarding houses in New York State's
Ulster and Sullivan counties. Before long, hotels and their
Jewish entertainers year-round converted the Catskills in the
public mind from simply "the mountains" to "the borscht belt."
For Louis Selmanowitz's daughter, whose father sometimes
inspected kosher hotels in the vicinity, being hosted in the
"Jewish Alps" and getting passes to weekend shows at resorts
like Grossinger's remains a fond memory of youth.[47]

---

[46] Naturalization Service, Petition and Record files, petitions #231999 and
#232000, NARA-NE; Victor Selmanowitz, interview. While Abraham
Selmanovitz, upon becoming a citizen in 1927, had given Benny's birthdate
as Nov. 15, 1902, Benny now wrote down 12 Feb. 1904. (The latter is
obviously in error, since younger brother Moshe was born that year.)

[47] Sorin, *A Time for Building*, 157-58; Livia Straus, conversation with the
author, 26 Nov. 1997.

For Morris, the name soon replacing "Moszak" (Moshe), America beckoned in more radical measure. At first, along with many of his immigrant contemporaries, this Selmanovitz son worked in the garment industry. He also served as a *kashrut* supervisor in different catering halls. When living at home, Morris retained the facade of Sabbath observance. When he married and left Williamsburg for the Bronx, however, Morris became openly non-observant. His wife, who worked in a sweatshop, met the young man via a "Brighton Beach-Rockaway Romance" common to the second generation: walking on the boardwalk in Rockaway. They had two sons and a daughter; she died tragically as a teenager. One son went on to become a professor of mathematics in California, while the other lives in Florida; Tillie, Morris's widow, resided there as well.[48]

Louis (Aryeh Leib), the next child born to Abraham and Chana, is remembered by all with great fondness. Portrayed as a tall, handsome man, meticulously dressed, very bright, and gentle, he seems to have been everyone's favorite. Louis graduated *Beit Midrash le-Morim* of Yeshiva University (Yeshiva's status upgraded by the New York State Department of Education in 1945) with a teacher's certificate. Never putting the degree to professional use, he also attended Columbia College at night, pursuing premedical studies. Needing to earn money, Louis tried his hand at various schemes. A cousin, Joseph Fox (formerly Fuks), had made arrangements to produce a Yiddish film starring the world-renowned cantor Yossele Rosenblatt. (During the filming, Rosenblatt died; his funeral was recorded in this musical travel log of Palestine.) Using the name Louis Solomon, Louis traveled to Canada and some U.S. cities to promote the film, "The Dream of My People," which had been finished in Palestine in 1934.

He also worked part-time as a *kashrut* inspector, which is how Louis met his wife. Ethel (Esther Rivka) Simon, who then

---

[48] Victor Selmanowitz, interview.

lived on Rogers Avenue in Flatbush, was in her uncle's butcher shop one day when Louis entered for an inspection. He spoke with the young woman and a courtship followed. Enrolled in New York University, Ethel was studying to be a teacher. They married on March 14, 1937 in Grand Street's Grand Paradise Hall, with Rabbi Revel in attendance. At this point, Louis dropped out of college to support a family and went to work full-time for the *kashrut* division of the state's Department of Agriculture. Their oldest child, Victor, was born in 1938, and the second, Livia, in 1943.[49]

Louis was a modest, sentimental, and loving person. When away from home on work trips, he would write Ethel letters, bringing flowers and gifts for the children when he returned. His sister Bertha remembers him buying her a special gift, a fur coat, when she made the Dean's List at Hunter College. He always tried new things, and brought home one of the earliest television sets available on the market. During World War II, Louis served in the National Guard in upstate New York. All personal hope to be a physician ended forever, these aspirations being transferred to his son Victor.

Louis had a deep sense of respect for his parents, whom he loved dearly. He followed their example in maintaining an Orthodox Jewish home, although of a modern cast, and helped found the Young Israel of Vanderveer Park. When his son Victor, a very mischievous child in the throes of third-generation rebellion, had to be admonished, Louis would invariably respond with a question: "What would *zayde* (grandfather) say?" Louis visited his parents on a weekly basis, and would hurry to 214 Rodney St. when they had any need. After his father died, Louis was the first child his mother would telephone for help. He spent a great deal of time with her until his own illness.

---

[49] Victor Selmanowitz, interview; *Courier*, 18 Dec. 1934; Victor Selmanowitz MSS.; Selmanovitz-Simon wedding invitation, 14 Mar. 1937, Revel Collection, folder 5/1-7, General Correspondence "S", 1930-1940, Yeshiva University Archives.

In 1954, Louis was appointed head of the *kashrut* division of the New York State Department of Agriculture. A break in the dark clouds of financial stress, which long hovered above him, seemed finally at hand. Despite these tensions, Louis had always committed whatever his means allowed to a yeshivah education for his son and daughter. Yet now, with respite in view, he began feeling ill. Louis resigned from his position, too weak to work. Mother Chana would make special foods for him to eat in the hopes of whetting his appetite and thus strengthening her son. The illness was at last diagnosed as Hodgkin's disease. Louis died in 1957 at the age of 47.[50]

Selmanovitz's next son, Jack (Yaakov), became a diamond cutter. He learned this profession with his older brother Benny, although the latter never worked in that trade. During World War II, many members of the Orthodox community entered the diamond business, since commerce with European centers such as Antwerp was severed. Jack enjoyed the reputation of having great strength, able to tear telephone books in half. This physical prowess was inherited from his mother's family, who counted among their numbers an Olympic wrestler. Jack married and had one child, Barry. Unfortunately, the boy had mastoids as a child and later developed rheumatic heart disease. Taught a great deal at home, he later proved to be an outstanding success in school. After completing training for psychiatry, Barry committed suicide. Jack eventually separated from his wife, after which he went to live with his widowed mother. In time, he returned to the Orthodox Jewish practices of his youth.[51]

Miriam, ten months younger than Jack, married Irving Rosenfeld. Abraham and Chana's second daughter, bright and attractive, had graduated with a B.A. degree from Brooklyn College. She met Rosenfeld while he was serving

---

[50] Livia Straus, conversation with author, 26 Nov. 1997; Bertha Machlis, interview with Idelle Rudman.

[51] Victor Selmanowitz, interview.

in the U.S. Air Force during World War II. The two eloped, a match outside the Orthodox fold. With her husband a dentist, Miriam acted as the office receptionist. Unfortunately, medical problems prevented Miriam from having children.[52]

Bertha (Brakha), the next Selmanovitz child, graduated from Hunter College and took a Hebrew teacher's degree from the Jewish Theological Seminary. She married Julius Machlis, a cantor and salesman in the fabric trade. He had also been a Hebrew teacher and principal of a Hebrew school. They had two sons, Joel and David (Peter). Now widowed, Bertha lives in Lawrence, New York. Active in various Jewish organizations, she has been honored many times by her local synagogue and other charitable groups. Her interest in studying Torah has not diminished, and she remains active in the Orthodox Jewish community.[53]

The youngest of the brood enjoyed a special relationship with her father. From spending all of a weekly five-dollar allowance on candy for the parent she adored, to combing his hair and beard as he lay down on the sofa, Vita (Ita) did all to please him. He, in turn, regularly sat the little girl on his lap, and supported her subsequent use of makeup when a zealous young relative raised objection. In Vita's eyes, her father remained "the sweetest, softest person in the world."

One *Rosh ha-Shanah* night, Vita, then still a teenager, met her future husband, Nathan Friedman. After two years at Hunter College, she married the accountant-postal worker. Nathan respected his father-in-law immensely, years later recalling the sage's gifts of charity worldwide and the "brilliant masterpieces" which the rabbi delivered in *shul* on Shabbat and religious holidays. The couple moved to Brighton Beach, where Vita worked tirelessly to build the local synagogue center. While Nathan also volunteered his services for the next thirty-five years to the Knights of Pythias, his wife offered her

---

[52] Livia Straus, conversation with author, 26 Nov. 1997.

[53] Bertha Machlis, interview with Idelle Rudman.

talents to a Jewish home for incurables. The loving pair had three children, Joan, Barry and Shelly. Currently, Vita and Nathan live in Las Vegas, choosing a more liberal religious lifestyle while "trying to be as kosher as we can be in a non-kosher town."[54]

All eight Selmanovitz children had married by 1946, when Abraham, long a heavy smoker, lay ill with cancer. Yet even then, his sense of humor surfaced. During a visit to the hospital, a former student queried how his *rebbe* would deal with female nurses. Responded the patient: If they were very good, caring, and attractive, and in fact appeared to him as *mal'akhim mi-ma'al* (angels from heaven), who was he to question the One above?[55]

A frequent visitor to the stricken victim was Rabbi Joseph Baer Soloveitchik, who told his students to inform him of any change in Selmanovitz's condition. Since assuming Rabbi Moshe's position as *rosh ha-yeshivah*, Soloveitchik continued the warm, close relationship with Selmanovitz that his father had treasured. It was through Joseph Baer's personal invitation that Selmanovitz came to Boston to eulogize Rabbi Moshe in an *azkarat sheloshim* (a memorial service held one month after the Jewish individual's death). The older man, in turn, showed his deep respect for the new senior *rosh yeshivah* by having him come to Williamsburg every year and give a public *shiur* (Torah lecture) at the Poilisher Shteibel. Students from all the local yeshivas came to hear this annual discourse, where standing room only prevailed. For Soloveitchik, Selmanovitz's most admirable characteristic was his rapport with, and respect for, the students of RIETS, and he remained forever grateful to the individual who resolutely championed the Soloveitchik dynasty there.[56]

---

[54] Vita and Nathan Friedman, telephone interview.

[55] Livia Straus, correspondence with author, 8 July 1998.

[56] Philip Reiss, interview; Maurice Wohlgelernter, interview.

On October 4, 1946, at 9:25 in the morning of Yom Kippur eve, Rabbi Abraham Isaac Selmanovitz passed away after a long illness. The funeral was held that same Friday, just several hours preceding the holiest 25-hour-period in the Jewish year. The pressure of time notwithstanding, hundreds of people attended the services, including members of the community and of the two *shuls* Selmanovitz served as rabbi, as well as students of RIETS and other *yeshivot.* Administrators from Yeshiva University, headed by President Belkin and Dean Samuel Sar, came, as did representatives of Yeshiva Torah VoDa'ath and the *Agudat ha-Rabbanim.* The leaders of the *Novominsker, Modzitser,* and *Daliner* Hasidic dynasties also arrived to pay their last respects. Williamsburg's streets were "black with people," recalled one on-looker of the moving farewell, distinguished by a bearded mass attired in the same color hats and gabardines. The cortege ended in Beth David Cemetery, located in Elmont, Long Island, with burial taking place in the section reserved for the Hasidim of *Gur.*[57]

Rabbi Joseph Baer Soloveitchik, present when Selmanovitz breathed his last, was the major eulogist that day. He had specially flown in from Boston and returned shortly before Yom Kippur began. The city's chief rabbi was given a police escort, sirens blaring, from Boston's airport in order to be able to arrive in *shul* for *Kol Nidrei,* marking the commencement of evening prayers; so pressed was Soloveitchik for time that he was unable to partake of the customary pre-fast meal.[58]

Orthodox Jewry in America took note of this loss in its ranks. The *Morgen Zhurnal* (Morning Journal) spoke about the 69-year-old deceased as a *gaon* (luminary) of Torah, both in the realm of *beki'ut* (expertise in the sources) and in that of

---

[57] Microfilm no. 651, Death Certificate #19157, New York City Dept. of Records and Information Services, Municipal Archives, New York; *Morgen Zhurnal,* 6 Oct. 1946; Louis Brenner, telephone conversation with author, 17 Feb. 1998.

[58] Shulamith Meiselman, interview.

harifut (incisiveness of mind). Eloquent notices appeared in the *Morgen Zhurnal*, the principal Yiddish-language newspaper for the Orthodox, from the *Agudat ha-Rabbanim* and the Talmud Torah Anshei Emes, as well as from the executive of the *Vaad ha-Rabbanim* of Williamsburg.[59]

One month later, a memorial service was held in the Harry Fischel Synagogue of Yeshiva College. Rabbi Joseph B. Soloveitchik spoke about his father's relationship with Selmanovitz, their two identities "merged into one." He vividly portrayed for the more than three hundred people in attendance a picture of the way they knew the deceased best: "smiling, erect, and with the dignified bearing of a great scholar and educator." Personally, confessed the speaker, the departure of Rabbi Selmanovitz left him with "his arms outstretched in vain" and with the feeling of an irreplaceable loss. Rabbi Aaron Burack, a RIETS colleague of Selmanovitz, eulogized his good friend as a great teacher devoted to his pupils, and noted that he gave a large portion of his small income to charity and was to a large degree responsible for the *Gerer Rebbe*'s escape to Palestine.[60]

Rabbi Dr. Sidney Hoenig, often a houseguest at 214 Rodney St., also spoke. Leader of the Young Israel of Williamsburg, Hoenig had learned much from Selmanovitz, taking note of his practice as a communal rabbi. Before the Passover holiday, in particular, Hoenig would spend hours watching Selmanovitz write out the *shtar mekhirat hametz*, the pre-Passover contract with a Gentile for selling him Jewish-owned leavened foods that are forbidden to them during the holiday. Hoenig, who also taught Jewish history at Yeshiva College, would accompany the older man on the train every day to RIETS. To the assembled at the memorial service, Hoenig pointed out that Selmanovitz gave unselfishly to others;

---

[59] *Morgen Zhurnal*, 6 Oct. 1946.

[60] *Commentator*, 5 Dec. 1946, p. 1.

he found time for his personal study either during the late evening or the early hours of the morning.[61]

The deceased was also able to leave an estate of some worth. The record on file gave a sum of $23,586 in cash, deposited in various banks. (There were no stocks and bonds or a life insurance policy.) The actual and assessed value of 214 Rodney St. came to $5,500. A mortgage on that property in the sum of $4,600 left an equity of about $900. Debts for medical expenses ran to $2,700; other expenses such as the funeral and incidentals amounted to about $500. One-third of the estate would go to his wife, their eight children to share the remainder in equal measure.[62]

"My *sefer Torah* is gone!" So Chana Selmanovitz cried out when her beloved mate of fifty-two years was no more. In Chana's perception, the holiest emblem of Judaism and the image of her husband who lived by its precepts were always one and the same. A few years later, in light of the projected Brooklyn-Queens Expressway, the house in Williamsburg (like the Poilisher Shteibel) was sold to the city. Chana went to live near her daughters Miriam and Vita in the Brighton Beach section of Brooklyn. She died in 1974, at the ripe age of ninety-four, and was buried in the women's section of the same *Gur* cemetery grounds where her Abraham lay at rest.[63] Thus drew to a close the story of one Jewish family's first generation in twentieth-century America.

Rabbi Abraham Isaac Selmanovitz exercised great impact on those who made up his self-contained universe. In such Orthodox fastnesses as Opoczno, Williamsburg, and RIETS, his *yihus* (lineage) rested on his being a traditional scholar of

---

[61] Ibid.: Ya'akov Hoenig (son of Sidney), interview with Idelle Rudman, 17 Sept. 1996.

[62] File 9582-46, Kings County Surrogate's Court archives, Record Room 109, New York State Supreme Court, Brooklyn, New York.

[63] Victor Selmanowitz, interview. The location of the former house in Williamsburg currently lies where the Brooklyn Queens Expressway bisects Rodney Street.

impeccable character. A commanding voice matched the tall frame, exuding authority and even charisma for hundreds who shared his certitudes. In Rabbi Joseph Baer Soloveitchik's eloquent characterization, Selmanovitz's "great spiritual value" lay in his being "a humble man who concealed his virtue." This sage's desire for knowledge "sublimated the desire for material wealth" that attracted so many of his generation. Looking at Selmanovitz's stately figure, Soloveitchik aptly saw "not the skyscrapers and concrete of the huge metropolis, but the Torah communities of Warsaw and Lodz."[64]

Yet, the unfettered reality that was America, given the acceptance and affluence so foreign to the Jewish experience in Eastern Europe, suggested countless alternatives for future exploration. The variegated richness of the new and the untried attracted some younger, adventurous spirits within the Selmanovitz family. Along with the large majority of their Jewish contemporaries in the United States, they would jettison the life of enclosed Halakhah (law) and prudence for personal achievement and happiness. The insular lifestyle of precincts like Williamsburg was to be abandoned for seemingly endless vistas that appeared on the horizon.

Selmanovitz lamented the consequences. In one *derashah* (homily) at the Poilisher Shteibel, he reminded his listeners of the liturgical phrase in Hebrew "*ashamnu mi-kol am*" (we have become more guilty than any nation). "Surely this confession to God appeared to be without grounds!" he wondered. Yet, the rabbi went on in his trademark Yiddish, the assertion possessed a sad validity: Unlike other nations that had progressed over time from a culture of thievery to one of educational attainment, Jews were renouncing the incomparable Torah and Talmud of their ancestors for the seductive forces of materialism and pleasure. Their prayers, their homes,

---

[64] Moshe Wolfson, telephone interview with author, 17 Feb. 1998; *Commentator*, 5 Dec. 1946.

their lives – all were a greatly weakened version of the proud traditions of yore.[65]

One of the last scions of Polish Jewry, Selmanovitz could not stem the tide. Aided by his loyal Chana for more than a half-century, this guardian of Orthodox tradition chose a path of upright, rigorous commitment. Few did so, with palpable results. Modernity, as he foresaw, would bring spectacular success to Jews, but concomitantly give rise to a diminished Judaism. Some of his own children reflected the same trend. The Jewish people's survival on these welcome shores now rested with the next generation.

---

[65] Beryl Schwartz, telephone interview with author, 17 Feb. 1998.

Maimonides on
Pride and Anger*

Bezalel Safran

– I –

A most intriguing contradiction in Maimonides' *Mishneh Torah*
has attracted a great deal of scholarly attention.[1]

For all psychological traits and predispositions, including
pride and anger, the core of Maimonides' curative ethical program
is Aristotle's golden mean.[2] Concerning pride and anger,

---

* This article has benefited from helpful criticism and comments by
Profs. James Diamond, Warren Harvey, Moshe Idel, David Novak, Esther
Starobinski-Safran and Michael Shmidman. Any remaining defects are
the responsibility of the author.

[1] See R. Eisen, "Lifnim mi-Shurat ha-Din in Maimonides' *Mishneh Torah*,"
Jewish Quarterly Review 89:3-4 (1999): 298 n. 21. According to H. Davidson, "The Middle Way in Maimonides' Ethics," *PAAJR* 54 (1987): 42, "The
contradiction is flagrant" and "is amenable to no satisfactory explanation"
(44 n. 49).

[2] On the influence of Aristotle's *Ethics* on Maimonides' formulation of
the golden mean, see A. Kirschenbaum, "*Middat Hasidut* and Supereroga-
tion," [Hebrew] *Da'at* 44 (1999): 26-27 n. 102; M. Fox, "The Doctrine of the

Maimonides states this twice, in *Hilkhot De'ot* 1:4, and even more emphatically, in *Hilkhot De'ot* 2:2. In *Hilkhot De'ot* 2:3 however, the very next passage, Maimonides contradicts himself, stating that pride and anger must be totally suppressed, i.e., that the principle of the golden mean is not applicable to them.[3]

Mean in Aristotle and Maimonides: A Comparative Study," *Interpreting Maimonides* (London and Chicago: University of Chicago Press, 1990), 93-123; B. Safran, "Maimonides and Aristotle on Ethical Theory," *Studies in the Literature of Jewish Thought Presented to Rabbi Dr. Alexandre Safran*, ed. M. Hallamish (Ramat Gan: Bar-Ilan University Press, 1990), 133-61; H. Davidson, 59, who points out that Maimonides learned of Aristotle's doctrine from Alfarabi; see further in S. Harvey, "The Source of the Citations from Aristotle's *Ethics* in the *Guide* and in the *Moreh ha-Moreh*," [Hebrew] *Joseph Sermonetta Memorial Volume*, ed. A. Ravitzky (Jerusalem, 1998), 99-102, on the indirect nature of Aristotle's influence on Maimonides.

[3] The possibility that the contradiction is a pedagogical one of the "fifth kind" (see the end of Maimonides' introduction to the *Guide*), whereby an "impressionistic" initial presentation of asserting justifiable anger (*Hilkhot De'ot* 1:4) is refined by a second presentation of feigning this justifiable anger while remaining outwardly calm (*Hilkhot De'ot* 2:3), is implicitly rejected by Davidson, 42-43.

Conceivably, one might try to argue that *Hilkhot De'ot* 2:2 refers to the discipline of psychology, not ethics, disposing of the contradiction in this way. However, *Hilkhot De'ot* 1:4 clearly refers to the discipline of ethics: "Thus a man should not be choleric, easily moved to anger, nor be like the dead without feeling; but should aim at the happy medium; be angry only for a grave cause that rightly calls for indignation, so that the like should not be done again" (translation from I. Twersky, *A Maimonides Reader* [New Jersey, 1972], 52). One might say, that included in this passage is not only the mean concerning anger but concerning pride as well. Not to "be like the dead without feeling" means to have a measure of self esteem. It is this justifiable pride which is at the root of justifiable anger. See S. Schimmel, *The Seven Deadly Sins* (New York, 1992), 92.

The most recent attempt to resolve this "flagrant" contradiction is Kirschenbaum, 29-30. His ultimate solution, however, seems to ignore the fact that in *Hilkhot De'ot* 2:2 (which he had just cited), Maimonides advises, even concerning pride and anger, that after taking the extreme therapeutic approach, one return to the mean.

This article deals with what Kirschenbaum calls the "thought" of Maimonides concerning the *hasid* (26-30). For a presentation of Maimonides' halakhic treatment of "*middat hasidut*," see 30-38.

Furthermore, in *Hilkhot De'ot* 1:5, there is another, structurally analogous direct contradiction: "Whoever is particularly scrupulous and deviates slightly from the mean, in one direction or the other, is called a *hasid*." The very next sentence, however, reads: "For example, if one distances one's self from the other extreme and is exceedingly humble, he is deemed a *hasid* and this is the quality of *hasidut*." Is *hasidut* a slight deviation from the mean or an extreme one?

Hilkhot De'ot 1:6 is a contradiction-riddled discussion:

> We are bidden to walk in the middle paths (*ha-derakhim ha-elu ha-beinonim*), which are the right and proper ways, as it is said, "And you shall walk in His ways" (Deut. 28:9). In explanation of the text just quoted, the Sages taught, "Even as God is called gracious (*hanun*) so be you gracious; even as He is called merciful, so be you merciful; even as He is called holy, so be you holy." Thus too, the prophets described the Almighty by all the various attributes "long-suffering (*erekh appayim*) and abounding in kindness (*rav hesed*), righteous and upright, perfect, mighty and powerful," and so forth, to teach us that these qualities are good and right and that a human being should cultivate them, and thus imitate God, as far as he can.[4]

This passage appears to introduce the concept of emulating God according to the mean, the way of the *hakham*,[5] but goes on to catalog qualities that Maimonides himself defines in accordance with the extreme, the standard of *hasidut*.

For example, Maimonides explains the sense in which God is *hanun* in *Guide* I:54:

> When we give a thing to somebody who has no claim on us, this is called grace (*haninah*) in our language, as it

---

[4] Translation in *A Maimonides Reader*, 53.

[5] On the way of the *hakham* as the way of the mean, see *Hilkhot De'ot* 1:4.

says, "Grant them graciously" (Judges 21:22) – [so is the term applied to Him:] ... For He, may He be exalted, brings into existence and governs people that have no claim upon Him with respect to being brought into existence and being governed. For this reason He is called gracious (*hanun*).[6]

The notion of God as *hanun* is identified in *Guide* III:53 with God as *hasid* and *rav hesed*:

It is known that beneficence ... [is] consisting in the exercise of beneficence toward one who has no right at all to claim this from you.... In most cases, the prophetic books use the word *hesed* in ... [this] sense. Therefore, every benefit that comes from Him, may He be exalted, is called *hesed*. Thus ... He, may He be exalted, says in an enumeration of His attributes, "And abundant in loving kindness" (*rav hesed*).... Accordingly, He is described as *hasid* [one possessing loving-kindness] because He has brought all into being.[7]

God's attributes of *hanun* and *hasid* are considered by Maimonides as synonymous and both are cited in the version of *Sifre* quoted by Maimonides in *Sefer ha-Mizvot* (positive precept 8) as Divine ethical standards to be emulated. And when Maimonides and the Rabbis speak of exercising *haninah* and *hasidut* just as God does, the meaning is "giving a thing to somebody who has no claim on us."

Clearly, the attributes of *hanun* and *rav hesed* (which Maimonides cites in *Hilkhot De'ot* 1:6) are *hasidic* traits. They call for the total suppression of self-interest and angry resentment, even in the face of justified anger, which according to the mean would be permitted (*Hilkhot De'ot* 1:4). This is reflected in Maimonides' prooftext (cited in *Guide* I:54) for the meaning of

---

[6] Maimonides, *The Guide of the Perplexed,* vol. 1, trans. S. Pines (London and Chicago: University of Chicago Press, 1963), 125.

[7] *The Guide of the Perplexed,* vol.2, 630-32.

haninah from Judges 21:15-23. The passage tells of a communal effort undertaken at a time of national emergency. The
elders of Israel advise the ostracized tribe of Benjamin to kid-
nap Shilonite women and marry them, in order to insure that
their tribe not become extinct. To counteract the anticipated
angry remonstrations of the women's parents, the elders are
prepared to say, "Grant them [the women] graciously unto us
(*hanunu otam*)."

Maimonides considers this case a paradigm of *haninah*.
The elders – or the tribe of Benjamin – have no legal or moral
claim whatsoever on the women's families. They can only appeal to a standard of *haninah* or *hesed*. As *honenim*, the
wronged parents are expected to acquiesce in the face of the
provocation they are experiencing. *Haninah* entails suppression of anger, just as God suppresses His anger (Exodus
33:14,19) and exercises grace. Just as *hanun* and *rav hesed*
are hasidic traits, so is *erekh appayim*. Three out of the ten
attributes mentioned in *Hilkhot De'ot* 1:6 are *hasidic*. How are
they supposed to demonstrate that "we are bidden to walk in
the middle paths which are the right and proper ways"?

Such direct contradictions, back to back and in triplicate,
do not appear concerning any other discussion in *Mishneh
Torah* and dealing with them invites a special approach. They
appear to be what Maimonides characterizes in the
introduction to the *Guide* as intentional contradictions (of the
"seventh kind"). As has been pointed out,[8] when Maimonides in
the *Guide* deals with theoretical philosophical issues, the
exoteric and the esoteric tracks are mutually exclusive and
only the esoteric may be deemed to be "true." However,
concerning moral questions, an intentional contradiction does
not generate mutually exclusive premises. Both premises are

---

[8] Howard Kreisel, "The Problem of Contradictions in Maimonides' Approach
to Ethics," in *Maimonides' Political Thought* (New York: State University of
New York Press, 1999), 176, 183-85.

true if they be considered from different perspectives.[9] It is the thesis of this article that the two tracks suggested by the intentional contradictions in the first two chapters of *Hilkhot De'ot* are the anthropocentric orientation of the *hakham* and the theocentric one of the *hasid*. Furthermore, the orientation of the *hakham* is intended for one historical period, the *hasidic* track, for another.

The world-view of the philosophical *hakham* (reconstructed from *Hilkhot De'ot* references as well as the "Eight Chapters," the *Commentary on Avot* and the *Guide*), in context of Aristotle's ethical theory, was dealt with in great detail elsewhere.[10] Certain points will be highlighted here. The *hakham* aims to achieve a moral-psychological balance between contrary extremes in his psyche. To attain this "intermediate state" of the soul, therapies are recommended which ultimately create an autonomous ethical personality free to "calculate" and "decide" his moral options. While the mean is always the goal, in order to achieve it, one may have to go to the other extreme temporarily, or tilt in one direction, in order to ascertain that the mean is not violated (one who does such "tilting" is sometimes called *hasid*, as in *Hilkhot De'ot* 1:5).

For both Aristotle and Maimonides, the theory of the mean is eudaemonistic, i.e., it enables the *hakham* to attain bliss in this world, "perfection of the body, and

---

[9] It follows from Kreisel's approach that in intentional contradictions concerning moral questions, there will not be "very obscure matters" where "it is necessary to conceal some parts and to disclose others," nor must "the vulgar in no way be aware of the contradiction," meaning that "the author ... uses some device to conceal [the contradiction] by all means." The contradiction is blatant and signals that there are several equally valid strata of meaning. (The sentences in quotes are sentences taken from Maimonides' characterization of the "seventh kind" of contradiction at the end of his introduction to the *Guide of the Perplexed*, vol. 1, 18.)

[10] B. Safran, ibid.

perfection of the intellect."[11] In that sense, it contributes to self-fulfillment, it is man-centered. An example of anthropocentric moral-psychological analysis is Maimonides' – and Aristotle's – analysis of the mean vis-à-vis pride and anger.[12] Pride is a virtue for Maimonides' *hakham* if it is maintained according to the mean (*Hilkhot De'ot* 2:2). For Aristotle too, pride is a virtue and is considered on two levels: one, pertaining to the honor earned by the perfectly virtuous person, where pride is unquestionably justifiable; the other, regarding the individual who only approximates a virtuous state, where he speaks of the quest for "small honors."

The former relates to one who thinks himself worthy of great honor, and is really worthy of it. Having achieved virtue, he has a clear sense of his superiority and of getting what is due to him; if he is honored by just anyone, he will actually disdain it, for that is not what he is worthy of. It follows that he considers it praiseworthy to display his greatness – but only among equals. Dishonor to his person will justify anger and vindictiveness.

The vice of deficiency lies in pusillanimity, when one thinks he is worthy of less than he is in fact worth. That deficiency appears suspicious and indecisive. The vice of excess, vanity, results from exaggerating one's worth.

Regarding the "many" who have not achieved perfect virtue, Aristotle extrapolates from the actualized ideal of the perfectly virtuous one, "also we can desire honor more or less than is right, and we can desire it from the right sources and in the right way."

Anger also has its place; there are times when it is justified according to Maimonides (*Hilkhot De'ot* 1:4), and

---

[11] On how "the perfectly balanced Law" relates to the *hakham's* philosophy and enables him to achieve bliss, see ibid., 157-60.

[12] The generalizations about the mean of pride and anger in Aristotle's *Ethics* are documented; ibid., 148-51.

according to his source, Aristotle: "The person who is angry at the right things and towards the right people, and also in the right way, at the right time and for the right length of time, is praised."

To suppress anger completely, Aristotle maintains, is slavish and betrays foolishness, insensitivity and weakness. The mean is mildness, which curbs "excessive" outbursts of bitter or irritable people in accordance with reason and tends towards a readiness to pardon.

The *hakham*'s – or the philosopher's – pride and anger, if legitimately exercised, help them defend their honor in the face of provocation and "adorn" their achievements in the face of that claim. They define their place in society, their identity, in relation to others. They meet their ego needs by being self-respecting and assertive and judging from Aristotle's examples, this may also help in venting frustration and resentment (e.g., the wrath of Achilles in the Iliad).

If Maimonides' *hakham*, following the self-interested track, is man-centered, Maimonides' *hasid* or *zaddik* is God-centered (*Hilkhot De'ot* 2:3).

We are forbidden to apply the mean to pride; it is to be totally eliminated. In *Hilkhot De'ot* 2:3, explaining why pride, in the case of the *hasid*, must be completely eradicated, Maimonides paraphrases a Talmudic statement (*Sotah* 4b): Every man in whom is haughtiness of spirit is as though he had denied the fundamental principle (i.e., the existence of God), as it is said (Deut. 8:14): "But your heart may then grow haughty, and you may forget God your Lord...."

The Talmudic context from which Maimonides cites in *Hilkhot De'ot* 2:3 contains three other statements censuring a haughty spirit – with different prooftexts. Maimonides selected this particular one because it best epitomizes the conceptual framework he has constructed for the *hasid* – both in terms of the larger context of Deuteronomy 8:14, and of Maimonides' understanding of how pride denies the existence of God.

If Deuteronomy 8:14 be considered in context – as Maimonides insists prooftexts should be studied[13] – the nexus between pride and obliviousness of God is greatly clarified. While Deuteronomy 8:15-16 recalls the forgotten feats that God has wrought for his people, Deuteronomy 8:17-18 concentrates on the rationalization employed to justify pride:

> And you will say in your heart, it was my strength and personal power that brought all that prosperity (*hayil*). You must remember that it is God your Lord who gives you the power to become prosperous.

If pride results in forgetfulness of God's role in one's success, humility generates a memory and an awareness of one's dependence on the power of God.

For Aristotle's paragon of virtue, the mean is achieved through one's own powers (book three of *Ethics*) and pride is therefore understandable, even necessary.

Maimonides' *hasid* or *zaddik*, however, does not claim credit for his achievements, not even for his spiritual prowess. Commenting (*Hilkhot Teshuvah* 6:5) on the verses (in Psalms 25:8-9) "Good and upright is the Lord, therefore he shows sinners the way; He guides the lowly in the right path, and teaches the lowly His way," Maimonides maintains that God enables the religious effort. It is true (*Hilkhot Teshuvah*, ch.5) that man has his free will to accomplish, but God supports that will and therefore makes possible its realization:

> [Psalms 25:8-9 shows] that He gave power to learn and to understand [the right way]. For this quality is [residing] in every person, that so long as he is drawn by the ways of wisdom and righteousness [asserts his free will] – he craves them and pursues

---

[13] B. Safran, "Maimonides on Free Will, Determinism and Esotericism," *Porat Yosef: Studies Presented to Rabbi Dr. Joseph Safran*, ed. B. and E. Safran (New Jersey, 1992), 122 n.4.

them [through a Divine nudge]. And this is what our
Sages of blessed memory said: "If one comes to
purify [one's self] he is being aided" (*Yoma* 38b) [from
above], that is, he will find himself helped concerning
this matter.

This sense that he is being helped in his spiritual achievement renders his self-satisfaction presumptuous.[14][15]

The *zaddik* must also totally eradicate his anger
(*Hilkhot De'ot* 2:3) because anger is "idolatrous." This reason
harks back to the *Commentary on Avot* where Maimonides
explains that anger and a religious disposition are mutually
exclusive; anger and idolatry are identical.

Commenting on the Mishnah in *Avot* 2:13, "do not be
prone to anger," Maimonides explains:

---

[14] The concept "theocentric" or "God-centered" is used differently here and
in Daniel Frank's "Humility as a Virtue: a Maimonidean Critique of
Aristotle's *Ethics*," *Moses Maimonides and His Time*, ed. Eric L. Ormsby
(Washington, DC: The Catholic University of America Press, 1989), 89-99.
For Frank (98), the *hasid*'s "ethical theocentrism" consists in the fact that
"God, not man, is the author of the moral law" and as a result, the *hasid*
turns extremely humble as he realizes "that man's ultimate felicity
depends upon obedience to this (Divine) law, and to nothing else." For us,
God-centeredness stems from the deep existential awareness of the *hasid*
that "he finds himself helped concerning this matter" (of his achievement).

[15] This is a moderate interpretation of Maimonides' insistence on the total
suppression of pride. A more radical interpretation also suggests itself.
After all, Maimonides adopts the Talmudic position that not even a modicum of pride ("an eighth of an eighth," *Sotah* 5a) is justifiable. This may
intimate that one has no share whatsoever in one's achievement; it is all
God's doing. It is not merely that God helps in man's undertaking; it is God
who achieves through man.

This theme deserves a full treatment (forthcoming), which requires the use
of Judah Alharizi's translation of the *Guide* (Tel Aviv: Mahberot le-Sifrut
and Jerusalem: Mossad ha-Rav Kook, 1953) where this idea is systematically developed. For a terse suggestive introduction to themes in Judah
Alharizi's translation, see A. Kaminka, "Introduction to Tahkemoni,"
Tahkemoni (Warsaw, 1898); and *Moreh Nevukhim*, trans. and ed. Michael
Schwartz (Tel Aviv: Tel Aviv University Press, 2002), 746-47. In this connection see also B. Safran, "Maimonides on Free Will," 111-28.

> Do not dispose yourself to irritability and anger.
> They [the Rabbis] already urged concerning the
> reprehensible nature of anger, saying that everyone
> who gets angry is like a worshiper of idolatry. They
> related it to what was said (Psalms 81:10), "you shall
> have no foreign god, you shall not bow to an alien
> god," that is to say, that the two things (anger and
> worship of an alien god) are identical.

There is no explicit rabbinic statement which expresses
the identity Maimonides claims. In order to arrive at this
"rabbinic" precept, he improvises on the following Talmudic
passage (*Shabbat* 105b):[16]

> R. Simeon b. Eleazar said ... He who rends his
> garments in his anger, he who breaks his vessels in
> his anger, and he who scatters his money in his
> anger, regard him as an idolater, because such are
> the wiles of the Tempter (*yezer ha-ra*). Today he says to
> him, "Do this"; tomorrow he tells him, "Do that," until
> he bids him, "Go and serve idols," and he goes and
> serves [them]. R. Abin observed: What verse [intimates
> this]? "There shall be no strange god in thee; neither
> shall you worship any strange god" (Psalms 81:10).
> Who is the strange god that resides in man himself?
> That is the Tempter.[17]

The difference between the Talmudic text and
Maimonides' insight is remarkable. For R. Simeon b. Eleazar,
anger and idolatry are not one and the same. R. Simeon
is concerned about the loss of self control which anger betrays.
A lack of moral discipline initially leads to minor lapses,
but may ultimately degenerate into a total breakdown of moral
and religious values. Psalms 81:10 reinforces this concern.

---

[16] N. L. Rabinovitch, *Yad Peshutah, Hilkhot De'ot* (Jerusalem, 1987), 40-41.

[17] Translation in *The Babylonian Talmud, Seder Mo'ed*, vol. 1, trans.
H. Freedman (Soncino Press, 1938), 510.

The "foreign god" of unfettered, angry self-indulgence will eventually metamorphose into the "alien god" of idolatry.

Maimonides, however, sees these two mental aberrations not as discrete points in a time continuum – one lapse will gradually lead to the other – but as identical. Anger consists in worshiping a foreign god because in some sense (to be clarified) it represents oblivion to the One. The two parts of Psalms 81:10 are read as a parallelism. Allowing the strange god within – the *yezer ha-ra* – to predominate, is an act of idolatry. *Yezer ha-ra*, according to Maimonides' comments on *Berakhot* 9:5, consists precisely in such eruption of anger and irascibility, and Psalms 81:10 treats this outburst, according to Maimonides' reading, as a religious defection. It remains to elucidate the sense in which Maimonides considers anger as "idolatrous."

A passage which should be considered in this connection is that very comment to *Berakhot* 9:5. The Mishnah says that one should offer a blessing to God when one experiences the bad (when one recites, "blessed are You, the True Judge") as well as when one experiences the good (when one recites "blessed are You, Who is good and does good"). A biblical text (Deut. 6:5) and its exegesis is offered by the Mishnah as proof for its precept. "And you shall love the Lord your God with all your heart, and with all your soul, and with all your *me'od.*" The rabbinic exegesis ensues, "with all your heart" – with your two inclinations (*yezarim*), the good and the bad; "and with all your soul" – even if He takes away your soul; "and with all your *me'od*" – with your money. Another interpretation for "and with all your *me'od*" – in regard to every measure (*middah*) that He metes out to you, acknowledge Him verily (*me'od*) in everything.

Maimonides' comments to *Berakhot* 9:5 can be read as a short, coherent essay, highlighting the philosophical and ethical issues in the Mishnah. He begins by epitomizing the Mishnah's thesis: there is "good" in everything which God generates, whether it is immediately fathomed or not, a notion discussed at length in *Guide* III:43 and III:25. In light of this "good," grief is an inappropriate response. The rabbinic perspective on Deuteronomy 6:5 is introduced with the idea that "everything which befalls one in this world, be it favorable or evil, should be perceived as a proximate cause for the attainment of true bliss" – a paraphrase of the fifth of the "Eight Chapters." With this leading sentence, Maimonides proceeds to focus on two elements of the rabbinic comment, and to collate them into a unified statement.

> [Love God ... with both the good and bad inclinations,] that is to say, that he should put in his heart a love of God and faith in Him, even at a time of rebelliousness and anger and resentment, for all this is the evil inclination – *yezer ha-ra* – as the Rabbis said, "in all your ways will you know Him" (Proverbs 3:6) – even concerning a matter of transgression.

Immediately following this comment, he adds:

> And the explanation of *middah*, is way. That is to say, in whatever situation you will be, praise Him and thank Him. (The unmentioned referent is, of course, the rabbinic comment on "your *me'od*" – in regard to every measure – *middah* – acknowledge Him verily.)

Having established the common theme running through the different parts of the Mishnah, Maimonides may now go on to integrate his two comments – on the two *yezarim* and on *middah* – into one thematic unit.

Loving God "at a time of *yezer ha-ra*" refers to a time when one finds oneself beset by anger or resentment. Anger or resentment may be a response to natural causes, which, according to *Guide* II:48, are to be viewed as "acts of God." But the anger may be a reaction as well to human provocation, such as a time when one experiences a hurt caused through another's insult, for example, or worse. "In all your ways you will know Him," in these circumstances means that this particular anger-producing situation, too, should be related theocentrically. Joseph's view of his brothers' folly as God's work (Genesis 48:7) and David's acquiescence in the defiance of political foes (2 Samuel 16:10) are two of Maimonides' examples (*Guide* II:48) for a "loving" relationship to the Source; in other words, a knowledge of God in all "His ways," instead of venting anger and resentment. Even volitional acts by antagonists should be traced back to the First Cause, Maimonides insists in *Guide* II:48,[18] a chapter which he considers the most important in the *Guide*. Taken moralistically, these provocations are outrageous. Taken religiously, theocentrically, they reflect God's Will executed through His messengers. Maimonides maintains that the moralistic response needs to be suppressed in favor of the religious one.[19]

To vent anger – rather than to relate to Him through His "ways" – is "idolatry." The worship of an "alien God" through an angry outburst, consists in relating to the anger-provoking situation as an independent reality, rather than as rooted in the Source. The resentment expressed through anger is a resentment of God, hence "idolatrous."[20]

---

[18] *Sefer ha-Hinnukh*, in his attempt to explain the prohibition against vindictiveness (precept 241), seems to apply Maimonides' reasoning in *Guide* II:48 practically as well, not merely theoretically. Appearances notwithstanding, it is not the individual actor's free will that is responsible for the harm done, but God's Will exclusively. (Maimonides too insists in *Guide* II:48 that the actor's free will is frustrated by the Divine in the examples he cites.) The "human" provocation is really a message from God, penalizing one for a sin. Like Maimonides, the author of the *Hinnukh* points to David's encounter with Shim'i ben Gera as an example of how David related to the Sender and not to the human agent. Maimonides' deep influence on *Sefer ha-Hinnukh* was documented by the author himself in his introductory letter. See also *Sefer ha-Hinnukh*, vol. 1 (Jerusalem: Makhon Yerushalayim, 1988), 16, where much further corroboration is provided for *Sefer ha-Hinnukh*'s dependence on Maimonides, including the *Guide of the Perplexed*.

[19] On the apparent "passivity" of this approach, see end of n. 83.

[20] The term "idolatry" is used differently here and in Daniel Frank's article, "Anger as a Vice: A Maimonidean Critique of Aristotle's *Ethics*," *History of Philosophy Quarterly* 7:3 (July 1990): 269-81. For Frank (278), the injunction against anger as idolatry is ultimately related to a new ethical

Love of God, as we just saw in the *Commentary on the Mishnah* (*Berakhot* 9:5), consists in acquiescence in God's Will. This sense carries over to *Hilkhot De'ot* 2:3, where the rabbinic statement (*Yoma* 23a, *Gittin* 36b) about the "lovers of God" who "are insulted and do not respond in kind," is focused by Maimonides on the *zaddikim*. It is Maimonides who adds the term *zaddikim* to the rabbinic statement.[21]

Zaddik now emerges as the term that (alongside *hasid*) epitomizes a theocentric stance – rather than a self-interested, self-centered one – in relating to one's

---

standard, imitation of God's ways. For us, idolatry and anger are actually coterminous.

[21] According to Gershom Scholem in his essay, "Three Types of Jewish Piety," *Eranos – Jahrbuch 1969*, vol. 38 (Rhein-Verlag Zürich: 1972): 341-43, there is a distinction between a *zaddik* and a *hasid* in the ethical literature of Judaism. Being a *zaddik* means less than being a *hasid*. "Whereas the Zaddik is the ideal embodiment of the *norm*, the Hasid is the exceptional type of man. He is the radical Jew who, in trying to follow the spiritual call, goes to extremes." One's "imperviousness to insult and the bearing of shame without flinching" is perceived as a trait of the *hasid*. Clearly, Maimonides does not make this terminological distinction here. The *hasid* and *middat hasidut* of *Hilkhot De'ot* I:5 are here (end of *Hilkhot De'ot* 2:3) characterized by the term *zaddik*. Scholem, however, cites Maimonides (*Commentary on Avot* 5:7; Scholem apparently employs the numbering of *mishnayot* in *Avot* which appears in the Vilna Talmud, not in the edition of Maimonides' *Commentary on Avot* published by Mossad ha-Rav-Kook, nor in that published by Yosef Kafih) as distinguishing between a *zaddik* who gives equal attention to every commandment and a *hasid*, "who singles out one commandment in order to exalt it, to go to extremes in its performance and thus leave the middle road." But Maimonides does not make this terminological distinction in the alleged source. Nor does Scholem's distinction between *zaddik* and *hasid* appear in Maimonides' *Commentary on Avot* 5:10-14 where he discusses the distinction between *hasid* and other terms (not *zaddik*) and the *hasid* there is not depicted in the same way as Scholem would have Maimonides depict him. Furthermore, the term *hakham* with which *Avot* 5:7 is concerned, is more relevant to the first type of Jewish piety – in contradistinction to the *zaddik* and *hasid*. Scholem's formulation of Maimonides' *hasid* is however reminiscent of Maimonides' account in his comments on *Makkot* 3:17.

For another approach, see Isaiah Tishby, *Mishnat ha-Zohar*, vol. 2 (Jerusalem, 1975), 655-58 (specifically, 656 n. 6), who points out that often Maimonides, as well as other medieval ethical writers, uses *zaddik* and *hasid* interchangeably.

environment. Though invoked by Maimonides in context of total eradication of anger, it is equally applicable to total eradication of pride. Anger, after all, is injured pride – an aspect of "*havlei ha-zeman*" – which we will find Maimonides present as the "insignificant matters," such as hurt, pride, self-satisfaction, angry resentment and so on.

Two *Mishneh Torah* passages will now be cited. The first (*Hilkhot Mezuzah* 6:13) formulates the theme of the theo-centric stance abstractly, the second (*Hilkhot De'ot* 7:7), concretely.

At the end of the *Laws of Mezuzah*, Maimonides suggests a symbolical explanation for the mnemonic sign placed on the doorpost.

> Whenever one enters and exits, one will encounter the unity of God's name, will recall His love, and awaken from his slumber and consuming preoccupation (*shegiyotav*) with meaningless temporal concerns (*havlei ha-zeman*). Let one know that there is nothing that endures eternally, save knowing the Rock of the World (*Zur ha-olam*). [Recognizing that] one will imme-diately retrieve one's (religious) awareness (*hozer leda'ato*)....

Going in and out of one's home – experiencing domestic or public situations – one is reminded to maintain a perspec-tive: to focus on the eternal reality of *Zur ha-olam*, even as one fights the great attraction of *havlei ha-zeman*. The term "*havlei ha'olam*" is defined by Maimonides (*Laws of Forbidden Rela-tions* 13:15) as either apprehension or fear in the face of tem-poral provocation or the desire for self-aggrandizement in a time of leisure. These preoccupations should be rechanneled to *Zur ha-olam*. *Zur ha-olam* as an appellation for God, refers, according to *Guide* I:16, to His being the "principle and the efficient cause of all things other than Himself."[22]

---

[22] *The Guide of the Perplexed*, vol. 1, 42.

The second *Mishneh Torah* passage (*Hilkhot De'ot* 7:7) reads:

> He who takes vengeance of his fellow, violates the pro-
> hibition of "You shall not take vengeance" (Lev.19:18)
> and though one is not flogged for the violation, it is an
> extremely evil inclination. It behooves one rather to re-
> strain one's inclination (*leha'avir al midotav*) in all tem-
> poral matters (*divrei ha-olam*). Everything, for those
> who understand (*ha-mevinim*), is meaningless (*hevel*)
> and illusory (*havai*), and not worthwhile to take revenge
> because of it ... Thus did David say by virtue of his
> good ethical traits (*be-de'otav ha-tovot*), "Did I repay my
> [former] friend [who turned against me] in kind, or did I
> not rescue my enemy though he was undeserving?"
> (Psalms 7:5) [David said this in illustration of his asser-
> tion that his hands do not bear the guilt of wrongdoing,
> 7:4.]

David emerges in this passage as an exemplar. He is among those who understand that his social or personal frustrations are an aspect of an illusory reality and point higher ("*ha-mevinim*").[23] That his trusted ally turned against him is

---

[23] The discussion in the body of the text of David's deep understanding of the higher spiritual dimension on which he is to focus may be correlated with Maimonides' epistle on his own suppression of anger (Moses Maimonides, *Iggerot*, ed. D. Z. Baneth [Jerusalem, 1985], 89, 90; *Iggerot ha-Rambam*, vol. 1, ed. Y. Shilat [Jerusalem, 1987], 420-22). Maimonides says that it behooves one who wishes to be truly human to contemplate how he could improve his ethical qualities and acquire intellectual traits rather than preoccupy his mind with vanity, e.g., being vindictive. Accordingly, *Hilkhot De'ot* 7:7 addresses itself precisely to the ethical, intellectual-spiritual modes of transcendence of revenge.

Another epistle (Epistle 6; Baneth, 63-64, 75, 79; Shilat, vol. 1, 308-09) seems to confirm our interpretation of *Hilkhot De'ot* 7:7 in the sense of moving from an illusory reality to a higher, Divine realm. Maimonides pleads with his disciple to emulate him, to take abuse, not be abusive in return, and not speak irresponsibly. Then he appears to immediately ex-plain: Visualize God before you first, and the censure of your critics last. (Note that while *Hilkhot De'ot* 7:7 concerns itself with ethical and intellectual-spiritual goals, *Hilkhot De'ot* 7:8 deals with ethical-social motives exclusively.)

meaningful only from a temporal perspective (it consists in
"*havlei ha-zeman*"). Its ultimate significance lies elsewhere, in a
different dimension.

The higher dimension on which David focuses is expli-
cated by Maimonides when he invokes a provocation analogous
to Psalms 7:5, in *Guide* II:48. Among the examples of Divine
Will determining human volition is the account of Shim'i son of
Gera verbally abusing King David and stoning him (2 Samuel
16:5-8).[24] Responding to his bodyguard's impulse to behead
the rebel (16:9), the king says that Shim'i curses because "the
Lord said to him, curse David," (16:10) and demands that his
offender be left alone.

Finally, it should be noted that the term *ha-mevin* or *ha-mevinim* (in *Hilkhot
De'ot* 7:7 as well), is frequently related, according to I. Twersky (*Introduction to the Code of Maimonides* (New Haven: Yale University Press, 1980),
471 n. 284), to the one who apprehends esoteric allusions in Maimonides'
writings. For our purposes, it is intriguing to pursue Twersky's citation (in
the above-mentioned n. 284) from *Teshuvot ha-Rambam*, vol. 2, ed. J. Blau
(Jerusalem, 1989), no. 436, p.715. A careful reading of the context, taking
account of the apparent incongruity of "*litol*" (or "*limol*"), the meaning of the
"way of truth" (see B. Safran, "Maimonides on Free Will, Determinism and
Esotericism"), n. 16 of the responsum referring to the beginning of *Hilkhot
De'ot* instead of *Hilkhot Teshuvah* 5:4 – and the link to esotericism – would
reinforce the connection (in *Hilkhot De'ot* 7:7) between *ha-mevinim* and a
theocentric perspective on "human" provocation.

Ha-mevinim in *Hilkhot De'ot* 7:7 should then certainly not be interpreted as
Stoic philosophers who are aware of the pettiness of those things that most
frequently provoke our anger (see the passages from Seneca quoted in
S. Schimmel, 102-3), but rather as *hasidim* moved by Maimonides' religious motives. Analogously, Maimonides' own forgiving attitude and
patience in the face of human abusiveness, a patience motivated by "[age,
experience and] philosophical speculation," should similarly be explained
in terms of the theocentric vantage point rather than as a mere philosophical moral stance. (However, see Baneth, 49, note to line 5; *Iggerot
ha-Rambam*, trans. and ed. Yosef Kafih [Jerusalem, 1987], 125 n. 4.
Kafih's reference to *Guide* III:51 pertains only to the intellectual perfection
that comes with age, "when the faculties of the body are weakened and the
fire of the desires is quenched.")

[24] This incident was already mentioned in note 18 and in the body of the
text covering that note. It is repeated here for a somewhat more detailed
account of its relevance to *dumiyah*.

Focusing on the Divine Will activating the proximate causes, David "blocked out thoughts" of anger and resentment at the provocation. He hears not "meaningless" curses, but is among those who understand *(ha-mevinim)* the confrontation as a summons to connect with the Divine Cause. David may or may not perceive the message implicit in the event *(Guide* 11:18), but understands *(Guide* III:25) that it emanates from the wise, purposive will of the Creator.[25] It is to Him that he relates; it is He that he contemplates.

Maimonides relates this religious attitude of "blocking out" and "connecting" to the root *dom*, whose noun form is *dumiyah.*

Interpreting the Mishnah *(Avot* 3:3) that portrays one engaged in Torah all by himself, Maimonides begins by focusing on the term *dom*, in the biblical prooftext. Lamentations 3:28 is adduced by the Mishnah to evoke the loneliness of one *osek ba-Torah* – a person preoccupied with Torah. "He will sit alone and be silent *(ve-yidom)*, because he accepted upon himself [keeping the Torah]." *Ve-yidom* is explained by Maimonides as being silent and is linked up with Leviticus 10:3, *"va-yidom Aharon"* – and Aaron was silent. But that does not exhaust the sense of the term. Maimonides goes on to cite the *Targum*'s comment that Aaron's silence in the face of his children's death was deemed praise. The *Targum* translates "and Aaron was silent," as "and Aaron praised *(ve-shabbah).*"[26] Finally, considering the latter part of the verse

---

[25] According to *Sefer ha-Hinnukh*, the message was a penalty for sins.

[26] A resemblance between Maimonides' comments on *Avot* 3:3 and those of Rabbi Menahem ha-Me'iri *(Beit ha-Behirah* on *Avot* 3:3), although they both cite the *Targum* for *dom*, is only superficial. While Me'iri interprets *dumiyah* as speech of praise, Maimonides stresses acquiescence in faith. A very careful reading of Maimonides' *Commentary on Avot* 3:3 would corroborate this observation. See *Mishnah Im Perush Mosheh ben Maimon*, vol.1, ed. M. D. Rabinovitz (Jerusalem: Mossad ha-Rav Kook, 1961), 73 n. 2; *Mishnah Im Perush Mosheh ben Maimon, Seder Nezikin*, trans. and ed. Yosef Kafih (Jerusalem: Mossad ha-Rav Kook, 1965), 281 n. 5.

from Lamentations – "because he accepted upon himself" –
Maimonides observes: "it is as if the acceptance of the Torah is
incumbent upon him exclusively."

Maimonides' first encounter with the term *dom* is
highly suggestive. His invocation of Leviticus 10:3 and its
Targumic interpretation – silence in the face of adversity is
tantamount to religious praise – suggests that Lamentations
3:28 is also to be considered in its own thematic context,
acquiescence in the tragedy of destruction.[27] His last
comment intimates that the Mishnah's protagonist's lonely
preoccupation with Torah (*osek ba-Torah*) consists in just such
acquiescence to the Divine Will.

Maimonides' citation not only of verses, but implicitly of
their context as well, as we have seen,[28] is a crucial medium
for communicating his message, making the larger frame of
Lamentations 3:28 highly instructive.

---

[27] *Dom* and *dumiyah* have been selected as the appropriate terms to
epitomize Maimonides' stress on silent acquiescence for several reasons.
Aside from his suggestive citation of *va-yidom Aharon*, there is his
development of the theme of "listening, being silent (*dumah*), and enduring"
the Arab provocations, at the end of the "Epistle to Yemen" (see A. Halkin,
ed., *Iggeret Teiman* (New York, 1952), 96-97 n. 142). There is reference in
the body of the text of this article to *Gittin* 7a, which employs the root *dom*
in Maimonides' sense. Another Talmudic passage, which Maimonides
appears to have internalized, is *Berakhot* 17a, "to those who curse me, let
my soul be silent – *nafshi tidom*." While he does not quote this passage
explicitly, echoes of this Talmudic phrase resonate in his letters. See A. J.
Heschel, "Did Maimonides Believe that He Had Attained the Rank
of Prophet?" [Hebrew] *Jubilee Volume in Honor of Louis Ginzberg*, vol. 2
(New York, 1950), 178 and notes; Shilat, vol. 1, 304, particularly line 8,
and notes; Shilat, vol. 2, 436.

Once these above-mentioned passages are considered, the usage of
dumiyah in *Guide* I:59 may be invoked as well, and then related to
Guide III:51, i.e., to contemplation without words as the truest sense of
avodah. (I am grateful to Prof. Warren Harvey for suggesting the inclusion
of *Guide* I:59 and *Guide* III:51 in this discussion).

[28] See note 13.

Notwithstanding excruciating suffering and helplessness (Lamentations 3:1-21), the Jeremiad still manages to exude hope in God's compassion and expected salvation (3:22-26). Verse 27 commended the person who has borne a yoke from early youth, thus becoming – in the larger context of the chapter – an early initiate in bearing his burdens with equanimity. The cited verse 28, describes this person's lonely acquiescence in God's Will, his struggle to be engaged in Torah, i.e., as Maimonides implies, in a reality generated by God's "commanding" presence. This unstinting, unresenting acquiescence is the ultimate praise of God. The meaning Maimonides assigns to this verse provides direction and focus for those that follow.

The person who "praises" God will place his mouth in the dust – i.e., will bite his plaintive tongue – for there is yet hope (3:29). He will even offer a cheek to his tormentor (3:30), knowing that God will not abandon him (3:31). For even if He chastises, He will yet have compassion (3:32). The tormentor did not persecute of his own heart's desire (3:33). It was the Will of God. When the tormentor subdued his prisoners (3:34), it was in order that the focus of their trial be shifted to the presence on High (3:35). It is God who is judging, not the persecutor – and the attention of the one tried should be riveted on Him. God did not intend to set man off course through his trial (3:36). Staying on course requires one to consider: who would cause something to be if God had not commanded it? (3:37). From the mouth of the One on High will not emanate both evils and good (3:38). Only good emanates from Him, and in hopeful acquiescence – rather than desperate resignation – man connects with His will, the Source of good. In what can a living person find pain? In errancy from God (3:39). Let us therefore search our ways and return to God (3:40), raising our head to God in Heaven (3:41).

These verses read in light of Maimonides' comment to *Avot* 3:3 and further elucidated by *Guide* II:48 and *Hilkhot Teshuvah* 5:2, concretize his understanding of *dumiyah* as a religious stance. *Dumiyah* – in fact, and in the contexts Maimonides evokes – means both silence and hope.[29]

Maimonides' notion of *dumiyah* reflects his presumed understanding of a Talmudic anecdote which employs the term *dom* and its thematic associations as its central motif.

A story is told (*Gittin* 7a) of Mar Ukva soliciting R. Eleazar's counsel regarding a distressing personal situation. "Certain men are annoying me and I am able to get them into trouble with the government, shall I do so?"[30] Instructed to restrain himself although the wicked is before [him], Mar Ukva insists the situation is intolerable. He is now admonished to restrain himself in the face of God and hope for relief, which comes immediately.[31]

R. Eleazar's recommendation for restraint is couched in a verse from Psalms 37:7, "be silent unto God (*dom la-Hashem*) and hope unto Him [do not be angry because of the prospering man who carries out evil schemes]."[32] Transposed into advice for coping with his present hardships, the verse implies that Mar Ukva must acquiesce. In his "silence," he should relate not to his tormentor (do not be angry at the scheming man) but to

---

[29] For biblical parallels and kabbalistic analogues (albeit the kabbalistic are more far reaching) see M. Hallamish, *"Al ha-Shetikah ba-Kabbalah u-va-Hasidut,"* *Dat ve-Safah*, ed. M. Hallamish (Israel, 1981), 80, 87.

[30] The translations in this paragraph are from *The Babylonian Talmud, Seder Nashim IV, Gittin*, trans. M. Simon (Soncino Press, 1936), 22.

[31] The Talmudic story ends with the detail that in the heels of Mar Ukva's presumed acquiescence, the provocateur is to be punished. Maimonides too reflects this belief when in one of his epistles (Shilat, vol. 1, 304), he cites another Talmudic phrase (*Berakhot* 19a), that (following *dumiyah*) God Himself avenges the honor of a Torah scholar.

[32] The bracketed part of the verse is not cited in the Talmudic passage, but the larger context sheds light on the spirit of R. Eleazar's counsel.

the Divine Will (be silent in the face of God) who is alone responsible for Mar Ukva's plight.

Maimonides' directive of *dumiyah*, to acquiesce in the work of the Divinely directed messenger – is a theoretical account of R. Eleazar's prescription. R. Eleazar too, is advising his questioner to strip the irritating experience of its natural, "realistic" trappings and convert it into an image of the Divine – "be silent unto God." Mar Ukva is instructed to train his mind that confronting him is not the troublemaker, who is only an agent, but rather his Sender.[33]

---

[33] The Tosafists, *ad loc.*, offer a different interpretation of the root *dom*. However, it would seem that in context of two subsequent passages involving *domem* in *Gittin* 7a – in close proximity to the Mar Ukva passage – *dumiyah* as acquiescence is a most plausible meaning. (This "contextual" point is made in passing by Maharam Schiff, *ad loc.*) Significantly, *dom* of Psalms 37:7 is juxtaposed in *Zevahim* 115b with the acquiescence of "*va-yidom Aharon.*"

Maimonides' presumed reading of the Mar Ukva passage is echoed in a later writing. *Dom* and *hitholel* are apparently understood as acquiescence achieved through self "deadening" (*hithalelut*). Mar Ukva's preoccupation with the antagonist (*atah rozeh she-titpa'eil mi-menu*) should be related rather to God (who is the Source; *hityahes lo yitbarakh*) and not turn to self-indulgence (*ve-lo le-azmekha*). The writer, through an allusive presentation, seeks to resolve "all the feelings" (*kol ha-hargashot*) which occur in this passage. See *Hiddushei Ge'onim* (*Iyei ha-Yam*) on *Ein Ya'akov, Gittin*, part 3 (Israel, 1973), 2 (bottom) – 5 (top).

As was indicated at the beginning of this note, there are two other passages in *Gittin* 7a, in proximity to the Mar Ukva passage, which deal with the state of *dumiyah*. The first is: "Whoever has cause for indignation against his neighbor and yet holds his peace (*domem*), He that abides for all eternity shall espouse his cause." In terms which are reminiscent of our account of Maimonides' conception, *Iyun Ya'akov* (*Ein Ya'akov*, 3) explains that God takes up the cudgels for the victim because he transports himself from "this world" to a higher "next world." See, in this connection, Rabbi Judah Loew of Prague's comment to the Mar Ukva passage in, "*Netiv ha-Bittahon*," *Netivot Olam*, part 2 (New York, 1969), 235. Through the trust of *dumiyah*, an individual gives himself over to God. His personal struggle then becomes God's struggle and he prevails because (the realm of) trust transcends (the realm of) reason.

Our focus on the Mar Ukva passage is a theological one. For halakhic perspectives, see *Ozar Mefarshei ha-Talmud, Gittin*, part 1 (Jerusalem: Makhon Yerushalayim, 1998), 275-78, 291-92.

– II –

The way of the *hasid* is a radical ethic.[34] It is not the generally accepted standard of behavior in society, even in Halakhah.[35] This can be exemplified within Maimonides' writing. In *Guide* II:48 he views Shim'i ben Gera's abuse of King David as traceable to God's Will and implies that the appropriate response is to acquiesce in God's "ways," i.e., to leave Shim'i alone. Yet in *Hilkhot Melakhim* 3:8 he points to Shim'i ben Gera as the paradigmatic example of a rebel against the king: "Whoever rebels against the king of Israel, the king has license to execute him ... Similarly, whoever humiliates the king or abuses him verbally, the king has license to execute him, as [in the case of] Shim'i ben Gera."

To cite a Talmudic example of the dissonance between the ways of the *hakham* and the *hasid*: In the larger context of the Mar Ukva passage mentioned earlier (*Gittin* 7a), the Talmud speaks of other applications of *dom*: "Whoever has

---

[34] See note 21.

[35] For an exposition of the various definitions in rabbinic literature of the *hasid*, see E. Urbach's article on *hasidim* in *Encyclopedia Judaica*. The image of the *hasid* was not identical at all times during the rabbinic period. The sources reflect the diversity of religious types, each distinguished in its own way, but "common to all is a divergence from what was regarded as conventional behavior and the normal standard." Concerning the theme discussed in our article, shows Urbach, the term *hasid* came to refer to an exemplary temperament. "He whom it is hard to provoke and easy to pacify is a *hasid*" (*Avot* 5:11). R. Alexandri said that "whoever hears someone curse him and keeps silent is called a *hasid*" (*Midrash on Psalms* 16:11). For a bibliography and brief highlighting of the phenomenon of hasidism through the ages, see A. Kirschenbaum, 9-10.

Maimonides does not simply reproduce these rabbinic statements and others; rather, he places them into a coherent system, makes them legitimate halakhic options, and in incorporating them into his halakhic code, he endows them with a weightiness, a binding force and a wide currency. (See I. Twersky, *Introduction*, 461-62; A. Kirschenbaum, 31-38.) Arguably, Maimonides converted hasidic doctrine from something esoteric to a potential socio-cultural phenomenon and in this way may have contributed to a spiritual reorientation. (I am indebted to Prof. Moshe Idel for the observations in this paragraph.)

cause for indignation against his neighbor and yet holds his peace (*domem*), He that abides for all eternity shall espouse his cause ... If a man has just cause of complaint against his neighbor for taking away his livelihood and yet holds his peace (*domem*), He that abides in the [burning] bush will espouse his cause."[36] Rashi explains the offense in the latter case: "he robs him, depriving him of his sustenance."

These unique formulations of hasidic acquiescence in the Talmud run counter to the general spirit of biblical and Talmudic jurisprudence and the legal codes, which state that one may seek relief from the courts when one is robbed or exploited.[37] Halakhah in these cases reflects the orientation of the *hakham*.[38] In his own way, the *hakham* seeks a

---

[36] Translations are from *The Babylonian Talmud*, Gittin, 23.

[37] Commenting on the second instance of *domem* in *Gittin* 7a, a translator and interpreter of the Talmud opines that "the Gemara would seem to be speaking here of someone who cannot seek relief from the courts either because his grievance – though justified – is not something for which the courts can intervene, or because he lacks sufficient evidence for the courts to act." See *Talmud Bavli, Gittin*, vol. 1, trans. Y. Isbee (New York: Mesorah Publications, 1993), 7a[(2)]. However, since we have here a sweeping statement, unqualified (by whether the court can intervene or whether there is sufficient evidence), it seems more plausible to assume that the individual in question is a *hasid* in *dumiyah* who does not avail himself of the resources of the court.

This is corroborated by *Iyun Ya'akov* (3), who, concerning the previous *domem*, writes that he forfeits the opportunity to have his grievance redressed by a mundane court (*zeh lo hafez be-din shel mattah ve-eino zo'ek alav le-din*); consequently God fights for his claim through a heavenly judgment, *din le-ma'alah*. Another perspective on this first *domem*, says *Iyun Ya'akov*, is that he is "other-worldly": he suppresses the "jealous" inclination to assert his self-interest. God, therefore, acts for him. It would stand to reason that these selfsame self-effacing traits of the first *domem* are shared by the second and indeed, *Iyun Ya'akov* (4) pursues this line of thinking and describes the latter *domem* too as surrendering his just claim (*shotek*), walking the spiritual hasidic track instead. Silent, he trusts that God's providence extends to those who have been humbled and that He will provide his sustenance from another place.

For ostensibly similar approaches to the second *domem*, see *Ozar Mefarshei ha-Talmud*, 283 n. 72.

[38] See note 11.

relationship with the Divine, but does not insist on a direct experience of Him through His "mediating" ways[39] (except in prayer and fasting in response to troubles besetting the community or the individual).[40]

But the religious mind evolves, according to Maimonides.[41] Explaining why Jews had to be redirected only gradually from the pagan sacrificial cult to which they were exposed, Maimonides says that banning sacrifices abruptly would have been useless. It would have been analogous

> to the appearance of a prophet in these times who, calling upon the people to worship God, would say: "God has given you a law forbidding you to pray to Him, to fast, to call upon Him for help in misfortune. Your worship should consist solely in meditation without any works at all." Therefore He, may He be exalted, suffered the ... kinds of [pagan] worship to remain, but transferred them from ... unreal things to His own Name, may He be exalted, commanding us to practice them with regard to Him, make He be exalted (*Guide* III:32).[42]

One may infer that the imagined message of the prophet "in these times" is an ideal for Maimonides. But why? Is prayer and fasting in time of need not the way of relating to the Divine efficaciously?[43] It would appear that the higher mode of religious service, which the prophet teaches, is connecting with God through His "mediating ways." Prayer and fasting relate to the undesirable mundane reality as a challenge to be overcome; the *hasid* in *dumiyah*, however, perceives this reality as God Himself, focusing on its source.[44] This focus on God's

---

[39] See the discussion on "mediating ways" in the next section.

[40] See *Hilkhot Ta'aniyot* 1:1-4.

[41] See the discussion by M. Kellner, *Maimonides on the "Decline of the Generations" and the Nature of Rabbinic Authority* (Albany, NY, 1996), 70-75, 78-79.

[42] *The Guide of the Perplexed*, vol.2, 526.

[43] See note 40.

[44] See note 67.

"mediating ways" is amplified by Maimonides in his account of Exodus 33:13-23, where the individual's religious struggle is accentuated. While God may not be conceived in His essence (*Guide* I:54 and I:21) and Moses' request to know Him as such cannot be granted (Exodus 33:20), there is a spiritual station (*makom*: Exodus 33:21, *Guide* I:8) to which Moses may yet attain.

He should stand (*nizavta*) on the Rock (33:21). And when God's "honor" passes, he will be placed in the deep crevice of the Rock, protected all the while by God's "palm" (33:22). God will then remove His "palm," enabling Moses to see His "rear" (*ahor*), but His face (essence) will not be seen (33:23).

Nizavta – you will stand – is related by Maimonides (*Guide* I:15) to the meaning he assigns to *amod* (*Guide* I:13), namely, to be stable, to endure, to withstand. Exposed to "all God's ways" (33:19), identical with God's "honor" (in the first sense of *Guide* I:64), he is assured of a spiritual station (*makom*). Being there, he can endure "all God's ways" upon the Rock, i.e., by relating his experiences to the *Zur*,

> the principle and the efficient cause of all things.... The verse "And thou shalt stand erect upon the rock," means, Rely upon, and be firm in considering, God, may He be exalted, as the first principle. This is the entryway through which you shall come to Him, as we have made clear when speaking of His saying (to Moses), "Behold there is a place by Me" (*Guide* I:16).[45]

This last reference ('as we have made clear') is to the immediately preceding *Guide* I:15:

> "[God] stood erect upon it" signifies God's being stable, permanent and constant; not the erect position of a body. The same meaning is to be found in the verse: "And thou shalt stand erect upon the rock."

---

[45] *The Guide of the Perplexed*, vol. 1, 42. Compare with *Hilkhot Teshuvah* 3:7: "one must affirm that God is ... *Zur la-kol*."

This "same" meaning is that "standing upon the Rock," Moses should aim to maintain his stability – to endure and to withstand – even if God's "ways" appear challenging.

The upshot of the lesson of the Rock is that in effect, the endurance, the acquiescence modeled on God's *haninah* (Exodus 33:19, 34:6) is intimately coupled with a relationship to the *Zur* , the first principle (Exodus 33:21-22). It is not, in Maimonides' view, a quietist stance, but an intensely active attempt by the individual to find stability through struggling to remain with the Source – rather than to lapse into anger or resentment. Standing on the Rock for Moses represents the "entryway through which to come to Him."[46]

Moses finds himself comfortably ensconced in the depth of this Rock when God protectively covers him (Exodus 33:22). But even after God's "palm" is temporarily withdrawn and it initially feels as if God "had turned [His] back, because of [his perceived] remoteness from the existence of God" *Guide* (I:37),[47] even then Moses should realize that he is actually in communication with God's *ahor* (Exodus 33:23), i.e., with things that follow necessarily from His will:

> In this sense it is said: And thou shalt see My back, which means that thou shalt apprehend what follows Me, has come to be like Me, and follows necessarily from My will – that is, all the things created by Me (*Guide* I:38).[48]

If we now reflect about the totality of the revelation vouchsafed to Moses, we need to re-integrate the various interpretive fragments (different chapters in the *Guide*) dealing with

---

[46] Compare with H. Kasher, "Maimonides' Interpretations of the Story of the Divine Revelation in the Cleft of the Rock," [Hebrew] *Da'at* 35 (Summer 1995): 43.

[47] *The Guide of the Perplexed*, vol. 1, 86.

[48] Ibid., 87.

the insights he had apprehended (in reference to Exodus 33:13-23) and relate them to each other.

What emerges is that the lessons were two-tiered: some were for Moses and some for the people. Moses succeeded in intuiting the coherence and inherent meaningfulness of "all of God's ways" (33:19, *Guide* I:54).[49] He grasped "their nature and the way they are mutually connected so that he will know how He governs them in general and in detail."[50] Only Mosaic prophecy could fathom these depths: "He is trusted in all My house,"[51] that is, he has grasped the existence of all My world with a true and firmly established understanding."[52] With this prophetic conviction of God's goodness which is expressed in His world (Gen. 1:31 is invoked here in relation to Exodus 33:19 – "all of [God's] goodness" – and twice in *Guide* III:25), Moses has an advantage. It is true that he may know only God's attributes of action, His "ways" and not His essence, but he can always struggle to discover the underlying Divine goodness inherent in the "ways," which he is now confident he will find. The "*ahor*" may sometimes appear threatening, but always holds out the promise of spiritual rejuvenation if he will "stand" on the "Rock."

What is there in all of this for the people? "Consider that this nation is [Your] people" (Exodus 33:13), Moses pleads. To this end, I need to know You, i.e., Your ways, because "I need to perform actions that I must seek to make similar to [Your] actions in governing them."[53] On one level, Moses needs to know and emulate God's "ways" (thirteen attributes of Divine action) in order to rule the people as God would rule them.

---

[49] The "display to him of all existing things" is identified with the revelation of God's "ways" in *Guide* I:54.

[50] Ibid.

[51] See the context of Numbers 12:7. It introduces the notion of the superiority of Mosaic prophecy.

[52] *The Guide of the Perplexed*, vol. 1, 124.

[53] Ibid., 125.

But there is another level as well: *they* need to rule themselves according to these "ways." A strange transition at the end of *Guide* I:54 is actually very enlightening.[54] "Those [thirteen attributes of] actions are needed for the governance of cities," says Maimonides. And the very next sentence goes on to say: "For the utmost virtue of man is to become like unto Him, may He be exalted, as far as he is able; which means that we should make our actions like unto His, as the Sages made clear ... They said: He is gracious, so be you also gracious; He is merciful, so be you also merciful."[55] Maimonides seems to be saying (through this transition) that the "governance of cities" in accordance with the internalized "thirteen attributes" of the prophet-governor impacts morally on the people.[56] They learn

---

[54] H. Davidson (66 n. 122) states that at the conclusion of *Guide* I:54, "Maimonides is laying down a desideratum for all men," though Maimonides speaks earlier in *Guide* I:54 of the special applicability of walking in God's ways to the "ruler ... if he is a prophet." However, Davidson does not deal with the intent of the awkward transition at the end of *Guide* I:54.

[55] *The Guide of the Perplexed*, vol. 1, 128.

[56] Ibid., 126.

Parenthetically it might be observed that the total suppression of anger by the prophet-governor, an important theme in *Guide* I:54, may shed light on *De'ot* 2:3. In this chapter of the *Guide*, Maimonides makes it clear that not everyone is expected to eradicate their anger completely; only a Moses-like leader is expected to do so. The people are then inspired by this leader's behavior to do the same, as Maimonides implies (at the end of the chapter, according to our interpretation). This may have repercussions for *De'ot* 2:3. Total suppression of anger is presented as a categorical imperative in *De'ot* 2:3, but it ought to be read in context of other, more restrictive Maimonidean discussions on the regulation of anger, such as I:54.

Furthermore, Maimonides (in the fourth of the "Eight Chapters") explains Moses' error in Numbers 20:12 as anger; it did not behoove "someone like Moses," from whose "every motion and word" everyone was learning, to lose his calm. Relative to his moral stature and his position in the community, his lapse into anger was considered a desecration of the Name. The implication is clear – that such a penalty would not be imposed on the common people. Once again, the regulation of anger (and in the fourth chapter Maimonides discusses justified anger according to the mean, not its total suppression) may not be universally relevant. Later on in the article, the point is made that Maimonides considered the imperative of the total

to emulate God's moral traits by emulating the prophet, just as the prophet was taught to emulate God by God Himself. (It may be, in light of Maimonides' transition, that "governance of cities" or "in governing them" has a double meaning: ruling them administratively and by moral example).

The notion that the prophet-governor has ethical-spiritual influence over his community has already been articulated in Maimonides' earlier writing. In the fourth of the "Eight Chapters," he writes that unjustified anger by Moses was deemed a desecration of the Name (on his level) "because everyone learns from all of his movements and words and through them they hope to achieve bliss in this world and in the next."[57] In *Hilkhot Teshuvah* 9:2, Maimonides describes King Messiah as a wise, popular teacher of God's Way, *derekh Hashem*.[58]

In review, it follows from this discussion that when Maimonides speaks in *Guide* I:54 of the knowledge of God's actions, he means two different things. For Moses, there is a profound theoretical knowledge, apprehended prophetically, of the order and rationality of God's world. This insight has repercussions for his Rock experience. Furthermore, there is a summons to personalize the "thirteen attributes" and employ them in "governing." For the people, the "thirteen attributes"

---

eradication of anger as directed only to people like himself and his close, like-minded students. See note 83.

For other indicators which tend to limit the scope and applicability of *De'ot* 2:3 and redirect its focus, see note 82 (all of it), 83, 94 and the correlation of *zaddikim* and *behirei zadikaya* in the text of the article (as covered by notes 69, 70, and 71).

Given these considerations, already at this juncture in the article, we may perhaps anticipate, along the lines of I:54, that it may take a future King Messiah to inspire a society to emulate his own example of self-transcendence. (For much of the insight contained in this note I am indebted to Profs. Michael Shmidman and Moshe Sokol.)

57 *Mishnah Im Perush Mosheh ben Maimon, Seder Nezikin*, trans. and ed. Y. Kafih (Jerusalem: Mossad ha-Rav Kook, 1965), 255.

58 *Derekh Hashem* will be shown, later in the article, to be the way of hasidic *dumiyah.*

of Divine action, taught by the example of the prophet, are ultimately known experientially. And *haninah, erekh apayyim,* and *rav hesed* (three of the thirteen attributes) demand that one acquiesce hasidically in the face of human abusiveness.[59] God is gracious though we are undeserving (*hanun*), so must we be gracious though the provocateur is undeserving. In response, then, to his request for the revelation of God's "ways" for the people (33:13), Moses received both a picturesque and a theoretical version of the same lesson.[60] The version of the Rock came first. It presented in concrete form how God's "honor" emanating from the "Rock," sometimes beclouded by the darkness of "*ahor,*" required Moses to "stand" firmly in his "place" and not to totter.[61] This theme was conceptualized when the "thirteen attributes," particularly the three above-mentioned, were revealed abstractly for emulation (34:6).[62]

---

[59] See the elucidation of these three hasidic attributes at the very beginning of this article. The implication of these traits for Maimonides' overall conception will be spelled out at the end of the article.

[60] *The Guide of the Perplexed,* vol.1, 125. Our discussion has confirmed that Moses requests knowledge of the "ways" not just to govern, but for the people to internalize as well. 1. His own internalization of the "ways" reflects an ethical model for the people (end of *Guide* I:54 and fourth of the "Eight Chapters"). 2. "Governance of the people" therefore may imply their own self-regulation through these "thirteen attributes."

[61] On concretization of abstract ideas, see Maimonides' account in *Guide* II:31 (vol. 2, 359), on how opinions need to be "accompanied by actions that strengthen them, make them generally known, and perpetuate them among the multitude."

[62] It is possible to correlate the primacy of the hasidic acquiescence of these three traits with H. Davidson's (66-68, 71-72) claim that the directive to emulate God's attributes in the *Guide* focuses specifically on the creation of a "dispassionate" ethical personality just as God is "dispassionate." How *Hilkhot De'ot* 1:6-7 relates to this idea is discussed at the end of our article.

Actually, a close look at the thirteen attributes which Maimonides enumerates (*She'eilot u-Teshuvot Rabbeinu Mosheh ben Maimon – Pe'er ha-Dor,* ed. D. Yosef [Jerusalem: Makhon Yerushalayim, 1984], no. 90, p.194) reveals that nine of them are overtly hasidic, i.e., they are in consonance with the hasidic criterion of bestowing good on the "undeserving." With more data, more attributes could perhaps have been classified as such.

Sensitized by the Mosaic conviction of the ultimate goodness of Divine "ways," the people as well were encouraged to persevere, notwithstanding their travails, and attempt to find repose in the "crevice of the Rock."[63] The revelation of the "attributes" verbalized what Moses had already portrayed for them pictorially.

To transpose what we have just learned in terms of our previous discussion, Moses and the people learned that the experience of *"ahor"* can turn into an "entryway to God," if one combines *dumiyah* with a focus "on High." To do otherwise, i.e., to allow the "veil"[64] of resentment in the face of provocation to infiltrate the "crevice of the Rock," will create a remoteness between man and God, even as knowing God through His ways – and silencing the anger they arouse – creates closeness.

> "Show me now Thy ways, that I may know Thee" and so on (Exodus 33:13). Consider the wondrous notions contained in this dictum. For his saying, "Show me now Thy ways, that I may know Thee," indicates that God, may He be exalted, is known through His attributive qualifications; for when he would know the "ways," he would know Him. Furthermore his saying, "That I may find grace in Thy sight," indicates that he who knows God "finds grace in His sight" and not *he who merely fasts and prays*, but everyone who has knowledge of Him [in context: through His "ways"]. Accordingly, those who know Him are those who are favored by Him and permitted to come near Him, whereas those who do not know Him [through His "ways"] are objects of His wrath and are kept far away from Him. For His favor and wrath, His nearness and remoteness, correspond to the extent of a man's knowledge or ignorance [in context: of His "ways"] (*Guide* I:54).[65]

---

[63] As was already emphasized, the theology of the *Zur* was a mode of granting Moses' request to provide access for the people, too, to the "ways" of God.

[64] On "veils" see the seventh of the "Eight Chapters."

[65] *The Guide of the Perplexed*, vol. 1, 123-24.

The theme of God's "ways" being generated by the *Zur*, provoking and stimulating a religious response, was introduced in order to make intelligible a "prophetic message" (*Guide* III:32)[66] that mere prayer and fasting are inferior to "meditation without any works at all," i.e., to experiencing God's "ways" as God.[67] In the foregoing passage from the *Guide*, Maimonides spells out the definition of "meditation" explicitly: it is "knowing God through His ways" that is superior to prayer and fasting. And in *Guide* III:32 he implies (in context) that the prophet's may be a jarring message in Maimonides' time, but could conceivably be a popular teaching in a later time. When is that time?

Maimonides seems attuned to this concern, when in *Guide* I:30 he appears to embrace Jonathan ben Uziel's idea that the Messiah will communicate a new teaching.[68]

> Jonathan ben Uziel, peace be on him, translates the verse, "with joy shall ye draw water out of the wells of salvation," by the words: With joy shall you receive a new teaching from the chosen of the righteous. Consider accordingly that he interprets the word water as being the knowledge that will be received *in those days*. And he takes the Hebrew word for wells –*ma'yene* – to be the equivalent of *me'eyne ha'edah*; I mean thereby the notables who are the men of knowledge. And he says: From the chosen of the righteous, as *righteousness (zedek)* is true salvation. See accordingly how he

---

[66] See note 42.

[67] Maimonides does not mean to do away at a future time with prayer and fasting. He is suggesting that knowing Him through His "ways" will then enhance the experience of prayer and fasting. By analogy, see I. Twersky, *Introduction*, 363 n. 18. "The goal of all commandments is fear and love of God, but the consequence of this fear and love is not only *vita contemplativa* but a deepened, more sensitive, highly motivated performance of laws."

[68] That the Messiah will communicate a new teaching appears to be a theme of several *midrashim*. See *Kohelet Rabbah* 11:12; *Otiyyot de-Rabbi Akiva* in *Batei Midrashot* 2, ed. S.A. Wertheimer (Jerusalem, 1980), 367-68 n. 74; *Seder Eliyahu Zuta*, 20.

interprets every word in this verse with a view to the notion of knowledge and learning. Understand this.[69]

If we hypothesize that the "chosen of the righteous" (*behirei zadikaya*) – whose *zedek* consists in salvation – are identical with the *zaddikim* of *Hilkhot De'ot* 2:3, who un-flinchingly acquiesce in the face of God's "ways" (recalling that it is Maimonides who calls them *zaddikim*),[70] we will find con-firmation in *Guide* III:11.[71] In contrast to the anthropocentric *Guide* III:33,[72] where "mutual envy, hatred, and strife" are attributed to unrestrained hedonistic appetites, *Guide* III:11 offers a new analysis of the problem of "enmity and hatred," i.e., men do not yet have "cognition of the truth;" they do not yet have the "knowledge concerning the true reality of the Deity" that they will have in the Messianic Period.

Maimonides does not spell out the contents of that "new knowledge," but he hints at it.

---

[69] *The Guide of the Perplexed*, vol. 1, 64.

[70] See the body of the text covered by note 21. This article assumes a tense complementary relationship between the *Mishneh Torah* and the *Guide*. For this reason, both sources are integrated here. For a broader range of views on this topic, contrast the approaches of I. Twersky, *Introduction*, 447-48, 464-68; J. Levinger, "Al Ta'am ha-Nezirut be-Moreh Nevukhim," *Bar Ilan – Sefer ha-Shanah le-Mada'ei ha-Yahadut ve-ha-Ruah* 4-5 (1967): 299-305; and H. Davidson, 39-72. For an interesting perspective, see David Hen-shke, "On the Question of Unity in Maimonides' Thought," *Da'at* 37 (Sum-mer 1996): 37-51.

[71] *Guide* I:30 and *Guide* III:11 are also conjoined by Maimonides' focus on a common biblical context that is in the background of these two chapters. The messianic vision of Isaiah 11-12 pervades these chapters: Isaiah 12:3 leaves its mark on *Guide* I:30, Isaiah 11:6 and 11:9, on *Guide* III:11. It is noteworthy that R. David Kimhi, in his interpretation of Jonathan ben Uziel's comment on Isaiah 12:3, also connects Isaiah 12:3 and Isaiah 11:9.

[72] The contradiction between the anthropocentric *Guide* III:33 and the theocentric *Guide* III:11, opens up an approach through which to pursue further Yonah ben Sasson's thesis (*Tarbiz* 29 [1960]: 268-81), which he applies to the reasons of the law only, as the esoteric message of the *Guide*. Subtle contradictions are entailed in the *Guide*'s discussion, in contrast to the back-to-back contradiction in the *Mishneh Torah*, because it is in the *Guide* that some of the more sensitive theological issues are broached. See notes 8 and 9.

> If there were knowledge, whose relation to the human
> form is like that of the faculty of sight to the eye, they
> would refrain from doing any harm to themselves and
> to others. For through cognition of the truth, enmity
> and hatred are removed and the inflicting of harm by
> people on one another is abolished. It holds out this
> promise, saying: "And the wolf shall dwell with the
> lamb...."

And later,

> the cause of the abolition of these enmities ... will be
> the knowledge that men will then have concerning the
> true reality of the Deity. For it says, "They shall not
> hurt nor destroy in all My holy mountain; for the earth
> shall be full of the knowledge of the Lord, as the waters
> cover the sea." Know this.[73]

Maimonides seems to be saying that in the Messianic
Period, through knowing God by knowing His ways ("the true
reality of the Deity"), enmity and strife will be eliminated. The
offender will not be perceived as an independent reality but
rather as an agency of the Divine. In this way, "the inflicting of
harm by people on one another is abolished," the "illusory reality" of the abuser gives way to the "true reality of the Deity"
behind the abuser. (We recall that in *Guide* II:48, not only
natural occurrences are considered "acts of God," but even
human, ostensibly voluntary actions, are traced to the Divine
Will. Maimonides points out that *Guide* II:48 deserves more
attention than any other chapter of the *Guide*.) In this sense,
"they would refrain from doing any harm to themselves and
others," for they would perceive themselves not as autonomous
actors, but as functions of the Divine Will.[74]

---

[73] *The Guide of the Perplexed*, vol. 2, 441.

[74] For different emphasis in the understanding of *Guide* III:11, see A.
Ravitzky, "To the Utmost of Human Capacity: Maimonides on the Days of
the Messiah," [Hebrew] *Meshihiyut ve-Eskhotologi'ah* (Jerusalem: 1983),
193-94, 196-98; and W. Harvey, "Maimonides' Political Philosophy and its
Relevance for the State of Israel Today" (*Occasional Papers, The Dean*

But this perspective is only half of the "new teaching," which the "chosen of the righteous" convey in the Messianic Period. As it stands, it may lead to absurdities if every abuser will maintain that he is a Divine reflex. The complementary perspective, not discussed in *Guide* III:11, but in *Guide* III:17 as well as in the eighth of the "Eight Chapters" and in *Hilkhot Teshuvah* chapter 5, is the principle of free will. Maimonides, in effect, insists on an antinomy (as did R. Bahya ibn Paquda).[75] Vis-à-vis himself, the abuser is held to account; vis-à-vis his fellow, he is a Divine agent. This antinomy is at the core of *Guide* II:48 where volitional acts are traceable to the First Cause.[76]

Maimonides once again exemplifies this sort of antinomy when in *Hilkhot Melakhim* 11:4 he discusses Jesus' culpability from the perspective of his own failures, and his historical accomplishments from the perspective of God's Will. The latter are traceable to God's transcendent "thoughts and ways" (Isaiah 55:8). Elsewhere (*Hilkhot Teshuvah* 5:5), Maimonides once again maintains the antinomy of man's free will and God's inscrutable foreknowledge, again invoking Isaiah 55:8.

In pre-Messianic Days, the antinomy of human freedom, on the one hand, and Divine Will and foreknowledge, on the other hand, is theoretical; in Messianic Days people will be motivated to act on the basis of both, and notwithstanding the logical difficulty, they will "see" ("... faculty of sight to the eye," *Guide* III:11) that this orientation is the ultimate bliss.

The insights of the new messianic teaching contained in *Guide* I:30 and *Guide* III:11 were foreshadowed by Maimonides

---

Ernest Schwarcz Memorial Lecture, CUNY, Queens College, Center for Jewish Studies, 15 November 2000), 14.

[75] *Hovot ha-Levavot*, trans. and ed. Y. Kafih (Jerusalem, 1973), 172-73.

[76] Compare this suggestion with studies on *Guide* II:48 mentioned by M. Sokol, "Maimonides on Freedom of the Will and Moral Responsibility," *Harvard Theological Review* 91:1 (1998): 25 nn. 2, 8. See also J. Levinger, *Ha-Rambam ke-Filosof u-khe-Posek* (Jerusalem, 1989), 49-55.

in his comment on the Mishnah in *Eduyot* 8:7 and in the *Mishneh Torah.*

Quoting interpretively from *Eduyot* 8:7, Maimonides states in *Hilkhot Melakhim* 12:2 that at the very beginning of the Messianic Era, a prophet, Elijah, will arise to guide Israel and set their hearts aright. His mission will be to bring peace to the world. What his message of peace will consist of and why it is entrusted to him, are elaborated in Maimonides' comment to the Mishnah in *Eduyot* 8:7.[77] Elijah will come in order to make the world fit for the coming of Messiah. He will accomplish this by removing the injustice of hatred from among people.[78] Hatred of one's fellow is considered an injustice because it is in vain that one hates the other.[79] And Maimonides repeats: one perpetrates an injustice in hating another person.

Maimonides' assertions in his *Commentary on the Mishnah* become intelligible if we read his somewhat cryptic observation in light of *Guide* III:11. At first blush, the problem

---

[77] It is puzzling why the *Rambam la-Am* edition of *Mishneh Torah* (Jerusalem: Mossad ha-Rav Kook, 1987), in its comments to *Hilkhot Melakhim* 12:2 (notes 16 and 17), follows Rabad's explanation of the nature of the messianic peace and not Maimonides' own, in his comments on *Eduyot* 8:7.

[78] Y. Kafih (*Mishnah Im Perush Mosheh ben Maimon*, vol. 4 [Jerusalem: Mossad ha-Rav Kook, 1964], 336-37) translates the Judeo-Arabic word as "*avel.*" The printed medieval commentary on the Mishnah translates the word derivatives variously as *hamasim, homes, ra'ot, oshek*, and *hit'ashkut*, apparently to the same effect as Kafih.

[79] Maimonides employs the Hebrew phrase "*sin'at hinam*" in his Judeo-Arabic comments on *Eduyot* 8:7 and Kafih follows suit (ibid., 337). The printed medieval commentary accentuates the vanity of the hatred by translating: "*aval ha-hit'ashkut ve-ha-ra'ot hem ha-sin'ot she-bein benai adam lefi she-hem hinam.*"

The phrase "*sin'at hinam*" has become dulled in the literature and in common parlance to the extent that it means simply hatred. Maimonides seems here to rediscover the pristine meaning of the phrase. For an illustration of sensitivity to the problem, see *Talmud Bavli, Yoma*, vol. 1 (New York: Mesorah Publications, 1998), 9b[(2)]. See also, Michael Zvi Nehorai, "*Sin'at Hinam*," *Da'at* 36 (Winter 1996): 5-14, especially, n. 2.

with Maimonides' comment is, what if one's hatred is not in vain, if there is cause for the hatred. The answer is that from the point of view of the abused party, the apparent cause is illusory because the ultimate cause is the Divine. Hatred as a response to abuse therefore becomes unjust. Elijah teaches this peace doctrine in order to make the world fit for Messiah, to sensitize society to the messianic teaching. Messiah's pedagogical task does not begin *de novo*; he may build on Elijah's preparatory work.

– III –

A point of departure for examining the difference between the pre-messianic and messianic ethical conceptions of Maimonides is *Hilkhot Berakhot* 10:3.

> If one hears good news, one offers the blessing, blessed are You ... Who is good and does good; if one hears bad news – one offers the blessing, blessed is the True Judge. One is obliged to offer a blessing over the bad with equanimity (*be-tuv nefesh*), just as one would offer a blessing over the good with joy (*simhah*), as it is said, "and you will love the Lord your God ... with all your *me'od*, verily" (Deut. 6:5; in response to whatever measure – *middah* – He metes out to you). Within this category of enhanced love (for God) that we are commanded (to harbor), is (the idea) that even at a time when one feels straitened, one should *modeh* and praise (*ve-shabbah*) in joy.

Given the context of straitened circumstances, "praise" should be rendered in the sense of *dumiyah*, as in Maimonides' *Commentary on Avot* 3:3 (mentioned earlier), *va-yidom Aharon – ve-shabbah Aharon*. The term "*yodeh*" should, in the same vein, be rendered as acknowledge (the Source) rather than as thank.[80] "*Yodeh*" in *Mishneh Torah* is employed in

---

[80] One might suggest that a usage of "*lehodot*" as a composite of both senses is reflected in *Hilkhot Berakhot* 10:8. Four (individuals) are required "*lehodot*" – a sick person who was healed, a freed prisoner, sea voyagers

both senses – admit and acknowledge on the one hand, thank on the other – and the former is the appropriate sense here, given the straitened circumstances.

The *dumiyah* underlying *Hilkhot Berakhot* 10:3 is normative even in the pre-Messianic Period: one encounters unfortunate natural occurrences as "acts of God."[81] The spiritual advance that takes place in the Messianic Period is experiencing human provocation as well, as a meeting with

---

upon their return, and wayfarers who arrived safely. The source for this requirement is a Talmudic (*Berakhot* 54b) rendering of Psalms 107. Maimonides (in *Guide* II:48) elucidates Psalms 107:25 as a "natural" act traceable to the Divine Will through His "ways," the intermediate causes. This elucidation is paradigmatic. "*Lehodot*" would then mean acknowledging as well as thanking the Source of the happenings, even as one praises (*ve-shabbah*), i.e., acquiesces (*dom*), in God's "ways" or *middot*.

[81] See *Guide* III:23, vol. 2, 492-93, concerning Job, who lost his "health, wealth and children," but at the end of the book, when "he knew God with a certain knowledge [rather than through the "traditional stories"] ... admitted that true happiness, which is the knowledge of the Deity, is guaranteed to all who know Him and that a human being cannot be troubled in it by any of all the misfortunes in question." Correlate this statement with that at the end of the chapter:

> Our intellects do not reach the point of apprehending how these natural things ... are produced in time.... How then can we wish that His governance of, and Providence for them may He be exalted, should resemble our governance of, and providence for, the things that we do govern and provide for? (496)

We need rather to affirm that He is aware of and is responsible for what is happening. Our only response can be that of "those who do out of love and are joyful in sufferings." Whereas in *Hilkhot De'ot* 2:3, this latter rabbinic statement is a response also to human provocation, in the case of Job it is specifically a response to natural occurrences. And while there is a strong religious element in the response of "doing out of love and rejoicing in suffering," there is also a noticeable anthropocentric component. See *Hilkhot Avel* 13:11:

> One should not indulge in excessive grief over one's dead, for it is said: "weep not for the dead, neither bemoan him" (Jer. 22:10), that is to say [weep not for him] too much, for that is the way of the world, and he who frets over the way of the world is a fool.

A "fool" would seem to be the opposite of the anthropocentric *hakham*. In the track of the theocentric *hasid*, to be mentioned now, there is no anthropocentric ingredient.

the Divine (*Hilkhot De'ot* 2:3[82] and *Guide* III:11). The intentional contradiction identified at the beginning of the article signals two tracks – a pre-messianic anthropocentric track and a messianic theocentric one: in the latter, the ideal *zaddik*'s (or *hasid*'s) experience of "insult and humiliation without responding in kind" – as "love of God" – is now approximated by everyone.[83] This messianic, theocentric

---

[82] When Maimonides speaks in *Hilkhot De'ot* 2:3 of "teaching oneself not to get angry even in response to something that warrants anger" and "orienting oneself not to feel anything even in response to things that provoke anger," he refers to anger generated by human provocation. This can be inferred from his references to *Yoma* 23a, about those who are insulted and do not insult in return and to *Pesahim* 66b, about scholars and prophets who lose their scholarship and prophecy when they become irritated at provocateurs.

The intentional contradiction emerging from *Hilkhot De'ot* II:3 signals a new perspective for this passage and the conceptual identity of *Guide* III:11 with *Hilkhot De'ot* II:3 tells us that this new perspective is messianic.

[83] Maimonides has been, in effect, portrayed in this article – both in terms of his theory and his practice (on the latter, see notes 23 and 27) – as the ideal *zaddik* or *hasid*, and while, on the face of it, he formulates *Hilkhot De'ot* 2:3 as a law for everyone, he makes it clear in a letter that the ideal of "those who are insulted but do not insult in turn" is elitist; it is intended for the likes of his close disciples only (Shilat, vol. 1, 308), just as is the theocentric way of relating abuse to the ultimate Sender (see note 23; Shilat, vol. 1, 308-09). The majority of the Jewish nation – the religious leadership as well as the masses – cannot be expected to be sensitive to ethical-spiritual values of this sort. "Fear of heaven" for the religious institutional "establishment" entails only observance of the severe prohibitions, while religiously regulated speech as well as moral traits are not deemed prerequisites to religiosity. In brief, says Maimonides, one cannot demand of Jewish society as a whole to be on the level of R. Hanina ben Dosa or R. Pinhas ben Yair; furthermore, even those who are not on the spiritual level of the latter, cannot be said, strictly speaking, to lack *yir'at shamayim*.

What Maimonides says, as was indicated in the body of the article, is that *De'ot* 2:3 is not legislation for the "here and now." *Hilkhot De'ot* 2:3, conjoined with *Guide* III:11, *Hilkhot Melakhim* 12:2 and Maimonides' comments on *Eduyot* 8:7, is a messianic vision. What is normative for Maimonides and R. Yosef ben Yehuda in their time (since, because of their moral stature, it behooves them to deport themselves in this way), becomes normative for the whole of Jewish society when they will "see" the Divine reality more clearly in the messianic future (*Guide* III:11).

track can meaningfully find its context in a *Mishneh Torah* endowed by scholars with a messianic significance.[84]

What still needs to be resolved is an apparent contradiction in one of Maimonides' letters to R. Pinhas ha-Dayan (Shilat, vol. 2, 436-38). Maimonides begins by repeating what he indicated in several letters (Shilat, vol. 1, 304, note to line 5) that he is always calm in the face of abuse. Yet, in the very next paragraph he tells of his anger when he received R. Pinhas ha-Dayan's most recent communication. How is this to be reconciled with his general practice and his contention in *Hilkhot De'ot* 2:3 that anger is never justified? The answer seems to be that his correspondent informed him of a case where a halakhic tradition was "invented" in Alexandria. (I am indebted for this suggestion to Rabbi Mordechai Ochs.) This catapulted Maimonides into the role of a (titular) head of a community who needed to assert his authority when there was a breach of discipline. In such circumstances, says Maimonides in *Hilkhot De'ot* 2:3, "he should make a show of anger before them, so as to correct them, but in reality, his mind should be composed like that of a man who simulates anger and does not really feel it" (translation from I. Twersky, *A Maimonides Reader*, 55). This composure, reflected in the first paragraph of the letter, would then presumably spill over into the second paragraph, even as he forcefully took his stand.

Vis-à-vis Maimonides standing up for halakhic principle in "anger," it should be emphasized that acquiescence in the face of abuse for Maimonides should not be equated with passivity or inaction or not rising up against injustice. Commenting on a contentious relationship with a difficult personality, Maimonides warns (after advising to acquiesce in the abuse) that if it is impossible to make peace, one should "not attack him at all. It is possible to respond to, to criticize and to oppose – courteously and while maintaining friendliness" (Baneth, 64; Shilat, vol. 1, 309).

[84] I. Twersky has focused on the possible messianic dimension of *Mishneh Torah*, critically adducing the scholarly investigations of that issue. See I. Twersky, "Maimonides' *Mishneh Torah* – Its Purpose and Function," [Hebrew] *Proceedings of the Israel Academy of Sciences and Humanities* 5:1 (1972): 5-7. (The aforementioned article was translated into English by I. Abrahams, in his "The *Mishneh Torah* of Maimonides," *Proceedings of the Israel Academy of Sciences and Humanities* 5:10 [1976]: 7-9.) See also I. Twersky, *Halakhah ve-Hagut: Kavei Yesod be-Mishnato shel ha-Rambam*, vol. 1 (co-author, Michael A. Shmidman) (Tel Aviv: The Open University of Israel, 1992), 145-46. For example, C. Tchernowitz proposed a "politico-eschatological theory," i.e., that the *Mishneh Torah* was intended to serve as the constitution for the messianic kingdom of Israel, a goal to which Maimonides aspired. This would explain the unprecedented concern with "messianic laws" and his preoccupation with the laws of agriculture, sacrifices and levitical purity.

Twersky's own view is that "while there is a kernel of truth here [in the messianic perception of *Mishneh Torah*], a perception which is important

– IV –

Having dealt with the intentional contradiction between *Hilkhot De'ot* 2:2 and *Hilkhot De'ot* 2:3 through the distinction between the anthropocentric track of the *hakham* and the theocentric track of the *hasid*, we may now proceed to tackle the related two contradictions within *Hilkhot De'ot* 1:5 and within *Hilkhot De'ot* 1:6 (mentioned in the very beginning of the article). *Hilkhot De'ot* 1:5 foreshadows the contradiction between *Hilkhot De'ot* 2:2 and *Hilkhot De'ot* 2:3 signaling the two tracks; *Hilkhot De'ot* 1:6 does the same with an added dimension. Once we are sensitized to the differences between the anthropocentric and theocentric ideals of the *hakham* and the *hasid*, respectively, we appreciate the expression *le-hidamot elav* at the end of *Hilkhot De'ot* 1:6 in a more nuanced way.

The meaning of this phrase is two-tiered. It means, on the level of the *hakham,* to emulate God's compassion and charity and righteousness as in *Hilkhot Avadim* 9:8; the prooftext from Job 31:13 is borrowed from Job, the *hakham*.[85] But "*imitatio dei*" for Maimonides, also holds significance on the level of the *hasid*. In *Hilkhot De'ot* 1:6, the *hasid* who suppresses his anger or resentment is *honen* (*Guide* I:54) or hasidic (*Guide* III:53) because he intimates God's suppression of anger in the face of people's provocation (*Guide* I:37).[86]

---

for understanding Maimonides ... it is still a far cry ... to a calculated eschatological endeavor, to a serious attempt to anticipate the Final Redemption by preparing a constitution for the restored Jewish State" (I. Twersky, "The Mishneh Torah of Maimonides," 9). The comprehensive scope of *Mishneh Torah* is explained as a quest for unfragmented Torah study.

For other perspectives on the *Mishneh Torah*'s messianic significance, see D. Hartman's "discussion" of Maimonides' "Episle to Yemen" in A. Halkin and D. Hartman, eds., *Crisis and Leadership: Epistles of Maimonides* (Philadelphia, 1985), 186; Warren Harvey, 13-14; M. Genack, "Rambam's Mishneh Torah: The Significance of Its Title," *Tradition* 38:2 (2004): 83 (in section on "King's Torah").

[85] On Job as *hakham*, see note 81.

[86] On the equation of *honen* and *hasid* see the discussion at the very beginning of this article.

Le-hidamot elav, for the *hasid*, would therefore mean not only imitation, but also acquiescence in God's Will, in God's "ways."[87]

Some problems remain. If, as just suggested, *Hilkhot De'ot* 1:6 is concerned with two types – *hakham* and *hasid* – how do we account for the phrase *ba-derakhim ha-elu ha-beinonim*, which seems to denote the mean? Furthermore, in *Hilkhot De'ot* 1:7, the attributes enumerated in *Hilkhot De'ot* 1:6 are again referred to as *ha-derekh ha-beinonit* and this way of the mean is identified with the "way of God." Why characterize the anthropocentric rather than the theocentric orientation as the "way of God"?

Maimonides' writing is finely crafted and has stimulated fine studies examining its diverse literary features.[88] In addition to his intentional contradictions, Maimonides also employs equivocation and "scattering" or fragmentation of his materials. As regards our problem, it may be argued that *beinonit* in medieval Hebrew is an equivocal term.[89]

---

[87] See R. David Kimhi's interpretation of *nidmeiti* in Isaiah 6:5 in the name of his father. Both *nidmeiti* and *lehidamot* are *nif'al* forms.

[88] L. Kaplan, "Rationalism and Rabbinic Culture in Sixteenth Century Eastern Europe" (PhD diss., Harvard University, 1975), 181-86. Kaplan discusses contradiction, scattering and fragmentation, allusion and equivocal terms as some of the devices of esoteric writing employed by Maimonides. On esoteric writing in Maimonides' halakhic works, see A. Ravitzky, "The Secrets of the Guide to the Perplexed: Between the Thirteenth and Twentieth Centuries," *Studies in Maimonides*, ed. I. Twersky (Cambridge, Mass., 1990), 202-4. (The article also demonstrates that for some scholars, *Mishneh Torah* themes may be transposed to the *Guide* and vice versa.) On the theme of the literary craft of the *Mishneh Torah* and the creation thereby of two levels of meaning in some halakhic contexts, one for the masses, one for the elite, see M. Kellner, "The Literary Character of the *Mishneh Torah*: On the Art of Writing in Maimonides' Halakhic Works," *Me'ah She'arim: Studies in Medieval Jewish Spiritual Life in Memory of Isadore Twersky*, ed. E. Fleischer, et al. (Jerusalem, 2001), 29-45. See also, D. Henschke.

[89] See Eliezer ben Yehuda, *Milon ha-Lashon ha-Ivrit ha-Yeshanah ve-ha-Hadashah*, vol. 1, 527-28, definitions one and three of the word *beinoni*.

When Maimonides says in *Hilkhot De'ot* 1:6-7 that the names by which the Creator is called constitute the *derekh beinonit*, he uses the term *beinonit* differently from the way he applied it to *de'ah beinonit*. *De'ah beinonit memuza'at* is a virtuous state of character regulated by the mean, intermediate between two contrary extremes (as it is *derekh emza'it*); *beinoni* in that sense denotes the mean. But *beinoni* in that sense hardly fits the context of *Hilkhot De'ot* 1:6-7, where some radical hasidic attributes (*kinuyim*) of God are identified with *derekh beinonit*. In that context, Maimonides intimates that *beinoni* is an equivocal term by creating a logical in-coherence in *Hilkhot De'ot* 1:6-7: hasidic traits as the way of the mean. It is the function of the incoherence precisely to signal the reader to study a contradiction-riddled passage closely and attentively and to discern that the difficulties can be resolved if we assume a *double entendre* for the term *beinoni*.

Maimonides defines and employs equivocal terms not only in the *Guide*, but is aware of them in *Mishneh Torah* as well.[90] If a meaning of *beinoni* be found which encompasses the way of the *hasid* as well, *Hilkhot De'ot* 1:6 becomes intelligible. Such a meaning would be "mediating between two things."[91] "Mediating" is an important concern for Maimonides when he discusses God's "ways," which are to be emulated or to be acquiesced in (as in *le-hidamot elav* at the end of *Hilkhot De'ot* 1:6, which supports both meanings). In *Guide* I:54 Moses may know God, not as He is in His essence, but only through His "ways," be they the ways which the *hakham* appropriates or the *hasid*. The response to Moses's request, "make Your ways known to me," is in effect, that God's "ways" mediate between God – as He is in His essential unknowability – and man. Man relates to the ineffable God by

---

[90] See *Hilkhot Tum'at Zara'at* 16:10.

[91] See Ben Yehuda, 528, definition 3. The excerpt is from Aharon ben Eliyahu the Karaite's, *Gan Eden* (1354).

experiencing His "ways" as rooted in Him, in the *Zur*.[92] It is noteworthy that some 150 years after Maimonides (perhaps under his influence), the term *beinoni* is used explicitly rather than implicitly to mean "mediating between two things or places."[93]

If the meaning of *beinoni* as "mediating between two things" be granted in *Hilkhot De'ot* 1:6, the related problem may be solved in *Hilkhot De'ot* 1:7. There too, we have seen, Maimonides refers to the attributes of God enumerated in *Hilkhot De'ot* 1:6 – including the hasidic ways – as the *derekh ha-beinonit*, which in turn is called, the "way of God," *derekh Hashem*. If the *derekh ha-beinonit* means also the "way" mediating between God and man, it may more justifiably be called the "way of God" (than if *derekh ha-beinonit* refers exclusively to the mean) because it is in consonance with a conceivable interpretation of the precept cited in *Hilkhot De'ot* 1:6, "and you should walk in His (mediating) ways." In any event, *Hilkhot De'ot* 1:6-7 are found to be "scattered" or fragmented between the mean (*ha-de'ot ha-emza'iyot, ha-derakhim ha-beinonim*) to be emulated and the mediating "ways" (*ha-derakhim ha-beinonim, ha-derekh ha-beinonit*) through which one relates to the Source, i.e., acquiescing in God's "ways."[94]

---

[92] Perhaps Maimonides employs this new sense of *beinoni* with *derekh* – rather than with *de'ah* – in anticipation of *Guide* I:54, where Moses may know God, not as He is in His essence, but only through knowing His "ways."

[93] See note 91.

[94] This understanding of *derekh Hashem* in *Hilkhot De'ot* 1:7 and its correlation in this article with Maimonides' messianic teaching in *Hilkhot De'ot* 2:3, *Guide* III:11, *Hilkhot Melakhim* 12:2, and comments on *Eduyot* 8:7, sheds light on *Hilkhot Teshuvah* 9:2, where Maimonides maintains that the Messiah will teach *derekh Hashem*.

Messianic teaching may thus be briefly epitomized as the doctrine of "God's ways" and brings to mind the discussion earlier of *Guide* I:54 and *Guide* III:32 (the latter, about the imagined message of the prophet in "these times"). This latter messianic message was related in the body of the text to

The initial contradiction with which this article began led us to discover the meaning of the messianic track in Maimonides' writing. The third contradiction helped us refine the notion of *derekh beinonit*. The theme of Messianic Days for Maimonides, is expressed through Isaiah 11:9, "For the earth shall be full of the knowledge of the Lord, as the waters cover the sea" (*Hilkhot Teshuvah* 9:2; *Hilkhot Melakhim* 12:2; *Guide* III:11).[95] What this means in pedagogic terms is the instruction of the "way of God" (*Hilkhot Teshuvah* 9:2), which is identical with the way the *hasid* achieves the "way of God" (*Hilkhot De'ot* 1:7), knowing God through His "mediating ways." As the Messiah, the ideal *zaddik*, teaches the meaning of relating to God through his "mediating ways," he elucidates the hasidic mode of *le-hidamot elav* (*Hilkhot De'ot* 1:6): "just as He is *hanun*, so you be *hanun*," i.e., just as God is gracious with one, though one does not deserve it,[96] so should one be gracious with others, though they do not deserve it. Reciprocating God's graciousness in this way, one is truly relating to the Source, for the "undeserving ones" are His agency.

Reflecting on the different texts cited in the article, Maimonides seems to be saying that this theocentric social ethic is the cornerstone of messianic theology. This is not a "*via passiva*," for, as mentioned earlier, it requires an intense struggle to find God in the provocative situation. Mental acquiescence and earnest focus on the *Zur* are very active

---

the notion in *Guide* I:54, that "knowledge of God's ways" is superior to praying and fasting (identical with the superiority of "meditation without any works at all" to praying and fasting). That this theme in *Guide* I:54 (as it was expounded) Maimonides deemed to be messianic, may be indicated by Samuel Ibn Tibbon's hint. What Judah Alharizi (*Moreh Nevukhim*, trans. J. Alharizi, 203) and Yosef Kafih (*Moreh ha-Nevukhim*, trans. Y. Kafih [Jerusalem, 1977], 85 n. 28) translate as *takhlit*, Ibn Tibbon translates as *aharit*.

95 *The Guide of the Perplexed*, vol. 2, 441.

96 See the explication of *hanun* at the beginning of the article.

modes of religious experience. It is through this experience, Maimonides posits, that "the earth shall be full of the knowledge of the Lord as the waters cover the sea."

The Contribution of the Dead Sea Scrolls to the Study of Hebrew Language and Literature

Lawrence H. Schiffman

A steady stream of documents has been discovered in the Judean Desert from the legendary entrance of the Bedouin boy into Qumran cave 1 in 1947, through "Operation Scroll" conducted by the Israel Antiquities Authority on the eve of the Israeli withdrawal from Jericho.[1] These finds have provided an altogether new corpus of documents for research into Hebrew language and literature (not to mention Aramaic, which is beyond the scope of this paper). In our lifetimes, this corpus has revolutionized our understanding of the linguistic situation in Palestine during the Hasmonean,

---

[1] For a survey of the history of the discovery of the scrolls, see L. H. Schiffman, *Reclaiming the Dead Sea Scrolls* (Philadelphia: Jewish Publication Society, 1994), 3-16 and the detailed account of S. J. Pfann, "History of the Judean Desert Discoveries," *Companion Volume to the Dead Sea Scrolls Microfiche Edition*, ed. E. Tov, S. J. Pfann (Leiden: E. J. Brill and IDC, 1995), 97-108.

Herodian and Roman periods,[2] and has given us an entirely
new sense of the scope and variety of compositions produced
by the Palestinian Jewish community during this period.[3]
We shall attempt here to survey the new materials and
their relevance, paying special attention to the wider historical
value of these new linguistic and literary discoveries and to
their significance as well for the history of Judaism. While
the term "Dead Sea Scrolls" is usually used to describe
only the Qumran scrolls, we will deal here also with the
finds from Masada and the Bar Kokhba caves as well.
Taken together, these three collections provide a sense of
the period as a whole and bridge the linguistic and literary
gap that stretches from the Bible to the Mishnah.

I. The Corpus

Only now, with the opening of the entire corpus of Judean
Desert texts to scholars, is it possible to gain an accurate
sense of the nature and significance of the entire collection.[4]
Indeed, this study would have been impossible before the
release of these newly discovered scrolls.

A. The Qumran Texts

The corpus of documents that emerged from the Qumran caves
is extensive and varied. Archaeological investigation of the

---

[2] On the history of Judaism in these periods, see L. H. Schiffman, *From
Text to Tradition, A History of Second Temple and Rabbinic Judaism*
(Hoboken, NJ: Ktav, 1991), 60-176.

[3] D. Dimant, "The Qumran Manuscripts: Contents and Significance," *"Time
to Prepare the Way in the Wilderness": Papers on the Qumran Scrolls by
Fellows of the Institute for Advanced Studies of the Hebrew University,
Jerusalem, 1989-90*, ed. D. Dimant, L. H. Schiffman, STDJ 16 (Leiden: E.
J. Brill, 1994), 23-58.

[4] See S. A. Reed, M. J. Lundberg and M. B. Phelps, *The Dead Sea Scrolls
Catalogue: Documents, Photographs and Museum Inventory Numbers*, SBL
Resources for Biblical Study 32 (Atlanta: Scholars Press, 1994).

buildings and caves of Qumran,[5] palaeographical examination[6] as well as carbon-14 tests[7] have established that the Qumran manuscripts were mainly copied in the second and first centuries B.C.E, with a few from the third century B.C.E., as well as several from the first century C.E. The composition of the texts dates anywhere from the date of the composition of the Torah in Israel's early history to about the turn of the century when the last of the Qumran texts were composed. The documents were gathered at Qumran, for the most part in cave 4, sometime after 134 B.C.E., when the Qumran sect established its central location, and before 68 C.E., when the Romans destroyed Qumran during the Great Revolt of 66-73 C.E.[8]

Most of the texts are in Hebrew, with some twenty percent in Aramaic and only a few in Greek. This breakdown already indicates that Hellenism only affected the community that collected and used these manuscripts in a limited way and that the community preferred both Hebrew and Aramaic, as was common among Jews in the Land of Israel at this time, to Greek.

Cave 4 shows clear evidence that it served as a library for those who inhabited the Qumran buildings. It is an artificially hewn-out cave with holes in its walls, which in antiquity held wooden supports for shelves. This cave must have been used regularly for storage of documents utilized by the members of the Qumran sect; it is located just a few minutes walk from the building complex.

---

[5] R. de Vaux, *Archaeology and the Dead Sea Scrolls* (London: Oxford University Press, 1973), 1-48, 95-102.

[6] F. M. Cross, "The Development of the Jewish Scripts," *The Bible and the Ancient Near East, Essays in Honor of W. F. Albright*, ed. G. E. Wright (Garden City, NY: Doubleday, 1961), 170-264.

[7] G. Bonani, et al., "Radiocarbon Dating of the Dead Sea Scrolls," *Atiqot* 20 (1991): 27-32; A. J. T. Jull, et al., "Radiocarbon Dating of Scrolls and Linen Fragments from the Judean Desert," *Atiqot* 28 (1996): 7.

[8] De Vaux, 106-9.

Some of the other caves, however, give an entirely different impression. Caves such as 1 and 11 look like refuges into which scrolls may have been thrown as the Romans were coming to destroy Qumran. Yet a profile of the contents of those caves is almost identical to that of cave 4.[9] Curiously, cave 7 contained only Greek manuscripts, a phenomenon which has no satisfactory explanation. Copies of some texts are found in several caves indicating that the various caves were all part of what had been one unified library in antiquity.

Throughout this study we will distinguish between texts brought to the Qumran community and those that were composed by its members.[10] Essentially, there are three classes of texts in this corpus. Each of these constitutes roughly one-third of the collection, excluding unidentified materials.

1. Biblical texts, covering some part of every book except Esther, which is probably missing only by chance.[11] Many of these manuscripts were certainly copied outside the domain of the sect.

2. Apocryphal compositions and other texts that were among the literary heritage of those who formed the sect or that were composed by similar groups. These texts were composed outside the sectarian center and brought there, although some of the manuscripts may have been copied there.

3. Sectarian texts that describe the teachings and way of life of a specific group of Jews, some of whom apparently lived at the sectarian center that has been excavated at Qumran. They include texts that outline the beliefs of the sect, their rules for entry into the group, their legal codes, and their liturgical compositions. We cannot be sure that all of them, or

---

[9] Dimant, 30-32.

[10] E. Tov, "The Orthography and Language of the Hebrew Scrolls Found at Qumran and the Origin of These Scrolls," *Textus* 13 (1986): 32-57; Dimant, 27-30.

[11] Cf. S. Talmon, "Was the Book of Esther Known at Qumran?" DSD 2 (1995): 249-67.

even most of them were copied at Qumran.

Although this three-fold division of the materials had been recognized early on, we did not truly appreciate the extent to which the collection contained general Jewish literature of the period, not specific to the Dead Sea sect, until the opening up of the entire corpus. This appreciation has helped greatly to provide a more accurate sense of the meaning of these documents for the general history of Judaism.

The biblical manuscripts, as mentioned, include segments from the entirety of Scripture, except for Esther. The Qumran biblical texts represent a number of different text types.[12] A large number resemble the later, Massoretic (received) biblical text possessed by the Jewish community throughout the ages. A fair number represent biblical texts written in a specific dialect of Hebrew used by the Qumran sect; these must have been used specifically within the community. A few texts represent the Hebrew text type from which the Greek translation of the Bible (Septuagint) was made, and a few represent forerunners of the Samaritan text of the Bible.

The specific documents of the Qumran community are a substantial part of the collection. These constitute some 191 manuscripts or about 115 works (some works are represented in multiple manuscripts). These works are distinguished by a number of characteristics: They generally reflect the practices and organization of the Qumran community; the history of the community and its own self-image; the theological views of the community; and the specific biblical interpretations of the community. Many of these ideas have parallels outside this community. It is the agglomeration of these ideas, as well as their specific linguistic character that identifies them as distinctively Dead Sea sectarian documents.

As already mentioned, there are many texts that reflect the general literature of the period. These texts have a similar

---

[12] E. Tov, "Groups of Biblical Texts Found at Qumran," *Time to Prepare the Way in the Wilderness*, 85-102.

profile to those found in the Masada excavations, which certainly cannot be identified with the Qumran sect.[13] Rather, the findings at both Qumran and Masada present samples of the literature that was shared by most Jews in the Second Temple period. These are apocryphal and pseudepigraphal documents – some of which were previously known in other languages and are only now available in their original Hebrew or Aramaic.[14] This class of texts has great significance for us in that we seek not only to describe the language and literature of the Qumran sect, but also to use their writings and the writings they collected as a means of uncovering information about a variety of Jewish groups of this period.

B. The Masada Texts

A much smaller collection of texts was preserved at Masada, the last fortress to fall in the Great Revolt of the Jews against the Romans in 66-73 C.E. According to Josephus[15] – whose dramatic account is doubted by many historians[16] – those who inhabited this fortress in its last stages were Sicarii.[17] Members of this Jewish revolutionary group had first attacked fellow Jews who cooperated with the Romans. Ultimately however, they turned their efforts to full-scale military operations against the powers of Roman occupation. Although Masada

---

[13] Yadin, however, was of the opinion that these texts had been brought to Masada by those who fled Qumran after its destruction in 68 C.E. See Y. Yadin, *Masada: Herod's Fortress and the Zealot's Last Stand* (New York: Random House, 1966), 172-74.

[14] Cf. Schiffman, *Reclaiming*, 181-210.

[15] *Wars of the Jews* VII, 252-406.

[16] A sense of the current debate regarding Masada can be gleaned from a series of articles by N. Ben-Yehuda, J. Zias and Z. Meshel, appearing under the title "Questioning Masada," *BAR* 24:6 (1998): 30-53, 64-68.

[17] Cf. M. Stern, "Zealots," *Encyclopaedia Judaica Yearbook* (Jerusalem: Keter, 1973), 135-40; D. M. Rhoads, *Israel in Revolution 6-74 C.E.: A Political History Based on the Writings of Josephus* (Philadelphia: Fortress Press, 1976), 78-80.

had been previously used in the Hasmonean and Herodian periods, the manuscripts found there were clearly brought there by the rebels.[18]

In contrast to the vast majority of Qumran documents, the Masada materials were found during controlled archaeological excavations led by Yigael Yadin in 1963-65. It goes without saying that all the manuscript materials found at Masada are dated prior to the year 73 C.E. and in fact, for the most part, they date to the first half of the first century C.E.

Manuscripts were found in several locations. One collection was found in a room in the casemate defense wall, and included a manuscript of part of the biblical book of Psalms. A few other fragmentary, "apocryphal" type items were found in the same place as well as part of the book of Leviticus.[19] These biblical texts were of the Massoretic variety and are essentially the same as our biblical texts except for some minor textual variations. An extremely important find from that same cache of scrolls was a manuscript of the *Songs of the Sabbath Sacrifice,*[20] a text also found at Qumran. The presence of similar material at both sites indicates that these texts were part of the common literature of late Second Temple Judaism.

A second casemate chamber yielded additional manuscripts,[21] among them a *Psalms Scroll* including part of Psalm 150 as well as the momentous scroll containing the end of the apocryphal book of *Ben Sira* in its original Hebrew.[22] Previously, only the Greek translation by the author's grandson and some medieval fragments from the Cairo Genizah were known.

---

[18] E. Netzer, *Masada III, The Buildings, Stratigraphy and Architecture* (Jerusalem: Israel Exploration Society, 1991), 615-55.

[19] Yadin, *Masada*, 168-74.

[20] C. Newsom in E. Eshel, et al., *Qumran Cave 4.VI, Poetical and Liturgical Texts, Part 1*, DJD 11 (Oxford: Clarendon Press, 1998), 239-52.

[21] Yadin, *Masada*, 174-79.

[22] Y. Yadin, *The Ben Sira Scroll from Masada* (Jerusalem: Israel Exploration Society, 1965).

Now, a large part of the original text was finally recovered.[23]

In one of the wall towers, a small fragment from a work closely related to *Jubilees*, similar to the *Pseudo-Jubilees* texts found at Qumran, was found.[24] Fragments of a *Leviticus Scroll* were also found near the northern palace villa.

In the outer wall of Masada, the rebels had adapted a building for use as a synagogue. Two scroll fragments were found here: one was part of Ezekiel and the other of Deuteronomy.[25] These two scrolls are virtually identical to the traditional text used by Jews to this day, with the exception of a few variants in the Ezekiel text.

C. Bar Kokhba Texts

This last corpus of texts emerged from the caves in which Jews took refuge during the Bar Kokhba revolt of 132-135 C.E. and where they seem for the most part to have met their deaths at the hands of the Romans. This group of texts is actually mislabeled. Most of these texts have nothing to do with the messianic rebel leader at all, although a few are actual military dispatches from him. The bulk are legal documents, written in Greek, Aramaic and Hebrew, the latter being the focus of this discussion.

These documents were discovered at a number of sites located along the western shore of the Dead Sea. We will treat here only the major collections, those of Wadi Murabba'at and Nahal Hever, and the so-called Nahal Se'elim texts.

The first of these areas to be discovered were the caves at Wadi Murabba'at in 1951. By the time the site was excavated,

---

[23] All of the known Hebrew fragments, ancient and medieval, are gathered together in *The Book of Ben Sira: Text, Concordance and an Analysis of the Vocabulary* (Jerusalem: The Academy of the Hebrew Language and the Shrine of the Book, 1973), 3-67.

[24] Cf. J. C. VanderKam in H. Attridge, et al., *Qumran Cave 4.VIII, Parabiblical Texts, Part I*, DJD 13 (Oxford: Clarendon Press, 1994), 141-85.

[25] Yadin, *Masada*, 187-89.

Bedouins had already removed most of the manuscripts; nevertheless, archaeologists recovered important fragments as well. The Murabba'at documents, fully published already in 1960,[26] included three biblical fragments, a set of *tefillin*, a *mezuzah*, and mostly documentary texts, many in Aramaic. Exceedingly important is the Hebrew *Scroll of the Twelve Prophets* found here which is virtually identical with the Massoretic text. The Hebrew materials included an unknown literary text, lists of names, abecedaries, letters, military dispatches from Bar Kosiba (the real name of Bar Kokhba), and contracts of various kinds.

The second of these collections stems from Nahal Hever. Israeli excavators discovered these materials *in situ* in 1960-61, again under Y. Yadin. This area yielded what are actually three collections of documents. One is the personal archive of the colorful lady, Babatha. This group of texts included Aramaic, Greek and Nabatean legal documents.[27] A second group consists of contracts written at Ein Gedi, mostly written in Hebrew.[28] Finally, this trove includes some personal letters from Bar Kosiba, mainly to his agents at Ein Gedi, in Hebrew and Aramaic. [29] Other caves in the area also yielded the Greek *Twelve Prophets Scroll*[30] and other Greek texts.

A third collection is generally designated as Nahal Se'elim. Yet these texts, which the Bedouins offered for sale in Jordan and claimed to have come from Nahal Se'elim, have been proven to have actually been discovered at Nahal Hever, across what was then the border in Israel. These materials include numerous documents in Hebrew, Aramaic and Greek.

---

[26] P. Benoit, J. T. Milik, R. de Vaux, *Les Grottes de Murabba`at*, DJD 2 (Oxford: Clarendon Press, 1960).

[27] Y. Yadin, *Bar Kokhba: The Rediscovery of the Legendary Hero of the Second Jewish Revolt Against Rome* (New York: Random House, 1971), 222-53.

[28] Ibid, 172-83.

[29] Ibid, 124-39.

[30] E. Tov, *The Greek Minor Prophets Scroll from Nahal Hever (8HevXIIgr)*, DJD 8 (Oxford: Clarendon Press, 1990).

A number of Hebrew letters to and from Bar Kokhba have been found.[31]

II. The Linguistic Situation

The discovery of such a large corpus of materials – Hebrew, Greek and Aramaic – certainly has stimulated discussion about the linguistic situation in Palestine in Late Antiquity.[32] To a great extent, this discussion has proceeded on the agenda set by New Testament studies that sought to establish the original spoken language of Jesus and the language in which early Christian traditions were initially transmitted. Jewish scholars dealing with this field were for their part influenced by nationalistic criteria, especially those scholars writing during the revival of Hebrew. Much of this discussion is rendered meaningless by the new texts. We will discuss this issue briefly, by placing the status of Hebrew – the subject of this study – at the center.

The most widely held assumption proceeds something like this: The spread of Aramaic throughout the Near East was greatly accelerated by the fall of the Neo-Babylonian Empire and the subsequent rise of the Achaemenid Persian Empire. This resulted from the use by the Achaemenid chancellery of the Aramaic language as a *lingua franca* to tie the disparate

---

[31] H. M. Cotton, A. Yardeni, *Aramaic, Hebrew and Greek Documentary Texts from Nahal Hever and Other Sites*, DJD 27 (Oxford: Clarendon Press, 1997). The Hebrew letter is found on page 104; Y. Yadin, J. C. Greenfield, A. Yardeni, B. A. Levine, *The Documents from the Bar Kokhba Period in the Cave of the Letters* (Jerusalem: Israel Exploration Society, 2002) 279-86, 293-99, 333-40.

[32] E. Schürer, *The History of the Jewish People in the Age of Jesus*, ed. G. Vermes, F. Millar and M. Black (Edinburgh:T. & T. Clark, 1979), 20-28; J. C. Greenfield, "The Languages of Palestine, 200 B.C.E.-200 C.E.," *Jewish Languages: Themes and Variations*, ed. H. H. Paper (Cambridge, MA: Association for Jewish Studies, 1978), 143-54 (note the response of F. E. Peters, 159-64); J. A. Fitzmeyer, *A Wandering Aramean: Collected Aramaic Essays* (Missoula, Mont.: Scholars Press, 1979), 29-56.

and far-flung empire together.[33] So far, so good. It is then maintained that the result of this development was the gradual replacement of Hebrew by Aramaic in the Land of Israel, a process that happened first in the northern and later in the southern parts of the country. It is assumed that the native language of Josephus and of Jesus and his disciples was Aramaic, and that Hebrew had fallen into disuse. Both Hebrew and Aramaic were understood to be on the run from the overpowering Hellenistic influence of *koine* Greek, both among pagans and even among Jews.

The material we have surveyed shows these last statements to be great oversimplifications of the situation. The evidence of the scrolls certainly indicates that in the fourth through early second centuries there was a great flowering of Aramaic literature.[34] These texts include occasional Persian loan-words (as is the case also in Second Temple Hebrew material) and clearly stem from the Achaemenid and early Hellenistic eras in which Persian influence in the Land of Israel was still strong. But by the time we reach the second century B.C.E., we again encounter a rich Hebrew literature. The earliest material from this period, such as *Ben Sira* and *Jubilees*, as well as other pre-Qumranian texts found amongst the scrolls, is all preserved in a form of late Massoretic Hebrew. These works come from circles for whom biblical Hebrew was very much a living literary language, even if we cannot be sure what languages they spoke in daily life.

When we reach the Hasmonean and Herodian periods, when the Qumran sectarian literature was composed, Hebrew writing occurs in at least two observable dialects. One is the same dialect as that of *Ben Sira* and *Jubilees* – a sort of late

---

[33] E. Y. Kutscher, "Aramaic," *EJ* 3, 266.

[34] B. Z. Wacholder, "The Ancient Judeo-Aramaic Literature (500-165 BCE), A Classification of Pre-Qumranic Texts," *Archaeology and History in the Dead Sea Scrolls: The New York University Conference in Memory of Yigael Yadin,* ed. L. H. Schiffman, JSPSup 8 (Sheffield: Sheffield Academic Press, 1990), 257-81.

biblical Hebrew, found in texts composed outside of the
Qumran sect but preserved in their collection. The other is
what we may term "Qumran Hebrew," with the strange endings
and grammatical forms which typify this dialect. This system of
writing – indeed it is more than just orthography as it affects
also morphology – is found only in the sectarian writings. This
orthography and morphology, along with certain specific usage
of terminology, are evidence of sectarian composition, primarily
between 150 B.C.E. and the turn of the era. This dialect is
largely judged to be an archaizing remnant of pre-Massoretic
Hebrew. It seems more likely, however, that we are dealing
here with a dialect invented by a group of hyper-sectarians,
who chose to separate themselves even by developing their own
linguistic system, at least for written material. In light of the
complete absence of this dialect from earlier texts, or from
inscriptions or other Second Temple period texts, we cannot
accept the notion that this dialect is actually ancient, or that it
represents a language pattern spread throughout the Judean
populace.

Two texts, the *MMT document*[35] and the *Copper Scroll*,[36]
have often been said to be in Mishnaic Hebrew.[37] Thorough
studies of these texts show this not to be the case. Although
these texts, like the *Temple Scroll*, include features of what we
later encounter as Mishnaic vocabulary as well as some
common grammatical elements, nevertheless, these texts
evidence many of the usual features of Qumran dialectology.[38]

In any case, we need to remember that these two Hebrew
dialects represent written dialects of Jews whose spoken

---

[35] E. Qimron and J. Strugnell, *Qumran Cave 4.V: Miqsat Ma`ase ha-Torah*,
DJD 10 (Oxford: Clarendon Press, 1994), 44-56.

[36] M. Baillet, J. T. Milik and R. de Vaux, *Les Petites Grottes de Qumran*,
DJD 3 (Oxford, Clarendon Press, 1962), 210-302.

[37] See E. Y. Kutscher, "Hebrew Language, Mishnaic," *EJ* 16, 1590-1607.

[38] Qimron, DJD 10.65-108 concludes that the grammar of *MMT* is closer to
Biblical than to Mishnaic Hebrew, although the vocabulary is closer to that
of Mishnaic Hebrew.

language we cannot determine. It is possible that those texts tending toward Mishnaic Hebrew are indeed evidence for spoken dialects, as had been suggested by some.[39] It may even be that many spoke Aramaic, if the evidence of the New Testament is to be accepted. That some Jews, even in the Land of Israel, were more at home in Greek than in Hebrew or Aramaic is clear from the presence of some Greek translation fragments at Qumran[40] and in the Bar Kokhba corpus. But certainly Hebrew was being used, and its use cannot be explained simply as a revival in the Maccabean period under nationalistic aegis. Indeed, the so-called revival was already in full force in the first half of the second century B.C.E., at what is supposed to be the height of the Hellenistic cultural on-slaught.

The Masada documents show the nature of the Hebrew used outside the confines of the Qumran sectarians (or others who may have followed them). The Masada collection includes Massoretic Hebrew biblical texts[41] as well as other apocryphal-type texts in Hebrew of a type similar to Massoretic Hebrew.[42] The *Ben Sira* text is the most notable text found at Masada, and from a linguistic point of view it is comparable to the fragmentary materials, such as the *Joshua apocryphon*.[43]

---

[39] G. A. Rendsburg, *Diglossia in Ancient Hebrew*, AOS 72 (New Haven: American Oriental Society, 1990), 7-15.

[40] Baillet, DJD 3.142-6.

[41] S. Talmon, "Fragments of a Psalms Scroll from Masada, MPsb (Masada 1103-1742)," *Minhah Le-Nahum: Biblical and Other Studies Presented to Nahum M. Sarna in Honour of his 70th Birthday*, ed. M. Brettler, M. Fishbane, JSOTSup 154 (Sheffield: Sheffield Academic Press, 1993), 318-27; idem, *Eretz Yisrael* 24 (5754): 99-110.

[42] S. Talmon, "Hebrew Written Fragments from Masada," *DSD* 3 (1996): 168-177.

[43] S. Talmon, "Qeta mi-Megillah Hizonit le-Sefer Yehoshua mi-Mezadah," *Shai le-Hayyim Rabin, Asufat Mehqere Lashon li-Khevodo bi-Mel'ot lo Shiv'im ve-Hamesh*, ed. M. Goshen-Gottstein, S. Morag and S. Kogut (Jerusalem: Academon Press, 1990), 147-57.

By the time we reach the collection of Bar Kokhba documents, Hebrew dialectology has taken a decided turn. While Aramaic is represented in letters, contracts and other documents, it is no longer used for literary texts; Greek is used extensively for legal documents.[44] By this time, direct Roman rule had brought the use of Greek into prominence, especially among those Jews who resided in the Roman province of Arabia, founded in 106 C.E.[45] Only the Massoretic type now represented Hebrew biblical texts. This collection did not preserve extra-biblical literary materials, but the free and easy use of Hebrew for letters indicates that for some Jews it was very much still a living language; others must have felt much more at home in Aramaic (perhaps especially in the north) and in Greek. But comparison with Talmudic literature, inscriptions and *Targumim* indicates that this was a period in which Aramaic was on the rise and was most probably the spoken language of the Jews of the Galilee, outside of the Hellenistic cities. But our texts indicate the continued survival and indeed even use of Hebrew as a spoken language.

It is important to emphasize that the Hebrew used in these texts is quite close to Mishnaic Hebrew, a situation that extends even beyond the legal formulary and technical language that is to be expected in some of these documents.[46] It is certain though, that Hebrew continued to be developed and to function as one of the languages of Palestine. Indeed, Talmudic evidence shows the same thing.

---

[44] N. Lewis, *The Documents from the Bar Kokhba Period in the Cave of the Letters, Greek Papyri* (Jerusalem: Israel Exploration Society, 1989), 35-133; Cotton, DJD 37.166-279.

[45] Cf. Cotton, DJD 27.148-52.

[46] Cf. E. Y. Kutscher, "Leshonan shel ha-Iggerot ha-Ivriyot ve-ha-Aramiyot shel Bar Kosiba u-Vene Doro, Ma'amar Sheni: Ha-Iggerot ha-Ivriyot," *Leshonenu* 26 (1961/2): 7-21; G. W. Nebe, "Die hebräische Sprache der Nahal Hever Dokumente 5/6Hev 44-46," *The Hebrew of the Dead Sea Scrolls and Ben Sira, Proceedings of a Symposium held at Leiden University, 11-14 December 1995*, STDJ 26 (Leiden: E. J. Brill, 1997) 150-57.

III. Literary Character

The Dead Sea Scrolls have presented us with a variety of Hebrew texts, which, from a literary point of view, present new genres or marked differences with previously known exemplars of the same genres. In this section we will mention some examples of this phenomenon, making specific reference to some of the newly released texts.

In the area of legal texts, the scrolls materials include a number of elements. But perhaps most important are the first post-biblical codes of Jewish law known to us. In one case, the *Temple Scroll*,[47] the redactor created a post-biblical code by rewriting the canonical legal texts from the Torah into a new document. Interestingly, the author of this text, finishing his work in about 120 B.C.E., had the benefit of previously existing sections of such a text, which constituted rewrites of sections of the Torah for the purpose of gathering and explaining the law on various topics. While these texts proceeded in the manner of the Torah itself, for the most part using its language, another trend is visible in the sectarian codes of the *serakhim*,[48] which are collections of laws on individual topics, such as the list, סרך, of Sabbath laws found in the *Zadokite Fragments*.[49] Here the language of the Bible can be detected behind the legal formulary of the new texts, but there are virtually no direct quotations of the Bible or reworkings of its actual text.

The early documents already display the two methods of presenting post-biblical law as understood by the later rabbinic teachers, the Midrash and Mishnah. Midrash is the arrangement of law according to the order of scripture and

---

[47] Y. Yadin, *The Temple Scroll* (Jerusalem: Israel Exploration Society, 1983).

[48] On this term, see L. H. Schiffman, *The Halakhah at Qumran* (Leiden: E. J. Brill, 1975), 60-68.

[49] Discussed in detail in Schiffman, *Halakhah*, 84-133.

Mishnah is that arranged by topic. Both types are in evidence in the sectarian literature of the last two centuries B.C.E.

Most of the legal documents present in the Bar Kokhba texts are written in Aramaic, the language used from time immemorial by Jews for such purposes. The few extant Hebrew legal documents from that corpus show us that Mishnaic legal terms, some of which are already in evidence in some sectarian texts as well, were in use in the legal practice of Jews from Judea. These contracts are, for the most part, the earliest preserved examples of these legal usages, predating the Mishnaic legal formulations to which they are parallel.

In the area of biblical interpretation, the *Pesher* literature presents us with a new genre from several points of view.[50] This is not the place to discuss the nature of the contemporizing exegesis found in these texts. What I want to concentrate on is the character of these documents as commentaries. Here, for some of the Minor Prophets, Isaiah and some Psalms, we have line by line commentary arranged in the form of lemma and comment, generally running in scriptural order. Specific terms are used, such as פשרו על – its interpretation is concerning, פשר הדבר – the interpretation of the matter is, which clearly separate the biblical from the non-biblical interpretive material. These are, from the literary point of view, the earliest biblical commentaries, as we know them. Yet at the same time, we should note the attempt of the so-called *Genesis Commentary* to provide plain sense commentary on the Bible.[51]

In the area of poetry, the scrolls texts offer a rich selection. Some of these texts are actually prayers or hymns, meant

---

[50] The *pesher texts* are collected in M. P. Horgan, *Pesharim: Biblical Interpretations of Biblical Books*, CBQ Monograph Series 8 (Washington, DC: Catholic Biblical Association of America, 1979). See also Schiffman, *Reclaiming*, 223-41.

[51] G. Brooke, in G. Brooke, et al., *Qumran Cave 4.XVII, Parabiblical Texts, Part 3*, DJD 22 (Oxford: Clarendon Press, 1996), 185-212. The extensive literature on this text and its mode of biblical exegesis appears on p. 185; see especially the articles by G. J. Brooke and M. J. Bernstein.

for liturgical use.[52] The scrolls provide us with the earliest post-biblical Hebrew poetry and this material clearly constitutes a bridge between the poetry of the Bible and that of the early *paytanim*. The poems in the scrolls are of varied character. The *Hodayot*[53] offer introspective religious poetry, which express the deepest longings of a sectarian author, thought by many to be the Teacher of Righteousness, the leader of the sect, and at the same time the deepest theological beliefs of the Qumran sect. The *Songs of the Sabbath Sacrifice*[54] describe the beauty of the innermost *sancta* of the heavens and have intimate links to the later *hekhalot* mystical poetry.[55] The *Daily Prayers*[56] set out morning and afternoon benedictions and the *Festival Prayer* texts[57] are for the various Jewish holidays. All of these poems, and many more, testify to a general loosening up of some of the rigid rules of biblical parallelism, and show the burst of creativity that Hebrew poetry experienced in the Second Temple period.

Closely linked to the poetry is the wisdom literature,[58] since some of the wisdom texts are poetic in character. *Ben Sira*, found at Masada and Qumran,[59] is a prime example of

---

[52] See B. Nitzan, *Qumran Prayer and Religious Poetry*, STDJ 12 (Leiden: E. J. Brill, 1994) 35-200.

[53] J. Licht, *Megillat ha-Hodayot mi-Megillot Midbar Yehudah* (Jerusalem: Mosad Bialik, 1957); cf. Nitzan, *Qumran Prayer*, 321-55.

[54] Newsom, DJD 11.173-401; cf. Nitzan, *Qumran Prayer*, 273-318.

[55] L. H. Schiffman, "*Merkavah* Speculation at Qumran: 4Q *Serekh Shirot Olat ha-Shabbat*," *Mystics, Philosophers and Politicians: Essays in Jewish Intellectual History in Honor of Alexander Altmann*, ed. J. Reinharz, D. Swetchinski and K. Bland (Durham, NC: Duke University Press, 1982), 15-47.

[56] M. Baillet, *Qumrân Grotte 4, III (4Q482-4Q520)*, DJD 7 (Oxford: Clarendon Press, 1982), 105-36.

[57] Baillet, DJD 7.175-215.

[58] Cf. Schiffman, *Reclaiming*, 197-210.

[59] J. A. Sanders, *The Psalms Scroll of Qumrân Cave 11*, DJD 4 (Oxford: Clarendon Press, 1965), 79-85 discusses an excerpt from *Ben Sira* included in the *Psalms Scroll* (11QPsᵃ).

this literature. The previously unknown *Sapiential Texts* are in reality an entirely new genre. They seem by their linguistic character and content not to be specifically sectarian texts. Rather, like the biblical wisdom texts, they give good advice to the typical family. They are set in the agrarian setting of the typical farmer of the period yet speak also of hidden wisdom which one is to probe. These texts are linked to the *Mysteries Texts*,[60] which in reality are also wisdom literature. The Qumran corpus shows the extent to which this wisdom literature continues to be a major genre in Jewish circles and helps as well to explain the strong wisdom trends evident in both the New Testament and Rabbinic literature.

It goes without saying that the genre of apocalyptic literature – however that term might be defined[61] – is greatly enriched by the new discoveries. The scrolls are replete with descriptions of revealed secrets and depictions of the end of days. We also hear descriptions of the eschatological war in the various versions of the *War Scroll*[62] and the associated texts and of the works of the Messiah.[63] From a literary point of view, the *War Scroll* points to the existence in this period of religious poetry from which the author derived the liturgical sections, as well as of military manuals that he used to pattern the military sections. This text, a marriage of these very

---

[60] J. T. Milik, in D. Barthélemy and J. T. Milik, *Qumran Cave I*, DJD 1 (Oxford: Clarendon Press, 1955), 102-7; L. H. Schiffman in T. Elgvin, et al., *Qumran Cave 4.XV, Sapiential Texts, Part 1*, DJD 20 (Oxford: Clarendon, 1997), 31-123.

[61] On apocalypticism at Qumran, see C. A. Newsom, "Apocalyptic and the Discourse of the Qumran Community," *JNES* 49 (1990): 135-44; J. J. Collins, *The Apocalyptic Imagination* (New York: Crossroad, 1984), 115-41; idem, "Was the Dead Sea Sect an Apocalyptic Movement?" *Archaeology and History in the Dead Sea Scrolls*, 25-51; idem, *Apocalypticism in the Dead Sea Scrolls* (London and New York: Routledge, 1997).

[62] Y. Yadin, *The Scroll of the War of the Sons of Light Against the Sons of Darkness*, trans. B. and C. Rabin (Oxford: Oxford University Press, 1962).

[63] E. Puech, *Qumrân Grotte 4.XVIII, Textes Hébreux (4Q521-5Q528, 4Q576-4Q579)*, DJD 25 (Oxford: Clarendon Press, 1998), 1-38.

different kinds of material, is therefore also testimony to texts which lie behind those preserved in the scrolls corpus.

In general, the scrolls provide us with an entire collection of texts of varied genres, showing us how the major types of literature found within the biblical collection developed in the Hasmonean period. The one major element missing from the scrolls, presaging the situation in rabbinic literature, is historical writing. One of the greatest disappointments about this collection is the absence of *1 Maccabees*, a Hebrew text composed in this period but preserved only in Greek, which may be absent because of the strong anti-Hasmonean stance of the Qumran sectarians.

IV. Language

Our perspectives on the history of the Hebrew language itself have also been greatly advanced by the finds in the Judean Desert. We shall here concentrate on just a number of examples of particular interest. Our discussion will be limited to only two aspects, the linguistic character of the sectarian scrolls and the Hebrew of the Bar Kokhba texts and its relationship to Mishnaic Hebrew.

A. The Sectarian Scrolls

While, as we already noted, many of the Qumran scrolls were written in a dialect of Hebrew virtually the same as that of the Massoretic Text of the Hebrew Bible, a second dialect is also preserved at Qumran – that of the sect's own compositions. These latter texts can be distinguished on the basis of certain specific linguistic features and also by the presence of the distinctive ideas of the sect. From the linguistic point of view, the following are some of the main features.[64]

---

[64] On Qumran Hebrew, see M. H. Goshen-Gottstein, "Linguistic Structure and Tradition in the Qumran Documents," *Aspects of the Dead Sea Scrolls*, ed. C. Rabin, Y. Yadin, Scripta Hierosolymitana 4 (Jerusalem: Magnes

These texts exhibit what we have come to term "long
pronominal endings," e.g., הואה, היאה, אותמה, אתכמה and the spelling
of כיא with final *alef*; we cannot be certain if these endings were
actually pronounced (we should note that they are pronounced
in Samaritan pronunciation today). In addition, final forms of
verbs, such as יכתובו, appear in medial position where we would
expect יכתבו. There is some evidence for such features in the
Massoretic Text or in the *qere/ketiv* notes. However, nowhere
else in Hebrew dialectology do we find these "survivals" of an
age gone by (if that is what they are), grouped so consistently
and turned into a full-fledged system of orthography and
morphology.

If indeed this is an archaizing language, as some have
suggested, we would understand easily the presence in the
sectarian lexicon of numerous biblical usages that are clearly
designed to replace well-known post-biblical Hebrew terms. For
example, הון, replaces ממון, "money," and ביד רמה replaces במזיד,
"intentionally." Many examples of this phenomenon could be
cited, as it is a regular feature of these texts.[65] At the same
time, the scrolls cannot help but reveal knowledge of contemporary terminology, especially regarding technical matters. We
find in the *Temple Scroll* such "later" terms as הניפת העומר, "the
waving of the sheaf," תערובת, "mixture," and התערב, "to be mixed,"
hence "to become impure."[66] Many of these usages point

Press, 1958), 101-37; C. Rabin, "The Historical Background of Qumran
Hebrew," *Aspects of the Dead Sea Scrolls,* 144-61; Z. Ben-Hayyim,
"Traditions in the Hebrew Language with Special Reference to the Dead
Sea Scrolls," *Aspects of the Dead Sea Scrolls,* 200-14; E. Y. Kutscher, *Ha-
Lashon ve-ha-Reqa ha-Leshoni shel Megillat Yesha'yahu ha-Sheleimah
mi-Megillot Yam ha-Melah* (Jerusalem: Magnes Press, 1959); E. Qimron,
The Hebrew of the Dead Sea Scrolls, Harvard Semitic Studies 29 (Atlanta:
Scholars Press, 1986); M. G. Abegg, "The Hebrew of the Dead Sea Scrolls,"
The Dead Sea Scrolls After Fifty Years, A Comprehensive Assessment,
vol. 1, ed. P. W. Flint and J. C. VanderKam (Leiden: Brill, 1998), 325-58.

[65] Cf. C. Rabin, *Qumran Studies,* Scripta Judaica 2 (Oxford: Clarendon
Press, 1957), 108-9.

[66] Listed in Yadin, *Temple Scroll,* 1.35-8.

toward the full Jewish ritual and legal lexicon of Mishnaic Hebrew. The *MMT* text, we should note, uses such terminology extensively in its polemics with the Pharisees. Examples include: ולד, "embryo, infant," יד, "handle," פרש מן, "separate from" and others. Examples such as these – and there are many more – indicate the extent to which much of the vocabulary and terminology found first in Tannaitic sources – even that which is not paralleled in the scrolls – is actually much older. It simply appears in Tannaitic sources for the first time in the extant literary corpus.[67]

The new texts from Qumran greatly enrich the lexicon of Hebrew with words not previously known, such as בחון, "expert," זיק, "dart," כידן, "sword", מדע, "fellow," מצול, "saved" and many, many more.[68] In all areas of vocabulary, whether religious, military, economic or social, we find new vocabulary items. It stands to reason that only a few of these locutions were inventions of the sectarian authors. For the most part, this material testifies to the wide vocabulary of Second Temple Hebrew, which included numerous terms, which for reasons of accident or because they entered the language later, did not appear in the biblical corpus.

B. The Bar Kokhba Period Documents

As mentioned above, the Hebrew documents in the Bar Kokhba collection ended forever the debate over whether Hebrew was a living language in the Mishnaic period, i.e., from the destruction of the Temple in 70 C.E. through the editing of the Mishnah c. 200 C.E. At the same time, this corpus supplied much new linguistic data, some of which challenged reigning views. Exceedingly interesting here is the appearance of ת instead of the more familiar את to signify the direct object.

---

[67] See also, J. F. Elwolde, "Developments in Hebrew Vocabulary Between Bible and Mishnah," *The Hebrew of the Dead Sea Scrolls and Ben Sira*, 17-55.

[68] Listed in Qimron, *Hebrew of the Dead Sea Scrolls*, 105-15.

From the point of view of orthography, none of the forms that typify Qumran sectarian Hebrew appear here. Despite the claims that Mishnaic Hebrew is characterized by the writing of של, "of," connected to the following word, as in the biblical example שלשלמה, "of Solomon" (Song 3:7), של appears in these documents both connected and as a separate word. Another touted characteristic of Mishnaic Hebrew, said to typify the best manuscripts, is the spelling ריבי for Rabbi, literally, "my master, my teacher." Here again, the scholarly consensus must be modified in light of the occurrence of רבי, which must have been pronounced *rabbi*, as appears most likely from the transliteration of this word in the Greek manuscripts of the New Testament. Other characteristics observed in Mishnaic manuscripts, like use of ן for biblical ם at the ends of words and the confusion of gutturals – the latter also found in Qumran sectarian Hebrew – are observable in these documents.

Among the linguistic usages of interest in these documents, we cite but a few examples: the occasional use of חנטין for חטים, "wheat"; חכיר, "rent"; the root מרק in the sense of "wipe off, erase," i.e., "pay" a debt; חרר (=ערר), "objection"; the verb תקן, "to tithe"; and the legal clause וקים עלי לעמת ככה, "it is accepted by me (i.e., I commit myself) regarding the afore-mentioned."

V. Concluding Remarks

We have surveyed here only the smallest part of the tremendous contribution that the Dead Sea Scrolls make to the corpus of material in the Hebrew language from the period of Late Antiquity. This treasure trove of material, stretching from the pre-Hasmonean period through the eve of the redaction of the Mishnah, provides new evidence for grammar, lexicography, literary structure, and for an understanding of the interplay of languages in the Jewish communities of the ancient Land of Israel. Needless to say, the scrolls are bringing about a reevaluation of many aspects of the history of Judaism and this in turn is providing a new backdrop for the evaluation of the linguistic and literary phenomena we have been studying here. Whatever the outcome of the many academic debates currently raging regarding the scrolls, their discovery certainly has reclaimed for us a new layer in the history of Hebrew language and literature. Like those before and after, this layer testifies eloquently to the linguistic and literary creativity of the Jewish people in their native language throughout their history.

Rashba

as

Halakhic Critic

of Maimonides

Michael A. Shmidman

In his wide-ranging study of the controversy surrounding the halakhic authority of Maimonides, R. Yizhak Ze'ev Kahana advances the following example of what he terms the "typical" attitude of Rashba to Maimonides' *Mishneh Torah.*[1] In the case of one who assumes an unfixed financial obligation (*davar she-eino kazuv*), e.g., if one obligates himself to provide food or clothing for another over a period of five years, Maimonides rules that he is not bound by the obligation.[2] Rashba, in a responsum, comments that these words of Maimonides "are

---

[1] I. Kahana, "Ha-Pulemos mi-Saviv le-Keviat ha-Halakhah ke-ha-Rambam," *Sinai* 36 (1955): 391-411 (esp. 398-400), 530-37; reprinted in idem, *Mehkarim be-Sifrut ha-Teshuvot* (Jerusalem, 1973).

[2] *Mishneh Torah, Hilkhot Mekhirah*, 11:16.

not, in essence, accepted by us as valid, and we act daily in
opposition to them."[3] It is interesting to note that Rabad
is similarly critical of this Maimonidean ruling. Yet just as
Rabad's critical *hassagot* should be seen as only one aspect
of Rabad's total role as both commentator and critic of the
Mishneh Torah, so too Rashba's criticism should be viewed
within the broader context of Rashba's overall approach to the
Mishneh Torah.[4]

Criticism and commentary are inseparable in *Mishneh
Torah* literature, and both are contained in the writings of the
twelfth and thirteenth century critics, fourteenth century
"arms-bearers," and the general halakhic literature of the period, including the writings of Rashba.[5] This essay attempts to
demonstrate how Rashba – in his responsa and codes – indeed
reflects this pattern of Maimonidean literature, and to determine more precisely his attitude toward the codificatory
method of the *Mishneh Torah.*[6]

---

[3] R. Solomon ibn Adret (Spain, c.1235-c.1310) *She'elot u-Teshuvot* (Jerusalem, 2005), II:89.

[4] See Professor I. Twersky's masterful analysis of Rabad as Maimonidean
commentator and critic in *Rabad of Posquieres*, revised edition (Philadelphia, 1980), part III.

[5] I. Twersky, "The Beginnings of *Mishneh Torah* Criticism," *Biblical and
Other Studies*, ed. A. Altmann (Cambridge, 1963); idem, *Introduction to the
Code of Maimonides* (New Haven and London, 1980), 518-31.

[6] Citations of Rashba's responsa follow the order of the standard
eight-volume edition (seven volumes plus *Teshuvot Meyuhasot la-Ramban*),
most recently published in Jerusalem (2005). On the history of the printing
of the various collections of Rashba's responsa, and the complex literary
issues associated with the standard edition, see: H. Dimitrovsky, *Teshuvot
ha-Rashba* (Jerusalem, 1990), vol. 1, introduction, 10-15; S. Z. Havlin,
introduction to *Teshuvot She'elot le-ha-Rashba ... Roma* (Jerusalem, 1977),
reprinted in *She'elot u-Teshuvot ha-Rashba* (Jerusalem, 2000).

References to Rashba's code of ritual law, *Torat ha-Bayit*, follow the pagination of standard editions, as recently reprinted in Jerusalem (2004).

I believe that the hundreds of citations from Maimonides' *Mishneh Torah* in
the above works present clear – if only preliminary – indications of distinct
patterns within Rashba's critique of the *Mishneh Torah*.

The Responsa

Rashba's role as defender and clarifier of the *Mishneh Torah* is evident in a significant number of responsa, almost equal to the number expressing clear disagreement. These positive or constructive types of comments, on occasion accompanied by faint praise (e.g., "he has determined well"),[7] may be classified further under a number of sub-categories. The most commonly-recurrent category consists of cases in which Rashba agrees with the Maimonidean ruling, and endeavors to sustain it by citing the appropriate talmudic source, elucidating Maimonides' interpretation of the sources, or supporting the ruling with additional proofs.[8] A typical example of this major category (responsum I:363) involves the priestly prohibition of "Do not drink *yayin ve-shekhar*, you, and your sons with you, when you go into the Tent of Meeting, lest you die ... (Leviticus 10:9)." The problem is whether this prohibition applies only to wine or, as Maimonides maintains, also to other intoxicating drinks. The questioner interprets the talmudic sources against Maimonides' opinion. Rashba responds: "It appears that Maimonides employed a different method in [interpreting] that law ... unlike the words of Rashi and Rabad; and he [Maimonides] is correct." He then proceeds to a lengthy interpretation of the talmudic source and its halakhic implications, concluding: "And so did Maimonides decide, and his words emerge properly according to this explanation of ours."

Among the smaller categories within this commendatory group are the following: instances in which Rashba supports Maimonides' halakhic ruling on the basis of principles of talmudic decision such as compliance with the majority opinion,[9] one instance in which Rashba prefers Maimonides' opinion on

---

[7] *Responsa*, I:535; V:10.

[8] See, e.g., I:124, 363, 405, 410, 706, 1218, 1252; II:320; III:245, 338; IV:254; V:10, 157, 276.

[9] I:411, 431.

the strength of empirical observation,[10] cases where he affirms
Maimonides' version of the talmudic text as the correct one,[11]
and a number of examples of Rashba defending Maimonides by
indicating scribal errors in the edition of *Mishneh Torah* cited
in the question.[12]

All this support of Maimonidean rulings does not imply
subservience, however, as will be demonstrated clearly soon
and as is evident already in some examples of the above categories in which Rashba essentially accepts Maimonides' decision, explains and supports it, but then adds a modification or
qualification. One example is responsum I:362, concerning a
kid roasted together with its forbidden fat. Here Rashba agrees
with and clarifies the statement of Maimonides, but then adds
the qualification that all this applies in regard to roasting; but
in cooking the law differs somewhat, "even though it does not
appear so from the words of Maimonides."[13]

Another category of more neutral or objective commentatorial responsa is comprised of statements clarifying aspects of
Maimonides' language, phraseology and opinions. In responsum I:500, for example, Rashba explains why Maimonides
chose to preface a ruling with the phrase "it appears to me,"
despite the fact that the explicit talmudic sources seem to
support such a ruling.[14]

Yet another, final category of commentatorial statements
consists of Rashba's replies to a series of questions concerning
apparent contradictions between Maimonides' halakhic decision in the *Mishneh Torah* and in his responsa, and between
different versions of the same ruling in different editions of the

---

[10] I:36.

[11] I:141, 328.

[12] II:98; III:126, 246.

[13] See also, I:321, 331.

[14] See also, I:168, 234, 320, 329, 368, 388, 1165, 1166, 1183; VI:177.

Mishneh Torah. Here Rashba fills the position of arbitrator, deciding which is the valid and authoritative ruling.[15]

Occasionally we encounter explicit expression by Rashba of his conscious role as commentator and defender. In responsum I:311, for instance, Rashba begins by concurring with the objections against Maimonides' decision, continuing: "However, I must ... pursue his merit [i.e., the merit of his words]" – and he proceeds to do so.[16]

At this point we turn gradually to Rashba's critical, openly negative *hassagot*. The transition is provided by a sizeable group of comments that are both commentatorial and critical in nature. This group may be divided into: cases where Rashba agrees with Maimonides in theory but differs in actual practice on the basis of locally accepted custom (e.g., responsum I:469, where – in accord with Maimonides – he is opposed in principle to the insertion of liturgical poems in honor of a groom or circumcision at certain points in the liturgy, but adds that the custom has become widespread "and allow Israel to act in accordance with their custom");[17] cases where Rashba affirms Maimonides' version and reading of a text, yet again records that the local custom differs;[18] and finally, instances in which Rashba personally disagrees with Maimonides and yet continues his quest for sources that might provide a tenable basis also for Maimonides' ruling, or for an interpretation that would reconcile Maimonides with the sources in question. One illustration of the latter category would be responsum I:311, previously cited, where Rashba sides with the questioner

---

[15] I:4-7. It should be noted that Rashba feels perfectly free to choose between the validity of earlier and later Maimonidean statements, sometimes affirming the earlier and other times preferring the later statement. This assertion of independence in approaching the decisions of the *Mishneh Torah* – already alluded to above – will be discussed more fully later.

[16] See also, V:70. The complete phrase in responsum I:311 is: אלא דבעינא למשכוני נפשין אדרב ז"ל לחזר אחר זכותו.

[17] See also, I:210, 398.

[18] See I:328.

against Maimonides' interpretation but attempts to "discover merit" in the ruling of the *Mishneh Torah*, concluding the lengthy explanation with: "So it appears to me to reconcile the matter in accordance with the ruling of the Rabbi [Maimonides]."[19]

In cases of the latter category, Rashba often must resort to admitted conjecture in order to salvage the validity of a Maimonidean ruling, usually prefacing such speculations with various words meaning "perhaps." A clear example is responsum I:320, where Rashba utilizes the word *u-lai* ("perhaps") no less than three times in qualifying the certainty of his proposed explanations.[20]

We now arrive at those statements of Rashba which clearly and definitively reject Maimonides' position. First, however, it should be emphasized that these negative criticisms are not gratuitous. Instead we encounter numerous references to the fact that Rashba's critical conclusions were preceded by an exhaustive search for possible justifications of Maimonides' position. In responsum V:16, for example, Rashba states: "I took pains to sustain his words and I was unable to do so"; also in responsum III:364: "I reviewed from every side, and I did not find a source upon which the Rabbi [Maimonides] could support [his view]."[21] Furthermore, in a number of responsa in which Rashba dismisses Maimonides' view, he first advances a possible basis for Maimonides' position before attacking its validity and then totally rejecting the opinion.[22]

The largest single category of criticisms contains rejections of Maimonides' positions as unsupported and untenable, without even suggestion of possible justification or text-support. These criticisms assume several forms: at times just a brief

---

[19]See also, I:309, 389, 392, 614, 884.

[20] See also, I:389, 392, 614. Speculative terms appear also in other categories, e.g.: I:168, 390; II:228, 230; III:364; V:158.

[21]See also, I:330, 331, 509; V:16.

[22] I:321, 390, 640 (=1168), 1090, 1249; II:228, 230; III:364; IV:145; V:158.

reference to the fact that Maimonides' opinion stands in opposition to the clear talmudic decision, or that he could not discover any source or line of reasoning; other times, a lengthy elaboration of the correct opinion followed or preceded by a categorical rejection of Maimonides' differing view, and supplemented occasionally by extensive refutation of the rejected opinion.[23] The use of the relatively mild phrases: "I am amazed at the Rabbi [Maimonides]," or "the words of the Rabbi [Maimonides] are astonishing" – the most critical expressions that Rashba ever utilizes against Maimonides – is to be found among this group.[24] Also among these animadversions appear frequent quotes from Rabad's *hassagot*, which are seconded by Rashba, or sometimes simply cited in lieu of his own criticism.[25] Nevertheless, Rashba does not automatically concur with Rabad's criticisms (just as he does not automatically prefer the views of the Rif or his own teachers over those of Maimonides),[26] and we find instances where he sides with Maimonides against the *hassagah* of Rabad.[27]

Attitude Toward
Maimonides' Mode of Codification

A major motivating factor in *Mishneh Torah* literature is the assertion of intellectual independence in halakhic decision-making, in response to the authoritarian air of Maimonides' Code. Rashba not only manifests this independence in his actual critique of Maimonidean rulings, as has been seen, but

---

[23] See I:29, 110, 160, 330, 331, 427, 507, 509, 569, 573, 717, 726, 794, 802, 920, 928, 981; II:42, 343; IV:89, 132; V:16, 180.

[24] See, e.g., I:509 (אני תמה על הרב הרמב"ם ז"ל); 1168 (גם אנו תמהנו על דבריו); II:228 (דברי הרב ז"ל בזה אינן אלא מן המתמיהין) IV:145 (דבריו מתמיהין).

[25] I:6, 110, 182, 331, 427, 507, 794; II:42, 343; IV:145.

[26] See examples cited by H. Tchernowitz, *Toldot ha-Poskim* (New York, 1947), vol. II, 122, nn. 13-14. See also *Torat ha-Bayit*, I:93a-b.

[27] *Responsa*, I:639; *Torat ha-Bayit*, I:32a.

also underscores it in some of the phraseology that he employs
in disagreement. In responsum I:726, for example, he states
concerning Maimonides' ruling: "We do not know his reasoning, nor have we seen any scholar or author who has written
thus; and [as for us], we shall rely on what is explained in the
Talmud." And again in I:920: "This is the correct interpretation
[and] even though Maimonides ... did not explain thusly, so did
we receive from our teachers and so is it written by us."[28]

Rashba also appears to share the general aversion to the
use of the title *Mishneh Torah* in halakhic contexts – because of
the aspirations it implied[29] – never using the Code's given
name. Instead, the terms *"Hibbur"* ("Compendium") or *"Hibbur
ha-gadol"* ("the great Compendium") sometimes are used to
designate the *Mishneh Torah;*[30] most frequent are direct references to the immediate section and chapter of the *Mishneh
Torah,* such as "chapter two of *Hilkhot Kelim.*"[31] This deliberate
avoidance of the official title of the work is particularly con-
spicuous when Rashba does refer to other works, like his own
Torat ha-Bayit or Nahmanides' *Torat ha-Adam,* by their given
titles.[32]

Further criticism of Maimonides' mode of codification,
particularly of his omission of sources and rationales,
is implied in a statement quoted by R. Asher ben Yehiel (Rosh)
in the name of "a great man in Barcelona" and attributed by
some to Rashba. The statement is found in a responsum of
R. Asher, in which R. Asher criticizes those who render
halakhic decisions on the basis of the *Mishneh Torah* without

---

[28] See also, *Responsa,* I:794, 802, 884.

[29] See Twersky, "Beginnings," 173, n. 55; idem, "R. Yosef Ashkenazi
ve-Sefer *Mishneh Torah* la-Rambam," *Salo Baron Jubilee Volume,* ed.
S. Lieberman (Jerusalem, 1975), vol. 3, 183-94; M. Genack, "Rambam's
Mishneh Torah: The Significance of Its Title," *Tradition* 38:2 (2004), 78-85.

[30] *Responsa,* I:4, 7, 253, 325, 1161.

[31] Ibid., I:195, 390, 392, 427 and many other examples.

[32] Ibid., I:59, 330, 392, 393, 443 and others.

prior knowledge of the underlying talmudic sources – "for he [Maimonides] wrote his work as if he were prophesying by the divine word, without reason or proof" – and then goes on to relate that:

> And so did I hear from a great man in Barcelona who was knowledgeable in three orders [of Talmud] and who said: "I am amazed at people who did not learn Talmud and who read the books of Maimonides and issue decisions and judge on the basis of his works and who think they comprehend them," for he said, "I know concerning myself that regarding the three orders that I learned, I understand when I read in his [Maimonides'] works, but regarding his books on the laws of *Kodashim* and *Zera'im*, I do not comprehend anything, and I know that so it is with them in all his books."[33]

Whether the phrase "a great man in Barcelona" actually refers to Rashba is highly questionable. Kahana, following J. Hayyim Michael, assumes that it does.[34] Kahana also refers to A. Freimann, however, who – in his biographical essays on R. Asher – obviously assumes that the "great man" is another rabbi whom R. Asher met while in Barcelona.[35] No one provides any proof either way, and the only evident clues are the account – recorded in *Shalshelet ha-Kabbalah* – of R. Asher spending eight days learning together with Rashba in Barcelona,[36] and the statement itself, which can be interpreted in different ways. The confession of ignorance of half the orders of the Talmud could be understood, on the one hand, as an expression of modesty on the part of Rashba,

---

[33] *Responsa* of R. Asher b. Yehiel (New York, 1954), 31:9.

[34] Kahana, 393, n. 10; J. Hayyim Michael, *Or ha-Hayyim* (Jerusalem, 1965), 542.

[35] A. Freimann, "Ascher b. Jechiel," *Jahrbuch der Judisch-Literarischen Gesellschaft*, vol. XII (Frankfurt, 1918), 251. (Hebrew translation, *Ha-Rosh* [Jerusalem,1986], 28.)

[36] Gedaliah ibn Yahya, *Shalshelet ha-Kabbalah* (Lemberg, 1866), section on R. Asher (unnumbered).

especially since most of his halakhic writings do concern
the other three orders.[37] On the other hand, aside from
commentaries and codes based on tractates *Berakhot*, *Hullin*
and *Niddah*, we also have Rashba's *Sha'ar ha-Mayim* on
the laws of ritual baths, *Piskei Hallah*, and scattered
responsa concerning non-practical laws in the orders of
Kodashim, *Tohorot*, and particularly, *Zera'im*. No other example
of the phrase "great man in Barcelona" exists among
the responsa of R. Asher to aid in clarifying the source of the
statement.

It is interesting to note one fact, however, that might
have direct bearing on this problem. In another responsum
of R. Asher, we encounter the very criticism leveled against
Maimonides and affirmed by the "great man," now directed
against Rashba (though only in regard to one specific decision
and not against an entire system of codification):

> I was unable to find a reason or proof for his [Rashba's]
> words.... And it is proper for he who says such aston-
> ishing things to advance support for his words ... for
> these are naught but "words of prophecy" and one
> should not hearken to him until he presents proofs
> that are straightforward to he who comprehends.[38]

Torat ha-Bayit

Similar criticism of Maimonides' system of codification is
implied by the nature of Rashba's own major code, *Torat
ha-Bayit*. This work (whose very existence spares Rashba's
Mishneh Torah criticism of any charge of being motivated by

---

[37] On the traditional restriction of talmudic studies in Spain to the practical "three orders," see Twersky, *Rabad*, 15 (and n. 80); idem, *Introduction*,
192-95.

[38] *Responsa* of R. Asher, 35:3. For poetic expression of R. Asher's respect
for Rashba, see ibid., 2:14-19.

arbitrary opposition to attempts at definitive codification) is composed of two parts. The longer *Torat ha-Bayit ha-Arokh* provides a detailed presentation of the talmudic and rabbinic deliberations underlying the specific halakhah, complete with names of authorities, citation of sources, and legal rationales, while the shorter *Torat ha-Bayit ha-Kazar* offers a capsule summary of the law, with minimal *apparatus criticus*. In his introduction to the work, Rashba recounts the factors that precipitated his composition of the code, and then elaborates upon his method of codification, stressing the necessity of citing authoritative sources:

> And I will write, with God's help – in the manner of [talmudic] deliberations – from whence these matters derive, in order that the reader shall find the source of the "water" and so that his "waters" will be trustworthy, from Talmud or from the words of the *rishonim*. And then I will write the halakhic decisions in concise form, as if[39] these matters were transmitted to us via tradition.

This programmatic statement is reiterated in Rashba's words of introduction to *"Bet ha-Nashim,"* the concluding section of *Torat ha-Bayit*:

> And I will write each matter at length, and I will examine it according to the Talmud and the words of the commentators, in order to apprehend the truth of the matter – with God's help – in accordance with [careful] investigation and via [talmudic] deliberation, until the reader ... will be able to discover on what basis I arrived at the halakhic decision.... And afterward I will write all the laws in brief form ... so that the reader may go through it quickly and find the matter that he

---

[39] Although the word באלו is found in standard editions of the *Arokh*, older editions of the *Kazar* (e.g., Berlin, Salonica, Prague) read: כאלו. See also, H. G. Zimbalist's edition of the *Arokh* (Tel-Aviv, 1993), and M. Elon, *Ha-Mishpat ha-Ivri* (Jerusalem, 1973), 1055-56.

> desires to deal with in concise form – if he wishes to
> rely upon what I saw fit to rely on.

The last phrase, in particular, again affirms the intellectual
independence of the individual, while rejecting the concept of
any one absolutely-binding code to which everyone, no matter
how learned, must unquestionably submit.

Rashba's insistence upon the *Torat ha-Bayit ha-Arokh*
to complement and underlie the *Kazar* raises a problem with
regard to another of his codificatory works, *Avodat ha-Kodesh*
(on the laws of Sabbath, festivals and *eruvin*), which is known
to us today only in the short, concise format typical of the
Kazar. Weiss suggests that Rashba deliberately altered his
method of codification – eliminating the longer part – upon
realizing the excessive difficulties involved in comprehending
the practical halakhah from the deliberations of the *Arokh*.[40]
Tchernowitz, primarily for reasons of lack of evidence to the
contrary, also leans to the view that no *Avodat ha-Kodesh
ha-Arokh* ever was composed.[41] It seems highly unlikely,
however, that Rashba suddenly would abandon his elaborately
and deliberately-developed system of codification, only to leave
himself an open target for the same criticism that was previously directed against the *Mishneh Torah* and which presumably was a factor in choosing his original system of codification.
Indeed, the indispensable role of the longer code in comprehending the shorter is stressed by Rashba in responsum I:273:

> And it appears that you do not have the *Arokh*. And my
> anger is upon those who copy the *Kazar* when no
> *Arokh* is to be found in the city, for I have set up the
> *Arokh* as a shield against the arrows of the critics who
> suspect that perhaps I wrote that which I wrote while
> in a slumber; and he who comprehends the *Arokh* will
> know what prompted me to say that which I stated.

---

40 I. Weiss, *Dor Dor ve-Doreshav* (Jerusalem, 1963-64), vol. V, 37.

41 Tchernowitz, 133-34.

Furthermore, among other existing codes from the pen of Rashba, we find that the *Sha'ar ha-Mayim* also consists of an *Arokh* and a *Kazar*, and the *Piskei Hallah* bears a close resemblance to the *Torat ha-Bayit ha-Arokh*. Finally, the *Or ha-Hayyim, Shem ha-Gedolim* and editors' introductions to more recent editions of *Avodat ha-Kodesh* all list references in halakhic works and even phrases in Rashba's responsa that persuasively point to the existence of a more detailed *Avodat ha-Kodesh ha-Arokh*, that subsequently must have been lost.[42]

Within the *Torat ha-Bayit (ha-Arokh)* itself, there emerges a pattern of *Mishneh Torah* criticism very similar to that encountered in the *Responsa*. Again we find Rashba carefully scrutinizing statements of Maimonides, offering agreement or positive commentary almost as often as critical disagreement. At times he simply cites a Maimonidean view and agrees with it, sometimes praising the view and advancing further support.[43] Other times he tries to suggest a basis or source for Maimonides' ruling, or simply clarifies the latter's position.[44] On the other hand, we also see Rashba dissenting, sometimes proposing a possible explanation for Maimonides' view and then rejecting its feasibility,[45] but more often just stating the correct opinion and then either rejecting the Maimonidean ruling or attacking it further.[46] Another example of implied criticism of the codificatory method of *Mishneh Torah* is to be found in the laws of *terefot* (*Torat ha-Bayit*, I:41b), where Rashba deliberates upon a difficulty in Maimonides' position, suggests a resolution of the problem, and then adds: "and it is

---

[42] *Or ha-Hayyim*, 579-80; H. Azulai, *Shem ha-Gedolim* (Brooklyn, 1958), 175-76; *Avodat ha-Kodesh*, ed. H. Zimbalist (Tel Aviv, 1973), introduction; *Avodat ha-Kodesh*, ed. S. Yungerman (Zikhron Yaakov, 1980), introduction.

[43] *Torat ha-Bayit*, I:4a, 8a, 9b, 30a, 35b, 36a, 37a, 42a, 86a, 86b, 87a, 94a; II:3b and others.

[44] Ibid., I:5b-6a, 25b, 41b, 64a, 88a; II:12a and others.

[45] Ibid., I:25b, 32b-33a, 41b, 45a, 51b, 78b, 90b; II:11b and others.

[46] Ibid., I:7a, 8b, 23a, 30a, 33b, 34b, 38a, 40b, 48b, 53b, 56b, 57b, 59b, 73b, 80a; II:3b and others.

possible that this was what the Rabbi [Maimonides] had in
mind, but he should have explained."

Our examination of the *Responsa* and *Torat ha-Bayit* has
demonstrated that Rashba reflects the general character of
Mishneh Torah literature: defense and commentary, dissent
and criticism; critique of the methodology of the work, together
with an effort to supply missing explanations and sources and
thereby uphold the authority of the Code; and all of this
founded upon a thorough, serious and independent study of
the *Mishneh Torah*. One might add, that Rashba's familiarity
with the *Mishneh Torah* appears to be quite extensive. He often
concludes the statement of a halakhic position with "and so
did Maimonides write," or otherwise inserts Maimonides into
the discussion even when the question is not directed specifically at a Maimonidean ruling.[47] At times he collates several
statements from different sections of the *Mishneh Torah* in
order to point out a possible contradiction or propose an
explanation.[48] Occasional lapses in this familiarity are noted by
later commentators. R. Vidal of Tolosa (*Maggid Mishneh*), at the
end of his introduction to *Sefer Zemanim* of the *Mishneh Torah*,
seems to consider Rashba an "expert" in Maimonides' Code,
but notes an instance in which Rashba inferred Maimonides'
position from one ruling without taking into consideration an
amplification of the same matter in a later chapter. Another
example is quoted by Kahana from the responsa of R. Levi ibn
Habib, who endeavors to justify his disagreement with Rashba
regarding the interpretation of a ruling of Maimonides:

> ... but what shall I do, for Rabbi Moses ben Maimon's
> own words in the beginning of the aforementioned
> chapter compelled me [to interpret in this way] as was
> explained, and the great Rabbi, Rashba, in accordance
> with his great erudition in Talmud – and those words
> which he wrote were clear to him according to his

---

[47] See, e.g., *Responsa*, I:183, 222, 319, 324, 404 and many others.
[48] See, e.g., ibid., I:390.

interpretation of the Talmud – did not wish to trouble himself to see all the statements of the Rabbi, our teacher, Moses ben Maimon, z"l, and there happened to him in this as occurred to him in another instance ... [the one cited by the *Maggid Mishneh*]."[49]

Aside from such isolated lapses, however, Rashba's *Mishneh Torah* erudition is evident.[50]

---

[49] Kahana, 399; *Responsa* of R. Levi ibn Habib, 138.

[50] Rashba's familiarity with the *Mishnah Commentary* of Maimonides is a more complex question. R. Malakhi ha-Kohen, *Yad Malakhi* (New York, 1945), 192, states that: "Rashba did not see the *Mishnah Commentary* of Maimonides; so wrote Radbaz...." In the published responsa, one finds – on the one hand – some support for the assumption that Rashba knew of, but did not have, the *Commentary*. In responsum I:390, after unsuccessfully attempting to resolve a difficulty in the *Mishneh Torah*, Rashba concludes: "and if you have in your possession his [Maimonides'] *Mishnah Commentary*, establish this matter with certainty and inform me." On the other hand, in several responsa Rashba explicitly states that he checked or was familiar with the *Commentary*. In responsum I:330, Rashba relates that: "afterward I examined the words of Maimonides in his *Mishnah Commentary* and found there that he explicitly prohibits, and these are his words...." Also in I:1149: "And I also found in his [Maimonides'] *Mishnah Commentary* that he wrote...." And again in I:325: "And Maimonides also ruled in accordance with the Rabbis, in his *Mishnah Commentary*."

The resolution of this difficulty apparently resides in the translators' introductions to early Hebrew editions of the various parts of the *Commentary*, cited by Y. Kapah in the foreword to his own translation of the *Commentary* (Jerusalem, 1963), vol.1, 8-10. In these introductions we read of a statement attributed to Rashba that: "these books [the *Mishnah Commentary*] are not available to us, and we never have become accustomed to learn Arabic," and we see Rashba actively promoting both the procurement of the *Commentary* and its translation from Arabic into Hebrew. Most of the translations appear to have been authored at the end of the thirteenth century, and we may assume that Rashba would have had more access to the text of the *Commentary* at that time.

Rashba also was familiar with numerous responsa of Maimonides. (See A. Freimann's introduction to his *Teshuvot ha-Rambam* [Jerusalem, 1934], 32.) Rashba apparently did not always have ready access to the responsum in question, for regarding one ruling of the *Mishneh Torah*, mentioned in both responsum I:29 and responsum I:160, he states (29): "And it would appear that he himself [Maimonides] retracted his position in a responsum," and (in 160): "And we heard that he retracted it."

Impact of Maimonides' Authority

A final question meriting consideration is whether and to what extent the widespread acceptance and veneration of the *Mishneh Torah* might have affected Rashba's attitude to and criticism of the work. The phenomenon of entire communities agreeing to decide all (or almost all) halakhic matters in accordance with Maimonides' Code is attested to in a number of the questions addressed to Rashba, and is essentially sanctioned by Rashba in a responsum.[51] One might reasonably suggest, therefore, that Rashba would not feel quite as free to express strong criticism as, for example, the Rabad clearly felt. We already have seen, however, how independent Rashba is in his overall critique of the *Mishneh Torah,* despite his awareness of and deference to the honored status of Maimonides – as evidenced further in a statement such as: "with all due respect, his [Maimonides'] words are not at all satisfactory in this instance."[52] In what concrete way, then, might such a limitation be manifested?

Choice of language is one possibility: Rashba is quite deferential to Maimonides, even while criticizing. The most common expression of disapproval is "his words are not clear to me," with an occasional "I am astonished at his words." In two cases, where Rashba notes what he considers to be an obvious and glaring error in halakhah, he respectfully suggests that Maimonides' words are "like an error which proceeds from the ruler."[53] Yet in the *Mishmeret ha-Bayit,* Rashba's rebuttal of the *Bedek ha-Bayit* of R. Aaron ha-Levi, Rashba is second to none in sharp, witty and quite caustic polemic,

---

[51] *Responsa,* I:253, 378, 1165 and Rashba's reply in 253. See also I. Baer, *A History of the Jews in Christian Spain* (Philadelphia, 1971), vol. 1, 220-21. On the "heroic image" of Maimonides in this period, see B. Septimus, *Hispano-Jewish Culture in Transition: The Career and Controversies of Ramah* (Cambridge, Mass., 1982).

[52] *Responsa,* I:1168.

[53] Ibid., I:160; *Torat ha-Bayit,* I:33a.

which prefaces most of his arguments of rebuttal. In fact, even the well-known criticism voiced by Rabad against Maimonides in the introduction to the *Mishneh Torah*: "It can only be that an overbearing spirit is in him," is echoed (in different phrasing) by Rashba – but against his contemporary R. Aaron ha-Levi, and not, as one sometimes might have expected, against Maimonides.[54] Perhaps here, then, current circumstances played some role in determining the choice and employment of critical language. One might object that Rashba's own obvious degree of respect for Maimonides would preclude any such strongly-worded refutations of the *Mishneh Torah*. One cannot automatically assume this, however, since we encounter numerous medieval examples of great reverence side by side with irreverently bold criticism;[55] and Rashba did have much to criticize as well as to admire about the *Mishneh Torah*.[56]

---

[54] *Mishmeret ha-Bayit* (printed in margins of *Torat ha-Bayit*), I:21a.

[55] See examples in Twersky, *Rabad*, 191-92.

[56] On the possible influence of the formidable authority of Maimonides on the tone of Maimonidean criticism, see my "On Maimonides' 'Conversion' to Kabbalah," *Studies in Medieval Jewish History and Literature*, ed. I. Twersky (Cambridge, Mass., 1984), 380.

The formidable authority of Maimonides may have played some role – among other factors – in several instances in which Rashba states his theoretical opposition to Maimonides' view and then defers to Maimonides in actual practice. Examples are responsum I:444, concerning forbidden foods, where Rashba concludes: "And also regarding the halakhic decision, were it not for the fact that the sage Maimonides already has ruled in accord with R. Judah, I would have said that we hold in accordance with R. Jose," and also two instances in *Torat ha-Bayit* (I:39b, 53a) concerning signs of *terefot* in chickens, where Rashba opposes Maimonides in theory but again yields to him in practice, concluding: "but what can we do, for the sage already has ruled." (On the general issue of instances in which Rashba hesitates to implement his theoretical position in practice or defers to earlier authorities, see H. Soloveitchik, *Pawnbroking: A Study in the Inter-Relationship Between Halakhah, Economic Activity and Communal Self-Image* [Hebrew] [Jerusalem, 1985], 116-17 and n. 56.)

Another factor that may influence a halakhic disagreement between Rashba and Maimonides is their differing philosophical orientations. See *Responsa*, I:413.

Master or Slave?

Rabbi Joseph B. Soloveitchik on Human Autonomy in the Presence of God[*]

Moshe Sokol

I. Introduction

Peter Berger, the sociologist of religion, has suggested that the theme of individual autonomy, more than any other, characterizes the worldview of modernity.[1] It is perhaps not surprising then, that R. Joseph B. Soloveitchik, amongst the most influential and creative of twentieth century Orthodox Jewish thinkers, would relate to it in the course of his writings. What is surprising, however, is the extent to which he does. No other theme so dominated R. Soloveitchik's thought as the

---

[*] A Hebrew version of this article first appeared in *Emunah be-Zemanim Mishtanim: Al Mishnato shel ha-Rav Yosef Dov Soloveitchik*, ed. A. Sagi (Jerusalem, 1996).

[1] P. Berger, B. Berger, and H. Kellner, *The Homeless Mind* (New York, 1974), 196.

problem of human autonomy in its many guises. Whatever
the putative subject, whether it is an analysis of faith
or prayer,[2] the quest for God or the nature of the halakhic life,[3]
all of R. Soloveitchik's major theological works are centrally
concerned with this issue. Even his treatment of Religious
Zionism reflects the same preoccupation.[4]

   Study of R. Soloveitchik's literary *oeuvre* reveals two
stages to his treatment of autonomy, an early and a late
phase. The early phase is embodied in *Halakhic Man*[5] and
"*U-Vikkashtem mi-Sham.*"[6] While the former was first published
in 1944 and thus is obviously early, the latter first appeared
in 1978 as a lengthy contribution to the rabbinic journal
Hadorom. Nevertheless, the consensus amongst students of
the matter is that at least an early version of the essay
was written shortly after *Halakhic Man*, thus pre-dating its
publication by some thirty years.[7] In both of these essays,
Rabbi Soloveitchik portrays the ideal Jew as resolving the

---

[2] For example, "*Ra'ayonot al ha-Tefillah*" in *Ish Halakhah – Galui ve-Nistar*
(Jerusalem, 1979), 239-71.

[3] For references, see below.

[4] "*Kol Dodi Dofek*" in *Be-Sod ha-Yahid ve-ha-Yahad* (Jerusalem, 1976).
I have in mind the distinction between the Man of Destiny and the Man
of Fate.

[5] Philadelphia, 1983.

[6] In *Ish Halakhah – Galui ve-Nistar* (Jerusalem, 1979), 115-235 (henceforth: *UVM*).

[7] See, e.g., L. Kaplan, "Rabbi Joseph B. Soloveitchik's Philosophy of
Halakhah," *Jewish Law Annual* 7 (1988): 143 n. 7; and A. Ravitzky, "Rabbi
J. B. Soloveitchik on Human Knowledge: Between Maimonidean and Neo-
Kantian Philosophy," *Modern Judaism* 6:2 (1986): 182 n. 17. I wish to
stress, however, that even if one regards *UVM* as late rather than early,
since it may have been substantially altered by R. Soloveitchik, its themes
are closely linked to that of *Halakhic Man* and treating them together
seems warranted. Some have suggested that, given the difficulties in dating
some of R. Soloveitchik's works, it may be best to analyze them not from
an evolutionary perspective, since this is difficult to ascertain, but from a
purely conceptual perspective. My basic analysis would be unaffected by
this approach, although I have used an evolutionary framework in this
essay.

autonomy/heteronomy polarity in favor of what might loosely be called "an autonomous stance towards God and life."

The late phase includes, most importantly, "Lonely Man of Faith,"[8] "Majesty and Humility" and "Catharsis."[9] Each of these three essays, in its own way, portrays Jews, and to a large extent all human beings, as embracing an antithetical stance towards life, in which dependence upon God, submission and self-sacrifice – all expressions of a heteronomous stance – are sustained in permanent dialectical tension with the majestic, creative and self-sufficient – all expressions of an autonomous stance. While a comparative study of the commonalities and differences amongst these late essays on the question of autonomy is a scholarly desideratum,[10] in this essay I shall focus on the early essays, in which Rabbi Soloveitchik presents a picture of religious experience that appears to embrace an ultimately non-conflicted personality whose fundamental stance towards life is the autonomous.

The questions I intend to address are: (1) How does Rabbi Soloveitchik attempt to solve the autonomy/heteronomy problem in these essays? (2) How successful are his solutions? (3) What do these attempts reveal about Rabbi Soloveitchik's own theological agenda and the relationship amongst his works?

II. Varieties of Autonomy

Both *Halakhic Man* and "*U-Vikkashtem mi-Sham*" are about topics at least *prima facie* unrelated to autonomy and heteronomy; the former portrays the inner world of the Talmudist and the latter the quest for *devekut*. Yet R. Soloveitchik devotes well over half *Halakhic Man* to exploring the role of creativity,

---

[8] *Tradition* 7:2 (1965).

[9] *Tradition* 17:2 (1978).

[10] See, for example, the brief survey in David Hartman, *Living Covenant* (New York, 1985), 77-88.

mastery and autonomy characteristic of Halakhic Man, since the inner world of the Litvak Talmudist, for Rabbi Soloveitchik, is largely defined by these characteristics. Similarly, the basic rift running through the quest for *devekut* as portrayed in "*U-Vikkashtem mi-Sham*" is a version of the problem of autonomy in religious context.

Why Rabbi Soloveitchik treats the problem of autonomy in such a fashion is an interesting question, but whatever the reason, this approach creates a difficulty for his interpreters: exactly how does R. Soloveitchik *understand* the very problem, or problems, of autonomy which, apparently, so exercised him? Before beginning with an analysis of the works represented even in the early phase, it would be helpful to delineate varying accounts of autonomy. For the purposes of this essay, I would like to distinguish amongst three different versions of the problem of autonomy which, in varying ways and degrees, seem to surface in R. Soloveitchik's writings: autonomy of *agency*; of *character* and *personality*; and of *intellect*.

Autonomy of *agency*, which I have elsewhere called "Nomic Autonomy,"[11] is the view maintained by Kant and his followers that a law is moral only if it is self-imposed by virtue of its rationality. The problem this raises for the halakhic Jew is two-fold. First, what is the status of moral Halakhah? Is it binding if not rationally self-imposed? If moral law is independently right, why is the divine command necessary? Second, what is the status of non-moral Halakhah? Are they mere obligations of interest and not true laws in the Kantian sense?

The second problem relates to autonomy not as a condition of moral agency, but autonomy as a condition of the

---

[11] "Religious Authority and Personal Autonomy" in *Rabbinic Authority and Personal Autonomy*, ed. Moshe Sokol (Northvale, NJ: Jason Aronson, 1992), 169-216.

ideal human *character and personality*. Isaiah Berlin called something akin to what I mean by this idea, "positive liberty" in his celebrated *Four Essays on Liberty*.[12] This tradition, which has its roots in Plato, the Stoic philosophers, and even such Romantics as Rousseau, maintains that the ideal human character acts out of motivations that express its true and deepest self. Joel Feinberg lists the following attributes as making up the autonomous character in this sense of autonomy: self-possession, individuality, self-determination or self-creation, authenticity, self-control, initiative, self-reliance, self-fidelity, and responsibility for self and independence.[13] In a religious and halakhic context, the problem then becomes to what extent can or should the ideal Jew embody some or all such virtues as he stands before an overwhelming, commanding God?

Related to autonomy of character, which has a moral dimension, is autonomy of *personality* and the concomitant behavior that flows from that personality. How should I *feel* and *act* standing before God? Should I feel and act self-confidently, masterfully and capably, or should I feel and act as an overwhelmed, insignificant creature before the Almighty God?

The third concept of autonomy, that of the *intellect*,[14] concerns the adequacy of the human intellect to arrive at the truth. To what extent can human beings know the truth about God, and to what extent is, or must, that knowledge be achieved through the processes of independent human reason? What happens if human reason reaches conclusions inconsistent with what the tradition teaches?

At this stage it must be stressed that each of these problems is, in fact, conceptually independent of the others.

---

[12] Oxford, 1969.

[13] *Harm to Self* (Oxford, 1986), ch. 18.

[14] What I call "epistemic autonomy" in the essay cited above, n. 8.

Thus, one might argue that the Jew must stand in prayer and at work overwhelmed by God, but one must come to this state, and remain in it, independently and authentically as an expression of one's true inner convictions. Similarly, one might argue that self-reliance and independent judgment on matters of faith are a vice, that one should blindly accept traditional authority, while nevertheless feeling empowered by God to conduct one's life and prayer with confidence and control. Again, one could affirm an autonomy of character and personality yet deny the Kantian autonomy of moral agency.

In any case, it should be clear that each of these kinds of autonomy bears its own problematics in a religious and halakhic context. The questions we must then address are: (1) Did R. Soloveitchik intend to resolve philosophically any of these problems, and if he did, which ones? (2) How successful are his proposals? At this point it is important to note that two models for responding to R. Soloveitchik's works are available to us. The first is to see R. Soloveitchik as a Jewish thinker struggling to resolve philosophically numerous problems raised by the encounter between Judaism on the one hand and modernity and secular philosophy on the other. The second model is to see R. Soloveitchik not as a Jewish philosopher, but as a contemporary figure struggling heroically to articulate a vision of Judaism – albeit in the language of philosophy – commensurate with his own inner religious and intellectual life.[15]

The usual view of R. Soloveitchik, of course, is that of a Jewish philosopher. The extensive, often highly sophisticated philosophical discussions and references, R. Soloveitchik's own

---

[15] For a fuller discussion of this distinction, which I call "Jewish-Philosopher-as-King" versus "Jewish-Philosopher-as-Hero," see my "*Ger Ve-Toshav Anokhi*: Modernity and Traditionalism in the Life and Thought of R. Joseph B. Soloveitchik," *Tradition* 29:1 (1994): 32-47; also in *Engaging Modernity*, ed. Moshe Sokol (Northvale, NJ: Jason Aronson, 1997), 149-165. See also below, in this essay.

advanced philosophical training, the philosophical formulation of the problems he addresses, all buttress this assessment. "*U-Vikkashtem mi-Sham*" tackles head on the problem of autonomy in a religious context, and *Halakhic Man*, too, engages the question of autonomy over and over again. That at least an early version of the former essay was written at about the same time as *Halakhic Man* lends further evidence to the assumption that *Halakhic Man* too is centrally concerned with the philosophical problems of autonomy. For all these reasons, I shall begin my essay with the following hypothesis: Rabbi Soloveitchik did indeed intend in both essays to provide a philosophical response to the many problems raised for Judaism by the modern value of autonomy. Evaluating the truth of this hypothesis may well turn out to shed light on the larger question raised above, about how best to understand the very enterprise in which R. Soloveitchik was engaged.

III. *Halakhic Man*: An Overview

As is well known, *Halakhic Man* proposes a pioneering phenomenological analysis of Litvak religiosity. Deploying the typological method that so characterizes his writings, Rabbi Soloveitchik maintains that Halakhic Man is a combination of two ideal types of persons, Cognitive Man and Religious Man. As will be seen, Halakhic Man is portrayed as fundamentally similar to Cognitive Man; nevertheless, he bears within him something of Religious Man as well, and it is to this type that I wish to turn first.

Religious Man yearns to break free from the chains of the physical world and find union with the transcendent God above. He apprehends the world not as an object of mastery and knowledge, but as a mystery that points to God, as well as a barrier that prevents Religious Man from finding Him. While R. Soloveitchik is at pains to point out that Religious Man seeks to cognize the world and understand it, the very lawfulness he discovers only compounds the most fundamental mystery, that there is any lawfulness at all.[16] Since his aim is *unio mystica*, Religious Man seeks a kind of self-annihilation:

> The will of Religious Man gradually wanes to nothingness, and his selfhood is inexorably extinguished inasmuch as he desires to immerse himself in the totality of existence and to unite with infinity.... What Religious Man wants is *unio mystica*, attachment to infinity and complete immersion and dissolution in the supernal realm.[17]

The experience of Religious Man is subjective and highly emotional. This subjectivity opens Religious Man to a life of inner turmoil and contradiction, to feelings of overwhelming attraction to God mixed with feelings of overwhelming awe and fear: "Religious Man is suspended between two giant magnets, between love and fear, between desire and dread, between longing and anxiety."[18]

R. Soloveitchik notes that the emotional state of such a person is tinged with melancholy, that it is filled with self-negation, the sense of lowliness, constant self-appraisal and fear.[19] Nevertheless, he extols the anguish of Religious Man's conflicts, remarking that they contain within themselves the "sweetness of eternity, a taste of the world to come."[20] Immediately thereafter he asserts:

> On the one hand, he [Religious Man] senses his own lowliness and insignificance, his own frailty and weakness.... On the other hand, he is aware of his own greatness and loftiness, how his spirit breaks through all barriers and ascends to the very heights.... Is he not

---

[16] *Halakhic Man*, 7, 11.

[17] Ibid., 78.

[18] Ibid., 67.

[19] Ibid., 74.

[20] Ibid., 67.

the crown of creation to whom God granted dominion over all the work of his hands? ... This antinomy is an integral part of man's creature consciousness.... The essence of the antinomy is rooted in the religious consciousness, the source of most of the antinomies and contradictions in man's outlook. From a religious perspective, man, in his relationship to the world, oscillates between the two poles of self-negation and absolute pride, between the consciousness of his nothingness and the consciousness of the infinity deep within him. Religious Man can never be free of this oscillation.[21]

Halakhic Man, portrayed throughout the essay as an autonomous, masterful, creative and assertive person, diverges from Religious Man on precisely these points, which at least suggests that the autonomy imputed to Halakhic Man is intended at least in part to respond to these features of Religious Man. This in turn implies that, from the point of view of autonomy in the life of Religious Man, at least two, and perhaps three issues concern R. Soloveitchik. First, Religious Man aspires to a negation of the self in God. This appears to undercut an affirmation of the autonomy of character. How can a self-reliant, self-determined, independent self aspire to its own annihilation? In addition, Religious Man's pervasive feelings of insignificance and lowliness undercut his autonomy of personality, and his response to the mystery of the universe and the unknowability of God undermines his autonomy of intellect.[22]

In contrast to Religious Man, Halakhic Man is projected throughout the essay as a pillar of autonomy in *each* of the three senses outlined above, and this is in large part due to his fundamental similarity to Cognitive Man. R. Soloveitchik's portrayal of Cognitive Man, as a kind of mathematical scientist,

---

[21] Ibid., 67-68.

[22] "Negative theology constitutes the greatest ideal of Religious Man," ibid., 12.

is heavily influenced by the Marburg School of Neo-Kantians, about which he wrote his dissertation and under one of whose leading interpreters he studied. Just as the mathematical scientist constructs reality through an ideal world of abstract, mathematically formulated rules, so too the Litvak Talmudist constructs his version of reality out of abstract, often quantitatively formulated halakhic principles. Just as all true human knowledge, for the Marburg Neo-Kantians, is ultimately a product of abstract scientific laws and their interrelationships, so too, for R. Soloveitchik, true Jewish knowledge of the world is ultimately the product of abstract halakhic principles and their interrelationships. In each case, knowledge of the details of reality derives from their subsumption under the general principle, which in science is wholly created by the scientist, and in Halakhah is at least partially created by the halakhist. This conception of the Litvak halakhist leads to a portrayal of the halakhist as autonomous, creative and masterful. Let us now examine each of the three species of autonomy to see how, for R. Soloveitchik, they are embodied in Halakhic Man.

IV. *Halakhic Man*: An Analysis

Autonomy of Intellect

Halakhic Man, says R. Soloveitchik, "recognizes no authority other than the authority of the intellect (obviously, in accordance with the principles of tradition)."[23] Evidence for this autonomy is adduced from the famous Talmudic debate about the oven of *akhnai*, in the context of which the Talmud asserts, "It is not in Heaven." "Even the Holy One, blessed be He," says R. Soloveitchik, "has, as it were, handed over His imprimatur, His official seal in Torah matters to man.... No other cognitive discipline has woven crowns

---

[23] Ibid., 79.

for its heroes to the extent that the Halakhah has done....
The glorification of man reaches here the peak of splendor."[24]
This autonomy is linked to a second characteristic of
Halakhic Man, his preoccupation with intellectual creativity.
"The essence of Torah," asserts R. Soloveitchik, "is intellectual
creativity."[25] Or again, "Halakhic Man is a man who longs
to create, to bring into being something new, something
original.... The dream of creation is the central idea in the
halakhic consciousness."[26]

Several problems emerge from this account of intellectual
autonomy in *Halakhic Man*. First, as Aviezer Ravitzky has
argued, the knowledge of reality advocated by R. Soloveitchik,
an Aristotelian/Maimonidean unity between knower and
object of knowledge is precluded by the very post-Kantian
theory of knowledge affirmed by R. Soloveitchik himself.[27]
Second, notwithstanding the fact that all scientists
must operate with some theory – some concepts – to get their
own theories going, scientists are not bound by any particular
starter theory or concepts. They are free to substitute or create
their own. The same cannot be said for the halakhist who,
as R. Soloveitchik himself notes, must operate "in accordance
with the principles of tradition," must work with the data
of Halakhah itself.[28]

---

[24] Ibid., 79-80.

[25] Ibid., 82.

[26] Ibid., 99.

[27] Ravitzky, ibid. See below for a fuller discussion of Ravitzky's argument in
the context of my analysis of *UVM*. Both Ravitzky and Kaplan point out
that the formulation of halakhic knowledge in "*Mah Dodekh mi-Dod*" may
avoid this problem. Below, however, I take issue with this claim as it bears
on *UVM*.

[28] For a discussion of this problem, see R. Shihor, "On the Problem of
Halakhah's Status in Judaism: A Study of the Attitude of Rabbi Joseph
Soloveitchik," *Forum* 30-31 (1978); Zvi Zohar, "*Al ha-Yahas Bein Sefat
ha-Halakhah le-Vein ha-Safah ha-Tiv'it*," *Sefer ha-Yovel li-Khevod ha-Rav
Yosef Soloveitchik*, ed. Sh. Yisraeli, et al. (Jerusalem, 1984); and L. Kaplan,
ibid.

Yet another point must be made. Creativity and intellectual mastery in themselves are not the most philosophically significant hallmarks of intellectual autonomy. As I noted above, the real nub of the problem of intellectual autonomy in a religious context is the extent to which I can be said to know X if X is contrary to what tradition teaches or what I know God to be or to have said. Where creativity in Halakhah – and surely there is much of that – does not run contrary to the teachings of accepted tradition, then it does not engage perhaps the most serious problem intellectual autonomy raises in a religious context. Where it does run contrary to accepted tradition, then even R. Soloveitchik himself admits of certain constraints. Thus, if every known halakhic authority from the Tannaitic period on down takes a certain position on a halakhic question, then no responsible halakhist, as autonomous and creative as he might be, will claim to know that the Halakhah is otherwise.[29]

In addition, R. Soloveitchik does not even take up what is perhaps the most sensitive dimension of intellectual autonomy, the theological. Can I be said to know that God is not provident over human beings, for example, if my independent reason leads me to that conclusion? Of course, R. Soloveitchik may have chosen not to take up this question since it falls outside the purview of his discussion of the characteristics of Halakhic Man as he sees them. Nevertheless, establishing the complete intellectual autonomy of Halakhic Man would require just such a discussion, and not only is that discussion absent, it seems unlikely R. Soloveitchik would accord Halakhic Man such autonomy were he to take it up.

---

[29] See Sokol, "Religious Authority," 194-95 n. 11. It should be noted that this is separate from the claim that one should act according to this knowledge and contrary to tradition. This latter question touches on the issue of moral autonomy.

Finally, if, as it appears, R. Soloveitchik does indeed mean to use Religious Man as a foil for the superiority of Halakhic Man in the arena of intellectual autonomy, then he is being somewhat unfair to Religious Man. This is because they both operate in different spheres. The autonomy of Halakhic Man emerges in the sphere of Halakhah, which is a cognitive-scientific discipline; the putative absence of autonomy for Religious Man emerges in the sphere of theology. But Halakhic Man may share Religious Man's lack of autonomy in the theological arena, and Religious Man may share Halakhic Man's autonomy in the cognitive-scientific arena.

Thus, R. Soloveitchik often cites Maimonides as an exemplar of Halakhic Man. But Maimonides is probably most famous in the history of Western philosophy for his advocacy of the doctrine of negative theology, and it is precisely this doctrine that is taken to be a characteristic of Religious Man's lack of autonomy.[30] Moreover, why can't Halakhic Man be as taken with the mystery of the universe as Religious Man, since he is not thereby surrendering whatever interest he might have in understanding the halakhic norms which govern that universe? Looking at this from the other side of the question, R. Soloveitchik is at pains to point out, as I observed above, that Religious Man too seeks the lawfulness of the cosmos, much as Cognitive Man does, although he is struck with the mysterious existence of such laws while Cognitive Man is not. Why then couldn't Religious Man be just as cognitive and masterful as Halakhic Man and the mathematician-scientist, at least when it comes to understanding the natural workings of the universe? In short, both Halakhic Man and Religious Man can occupy pretty much the same turf when it comes to intellectual autonomy.

---

[30] *Halakhic Man*, 11-12.

The Autonomy of Moral Agency

Probably the most famous form of autonomy in the history of philosophy is that of moral agency. Ever since Kant, theologians, Jewish and Christian, felt the need to account for the heteronomy of the divine command. Kant himself criticized Judaism directly, maintaining that it is "not really a religion at all, but merely a union of a number of people who, since they belong to a particular stock, formed themselves into a commonwealth under political laws."[31] A defense of autonomy in Judaism, then, would surely focus intensively on this problem, and to the extent that R. Soloveitchik wishes to argue for the autonomy of Halakhic Man in its classical post-Kantian sense, he would need to respond in depth to the Kantian challenge.

R. Soloveitchik does indeed appear to address this issue:

> Halakhic Man does not experience any consciousness of compulsion accompanying the norm. Rather, it seems to him as though he discovered the norm in his innermost self, as though it was not just a commandment that had been imposed on him, but an existential law of his own being. We do not have here a person who strains against the chains of the ethical and the reign of the norm.... Rather we have a blending of the obligation with self-consciousness ... *a union of an outside command with the inner will and conscience of man....* When Halakhic Man comes to the real world he has already created his ideal a priori image which shines with the radiance of the norm.... And this ideal world is his very own, his own possession; he is free to create in it, to arrive at new insights, to improve and

---

[31] *Religion Within the Limits of Reason Alone*, trans. R. Greene and H. Hudson (New York, 1960), 116. For a discussion of the Kantian thesis of autonomy and its implications for Jewish law, as well as bibliographic references to other discussions in Jewish theology, see Moshe Sokol, "The Autonomy of Reason, Revealed Morality and Jewish Law," *Religious Studies* 22 (1986): 423-37.

perfect.... *Therefore he is free and independent in his normative understanding* [emphasis added].[32]

R. Soloveitchik seems to be making two arguments. First, he suggests that Halakhic Man does not experience moral laws as heteronomous commands, but as expressions of what he independently believes to be right, on the basis of his own deep moral sensibilities. Second, since Halakhic Man creates his own ideal halakhic world, and that halakhic world embraces moral norms as well, then Halakhic Man experiences its norms as his own creation, and not as heteronomously imposed. What are we to make of these arguments?[33]

For Kant, the really critical issue in autonomous moral agency is rationality; unless an agent imposes the law upon himself out of an understanding of its rationality, then he is still acting out of some interest, whether it is the interest of satisfying his own conscience or the interest of obeying God. However, as Rabbi Soloveitchik formulates his own thesis, rationality plays no role: Halakhic Man simply experiences the law as his own. But if rationality plays no role in the self-imposition of the law, then he is still not an autonomous agent in the Kantian sense. By framing the argument in purely experiential terms, without reference to the philosophical underpinnings of Kant's thesis, the theological and philosophical problems raised by Kant are by-and-large circumvented.

If, on the other hand, Rabbi Soloveitchik does mean to assert that Halakhic Man experiences the law as rational, just as the Kantian moral agent would, then he would be conceding too much. In that case, he would essentially be agreeing with Kant's autonomy requirement, while maintaining that Halakhic Man is a good Kantian moral agent because he acts out of a rational understanding of the truth of the law.

---

[32] *Halakhic Man*, 64-66. See also 135-36.

[33] Rabbi A. I. Kook takes a position somewhat akin to the first argument of Rabbi Soloveitchik, although it differs in certain important respects as well.

But if this is so, how then would Rabbi Soloveitchik resolve all the many serious difficulties Kant's position raises for Jewish law? What if a real-life Halakhic Man does not experience some particular Halakhah in this way? More importantly, what is the moral status of Halakhah that does not emerge from the rational convictions of the agent, and what is the status of the divine command if a moral law is right, and is experienced as such, independently of the divine command? Are non-rational, ritual laws heteronomous, and obeyed out of mere interest, or do they have some special status? If they do have a special status, in what exactly does it consist?

Rabbi Soloveitchik himself appears to sense that there are certain difficulties with his arguments as they are formulated in the main body of his text, and in a footnote to the above-cited passage he comments as follows:

> The concept of freedom should not be confused with the principle of ethical autonomy propounded by Kant and his followers. The freedom of the pure will in Kant's teaching refers essentially to the creation of the ethical norm. The freedom of Halakhic Man refers not to the creation of the law itself, for it was given to him by the Almighty, but to the realization of the norm in the concrete world. The freedom which is rooted in the creation of the norm has brought chaos and disorder to the world. The freedom of realizing the norm brings holiness to the world.[34]

This formulation of the thesis considerably weakens the autonomy-affirming implications contained in the body of the text. Here the focus shifts from Halakhic Man's discovery of the norm in his own self to a distinction between the creation of the norm and its practical realization in the concrete world. Halakhic Man does not create the law, but freely chooses to act upon a law derived from God. Rabbi Soloveitchik thus explicitly

---

[34] Ibid., 153 n. 80.

denies Kantian autonomy. But then, in what philosophically interesting sense is Halakhic Man morally autonomous? Everyone, whether he is a Halakhic Man or not, is free to choose how to behave.

What distinguishes the Halakhic Man is that he does not feel himself compelled by God's will. But first, these same feelings might well be true of Religious Man as well, who wishes to absorb himself into the will and being of God. More importantly, Rabbi Soloveitchik casts the autonomy of Halakhic Man in experiential categories; his autonomy is a matter of how he feels about the law. But this is what I have called above the autonomy of personality, rather than the autonomy of moral agency. It turns out, then, that despite the appearance of engaging the problem of the autonomy of moral agency, and the appearance of affirming some version of that autonomy, in fact, Rabbi Soloveitchik has substituted the autonomy of moral agency with the far less philosophically problematic autonomy of personality. This is especially clear in the second of the two arguments Rabbi Soloveitchik deploys, building on Halakhic Man as a creator and master of an ideal halakhic world. Surely in this argument, the autonomy Halakhic Man is portrayed as experiencing is that of personality, deriving from the feeling of mastery that emerges from halakhic creativity.

Autonomy of Character and Personality

Even a cursory reading of *Halakhic Man* reveals just how much Halakhic Man as portrayed by Rabbi Soloveitchik embodies this version of autonomy. No better example of the self-control and self-possession of Halakhic Man can be found than the story Rabbi Soloveitchik tells of R. Elijah of Pruzhan, who delayed entering his dying daughter's room so that he might first put on the *tefillin* of R. Tam, thereby fulfilling even this *humra*, before becoming an *onen*, who is not halakhically

obligated to wear *tefillin*.[35] Even the normal fear of death does
not beset Halakhic Man, because he masters death through a
study of its *halakhot*.[36] Halakhic Man, in Rabbi Soloveitchik's
words, "fears nothing."[37] His religious experience, grounded as
it is in understanding, is deliberate, controlled and unwavering, not afflicted by alternating bouts of terror and love.[38]
Halakhic Man is intimidated by no one, no matter their
influence or worldly power;[39] he is also immune to the normal
temptations of the evil impulse.[40] Unlike Religious Man,
Halakhic Man is not passive and receptive, but active and self-
motivated. "Neither modesty nor humility characterize the
image of Halakhic Man. On the contrary, his most characteristic feature is strength of mind."[41]

These qualities of character and personality in part derive
from the masterful cognitive dimension of Halakhic Man and
his commitment to transforming and sanctifying the here-and-
now. In the second part of the essay, however, they are deepened and connected to his creativity. At one level, of course,
this creativity is purely intellectual and expresses itself in the
study of Torah. At another level, however, it involves self-
creation, which is how Rabbi Soloveitchik understands the
concept of repentance. Through self-creation, Halakhic Man,
who is now often called "the man of God," individuates himself,
separating himself from the species through dynamic reflection
upon and transformation of the self.

> Man, at times exists solely by virtue of the species....
> His roots lie deep in the soil of faceless mediocrity.... He

---

[35] Ibid., 77.

[36] Ibid., 75.

[37] Ibid., 74.

[38] Ibid., 85.

[39] Ibid., 89-91.

[40] Ibid., 65.

[41] Ibid., 79.

has no stature of his own, no original, individual, personal profile.... He is receptive, passive, a spiritual parasite. He is wholly under the influence of other people and their views. Never has he sought to render an accounting, either of himself or of the world; never has he examined himself.... He lives unnoticed and dies unmourned. Like a fleeting shadow he passes through life and is gone.

But there is another man, who does not require the assistance of others, who does not need the support of the species to legitimate his existence.... He exists not by virtue of the species, but solely on account of his own individual worth. His life is replete with creation and renewal, cognition and profound understanding.... He is dynamic, not static, does not remain at rest but moves forward in an ever-ascending climb. For it is indeed the living God for whom he pines and longs. This is the man of God.[42]

Rabbi Soloveitchik's formulation of these ideas is nourished by such diverse thinkers as Maimonides on the one hand and Max Scheler on the other, as the citations in the body of the essay and footnotes make clear. In some ways, his advocacy of these forms of autonomy in the person of Halakhic Man is the most persuasive in the essay, and I shall take up their significance towards the end of my discussion of *Halakhic Man*. Nevertheless, several points should be made, which taken together, I would argue, reveal a great deal about Rabbi Soloveitchik's treatment of autonomy in *Halakhic Man*.

It may be best to begin by re-examining the ways in which Halakhic Man is portrayed as superior to Religious Man in regard to autonomy of character and personality. Two issues emerge: Religious Man's negation of self in *unio mystica*, contrasting with Halakhic Man's affirmation of self; and

---

[42] Ibid., 126-28. Note the similarity to "Confrontation," and to the distinction between "Man of Fate" and "Man of Destiny" in "*Kol Dodi Dofek.*"

Religious Man's oscillation between extreme feelings of in-
adequacy and terror before God on the one hand and love of
God and self-worth on the other, contrasted with Halakhic
Man's constant feelings of mastery of God's wisdom and self-
worth in sanctifying the mundane. But consider for a moment
the first issue, Religious Man's quest for self-annihilation in
God. Does this really undercut autonomy of character and of
personality? Why can't an independent, self-possessed indi-
vidualist, at his own initiative, firmly choose a way of life which
realizes his highest, carefully considered and authentic desire
to submerge his self into God? Can't such an individual pursue
this quest for ultimate self-annihilation with assertiveness,
creativity and vigor, forcefully abandoning his own highly
personalized entanglements with this world and intensely
focusing his attention, with all the uniqueness of his personality and talents, exclusively upon God? Realizing the long-term
transcendentalist goal of Religious Man does not, it seems to
me, preclude an autonomous character and personality, and
perhaps may even require it.[43]

The second issue, the feelings of worthlessness and fear
characteristic of moments in the life of Religious Man, does
seem to stand in sharp contrast to Halakhic Man, as portrayed
by Rabbi Soloveitchik. But here several observations are
in order. Alan Nadler has shown that the writings of individuals Rabbi Soloveitchik himself regards as classic exemplars
of Halakhic Man, namely the Vilna Gaon and his followers,
reflect intense fear of sin and temptation, a sense of worthlessness before the Almighty God, an obsession with death and
the drive to transcend this world.[44] But all of these characteristics are supposed to reflect the inner life of Religious Man
rather than Halakhic Man. Since it is highly unlikely that

---

[43] Cf. *UVM*, 172, where, as a consequence of his love for God, man freely
chooses to lose himself in Him.

[44] Alan Nadler, "Soloveitchik's Halakhic Man: Not a Mithnagged," *Modern
Judaism* 13:2 (May 1993): 119-47.

Rabbi Soloveitchik was unaware of the texts and legends Nadler cites, Rabbi Soloveitchik's portrait of Halakhic Man as being devoid of these characteristics and emotions is therefore somewhat disingenuous.[45] The really interesting question is why Rabbi Soloveitchik chose to portray Halakhic Man as he did. Nadler himself cites this as evidence of Rabbi Soloveitchik's modernity, his novel contribution to Jewish thought in this area, which embraces such modern values as autonomy. But this alone would hardly explain why Rabbi Soloveitchik appears not to take into account the above facts. Clearly, something more is afoot.

This observation leads to another. Just how insulated is Halakhic Man from the sort of emotional turmoil characteristic of Religious Man? Although Rabbi Soloveitchik, of course, generally presents him as completely insulated, a closer look at the text reveals a decidedly more complex picture. A hint at this complexity may be found in Rabbi Soloveitchik's treatment of the recitation of *piyyutim*. Consistent with his overall approach to the inner religious life of Halakhic Man, Rabbi Soloveitchik remarks that, unlike Religious Man, who is wont to burst forth in song and psalms to God, Halakhic Man is "very sparing in his recitation of the *piyyutim*."[46] He follows this comment with a story about his father, who took away a Book of Psalms from his young son Yoseph Dov, who had been reciting them after the evening service on Rosh Hashanah, and handed him a volume of the Tractate *Rosh Hashanah* instead. Nevertheless, in a very different tone, some thirty pages earlier in the text, Rabbi Soloveitchik remarks that Halakhic Man

---

[45] Although Rabbi Soloveitchik focuses largely on the Brisker dynasty in his portrayal of Halakhic Man, and, it might be argued, their world view differed from that of the classic *mitnagdim*: (a) Rabbi Soloveitchik himself cites the Vilna Gaon as an example of Halakhic Man; and (b) Rabbi Soloveitchik might, himself, at least in a footnote, have made this distinction and have justified his claims about the Brisker dynasty in some way.

[46] *Halakhic Man*, 87.

"never accepted the ruling of Maimonides opposing the recital of *piyyutim*."[47] Quite the contrary:

> In moments of divine mercy and grace, in times of spiritual ecstasy and exaltation, when our entire existence thirsts for the living God, we recite many *piyyutim* and hymns, and we disregard the strictures of the philosophical *midrash* concerning the problem of negative attributes.[48]

Words far more fitting to the experience of Religious Man than Halakhic Man! Similarly, Rabbi Soloveitchik can remark that Halakhic Man is "beyond the maelstrom of the affective life, a true source of peace and tranquility."[49] Yet, on the other hand, consider Rabbi Soloveitchik's answer to the following rhetorical question:

> Is Halakhic Man devoid of the splendor of that raging and tempestuous sacred religious experience that so typifies the ecstatic Religious Man? Can he attain such peaks of enthusiasm that he will cry out in rapture "How manifold are Thy works, O Lord?" Is it possible for Halakhic Man to achieve such emotional exaltation that all his thoughts and senses ache and pine for the living God? Halakhic Man is worthy and fit to devote himself to a majestic religious experience in all its uniqueness.... However, for him, such a powerful experience follows upon cognition.... But since it occurs after rigorous criticism and profound, penetrating reflection, it is that much more intensive.[50]

While Halakhic Man's affective religious experience is indeed intensive, it is controlled and "strong as flint."[51]

---

[47] Ibid., 58.

[48] Ibid.

[49] Ibid., 73.

[50] Ibid., 83.

[51] Strictly speaking, this does not contradict Rabbi Soloveitchik's claim that Halakhic Man is outside the "maelstrom of the affective life." Nevertheless,

Further evidence of the real complexity of Halakhic Man's personality and character may be found in Rabbi Soloveitchik's own account of the way in which Halakhic Man is purported to overcome the emotional qualities of Religious Man. After describing how the experience of Religious Man is beset by oscillation between the poles of self-negation and terror before God, and self-affirmation and love of God, Rabbi Soloveitchik argues that Halakhic Man "has found the third verse," a solution to that affective oscillation. *"He too* [Halakhic Man] *suffers from this dualism, from this deep spiritual split,* but he mends the split through the concept of halakhah and law" (emphasis added).[52]

Here, Rabbi Soloveitchik explicitly admits that Halakhic Man does indeed suffer from the antithetical conflicts of religious life, even if he has found a strategy to mend them. Rabbi Soloveitchik continues in this vein by walking his reader through the experience of Halakhic Man as he reads the *ne'ilah* prayer, which asserts man's worthlessness. Rabbi Soloveitchik waxes eloquent in his heart-rending description of the despair and self-loathing Halakhic Man feels as he recites these prayers, how Halakhic Man later comes to feel an intense longing and yearning for God, the self-worth implied by this experience, and how awareness of the Halakhah assists in this process. But surely this means that Halakhic Man too, like Religious Man, at least sometimes suffers from the same conflicts, the same antithetical experiences of self-negation versus self-worth. What then distinguishes the two? Presumably, the key difference is that Halakhic Man recovers his equilibrium more quickly, and is able to sustain it much longer, than Religious Man. But this is a far cry from claiming that Halakhic Man is entirely insulated from emotional swings between self-negation and self-worth, and it is therefore a far

---

it does suggest that his affective life does indeed exist, and that it is far more complex and rich than one might expect.

[52] Ibid., 69.

cry from the claim that Halakhic Man is a perfect expression of autonomy of personality, as Rabbi Soloveitchik understood that concept.

In reality, this account of the inner life of Halakhic Man should come as no surprise. The very opening pages of Halakhic Man assert in the most forceful language that Halakhic Man is a conflicted personality.

> Halakhic Man reflects two opposing selves; two disparate images are embodied in his soul and spirit. On the one hand he is as far removed from Religious Man as east is from west and is identical, in many respects, to Cognitive Man; on the other hand he is a man of God ... if in the light of modern philosophy, Religious Man in general has come to be regarded as an antithetical being, fraught with contradictions ... who struggles with the tribulations of the dualism of affirmation and negation, approbation and denigration, how much more is this true of Halakhic Man?[53]

For Rabbi Soloveitchik, as explained in the opening pages of the essay, and in an extended three-page footnote on this theme, inner conflict is a virtue, not a vice.

> There is creative power embedded within antithesis; conflict enriches existence, the negation is constructive and contradiction deepens and expands the ultimate destiny of both man and the world.[54]

Were Rabbi Soloveitchik to have portrayed Halakhic Man as wholly insulated from a conflicted inner life, from such feelings as self-negation and worthlessness before God as against feelings of mastery and adequacy, then he would have been diminishing rather than enhancing the religious power and authenticity of Halakhic Man.

---

[53] Ibid., 3.

[54] Ibid., 4. See also 139-43 n. 4. See David Singer and Moshe Sokol, "Joseph B. Soloveitchik: Lonely Man of Faith," *Modern Judaism* 2 (1982): 227-71.

V. An Ethic vs. a Philosophy of Autonomy

What conclusions can be drawn from this lengthy analysis of *Halakhic Man*? The first point which should be made is that although *Halakhic Man* gives the appearance of grappling philosophically with some of the key philosophical and theological issues the modern value of autonomy poses to the believing Jew, this appearance is misleading. Rabbi Soloveitchik either avoids engaging, or takes a traditional position if he does engage, those dimensions of autonomy that are the most philosophically problematic for the traditional halakhic Jew. The hypothesis with which this section of the paper began, that Rabbi Soloveitchik intended to respond philosophically to the many problems autonomy poses for the religious Jew, has turned out to be wrong, at least for *Halakhic Man*. This leads naturally to the alternative model for responding to R. Soloveitchik's works suggested above.

I would argue that the best way to read *Halakhic Man* on autonomy is as a sustained polemic, a highly sophisticated, almost Midrashic attempt to capture what has been called the heroic quality of the life of the *talmid hakham*.[55] The exaggerations, the conceptual difficulties outlined above may be debilitating for a full-fledged philosophical theory of autonomy, but they are surely highly effective rhetorical devices. Despite the rich philosophical citations and discussion throughout the essay, I would argue that the repercussive stress on autonomy in *Halakhic Man* can be best appreciated and understood less in philosophical, than in both cultural and personal context.

---

[55] David Hartman, "The Halakhic Hero: Rabbi Joseph Soloveitchik, Halakhic Man," *Modern Judaism* 9:3 (1989). This essay is a response to Singer and Sokol, and Dorff's essay, cited below, n. 64. See also, for a different formulation, Moshe Sokol, "*Ger Ve-Toshav*," n. 15, where I make a distinction between what I call a Jewish-philosopher-as-king and a Jewish-philosopher-as-hero, and argue that Rabbi Soloveitchik embodied the latter rather than the former.

From a cultural perspective, modernity, as Rabbi Soloveitchik knew so well, sounded a clarion call for autonomy. While studying in Berlin, Rabbi Soloveitchik would have been exposed to how outsiders perceived the Talmudic enterprise: submissive, other-worldly, obscure, irretrievably old-fashioned. In the 1940's, the world of Brisk, which Rabbi Soloveitchik had left behind, was burning in the flames of the Holocaust. *Halakhic Man* is centrally concerned with memorializing that world by articulating its often-misunderstood power. If the figure of the *talmid hakham* in the 1940's was to receive the respect it deserved, Rabbi Soloveitchik knew it would have to be conveyed as embracing that value. Rabbi Soloveitchik, heir to the great Brisker tradition, understood just how independent-minded, majestic, creative and powerful – "autonomous" in a non-systematically philosophical sense – the Litvak *talmid hakham* was. Therefore, drawing upon his impressive philosophical erudition, and his accurate reading of the majesty of the Brisker Litvak life, Rabbi Soloveitchik set out to depict Halakhic Man in the most "autonomous" terms. This, then, is the apologetic agenda of *Halakhic Man*, the sort of agenda shared by some of the greatest Jewish thinkers of the past.

There is, however, another, non-apologetic agenda to *Halakhic Man* as well. In both cultural and personal terms, Rabbi Soloveitchik was arguing against what Lawrence Kaplan has called an "ethic of submissiveness."[56] This ethic takes submissiveness as a character trait, particularly in the context of the relationship to God and to rabbinic authority, to be a prime virtue. In many ways, *Halakhic Man* may be read as a sustained polemic against that ethic. To deepen this thesis, I

---

[56] "Da'as Torah: A Modern Conception of Rabbinic Authority" in *Rabbinic Authority and Personal Autonomy*, ed. Moshe Sokol (Northvale, NJ: Jason Aronson, 1992), 1-61.

would like at this point to introduce a distinction that I believe sheds light on Rabbi Soloveitchik's take on autonomy and that is, a distinction between a *philosophy* of autonomy and an *ethic* of autonomy.

By a *philosophy* of autonomy, I mean a systematic attempt to analyze the concept of autonomy and a proposal for a philosophical theory of autonomy consistent with, or implied by, the Jewish tradition in one or more of its various guises. By an *ethic* of autonomy, I mean the articulation of a positive attitude towards autonomy as an outgrowth of a certain view of Judaism. An ethic of autonomy need not emerge from a worked-through philosophical analysis, nor must it endorse autonomy unequivocally and systematically. By its very nature, an ethic of autonomy is defeasible and conditional, since it does not follow necessarily from a deep, philosophically comprehensive system or vision.

Rabbi Soloveitchik intended far more than an impassioned *apologia* for the religious and cultural significance of the Litvak personality. He sought to argue for what I shall now call an *ethic* of autonomy, as distinct from *philosophical* autonomy. That is, his objective was not only to defend his patrimony; he may have sought also to argue against a prevailing norm of submission within the traditional community, and argue for what he himself, or at least part of him, believed to be true about Judaism: its insistence on a this-worldly, assertive, cognitive stance towards the world. This is not the same as arguing for what I have been calling the autonomy of the intellect or of moral agency. It is somewhat closer to arguing for what I have called the autonomy of character and of personality, but not quite the same, since – as we have seen – his arguments do not fully justify the affirmation of those forms of autonomy in their fullest sense either. His is a polemic of the most sophisticated sort for a certain stance towards life and religion, what I am now calling an *ethic* of autonomy. In shaping this polemic, to whose truth an important part of him was deeply committed, he drew upon rich philosophical learning. But that is not the same as philosophically articulating a theory of autonomy. This is absent from *Halakhic Man.*

I have added the caveat, "an important part of him," because the tensions within the essay regarding the extent to which Halakhic Man is immune from the conflict and self-doubt of Religious Man reflect a deep ambivalence on Rabbi Soloveitchik's part towards the value of autonomy, even of character and personality, to which it had appeared he was so committed. This ambivalence emerges most fully in the late phase of his writing, but it is apparent that it was there from the very beginning. Indeed, I would argue that this ambivalence played an important role in Rabbi Soloveitchik's avoidance of engaging some of the critical philosophical issues involved in autonomy, as it played an important role in his consistent refusal to fully embrace even the less problematic areas of autonomy. Rabbi Soloveitchik's own personal religious experience, his own feelings of self-negation, fear of God and dependence upon Him, which emerge so forcefully in his later writings and which are hinted at in *Halakhic Man* as well, made it impossible for him, even in his earliest works, authentically to embrace anything more than a general, and conditional ethic of autonomy.

In light of an ethic of submissiveness which prevails in many quarters of traditionalist Orthodoxy, and in light of the disregard with which the figure of Halakhic Man is held in many modern circles, Rabbi Soloveitchik's formulation and advocacy of an ethic of autonomy with such power and sophistication is an achievement of considerable significance in the Jewish intellectual and cultural history of the twentieth century. This achievement, however, should not be confused with the formulation and advocacy of a systematic philosophy of autonomy which Rabbi Soloveitchik did not, and I would argue, could not, take on.

VI. *U-Vikkashtem mi-Sham*: Introduction

Perhaps the most ambitious, even audacious, essay Rabbi Soloveitchik ever published is "*U-Vikkashtem mi-Sham*," whose goal is nothing less than a phenomenological charting of the path to *devekut*. The title, drawn from Deuteronomy and recited as well in the annual *selihot* prayers, is aptly chosen, since the essay traces the human quest for God.

Given this objective, it is surely revealing that the central problematic in this quest, as Rabbi Soloveitchik articulates it, revolves around overcoming a dualism that bedevils humans in their search for God – the dualism between human freedom on the one hand and the heteronomous divine command and presence on the other. In short, we have yet another attempt to grapple with the problem of human autonomy.

The essay proceeds along three phases, as does the quest for God. The first phase is characterized by the autonomy/heteronomy duality; the second, which Rabbi Soloveitchik calls *hidamut* – emulation of God – consists in a partial solution to the duality; and the third phase, *devekut* – attachment to God – consists in its final resolution. As in *Halakhic Man*, Rabbi Soloveitchik at this early stage in his career, and in marked contrast to his later writings, wishes to project Judaism as coming to terms with, and finally resolving, the problem of human autonomy before a commanding God. I shall first consider in detail Rabbi Soloveitchik's formulation of the problem of human autonomy and heteronomy in "*U-Vikkashtem mi-Sham*," and then examine and evaluate Rabbi Soloveitchik's account of how the *hidamut* and *devekut* stages purport to resolve it.

Rabbi Soloveitchik's terms for the two antithetical experiences that characterize religious life are *toda'ah tiv'it* – the natural experience, and *toda'ah giluyit* – the revelational experience. He defines *toda'ah tiv'it* as follows:

> The explanation of *toda'ah tiv'it*: the spirit of man ascends to extraordinary distances. On the one hand,

there is a yearning implanted in the soul's existence to attribute the multiplicity in time-bound, finite existence to an unconditioned first existent, who is active both within and without the world. On the other hand, there is a by-product [in the universe] sealed with the seal of the Creator which signals to man a level of existence above and beyond it. In this framework, man's experience of the world is in essence and purpose the experience of God and the Creator of the universe. The initiative is man's; he must seek God.[57]

Three elements appear in this definition of *toda'ah tiv'it*: the experience of God is natural to man; the grounds for that experience are built into the very nature of the universe; and human beings must take the initiative in finding God. Later, Rabbi Soloveitchik argues that this experience is biological in origin, an instinctual human response to the universe.[58]

Whatever its biological origins, however, Rabbi Soloveitchik seems to identify all of human culture with *toda'ah tiv'it*. For Rabbi Soloveitchik, human culture is essentially the quest for self-transcendence,[59] and the content of human culture, namely the aesthetic, moral, philosophical and scientific experiences, all point to the existence of an infinite and unconditioned God, which grounds those experiences in a reality beyond themselves. Belief in the existence of God provides the only satisfactory answer to the question of why the world is such as to sustain scientific explanation, beauty, morality and the quest for truth, and why we are capable of these sublime experiences. For this reason, intuitively and sometimes even unmediated by reflection, God is simply perceived in these phenomena.[60]

---

[57] *UVM*, 148.

[58] Ibid., 156-61.

[59] Ibid., 124.

[60] Ibid., 133-34.

Thus far, I have focused on the content of *toda'ah tiv'it*. There is another dimension to *toda'ah tiv'it*, however, which may be even more important than content, and that is what I shall call "stance." It is a fundamental orientation to the world, or stance, which at a deeper level characterizes *toda'ah tiv'it*, and helps explain why *toda'ah tiv'it* has the content that it does. This stance may be best characterized as that of the autonomous personality. In describing the *toda'ah tiv'it* dimension of religious experience, which is of special concern to us in this paper, Rabbi Soloveitchik remarks:

> In this dimension, the religious experience manifests itself as an experience of absolute freedom. Man seeks God out of a thirst for freedom in life, to broaden and deepen his existence. The search for God is an emancipation from the distress of the tyrannical laws of nature which press down upon him.... When man yearns for his God, he arrives at the border of the absolute and eternal, and he feels no compulsory force.... The religious experience in this respect is an outbreak of wondrous force of the spontaneous metaphysical spirit in all its variegated character and stormy activities.... It leaps to the peaks of being out of a passion for victory and majestic flight.... The principle of principles is that man knows that religious life is an undetachable part of his essence; action is free, and is nurtured from the secret place of his existence. All the directions of his spirit, the speculative, the moral and the aesthetic are blended into one rich unity.... The spark of the creator is hidden inside him.

Freedom is so associated with *toda'ah tiv'it* that Rabbi Soloveitchik sometimes even uses the phrase "the experience of freedom" as its synonym.[61] The free, spontaneous quest for the "why" of the universe gives rise to human culture, which is the content of *toda'ah tiv'it*, as it gives rise to the experience of God as the final resting place of that quest. Thus it is the

---

[61] Ibid., 181.

autonomous "stance" of *toda'ah tiv'it* that is critical to explaining its content. Were man to experience the world bowed and submissive, completely trapped by the determinative forces of nature, he would never be led to the kind of reflection and awareness characteristic of *toda'ah tiv'it*.

Another dimension of the autonomous "stance" is the affective. The following passage, which argues for the importance of *toda'ah tiv'it* as a component of religious life, makes this point even more clearly than the passage quoted above:

> Man must serve God not just out of a feeling of compulsion and absolute decree, but out of a spontaneous inclination and yearning, rich in dimensions and joyous to the heart.... When he thinks of God only out of fear of punishment and with a cold intellect, without ecstasy, joy and passion, when his behavior and actions lack soul, interiority and vitality – then man's religious life is defective.... *Toda'ah tiv'it*, given to man by God, is the source of man's yearning for the infinite and for eternity. From it flow feelings of joy and excitement, from it the currents of satisfaction and sweetness in life flow, and it pushes man to share and join in the process of substantive creation.[62]

It is surely interesting to note that this account of the value of *toda'ah tiv'it*, and hence autonomy in Judaism, diverges from the autonomy of *Halakhic Man*.[63] In this passage, the stress is on passion, joy and spontaneity, qualities which, to a large extent, are lacking in Rabbi Soloveitchik's depiction of Halakhic Man. Thus "*U-Vikkashtem mi-Sham*" shifts its portrayal of the autonomous dimension of religious life in favor of the affective, joyous and spontaneous.[64]

---

[62] Ibid., 163-64.

[63] Elsewhere in *UVM*, *toda'ah tiv'it* is depicted as intellectual and cerebral, e.g., in the opening pages of the essay, and thus closer to *Halakhic Man*.

[64] See below for a possible explanation of this shift. It should be noted that Rabbi Soloveitchik's portrayal of the autonomous experience in human culture is somewhat over-romanticized. For example, one would

There is yet another respect in which the affirmation of autonomy in *"U-Vikkashtem mi-Sham"* diverges from that in *Halakhic Man*. Halakhic Man expresses his autonomy primarily as a creator of halakhic worlds; theory takes precedence over practice. This is not the case with *toda'ah tiv'it* in *"U-Vikkashtem mi-Sham,"* where technology and the practical transformation of the world are elevated to the status of a divine norm.

> God commanded man to participate in historical and social change, in scientific-technological development to improve the lot of man. Whoever separates himself from existence acts contrary to the command of the Creator: "Rule the land and conquer it."[65]

In both *Halakhic Man* and *"U-Vikkashtem mi-Sham,"* Rabbi Soloveitchik maintains that one of the central characteristics of Judaism is a this-worldliness. However, in *Halakhic Man*, the emphasis on this-worldliness is problematic, since it stands in tension with the overwhelmingly theoretical orientation of Halakhic Man, according to which even the Talmudic statement that the purpose of study is action is given a novel interpretation which stresses the intellectual.[66] *"U-Vikkashtem mi-Sham,"* which does not set out to portray the inner life of the Brisker Litvak, can, and indeed does, provide a far richer picture of autonomy. Thus, the this-wordliness of *"U-Vikkashtem mi-Sham"* is linked to an affirmation of all essentially human qualities, whose cultural expression ranges the full gamut of the human experience, including the aesthetic and the technological. Each of the three areas of autonomy delineated at the beginning of this essay is thus given

---

hardly associate joy with the lives of many artists and writers, where depression, melancholy and substance abuse is probably more common than Rabbi Soloveitchik's picture might lead us to believe.

[65] Ibid., 163-64.

[66] *Halakhic Man*, 64. See, e.g., Elliot Dorff, "Halakhic Man: A Review Essay," *Modern Judaism* 6:1 (1986): 94-95.

fuller and richer expression in *"U-Vikkashtem mi-Sham"* than in *Halakhic Man.*[67]

Notwithstanding the affirmation of autonomy in *toda'ah tiv'it*, strung out over the course of *"U-Vikkashtem mi-Sham,"* Rabbi Soloveitchik identifies numerous problems with the self-sufficiency of *toda'ah tiv'it* on account of which God chose to reveal Himself and His message to man. These include the impossibility for *toda'ah tiv'it* to lead to a clear knowledge of God and the dangers in using the sort of philosophical abstraction characteristic of *toda'ah tiv'it* which, Rabbi Soloveitchik claims, leads ineluctably to pantheism;[68] the existence of sin, which prevents man from finding God on his own;[69] the existence of the disorderly, of evil and deprivation in the universe, which frustrate man's independent quest for God;[70] the anarchy and self-interest which attach themselves to autonomous man, and which led to the Holocaust;[71] and the contradictions and inconsistencies he finds in his world view and life.[72]

For all these reasons, God chose to reveal Himself and His will to man in what Rabbi Soloveitchik calls *toda'ah giluyit.*

> The explanation of *toda'ah giluyit*: Man cannot come to God on his own with the initiative of his own spirit; existence is a sealed entrance without a passageway to the border of the absolute and eternal.... Therefore, God reveals Himself to human beings and tells them, "I am the Lord your God." This truth, continues *toda'ah giluyit*, can never be extracted from cognition. The inexplicable and awesome vision of revelation occurs

---

[67] Interestingly, the autonomy of character seems least apparent in *toda'ah tiv'it*, although, presumably, it would be linked to the moral dimension of human culture.

[68] *UVM*, 138.

[69] Ibid., 140.

[70] Ibid., 143.

[71] Ibid., 162.

[72] Ibid., 221.

without human compliance and without permission. To the contrary, man is frightened by the penetration of the hidden into his simple world, and he covers his face.[73]

Revelation, which typically occurs when man least expects it, when he is desperate and despairs of ever achieving salvation, is not experienced as an answer to his quest. It inexplicably pounces upon man, and he reacts in abject submission and terror.

> *Toda'ah giluyit*, in contrast with *toda'ah tiv'it*, bears no relation with the creative and free spirit of man, and is uninterested in the aspirations of cultural creativity and all its developments. The revelatory experience is a territory unto itself surrounded by walls, which is beyond the grasp of man.... It seeks to enclose all of human existence and fill its essence.... It is an experience of compulsion and subjugation; it is an absolute recognition of the obligations imposed by revelation which expropriates human will.... In the dimension of *toda'ah giluyit*, man accepts upon himself the yoke of the commandments against his will, and submits his arrogance and self-love to God.[74]

These words, and many passages elsewhere in the essay, are an eloquent description of the heteronomous religious experience, which stands in sharpest possible contrast with the autonomous stance characteristic of *toda'ah tiv'it*, and with all the forms of autonomy embraced in *toda'ah tiv'it*. Yet both *toda'ah giluyit* and *toda'ah tiv'it* are dimensions of the religious experience. Given the antithetical relation between them, is it any wonder that Rabbi Soloveitchik seeks some sort of resolution?

Interestingly, in *Halakhic Man*, the earlier work, this tension is given the shortest shrift. Halakhic Man is portrayed as

---

[73] Ibid., 148.
[74] Ibid., 154.

having already resolved the heteronomy-autonomy conflict, although, as we saw, this portrayal is somewhat disingenuous. Moreover, the autonomy embraced in *Halakhic Man* is largely a cerebral one, although again, as we saw, this is not the whole story. In "*U-Vikkashtem mi-Sham*," however, the heteronomy-autonomy conflict is laid out on the table in the most tragic detail, and the autonomous experience itself is portrayed in an emotionally far richer way, in which Rabbi Soloveitchik celebrates not only the intellect, but the spontaneous passion of the inner soul. It is as if Rabbi Soloveitchik is finally coming to terms with the true complexities of the spiritual life that he had left unexplored in *Halakhic Man*.

Several reasons for this evolution suggest themselves.[75] First, portraying Halakhic Man as fundamentally riven with conflict, and as spontaneous and emotional, would not have served the polemical purposes of *Halakhic Man*, as I pointed out above, nor would it have flowed from the model of the mathematician-scientist, which Rabbi Soloveitchik evoked to achieve those purposes. "*U-Vikkashtem mi-Sham*," which lacks, at least to the same extent, those polemical purposes, could finally engage what, I have argued, in fact troubled Rabbi Soloveitchik all along. Perhaps, too, there is a maturation in the thought of Rabbi Soloveitchik, a greater willingness to confront openly what he could not or would not confront somewhat earlier. Finally, it is possible that Rabbi Soloveitchik, who had already made his mark as one of the foremost philosophers of Halakhah, could now more comfortably relate to the fullest range of the religious experience, and finally engage the problem that so evidently troubled him deeply. Whatever the reasons for this evolution, however, and we can not really be certain what they are, there is no question that in "*U-Vikkashtem mi-Sham*," the problem of

---

[75] See below for further discussion of the relationship between *Halakhic Man* and *UVM*.

human autonomy and heteronomy, now more richly conceived than ever, occupies center stage.

VII. A First Solution: Emulating God

As I noted above, two solutions to the autonomy/heteronomy problem emerge in "*U-Vikkashtem mi-Sham*," one only partial, and the other complete. Each represents a different phase in the quest for God. The first and partial solution rests in the second phase of this quest, which Rabbi Soloveitchik calls *hidamut*, the emulation of God.

In this phase, the *toda'ah giluyit* and *toda'ah tiv'it* experiences evolve into the love and awe (*yir'ah*) of God, respectively. Whereas the *toda'ah giluyit* and *toda'ah tiv'it* experiences of the first phase are unrelated to one another, and are rooted in such biological instincts as terror and the need for security, love and awe of God by contrast emerge from human valuation. For this reason, they are two sides of the very same coin of religious experience. As man discovers more of God and His greatness, an outgrowth of the yearning for God characteristic of *toda'ah tiv'it*, he comes to understand God as the ground for all existence. This understanding of God's indescribable greatness leads to a powerful love of Him, a desire to become one with Him.

However, this very love and desire for unity with God yields awe of Him as well. The more one understands how truly great God is; the more one understands the vast chasm which separates one's own lowly self from God; the more one recognizes how unity with God entails self-negation; then, paradoxically, the more one feels distant from God, the more one feels driven from Him. Rabbi Soloveitchik goes so far as to claim, citing the kabbalistic concept of *tzimtzum*, that objective and experiential distance from God is metaphysically necessary for the existence of the cosmos and the individual.[76] In any case,

---

[76] Ibid., 169.

both awe and love flow from a deepened understanding of God and a deepened evaluation of his greatness.[77] Both these conflicting and dialectical experiences are ineradicable components of religious life.

If readers of this essay have the feeling that this dialectic between love and awe which stands at the heart of phase two of the quest for God has a familiar ring to it, they are correct. This is because it recapitulates the experience of Religious Man in *Halakhic Man*. Religious Man too, it will be recalled, suffered from exactly the same dialectic and exactly the same yearning for unity with God that leads to self-annihilation. The parallels are uncanny, down to the very same affirmation of the value of the dialectically torn and anguished life.[78] If Phase One in *"U-Vikkashtem mi-Sham"* represents human culture in its quest for God, Phase Two represents the classic type of Religious Man (although with some important modifications, as we shall soon see).

This observation is significant for evaluating the relationship between *"U-Vikkashtem mi-Sham"* and *Halakhic Man*, an issue I touched upon above, where I argued for an evolutionary understanding of the relationship between the two essays. An alternative model for understanding the relationship, one with wide currency among students of Rabbi Soloveitchik's thought, is that the two essays were originally written as companion pieces, in which *"U-Vikkashtem mi-Sham"* was intended to supplement the picture of religious life which appeared in *Halakhic Man*. Avi Ravitzky provides one formulation of this approach, according to which *Halakhic Man* analyzes the various components of the ideal personality, while *"U-Vikkashtem mi-Sham"* synthesizes the steps along the way

---

[77] Rabbi Soloveitchik locates his discussion of the love/fear dialectic in kabbalistic as well as medieval philosophic literature, most notably Maimonides.

[78] See above in this essay for references to *Halakhic Man*. In *"U-Vikkashtem mi-Sham,"* see 167-86 and especially 179.

to achieving this ideal.[79] According to this view, Halakhic Man is none other than the individual who has already achieved Phase Three in *"U-Vikkashtem mi-Sham,"* *devekut*, and has resolved all the tensions laid out with such drama in *"U-Vikkashtem mi-Sham."* The problem with this account, however, is that Rabbi Soloveitchik explicitly identifies Halakhic Man not only with the third, but also with the second of the two phases, in which the autonomy/heternomy dialectic remains unresolved, and which is, as I have just argued, by-and-large identical with Religious Man:

> The man of God [*Ish ha-Elokim*], *who is the Man of Ha-lakhah* [*Ish ha-Halakhah*] wrestles with his anxious dialectical experience, trapped in the brambles of opposites, without refuge or escape. "According to the pain is the reward." The service of the heart is commensurate with the split in the heart [emphasis added].[80]

Rabbi Soloveitchik goes out of his way here to identify Halakhic Man with the man of God torn asunder by the "strange" dialectic between love and awe of God. Unless we assume Rabbi Soloveitchik to have used the phrase "Halakhic Man" imprecisely, which seems unlikely,[81] Halakhic Man in *"U-Vikkashtem mi-Sham"* is far closer to Religious Man than to the Halakhic Man of *Halakhic Man*. This passage supports my earlier argument for a more nuanced reading of Halakhic Man even in *Halakhic Man*, as it supports an evolutionary reading of the relationship between the two essays. According to this account, Rabbi Soloveitchik's own conception of Halakhic Man

---

[79] Ravitzky, 160.

[80] *UVM*, 179. Note the parallels to *Halakhic Man*, 4. In *UVM*, 177-78, Rabbi Soloveitchik discusses the ways in which the Halakhah embraces this unresolved dialectic, and on p. 172 he asserts of the love/fear dialectic, "both form the fundamentals of the religious-halakhic experience."

[81] See n. 80. To this must be added: (1) the name Halakhic Man carries considerable weight in R. Soloveitchik's lexicon; (2) he borrows many of the concepts first developed in *Halakhic Man* for use in *UVM*, which suggests that in writing the latter essay he had the former essay very much in mind.

(and autonomy) undergoes development from *Halakhic Man* to "*U-Vikkashtem mi-Sham*," and the origins of this change are already immanent in *Halakhic Man*, if one attends to the tensions in Rabbi Soloveitchik's own portrayal of Halakhic Man in that essay.

In any case, with the analysis of love and awe in Phase Two, *toda'ah giluyit* and *toda'ah tiv'it* are brought closer together, since at this stage in their evolution they both emerge from common soil. Nevertheless, as Rabbi Soloveitchik himself notes, this is hardly a solution to the autonomy/heteronomy problem since in Phase Two, love and awe stand in unresolved dialectical tension with one another. What is interesting however, and this is a point that Rabbi Soloveitchik himself does not clearly stress, is that a subtle but radical transvaluation has taken place under our very eyes. At the first and lowest level of religious experience, *toda'ah tiv'it* was an expression of autonomy and *toda'ah giluyit* of heteronomy. However, at this next phase, love, although portrayed as an outgrowth of *toda'ah giluyit*, leads to self-annihilation in the overwhelming existence of God, and thus becomes an expression of the heteronomous experience. The autonomous quest for God paradoxically leads to the brick wall of the overwhelming greatness of God, which snuffs out the autonomous existence of the individual.[82]

Conversely, awe, although portrayed as an outgrowth of *toda'ah giluyit*, yields a drive to escape from God's overwhelming presence so as to preserve the possibility of the continued existence of the individual. Thus fear of God becomes an expression of the autonomous, and not heteronomous, experience. Indeed, Rabbi Soloveitchik's own analysis of the nature of awe of God yields the inevitable conclusion that its relationship to the fear of *toda'ah giluyit* is formal, or perhaps psychological, at best. As we have seen, awe is a consequence of both

---

[82] See, e.g., p. 172.

understanding and love, and these in turn are both consequences of *toda'ah tiv'it* rather than *toda'ah giluyit*. What then
has happened to *toda'ah giluyit* in this phase of the quest for
God? Apparently – and this point unfortunately is barely
alluded to – *toda'ah giluyit* serves to rein man in with unbend-
ing law as he seeks to escape from God in fear.[83] It thus
turns out that the heteronomy/autonomy problem Rabbi
Soloveitchik must solve, is now considerably more complex.
Not only must it resolve a revised version of the original
problem – God's law as constraining the impulse to run from
him, it must also resolve the higher-level tension between the
love and awe of God.[84] Let us now consider just how Rabbi
Soloveitchik attempts to at least partially achieve these goals in
Phase Two of the religious quest.

What distinguishes Phase Two from Religious Man, and
what brings him closer to Halakhic Man on the one hand and
constitutes a partial resolution to the autonomy/heterenomy
dialectic on the other, is *hidamut*, the emulation of God.

> Out of the dialectic of hope and despair, of *devekut* and
> separation, of closeness and distance, the idea of
> emulation grows. It compromises between the two
> sentences which contradict one another, between
> decree and free self-creation, between the yoke which
> binds man and spontaneity, between fear of the
> revealed decree and the beautiful vision of absolute
> freedom, between the revelatory experience [*toda'ah
> giluyit*] and the experience of freedom.[85]

Just how the idea of *hidamut* achieves this is somewhat
difficult to understand. Apparently it works something like
this: As man gets closer to God, in Phase Two, he feels more

---

[83] *UVM*, 180.

[84] It sometimes appears that Rabbi Soloveitchik conflates these two issues
in his discussion of *hidamut*; nevertheless, they are indeed conceptually
distinct, and should be treated as such.

[85] *UVM*, 181. Note that here Rabbi Soloveitchik uses the term "experience
of freedom" as virtually synonymous with *toda'ah tiv'it*.

comfortable with the revelatory experience, and he tries to link
it to his experience of God in the mode of love and *toda'ah
tiv'it*.[86] It is now possible for him to imagine that his obedience
to the law is a result of his own freedom, although he knows
that eventually he will be driven from God in awe, and will
obey the law because he must. Moreover, he partially recon-
ciles himself to the inevitable dialectic between closeness to
God and distance from him, and recognizes that the best he
can do as a humble, willing servant of God is to simulate God's
own behavior, exemplified in moral Halakhah, thereby simulat-
ing the radical freedom of God Himself. While he recognizes
that his behavior is not truly free, he feels somewhat comforted
by this acceptance of his fate and by his simulation of true
freedom.[87]

Rabbi Soloveitchik would be the first to admit that we do
not have a complete resolution to the autonomy/heteronomy
problem here, since the love-awe dialectic, with its consequences for *toda'ah tiv'it* and *toda'ah giluyit*, continues to rage
unabated. Phase Two seems to be no more than an attenuation
of the feeling of crisis attendant upon the swings between these
feelings. There is no conceptual breakthrough here, but a kind
of palliative for the wounded soul. While palliatives are surely
desirable for the tormented individual stuck on the path to
God, they do not provide us with a real resolution to the
theological problems that confront us. This is said to come only
with the ultimate stage in the quest for God, *devekut*, to which
we shall now turn.

VIII. The Second Solution: *Devekut*

Rabbi Soloveitchik's analysis of *devekut* appears to proceed in
three phases. In the first, the focus is on affect, the second, on

---

[86] Ibid., 234. But note that the mode of love eventually yields self-annihilation rather than closeness.

[87] Ibid., 180, 186.

epistemology, and the third, on the uniquely Jewish life-strategies that lead to and support *devekut*. Each is presented as an essential part of a solution to the autonomy/heteronomy problem.

Interestingly, Rabbi Soloveitchik's very definition of *devekut* is, at least at first, cast in affective terms, and designed primarily to respond to the love/awe, rather than *toda'ah giluyit/toda'ah tiv'it* polarity:

> What is *devekut* according to Judaism? Judaism says that the awesome fear of God, and escape from Him, are rooted only in the upper levels of the religious experience.... In the beginning, the yearning of love is attached to the repulsion of awe, but at the end a wave of pure love floats up burning with desire which expels the alarm and recoil.... The escapee suddenly feels the hand of the Divine Presence caress him like a merciful, refined mother, and he turns his face with trembling and mute wonder, covering himself with his cloak. He then uncovers a bit of his face and looks with a startled eye full of fear and astonishment, until his stare stumbles upon the smile of the Divine Presence revealing Himself, pursuing him, and immediately the escapee becomes full of love for the pursuer Who loves him without end.[88]

The experience of God as a merciful mother who pursues and loves him, enables man to overcome his feelings of awe and distance from God, in a burst of what Rabbi Soloveitchik in another passage calls "crazy" love.[89] This sort of experience of God reflects a conception of a God, Who wants not human defeat but human redemption and self-expression, and the ultimate human religious experience is therefore joy, an outgrowth of feeling loved and of loving.

This idea is an attractive one. The question is to what extent it helps solve the autonomy/heteronomy problem. If it is

---

[88] Ibid., 193-94.
[89] Ibid., 187.

to be taken as a report of the personal religious experience of someone, such as Rabbi Soloveitchik himself, who has gone through Phases One and Two, who has come so close to God as to experience firsthand the awe which follows upon the understanding of just how great God is, and who yet permanently overcomes that feeling of distance from God as a consequence of feeling loved and pursued by Him, then we can not help but take it at face value as a solution for that individual to the love/awe dimension of the autonomy/heteronomy problem. However, Rabbi Soloveitchik does not present his thesis as a personal report. Indeed, knowing what we do about the conflicted and anguished nature of Rabbi Soloveitchik's own religious experience, as evidenced by his later writings and the tensions within the earlier writings,[90] it seems unlikely at best that the ongoing joy, which he says characterizes *devekut*, could be an accurate characterization of his own life. What we really have here is a theory of *devekut*, although perhaps grounded in certain moments of Rabbi Soloveitchik's personal religious experience. How successful is it as a theory of *devekut*?

Perhaps a contrast with Maimonides would be helpful. On the one hand, Rabbi Soloveitchik opens his discussion of *devekut* with a quotation from Maimonides to describe the kind of intense love that characterizes *devekut*.[91] However, this Maimonidean text does not really imply that awe is absent from the experience of God, but only that love, at this stage of religious development, is always present. Love could, after all, be experienced together with awe. Indeed, that seems to be exactly what Maimonides himself thinks, based upon *Mishneh Torah, Yesodei ha-Torah* 2:1-2 – which Rabbi Soloveitchik

---

[90] Note too, his self-description as melancholic, at least as it appears in *Divrei Hashkafah* (Jerusalem, 1992), 135-36: "Certainly there is within me a spiritual inclination towards elegy, towards a religious melancholy."

[91] *UVM*, 187 quoting *Mishneh Torah, Hilkhot Teshuvah* 10:3.

himself quotes approvingly in his discussion of Phase Two.[92] Quite apart from the fact that Rabbi Soloveitchik cannot legitimately use Maimonides in support of the claim that awe always accompanies love, and also in support of the claim that it can exist independently (without at least making the case within the texts that the latter is a higher level than the former), there is another, greater, problem here. Maimonides' own logic behind the claim that awe always accompanies love seems beyond reproach, and Rabbi Soloveitchik himself buys fully into it. This logic is a metaphysical one. The chasm that separates God from man is so great, that it seems altogether unavoidable that the more one understands God, the more one will appreciate that chasm and feel himself distant from God. In appropriating the kabbalistic metaphysic of *tzimtzum* to help formulate the thesis that no independent existence is possible outside of God, it is extremely difficult to see how Rabbi Soloveitchik can escape its consequences for the inevitability of awe as a component of the religious experience.

Perhaps, however, Rabbi Soloveitchik does not mean his claims in this part of the discussion to contribute to a solution to the problem, but only to serve as a description of the state of *devekut*, however one resolves the tensions and overcomes awe of God. While this seems unlikely, given Rabbi Soloveitchik's presentation of his case, let us proceed on that assumption. He does admit that at this stage he has not yet explained the "epistemological-metaphysical" basis for *devekut*. This, Rabbi Soloveitchik attempts to achieve by introducing – with much fanfare – the thesis of the unity of the knower with the object of knowledge.

According to this view of human knowledge, articulated in the *Guide* (1:68) and widespread in other classical and

---

[92] See also *Guide* 3:52. While Maimonides seems to contradict himself on whether awe or love is the superior experience and the end of Torah, both are advocated.

medieval sources, there exists an object of knowledge independent of the knower, and a potential knower. As the potential knower comes to know the object of knowledge, to understand it, his intellect becomes, in this state of knowledge, that which is intelligible about the object of knowledge. Thus, the knower and object of knowledge become, in some sense, one. In the case of God, the situation is somewhat different, but the result is the same. God knows the world, as Maimonides says not only in the *Guide*, but in the *Mishneh Torah* as well (*Yesodei ha-Torah* 2:10), by virtue of His knowledge of Himself. Since the world depends upon God for the infinite varieties of its existence, God's knowledge of the world flows from His own self-knowledge. But this in turn implies that in knowing the world, man becomes one not only with the world, but with God Himself, since both God and man know the same object of knowledge, the intelligibility of the universe.

This is Rabbi Soloveitchik's first pass at formulating the "unity" thesis, and he devotes much of his energies to explicating it. However, interestingly enough, towards the very end of his discussion he seems to veer from this account and offer another.[93] Now, the "unity" thesis is deployed not for knowledge of the universe, which, Rabbi Soloveitchik says, is static and non-normative, but for knowledge of Halakhah. Rabbi Soloveitchik makes this shift to accommodate yet another unity at stake, and that is the unity between God's knowledge, will and action. Knowledge of the universe alone – scientific knowledge – has no normative and moral dimension. Knowledge of God's wisdom as reflected in his will towards the world and action in governing the world morally – all embodied in the Halakhah – does however, yield the desired unity with the fullest range of the God-expression, namely, wisdom, will and action. Therefore, it is only through knowledge of

---

[93] *UVM*, 204.

Halakhah that *devekut* is achieved.[94] In Rabbi Soloveitchik's words, we have the "wondrous identity of wills."[95]

Several problems with the "unity" thesis suggest themselves. First, as Ravitzky correctly points out, it is fundamentally at odds with the epistemology Rabbi Soloveitchik employs throughout his writings, namely, the by-now widely shared post-Kantian view that there is no pristine "object" out there which the knower becomes "united" with.[96] Rather, human cognition itself, and especially scientific theory, constructs in some sense its own structures whereby it responds to reality. But then this cognitive construct is itself a barrier between the thing itself and the knower, making unity once again impossible. In short, the epistemological framework for the "unity" thesis derives from pre-modern theories of knowledge, and this is a framework Rabbi Soloveitchik himself abandoned throughout his writings.

While this epistemological problem is serious enough for Rabbi Soloveitchik's discussion of scientific knowledge – the first formulation of the "unity" thesis – it is hard to see how even the second formulation of the thesis would fare much better. To be sure, in *"U-Vikkashtem mi-Sham,"* as in *Halakhic Man*, halakhic knowledge is portrayed as embracing exactly the same creation of cognitive constructs as the scientific creation

---

[94] There may be a logical inconsistency here, however. If God's thought is equal to His will and action, then that same equivalence must apply to all aspects of His thought, including thought about the universe. Therefore, God's thought about the universe must also have a normative dimension, exactly the view of Maimonides, and indeed of Rabbi Soloveitchik himself (See e.g., ibid., 223-25 and elsewhere). If so, it should be possible to derive norms from contemplation about the universe, e.g., God's mercy and compassion for the world. Thus, Rabbi Soloveitchik's move to halakhic knowledge appears to be unwarranted, if his whole aim is to get at the normative. Moreover, Rabbi Soloveitchik appears to contradict himself on this question, asserting here that norms cannot be derived from nature, but asserting elsewhere (ibid., 223-55) that they can.

[95] Ibid., 235.

[96] Ravitzky, ibid.

of theories, and thus, it might be argued, a pure idealism would be possible in the sphere of Halakhah. Nevertheless, Rabbi Soloveitchik himself admits elsewhere in *"U-Vikkashtem mi-Sham"* that the halakhist works with divinely revealed laws and categories, and creates his theories out of them.[97] How then is it possible for the halakhist to know those divinely revealed laws, and hence become one with God and achieve *devekut*, if his own halakhic knowledge serves as barriers between him and God's will as revealed in His law?[98]

But let us assume, for argument's sake, not only that the "unity" thesis is true, but that it is consistent with R. Soloveitchik's other writings. I must confess that I am uncertain just how much has been achieved in resolving the love/awe polarity. Although God's will becomes identical with mine as I contemplate and then act according to the Halakhah, wouldn't I still feel at times so in awe of God's greatness as I have come to understand Him; so in awe of His wisdom and goodness with which I struggle to identify, that I feel a great chasm between us, that I feel so inconsequential before Him? It

---

[97] *UVM*, 206.

[98] In this respect, I take issue with Ravitzky, who maintains that pure idealism is possible in the halakhic context. There is yet another problem with the unity thesis that should be mentioned, what philosophers sometimes call the "intentionalist fallacy." Suppose that I never heard of the "unity" thesis, or that I believe it to be false. Will I experience awe together with love? Presumably the answer would be "yes." I can not console myself with a conviction that I am one with God, since I do not share that belief, even if my own belief is false (since *ex hypothesi*, the "unity" thesis is true) and in fact, I am indeed one with God. The "unity" thesis can help solve the love-awe problem for the seeker after God only if he believes it to be true, since the problem is located in the consciousness of the seeker. Does the seeker ever feel distant from God or only love for Him? A solution to the metaphysical problem is thus not *ipso facto* a solution to the religious one. Given the obscurity of the doctrine and its heavily philosophical formulation, one wonders whether the prophets or the Talmudic Rabbis ever consciously believed it to be true, and therefore ever succeeded in achieving *devekut*. I mention this problem in footnote only, since it is perhaps unlikely that R. Soloveitchik himself would have thought in these terms.

is hard for me, at least, to see how the epistemology and metaphysics of the unity principle can undermine the feelings of awe which Rabbi Soloveitchik himself so passionately advocated and explained in Phase Two of the discussion. Nor is it clear to me whether the "unity" principle can stand up to the metaphysics which underlies that problem, the idea that in God's presence no independent existence is possible. Has Rabbi Soloveitchik so effectively formulated the autonomy/heteronomy polarity that even he has difficulty resolving it?

These considerations lead us to the final phase in Rabbi Soloveitchik's account of *devekut*, what I have called the uniquely Jewish life-strategies that support it. In this phase of the discussion, Rabbi Soloveitchik reverts to the *toda'ah tiv'it/toda'ah giluyit* polarity, which these life-strategies are intended to address.

> The Jewish yearning to elevate experience to the spiritual, which conjoins the natural yearning of man for God with his faith in revelation, finds its expression in three ways: (1) the rule of the intellect; (2) the elevation of the bodily; (3) the perpetuation of the word of God.[99]

In his discussion of the rule of the intellect, the first of the three ways, Rabbi Soloveitchik pretty much recapitulates the thesis he devoted *Halakhic Man* to, arguing for the masterful creativity and hence intellectual autonomy characteristic of Halakhic Man which, as we have seen, amounts to an affirmation of an ethic, but not a philosophy, of intellectual autonomy. In relating this thesis to the *toda'ah tiv'it/toda'ah giluyit* polarity, he argues further, that since Halakhic Man creates intellectual constructs out of the raw data of revelation, there is "a blending of two opposing principles: the revelatory principle and the intellectual principle."[100] While, as I argued

---

[99] Ibid., 204.
[100] Ibid., 206.

above, this point does not help with the metaphysics underlying the love/awe polarity, it may indeed assuage the terror and submission one initially feels at the revelatory experience, by making it, psychologically, one's own through creative manipulation and interpretation of its contents.

What I find puzzling about the thesis is that it does not seem to be conceptually bound up exclusively with the *devekut* stage. At Phase Two, or even Phase One, the seeker after God can study Halakhah as a Brisker and gain psychological mastery of *toda'ah giluyit*. The *sturm und drang* of the *toda'ah tiv'it/toda'ah giluyit* clash can find at least this (partial) attenuation of its angst wherever the seeker after God happens to be situated in his quest. How then does *devekut* per se represent a resolution to the *toda'ah tiv'it/toda'ah giluyit* polarity? If this idea is its long-awaited resolution, then it could have been introduced much earlier in the essay.[101] I shall suggest a possible solution to this puzzle shortly.

The same point can be made about the second of the three ways Rabbi Soloveitchik identifies, the elevation of the bodily. "The elevation of the body is the whole of the Torah; as for the rest, it is its commentary, go and study."[102] Sanctifying the physical by placing it under the guiding *telos* of the Law, Rabbi Soloveitchik argues, is the central motif of the Halakhah. Unlike classical philosophy and certain religions, Judaism chooses not to abandon the physical in search of the spiritual, but to embrace them both as a "single, complete unit of psychosomatic man who serves his creator with his spirit and his body and elevates the living to eternal heights."[103] This account of Judaism has implications for the *toda'ah*

---

[101] It is possible that Rabbi Soloveitchik indeed meant this discussion to be independent of the *devekut* stage. Its location in the essay, however, and Rabbi Soloveitchik's summary statement at the end of *UVM* which includes, at the *devekut* stage, language reminiscent of this discussion, make this suggestion unlikely.

[102] *UVM*, 207.

[103] Ibid., 215.

tiv'it/toda'ah giluyit polarity, Rabbi Soloveitchik argues, since the content of revelation is the natural. Halakhah is directed at the physical; hence it unites the revelatory with the natural.

Here too, this argument could be made independently of the *devekut* stage, since Halakhah concerns itself with the physical whatever one's station on the quest for God. But how successful is the argument itself? Much like the case with the first way, that of intellectual mastery, the idea of the elevation of the physical may also help assuage the initial terror and otherness one feels at the revelatory experience when one reflects about its aim at elevating one's life. But of course, the reverse is possible as well. One might find Halakhah's manifold and intricate laws governing behavior to be intrusive and overwhelming, thus leading to feelings of submission rather than autonomy – ostensibly, exactly the way Rabbi Soloveitchik himself first portrayed the *toda'ah giluyit* experience.

That the Halakhah is concerned with the natural is in itself neutral with respect to the autonomy/heteronomy question. It is only Rabbi Soloveitchik's spin on that concern which might help assuage feelings of terror and submission. In this way, Rabbi Soloveitchik's argument may thus beg the question against how to read Halakhah's reach, and is not so much proof that Halakhah solves the problem, as it is an eloquent polemic for reading the Halakhah in an ideal way, which might help those who have heretofore responded to it in self-negation. Such an individual, who feels at first overwhelmed by the Halakhah and responds submissively, then reads Rabbi Soloveitchik's interpretation of the Halakhah and is persuaded by it, may indeed find it easier to reconcile his self and body to its claims with self-affirmation rather than self-negation. At best, of course, this does not reconcile the full gamut of autonomies affirmed in *toda'ah tiv'it* with their negation in *toda'ah giluyit*, for which reason, perhaps, Rabbi Soloveitchik introduces the third way, the perpetuation of the word of God.

During the course of Rabbi Soloveitchik's extended discussion of this theme, he makes a number of points aimed at
overcoming the *toda'ah tiv'it/toda'ah giluyit* polarity, which I
shall summarize, and then comment on briefly. First, he
argues that prophecy occurs only after extensive preparation
involving the *toda'ah tiv'it* experience. Thus, revelation is
experienced as a natural outgrowth of *toda'ah tiv'it*, a response
by God to man's quest.[104] This, however, is a curious argument, since it essentially amounts to a straightforward denial
of the argument he made at the beginning of *"U-Vikkashtem
mi-Sham,"* that *toda'ah giluyit* is not experienced as a response
to man's quest. Presumably, Rabbi Soloveitchik knew even
then that prophecy required preparation. What then has
changed? What new insights developed during the course of
the essay that might have led to this reversal?[105]

Next, Rabbi Soloveitchik reverts to a claim he made earlier in *Halakhic Man*, that man experiences the law of *toda'ah
giluyit* as a true expression of his own deepest self. Therefore,
he experiences it not as heteronomous but as autonomous.
Moreover, he feels himself liberated from the demands and
drives of his physical existence in committing himself to
revealed law. He identifies with the law and makes it his own,
so that he feels free and joyous.[106] Here again, he repeats his
(problematic) claim that great Jews never experienced a
struggle with the *yetzer ha-ra*, since the law is experienced as
their own inner desire. Apparently, Rabbi Soloveitchik regards
these arguments as crucial, since he recapitulates their
essence in his brief summary of the entire essay in the closing

---

[104] Ibid., 217-21.

[105] He buttresses his case during the course of his discussion by
observing (*UVM*, 218) that according to Judaism there is no complete
metaphysical break between the natural and the supernatural, the finite
and the infinite and that they together make up a single homogeneous
whole. The meaning of this statement, however, is not altogether clear
to me.

[106] Ibid., 221-22.

paragraphs of *"U-Vikkashtem mi-Sham."* This in itself is somewhat curious, since in *Halakhic Man* he makes the same point without the entire, elaborate apparatus constructed in *"U-Vikkashtem mi-Sham."*

As I noted earlier, this at best amounts to an affirmation of the autonomy of personality rather than the autonomy of morality. But even understood as a claim for the autonomy of personality, its status in regard to resolving the *toda'ah tiv'it/toda'ah giluyit* polarity is much the same as that of his thesis concerning the elevation of the body. Surely, this is one ideal way to respond to Halakhah. However, it is not the only way, as Rabbi Soloveitchik himself explains at the beginning of *"U-Vikkashtem mi-Sham."* To fully justify his claim that this solves an aspect of the autonomy/heteronomy problem, Rabbi Soloveitchik would need to show that this is the only possible way to experience Halakhah and that in fact the Halakhah does represent the true inner desires of the Jew. As with the elevation of the physical thesis, we have here a stirring argument (in this case very brief) for an ideal vision of the Halakhah, which may indeed help assuage feelings of submission and self-negation for whoever experiences the Halakhah in this way.

Finally, Rabbi Soloveitchik argues that the natural experience yields the revelational experience, since "the moral law is in itself the law of existence, and ethical action permeates the great creation."[107] God's creation and governance of the world is an expression of His moral will and actions, and so through experiencing the world, one experiences the divine moral will, which turns out to be the content of the revelatory experience. As I argued above, however, following Ravitzky, this thesis is at odds with the post-Kantian theory Rabbi Soloveitchik himself affirms. Moreover, at best, it relates only to divinely revealed moral law, and not to the large class of non-moral laws that are part of revelation and Halakhah.

---

[107] Ibid., 225.

In the end, perhaps the best way to understand the function of the three ways in R. Soloveitchik's thinking is two-fold: strategic and descriptive. I have heretofore focused on the three ways as a strategy for solving the autonomy/heteronomy polarity, and tried to demonstrate some of the problems they encounter in achieving this end. However, the three ways seem to function also as an idealized description of how, according to R. Soloveitchik, the individual who has already achieved *devekut* lives and experiences his Judaism. The descriptive function would provide the link I sought between the first two ways and *devekut*: certainly they could be experienced independently of *devekut*, but *devekut* always includes them. Understood as description, they reveal R. Soloveitchik's vision of the ideal Jewish experience. Understood as a strategy, they play a role in helping he who seeks God to resolve the *toda'ah tiv'it/toda'ah giluyit* polarity tension in his religious life and thereby help him achieve *devekut*. For some people, then, they may indeed contribute, if only partially, to a resolution of the autonomy/heteronomy polarity which is the central problematic of "*U-Vikkashtem mi-Sham.*"

IX. Conclusion

What conclusions can be drawn from this analysis? I have tried to show that Rabbi Soloveitchik's many and varied attempts to address the autonomy/heteronomy polarities in "*U-Vikkashtem mi-Sham*" does not appear to stand up to his own way of formulating the problem. It is absolutely critical for us to remember that Rabbi Soloveitchik need never have embraced so overwhelmingly heteronomous a characterization of the revelatory experience to begin with. After all, someone with an affinity for autonomy has numerous possible options open to him. For example, he could argue that the aim of revelation is to empower the Jew by making him a covenantal partner with God.[108] Or, he might argue that the submission one must feel to God is but one small aspect of the complex religious experience, which is most characterized by dignity and assertiveness. Or again, he could argue that autonomy is a central value in the tradition, but a defeasible one under certain circumstances or at certain times.[109] Whether or not any of these approaches would ultimately work, is in part beside the point. After all, creativity is one of Rabbi Soloveitchik's strongest intellectual virtues, and without a doubt he could have arrived at alternative ways of thinking about the problem that would have been far less problematic.

It is precisely Rabbi Soloveitchik's own formulation of the nature of the revelatory experience, his own deep personal conviction that Judaism really does require its adherents to submit themselves in defeat before God, that led him to set up the polarity which, in the end, he found so difficult to resolve.[110] "U-Vikkashtem mi-Sham" takes an important step beyond Halakhic Man in laying bare the autonomy/heteronomy

---

[108] This is essentially the strategy of David Hartman in Living Covenant.

[109] For an extensive discussion of these issues, see Sokol, "Personal Autonomy and Religious Authority."

[110] Rabbi Soloveitchik's reasons for understanding the religious experience as essentially submissive (while also assertive) almost certainly rest in his own personal faith experience as much as they do in a dispassionate reading of the sources. Why his faith experience was such is itself an interesting question that cannot be answered with any certainty. One factor that may have contributed, however, is the challenge that modernity posed to his religious faith. Some of the greatest problems R. Soloveitchik would have had to confront are the claims of Wissenschaft scholarship in the study of the Bible, Talmud and Halakhah. Yet, at least in the case of biblical criticism, R. Soloveitchik says in "Lonely Man of Faith" (8-9) that he was never troubled by it. In this context, it is important to remember R. Soloveitchik's admiring portrayal of the simple faith of the "man-child" in "The Remnant of Scholars" (Epstein, Shi'urei ha-Rav [New York, 1974], 16). I have argued elsewhere (Singer and Sokol, Ger Ve-Toshav) that R. Soloveitchik's response to some of the challenges of modernity was a fideistic, traditionalist faith affirmation, which of course amounts to a submission of self and intellect to the claims of classic Judaism. Thus the challenges of modernity may have led him to embrace a submissive stance towards God in his own personal religious experience.

tensions which were in large part – but by no means completely – submerged in Rabbi Soloveitchik's idealized portrait of Halakhic Man. Surgically laid bare as they are in "*U-Vikkashtem mi-Sham*," Rabbi Soloveitchik has great difficulty in closing these gaping wounds.

The next and final step in this literary-philosophical evolution is thus hardly surprising. In all of Rabbi Soloveitchik's later works, no attempt at resolving the polarities is even made. Human beings, Jews included, are portrayed as fundamentally and irreconcilably conflicted beings who must live out the autonomy/heteronomy polarities in a dialectical fashion, fully embracing each side of the dialectic. This final conclusion was in fact immanent at the very beginning and represents, I would suggest, the most authentic expression of Rabbi Soloveitchik's own religious sensibilities, even early in his career.[111] The problems I have tried to identify throughout *Halakhic Man* and "*U-Vikkashtem mi-Sham*" may of course indeed be just that – theological and philosophical problems; however, they may also amount to more. They may reflect Rabbi Soloveitchik's own ambivalent feelings about the very enterprise in which he was engaged. At some level, he may have sensed some of these difficulties, for which reason, in part, he may have abandoned even the attempt at resolution. In other words, despite the apparently great disparities between the early and late writings, I am arguing that there is, perhaps paradoxically, greater unity to Rabbi Soloveitchik's works than first meets the eye.

---

[111] See above, n. 110.

May One Destroy a Neighbor's Property in Order to Save One's Life?

A Case Study in a Conflict of Duties and its Contemporary Implications for the Incorporation of Jewish Law into the Israeli Legal System*

Ronnie Warburg

More than forty years ago, Moshe Silberg, a former justice of the Israeli Supreme Court observed:

> Why should a man pay his debt or fulfill an obligation which he has undertaken? The Roman lawyers, as well as any modern lawyer, would be most surprised by such a question. It is clear, they would say, that the duty of payment of a debt is the correlative of the concept of ownership, and one cannot exist without the other ... In Jewish law ... when a person refuses to pay his debt ... the concern of the court is not the creditor's debt, his damages, but the duty of the debtor, his religious-moral duty....[1]

* I am grateful to the anonymous referees for a number of helpful comments on earlier drafts of this paper.

[1] Moshe Silberg, "Law and Morals in Jewish Jurisprudence," 75 *Harvard Law Review* (1961), pp. 306, 312-13, reprinted in Moshe Silberg, *Talmudic Law and The Modern State* (New York, 1973), pp. 61, 68-69.

Implicitly relying upon a Hofheldian analysis of rights and duties, Silberg argues that a statement about a right entails a statement about a duty and a statement about a duty entails a statement about a right.[2] Conceptually speaking, when dealing with a right-based system, one justifies the duty by pointing to the right; if one requires justification, it is the right that one must justify. However, when one is dealing with a duty-based system, such as the Jewish legal system, one must justify the duty and one cannot do so by pointing to the right. On a halakhic-legal plane, there is no difference between Jewish law and other legal systems. Clearly, the Jewish legal system, similar to other legal systems, recognizes the notion of property rights. However, from a halakhic-conceptual perspective, we are dealing with two different systems. Jewish law focuses upon duties and others focus upon rights. During the last forty years, contemporary decisors of Jewish law, Jewish historians, law professors and philosophers alike have either subscribed wholeheartedly or with certain reservations to Silberg's analysis. However, his conclusion that the Jewish legal system is duty-based has been affirmed by all.[3]

---

[2] For a brief summary of the relevant jurisprudential literature, see Alan White, *Rights* (New York, 1984), pp. 55-73. Compare Feinberg's suggestion that rights are logically prior to duties and serve as grounds for obligations in Joel Feinberg, *Social Philosophy* (Englewood Cliffs, NJ, 1973), pp. 58, 62; see also Phillip Montague, "Two Concepts of Rights," 9 *Philosophy and Public Affairs* (1980), pp. 372-73. Implicit in this understanding of the relationship between rights and duties is the notion that it makes a difference which is derivative from which. See Ronald Dworkin, *Taking Rights Seriously* (London, 1979), p.171; Jeremy Waldron, *The Right to Private Property* (London, 1988), pp. 69-73. In our presentation, we are focusing upon the jurisprudential, rather than the practical differences between the two legal systems regarding duties and rights.

[3] J. David Bleich, *Contemporary Halakhic Problems* (New York, 1995), p. 307; Michael Broyde, "Human Rights and Human Duties in the Jewish Tradition" in *Human Rights in Judaism: Cultural, Religious and Political Perspectives*, ed. Michael Broyde and John Witte (Northvale, NJ, 1998), pp. 273-82; Haim Cohn, *Human Rights in Jewish Law* (New York, 1984); Robert M. Cover, "Obligation – A Jewish Jurisprudence of the Social Order," 5 *Journal of Law and Religion* (1987), pp.65-74; Menachem Elon,

In earlier studies, contemporary decisors and scholars alike have either advanced theological and/or philosophical reasons, or legally analyzed substantive topics dealing with the law of obligations, criminal law, domestic relations and *tzedakah* to find support for their characterization of Jewish law as promoting a duty-centered legal system.[4] Whereas these studies provided a jurisprudential framework and an analytical examination of particular areas in Jewish civil law that corroborate their conclusion, our focus will be different. Rather than delve into the inner dynamics of a particular obligation, our presentation will address, from a *jurisprudential* perspective, how decisors addressed the interplay between *two conflicting duties* functioning within a particular context, i.e., the defense of necessity and its contemporary implications regarding the incorporation of Jewish law into the Israeli legal system.

Within a secular legal right-based system, our topic would be examined in the following manner: Consider Joel Feinberg's example of a conflict between the right to life and the right to property. A stranded backpacker imperiled by a blizzard breaks into another person's cabin, not only eats the food he finds there but also burns some of furniture to keep

---

Jewish Law (Philadelphia, 1994), pp.117-19; Martin Golding, "The Primacy of Welfare Rights," 1 *Social Philosophy and Policy* (1984), p.119; Isaac Herzog, *Main Institutions of Jewish Law*, vol. 1 (London, 1936), p. 46; Aaron Kirschenbaum, "The Good Samaritan and Jewish Law," 7 *Dine Israel* (1976), pp. 7, 15-18; Berachyahu Lifshitz, "Shetar and Arevut," [Hebrew] in *Memorial Volume to Gad Tedeschi* (Jerusalem, 1995), pp.35-39; David Novak, *Covenantal Rights: A Study in Jewish Political Tradition* (Princeton, 2000), pp. 3-12; Eliav Shochetman, *Ma'aseh ha-Ba be-Averah* [Hebrew] (Jerusalem, 1981), pp. 228-31; Suzanne Last Stone, "In Pursuit of the Counter-Text: The Turn to the Jewish Legal Model in Contemporary American Legal Theory," 59 *Harvard Law Review* (1990), pp. 813,865ff; Ephraim Urbach, *The Sages: Their Concepts and Beliefs* [Hebrew] (Jerusalem, 1975), pp. 337-39; Itamar Warhaftig, *Undertaking in Jewish Law* [Hebrew] (Jerusalem, 2001), pp. 31-35; Ronnie Warburg, "Child Custody: A Comparative Analysis," 14 *Israel Law Review* (1978), pp. 480, 490; Ernest Weinreb, "Rescue and Restitution," 1 *S'vara* (1990), p. 59.

[4] See ibid.

from freezing to death.[5] Does the backpacker's right to life justify infringing the cabin owner's right to his property? In a right-based system, which is equally predicated upon the logical correlativity of rights and duties, the nature, extent and value of the right can be spelled out only after explaining how this *right* is affected by apparent conflicts with other *rights*. Does the right to life take priority over property rights? The resolution of this question will explain jurisprudentially the contours of the particular property rights.

Adopting the perspective of viewing the Jewish legal system as duty-centered, how will the backpacker scenario be resolved? Does the obligation against theft assume priority over the duty to save one's own life? Or does the obligation to save one's life outweigh the proscription against theft and permit the taking of one's neighbor's property? The resolution of this question will illuminate the contours of property *obligations* in cases of property losses and the owing of compensation as a result.

1. A Rabbinic Overview

With these questions in mind, let us now direct our attention to the following Talmudic passage found in Tractate *Bava Kama*:[6]

> Scripture says: "And David longed, and said, Oh that one would give me water to drink of the well of Bethlehem, which is by the gate." And the three mighty men broke through the host of the Philistines and drew water out of the well of Bethlehem that was by the gate etc. What was his difficulty? ... R. Huna said: There

---

[5] Joel Feinberg, "Voluntary Euthanasia and the Inalienable Right to Life," 7 *Philosophy and Public Affairs* (1978), pp. 93-123. See also, Judith Thomson, "Rights and Compensation," 14 *Nous* (1980) pp. 3-15 and literature cited in n. 51.

[6] *Talmud Bavli, Bava Kama* 60b (translation culled from Soncino edition of the Babylonian Talmud).

were [heaps] of barley which belonged to Israelites but in which Philistines had hidden themselves, and what he asked was whether it was permissible to rescue oneself through the destruction of another's property. The answer they dispatched to him was: it is forbidden to rescue oneself through the destruction of another's property; you however are King and a king may break [through fields belonging to private persons] to make a way [for his army], and nobody is entitled to prevent him [from doing so].

This passage raises the question as to when one may take or destroy the property of others in order to save one's own life.[7] R. Huna posed the question, whether King David's army was allowed to appropriate the property of other Jews that the Philistines had been using as camouflage. The answer he received was that a king, by dint of his authority and given the exigency of *pikuah nefesh* (a life threatening situation) is empowered to confiscate private property. However, the defense of necessity will not apply to individuals. Consequently, an individual is not permitted to destroy the property of others in order to save one's own life.

On the other hand, there is another passage found in Tractate *Sanhedrin* that implies the legitimization of the defense of necessity regarding individuals. In the wake of the Hadrianic persecutions of the Jewish community in the Land

---

[7] Though this passage is the sole explicit discussion of the defense of tortuous necessity in the *Talmud Bavli*, nevertheless, there are additional passages that have been interpreted by post-Talmudic legists as addressing our issue. See various dicta in *Yoma* 83b; *Ketubot* 18b; *Bava Kama* 80a and *Temurah* 15b. For earlier treatments of our topic, see Bleich, *supra* n. 3, 309-10; Mark Dratch, "His Money or Her Life? Heinz's Dilemma in Jewish Law," 20 *Journal of Halacha and Contemporary Society* (1990), pp.11-13; Shlomo Eishon, "Fundamental Law: Human Dignity and His Freedom According to Jewish Law," [Hebrew] 16 *Tehumin* (1986), pp. 313-39; R. Zalman N. Goldberg, "The Commandment of Bestowal of Acts of Kindness: Monetary Aspects," [Hebrew] 7 *Shurat ha-Din*, pp. 376-95, 412-35; Shmuel Jakobovits, "Response to R. Goldberg," [Hebrew] 7 *Shurat ha-Din*, pp. 395-412; Kirschenbaum, *supra* n. 3, pp. 66-68.

of Israel in 135 C.E., the Talmud records the following Mishnaic tradition:[8]

> R. Yohanan said in the name of R. Simon b. Yeho-
> zadak: By a majority vote it was resolved in the upper
> chambers of the house of Nithza in Lydda that in every
> [other] law of the Torah, if a man is commanded:
> "Transgress and suffer not death," he may transgress
> and not suffer death, excepting idolatry, incest [which
> includes adultery] and murder.

In short, martyrdom is required in face of idolatry, incest
and homicide. Evidently, other transgressions, including the
proscription against theft, do not mandate martyrdom. Hence,
the inference to be drawn is that in instances of life threatening situations, one is permitted to appropriate someone else's
property.

In effect, one tradition affirms the defense of necessity between individuals whereas another rejects this defense. One
might try to resolve this problem by denying the existence of a
conflict between *pikuah nefesh* and the prohibition against
theft. Espousing this view, one response to our scenario would
be this rejoinder:

> Although it might seem at first blush to be a conflict
> between the imperiled party and the property owner,
> further consideration shows that this is not so. Since
> the proscription against theft does not apply in cases
> where the thief intends to pay, therefore, by definition,
> it follows that the imperiled party may appropriate the
> property provided that reimbursement is effectuated.[9]

---

[8] TB *Sanhedrin* 74b; *Talmud Yerushalmi* (hereafter: TY) *Shevi'it* 4:2, TY
Sanhedrin 3:6. For historical background, see Kirschenbaum, *supra* n. 3,
p. 24 n.66.

[9] Goldberg, *supra* n. 7, p. 385. For antecedents to this approach, see R.
Bezalel Ashkenazi (Egypt, 16th century) in the name of the Rashba and
Ritba, *Shitah Mekubbetzet, Bava Metzia* 41a, s.v. *tirgema, katav
ha-Rashba*. For an identical approach regarding stealing from a Gentile,
see R. Pesah ha-Levi Horowitz, *Sefer ha-Makneh, Kuntres Aharon*, 28:1;
R. Naftali Zvi Berlin (Galicia, 1808-1875), *Teshuvot Sho'el u-Meishiv*,

In the process of fulfilling the duty of saving a life, the duty against theft has not been violated. Hence, appropriation is sanctioned.[10]

Alternatively, this position can be explained based upon the Talmudic principle "*aseh doheh lo ta'aseh*" – when a positive and negative duty are in conflict and one or the other must be transgressed, priority is accorded to the fulfillment of the positive commandment.[11] Generally speaking, transgressing a negative act involves intent to transgress a proscription. However, if the individual does not intend to transgress, he is not deemed a transgressor. *A fortiori*, if the individual performs a positive act that implicitly attests to his affirmation of accepting a divine imperative while simultaneously committing a negative act, *ipso facto* he is not to be labeled a transgressor. Consequently, the positive act of *pikuah nefesh* nullifies the negative act of theft.[12] Alternatively, pursuant to the reasoning of the Ramban, given that a positive action is intrinsically more

---

Mahadura Kama, 1:126. According to R. Goldberg's resolution, one must die rather than steal. However, willingness to furnish compensation will sanction the act of theft and avoid death!

[10] For an explicit rejection of this view, see, for instance, R. Menachem b. Solomon ha-Me'iri (Provence, 1249-1316), *Beit ha-Behirah, Bava Kama* 60b.

[11] TB *Beitzah* 8b. For the general ramifications of this principle, see Michal Guttman, "The Rules Concerning *Aseh Doheh Lo Ta'aseh*," [Hebrew] *Jubilee Volume of Rabbi Moses Aryeh Bloch* (Budapest, 1905), 1-20; Israel Schepansky, "*Aseh* and *Lo Ta'aseh* Which is Stricter?," [Hebrew] 10 *Hadarom* (1959), pp. 110-14.

[12] *Teshuvot Sho'el u-Meishiv, Mahadura Tinyana*, 1:95. For further discussion, see R. Hayim Hizkiyahu Medini (Italy, 1832-1904), *Sedei Hemed, Ma'arekhet Alef*, Section 16; *Pe'at ha-Sadeh, Kelalim, Ma'arekhet Alef*, 19.

Despite initial reservations, R. Isaac Schmelkes (Poland, 1828-1906) argues that pursuant to the principle *aseh doheh lo-ta'aseh*, it is permissible to kill a *tereifah* (a person suffering from a fatal disease), to save human life. See *Teshuvot Beth Yitzchok, YD* 2:162:3. Cf. R. Yehezkel Landau (Prague, 1713-93), *Teshuvot Noda bi-Yehudah, Mahadura Tinyana, HM* 59. *A fortiori*, one may argue that it is permissible to steal in order to preserve human life.

significant than a negative act, therefore, the positive act of *pikuach nefesh* supersedes the negative act of theft.[13] While a negative act involves more strictures, i.e., *humrot*, than a positive act, nevertheless, the significance of love between God and man emerging from the performance of a positive act supersedes the fear of God engendered through the performance of a negative commandment.[14] Despite the priority granted to *pikuah nefesh* due to its classification as a positive commandment, according to both positions, logic dictates that appropriation must be provided for destroying a neighbor's property. However, others have contended that the principle of "*aseh doheh lo-ta'aseh*" is not to be invoked within the sphere of interpersonal relations, i.e., *bein adam le-havero*.[15]

Nonetheless, the overwhelming majority of decisors construe our scenario as a conflict between the property owner and endangered party. One view is offered by R. Dov Breisch Weidenfeld and is also the opinion of the Rashba.[16] The

---

[13] R. Moses b. Nahman (Spain, 1194-1270), *Peirush ha-Ramban al ha-Torah, Shemot* 20:8.

[14] For this understanding of the Ramban's posture, see *Sedei Hemed, Kelalim, Ma'arekhet* 70, *kelal* 41. For numerous sources in *Hazal* that prioritize *ahavah* (love) over *yir'ah* (fear), see Louis Ginzburg, "Serve from Love, Serve from Fear," [Hebrew] *Sinai* 52 (1963): pp. 38-51; Ephraim Urbach, *supra* n. 3, pp. 348-70. Given that the Ramban's view is counter-intuitive, one might suggest that his exegetical commentary reflects a theological rather than a halakhically principled position. For a trenchant criticism of his position, see R. Malakhi ha-Kohen (Italy, 18th century), *Yad Malakhi*, 1:515. For a similar criticism of such a position that predates the Ramban's, see *Peirush Rav Nissim Gaon* (Abramson edition), *Shabbat* 133a. For the historical context of R. Nissim's position, see Moshe Zucker, "The Rabbinic-Karaite Controversy Regarding *Aseh Doheh Lo-Ta'aseh*," [Hebrew] 6 *Dine Israel* (1975), p. 181.

[15] See R. Moshe Sofer (Hungary, 1762-1839), *Teshuvot Hatam Sofer, Kovetz Teshuvot* (5733), no. 7; R. Aryeh Balchover (Russia, 19th century), *Teshuvot Shem Aryeh YD* 64.

[16] R. Dov Weidenfeld (Israel, 1881-1966), *Teshuvot Dovev Meisharim* 1:20; R. Solomon b. Avraham Adret (Spain, ca. 1235-1310), *Teshuvot ha-Rashba* 4:17. For a discussion of the Rashba's view, see R. Avraham Sofer Avraham (Israel, 21st century), *Nishmat Avraham* 2, 157:1, pp. 63-64.

contradictory traditions emerging from these Talmudic discussions are reflected in the process of identifying the rationale of a particular viewpoint regarding contraception. In the case of a woman whose life would be endangered by pregnancy, there is a school of thought that prohibits the use of a pre-coital *mokh* (tampon-like device) because it involves the act of *"hashhatat zera"* (destruction of male seed). Aside from the issue of *"hotza'at zera le-battalah"* (improper emission of seed), R. Dov Breisch Weidenfeld initially considers invoking the norm that an individual is proscribed from saving one's life by destroying someone else's property, as suggested by the passage in *Bava Kama*. Hence, one would be prohibited from using a pre-coital *mokh* in cases of pregnancy hazard. However, upon further reflection, R. Weidenfeld concludes that though the destruction of seed constitutes theft of the husband's property, nevertheless, the prohibition against theft is *nullified*, i.e, *hutrah*, in cases of *pikuah nefesh* as suggested by the tradition recorded in Lydda: "There is nothing that overrides the saving of human life except idolatry, incest and murder."[17,18]

On the other hand, while affirming the tradition of Lydda, numerous decisors such as *Tosafot*, Rosh, Maharshal and Maharam Schick opine that one is permitted to appropriate a neighbor's property to save one's own life provided that monetary compensation is made to the property owner.[19]

---

[17] For a development of the notion of the Jewish legal system's recognition of a Jew's ownership rights in human reproductive material, see Ronnie Warburg, "Solomonic Decisions in Frozen Preembryo Disposition: Unscrambling the Halakhic Conundrum," 36 *Tradition* (Summer 2002), pp. 31-44.

[18] The normative significance of the tradition "nothing stands (overrides) in the face of *pikuah nefesh*," compels R. Moshe Feinstein (U.S., 20th cent.) to argue that R. Solomon b. Isaac (Rashi; France, 11th century), endorses this view. See *Rashi, Bava Kama* 60b, s.v. *va-yatzilah* and *Iggerot Mosheh YD* 1:214. However, the plain reading of Rashi's words as well as the consensus among decisors is to reject this interpretation of Rashi. See sources cited in *Nishmat Avraham* 2, 157:4.

[19] *Tosafot Bava Kama* 60b s.v. *mahu*; R. Asher b Yehiel (Spain, 1250-1327), *Piskei ha-Rosh, Bava Kama*, 6:12; R. Solomon b. Jehiel Luria (Poland,

In effect, the prohibition against theft is *suspended,* i.e., *dehuyah,* in cases of life-threatening situations.[20] Upon completion of the rescue operation, the property owner's title triggers the duty against theft.[21] Upon reimbursement, the *issur* (prohibition) against theft is extinguished.[22]

1510-1573), *Yam shel Shelomoh, Bava Kama* 6:27; R. Moshe Schick (Hungary,19th century), *Teshuvot Maharam Schick YD* 347-48. See also, *Shulhan Arukh HM* 359:4; *Sema, HM* 259:10.

[20] Whether *pikuah nefesh* nullifies (i.e., *matir*) or suspends (i.e., *doheh*) the proscription against theft (see text accompanying notes 16 and 19) is based upon the commentary of R. Akiva Eiger (Germany, 19th century), *Gilyon ha-Shas, Bava Kama* 60b. For the adoption of similar terminology, albeit addressing other issues, see R. Asher Weiss (Israel, 21st century), *Minhat Asher, Sefer va-Yikra,* no. 60, p. 321.

Whether mortal danger abolishes or suspends theft is equally a point of controversy in cases of duress. See R. Isser Zalman Meltzer (Israel, 1870-1953), *Even ha-Ezel, Hilkhot Hovel u-Mazzik* 8:1 in his explanation of the dispute between the Rambam and Raavad.

[21] Subscribing to the notion that the owner retains his proprietary title (see note 22), it has been advanced that our scenario is analogous to the opinion of R. Eliezer b. Samuel (Germany, ca. 1115-ca. 1198), *Sefer Yerei'im, Hilkhot Lulav* 124 and *Yerei'im ha-Shalem* 422. See R. Jacob Lifshitz, *Teshuvot Berit Ya'akov OH* 15. (For antecedents to the *Berit Ya'akov*'s approach regarding theft from a Gentile, see *Hiddushei ha-Ramban, Sukkah* 30b; *Hiddushei R. Akiva Eiger, Sukkah* 30b; *To'afot Re'im, Sefer Yerei'im ha-Shalem,* no. 422, p. 344; R. Shimon Shkop (Lithuania, 1860-1940), *Sha'arei Yosher* 2, 2:14-16; *Hiddushei R. Shimon Shkop, Bava Kama* 39:6.) Similarly, in our scenario, while the system sanctions the appropriation of another individual's property in cases of *pikuah nefesh,* nonetheless, the property owner retains title.

[22] There are two implications that flow from this conclusion: First, though permission is given to appropriate the property, title to the property remains with the original owner. See *Yoma* 83b ("if one was seized by ravenous hunger...") and ensuing discussion in *Rashi,* ibid., s.v. *ki peligei*; R. Judah Rosannes (Turkey, 1657-1727), *Parashat Derakhim, derush* 19; R. Arye Leib Heller (Poland, 1745-1813), *Avnei Millu'im EH* 28:3; R. Yom Tov Lipman Halperin (Lithuania, d. 1879), *Teshuvot Oneg Yom Tov YD* 111; *Even ha-Ezel, Hilkhot Nizkei Mamon* 8:1. (For a differing interpretation of this Talmudic passage, pursuant to Rashi's position [see text accompanying note 28], see R. Jacob Ettlinger [Germany, 19th century], *Teshuvot Binyan Tziyyon* 167.) Consequently, upon completion of the rescue operation compensation must be made. Second, generally speaking, "stealing with the intent to compensate" is proscribed (see *Shulhan Arukh HM* 359:2); nevertheless, in situations of *pikuah nefesh,* it is permissible

While affirming the tradition of Lydda, R. Moshe Sofer[23] and R. Yisrael Mintzberg[24] concur with the above conclusion, but for different reasons. In their minds, the issue is whether the positive commandment of human self-preservation nullifies the proscription against theft. The Talmudic response is: "*aseh doheh lo-ta'aseh.*" However, this principle is limited to cases where both the positive and negative acts pertain to man and his fellow man. If, however, the positive act relates to man and God and the negative act pertains to man and his fellow man, the positive act will not override the negative act. Consequently, for example, their contention is that one cannot fulfill the mitzvah of *netilat lulav* (taking a palm-branch on the holiday of *Sukkot*) through the negative act of theft. Analogously, even though saving one's own life involves the performance of a positive act, nevertheless, appropriating

---

(see *Shulhan Arukh HM* 359:4) with the proviso that compensation is forthcoming upon the completion of the rescue operation. See R. Avraham b. Zeev Borenstein (Poland, 1839-1910), *Teshuvot Avnei Nezer OH* 325; *Teshuvot Maharam Schick YD* 348. Alternatively, it has been argued that given the fact that the property owner is obligated to save his life, a fortiori, the individual may save his own life with his neighbor's property, provided restitution is made. See *Sedei Hemed, Kelalim, Ma'arekhet Alef*, section 19.

Whether an imperiled person who is unable to provide compensation due to being destitute or due to his inability to locate the property owner, may save himself with his neighbor's property is a matter of debate. See *Sedei Hemed, Kelalim, Alef* 16; *Teshuvot Binyan Tziyyon* 170; R. Bezalel Stern (Israel, 21st century), *Teshuvot be-Tzail ha-Hokhmah* 3:118; R. Judah Ayash (Israel, 1700-1760), *Teshuvot Beth Yehudah YD* 47; *Teshuvot Maharam Schick*, ibid.; R. Mordecai b. Moses Schwadron (Poland, 1835-1911), *Teshuvot Maharsham* 5:54; R. Yaakov Bloi (Israel, 1929-), *Pithei Hoshen, Hilkhot Genevah* 1:9, no. 21 and *Hilkhot Nezikin* 12:5, no. 11; R. Menasheh Klein (New York, 21st century), *Teshuvot Mishneh Halakhot* 6:424.

[23] *Teshuvot Hatam Sofer, supra* n. 15. Our formulation of the Hatam Sofer's posture has been enlightened by the words of the *Teshuvot Shem Aryeh*, *supra* n. 15. Adopting the Hatam Sofer's approach, see R. Shlomo Kluger (Galicia, 19th century), *Teshuvot ha-Elef Lekha Shelomoh YD* 200.

[24] R. Israel Zeev Mintzberg (Israel, 1872-1962), *Teshuvot She'eirit Yisrael OH* 13.

someone else's property in the process will not legitimate, in
the eyes of the *Hatam Sofer*, the performance of the positive
act. In both situations, the positive commandment of taking a
lulav or saving life cannot supersede the negative act of theft
by performing a positive religious act with one's neighbor's
assets. Hence, the principle of *"aseh doheh lo-ta'aseh"* is not to
be invoked.[25] However, if one is willing to provide compensation to one's fellow for destroying his assets in order to save
one's own life, the principle is applicable. In other words,
though generally a positive act between man and God will not
override a negative act between man and his fellowman in his
performance of *pikuah nefesh*, he is fulfilling a positive act
between man and his fellow man in his willingness to offer
reimbursement, while simultaneously fulfilling a positive act of
a rescue of life, an action between man and God. Hence, in
such a situation, the positive act of saving a life will supersede
the negative act of theft.

On the other hand, relying upon various precedents
which dissent from this well-established tradition of Lydda[26]
and accepting the plain reading of the above cited passage in
Bava Kama, Rashi and others argue that an individual is
prohibited from destroying private property in saving one's own
life.[27] In effect, according to this approach, theft is the fourth
cardinal sin that mandates martyrdom.[28] Hence, one cannot
transgress the prohibition of theft to save one's own life.

---

[25] For the inapplicability of this principle to theft, see Goldberg, *supra* n. 7, p. 384 n. 5.

[26] TY *Shabbat* 14:4; TY *Avodah Zarah* 2:2; TB *Ketubot* 18b (according to R. Meir); R. Moses Margoliot (Lithuania, ca. 1710-80), *Mar'eh ha-Panim*, TY *Avodah Zarah* 2:2, s.v. *lo sof*; *Shitah Mekubbetzet*, *Ketubot* 19a, s.v. *ve-od katav ha-Ramban*; *Teshuvot Oneg Yom Tov*, *supra* n. 22.

[27] Rashi, *supra* n. 18. Various decisors concur with Rashi's position. See *Teshuvot Binyan Tziyyon* 167-68; *Teshuvot Sho'el u-Meishiv*, *Mahadura Kama* 2:174 and *Mahadura Tinyana* 2:10; R. Joshua Ehrenburg (Israel, 20th century), *Teshuvot Devar Yehoshua* 3:24. For a differing interpretation of Rashi's posture, see *Teshuvot Maharam Schick YD* 347.

[28] TY *Avodah Zarah* and *Mar'eh Panim*, *supra* n. 26.

Alternatively, while theft does not constitute homicide per se, it is rather a stricture ancillary to the prohibition of murder (*abizrayhu de-retzihah*).[29] As is known, there is a Talmudic presumption that an individual will not freely surrender his possessions to a thief.[30] Hence, the act of theft is a life-threatening situation and is subsumed under the rubric of murder and thus, mandates martyrdom.

Consequently, an individual cannot save his own life by appropriating someone else's property and thereby creating a life-threatening situation for the property owner. One is precluded from saving one's life at the expense of the life of another individual. "Who can say that your blood is redder? Perhaps his blood is redder?"[31]

The preceding analysis suggests varying rationales for affirming or rejecting the defense of necessity between two individuals. Pursuant to one approach (from two differing perspectives), one can destroy property in order to save

---

[29] According to the Maharsham (*supra* n. 22), this conclusion is based upon the Talmudic dictum (TB *Bava Kama* 119a): "One who robs from his fellow anything worth a *perutah* or more – it is as if he had taken his soul from him." In fact, the Talmud equates poverty with death. See TB *Nedarim* 7b, 64b. See also R. Abraham b. David (Provence, 1125-1198), *Temim De'im* 203; *Teshuvot Hatam Sofer HM* 1; *Teshuvot Ohr Gadol* 1; *Teshuvot Beit Yehudah*, *supra* n. 22. For an identical characterization of an employer who withholds his employee's salary, see *Sifrei, Ki Tetzei* 279 and *Shulhan Arukh HM* 339:2.

Though this conclusion may seem to be counterintuitive, nevertheless, there are additional sins, such as public embarrassment and battery of a fellow man that have been interpreted in a similar fashion. See R. Yonah Gerondi, *Sha'arei Teshuvah, Sha'ar* 3, no. 139; *Teshuvot Devar Yehoshua supra* n. 27, at section 28; R. David b. Zimra (Egypt, 1480-1574), *Teshuvot ha-Radvaz* 3:626; Mordechai Halperin, "Harvesting Organs from Live Donors for Transplants," [Hebrew] 45-46 *Assia* (1999), pp. 321, 334 nn. 54 and 55.

[30] *Sanhedrin* 72a-b. Based upon this presumption, there exists a privilege of a lawful resident to use deadly force against a resident-intruder. For the scope of this privilege, see for example, R. Moses b. Maimon (Egypt, 1135-1204), *Mishneh Torah, Hilkhot Geneivah* 9:9-10 and commentaries *ad locum*.

[31] *Sanhedrin* 74a.

one's own life because the obligation to save human life either abolishes or suspends the proscription against theft. Either due to the *generic* nature of *pikuah nefesh* being a positive act or the *intrinsic* nature of *pikuah nefesh's* capacity to override certain divine imperatives, the saving of life abolishes or suspends the proscription against theft. According to an alternate approach, the prohibition against theft cannot be overridden even in case of a life-threatening situation either because it is categorized as a murder, one of the cardinal sins that require martyrdom, or because theft is the fourth cardinal sin that mandates martyrdom. In either case, one is obliged to allow oneself to be killed rather than commit a transgression of theft. Despite the divergent conclusions and concomitant rationales, the focal point and perspective are identical. Both approaches resolve the issue by focusing upon the diverse obligations (self preservation and theft) of *the imperiled individual* rather than the rights of the property owner.

There is an additional resolution to the seeming contradiction emerging from these two Talmudic passages that is predicated upon an individual's proscription from saving one's own life with the destruction of another's property. A different analysis of the doctrine of tortuous necessity places the matter in a totally different perspective – focusing upon *the obligation of the property owner*. To gain a better understanding of this posture, a brief review of the parameters of the duty to rescue is in order.[32]

The Talmud views the provisions regulating the duty to rescue as a resolution of the interplay between a positive and a negative commandment emerging from two different spheres of Jewish law, namely the law of finders and the rules of criminal omissions. As I formulated this position in another context:

---

[32] Ronnie Warburg, "A Parent's Decision to Withhold Medical Treatment – A Case Study in Competing Analogies," 17 *Dine Israel* (1993-94), pp. 35, 42-43.

The Talmud states: "From where do we know that if a man sees his neighbor drowning ... he is bound to save him? From the verse, "Do not stand idly by the blood of your neighbor." But is it [really] derived from this verse? Is it not rather from elsewhere? From where do we know [that one must rescue his neighbor from] the loss of himself? From the verse, "And you ought to restore him to himself." From that [latter] verse I might think that there is only a personal obligation, but that he [the rescuer] is not bound to take the trouble of hiring men [if he cannot deliver the victim himself]. Therefore, this [former] verse teaches that he [the rescuer] must [hire men]." If the duty of rescue would have been governed exclusively by the law of the finder, then the scope of a rescuer's involvement would have been limited to personal involvement. The law of criminal omissions mandates that an individual's duty in rescue is not eclipsed by personal involvement. The rescuer, while attempting to render assistance to the endangered party, is obligated to incur the expenditures required for the rescue.[33]

In sum, based upon the interplay of two conflicting duties operative in the law of criminal omissions and the law of finders, there emerges an individual obligation to expend funds in order to fulfill the duty of rescue.

Pursuant to this provision of the duty of rescue, in our scenario, both the property owner and imperiled party are equally obligated in the rescue operation. Whereas the endangered individual is obligated to save his own life, the property owner is duty bound to expend financial resources to save the individual in distress. According to one interpretation of Rashi,[34] Raavad,[35] and *Nishmat Kol Hai*,[36] the property owner's

---

[33] Ibid.

[34] Goldberg, *supra* n. 7, p. 384.

[35] *Hiddushei ha-Raavad, Bava Kamma* (1940), p. 359. Whether according to Raavad, the owner's property is subject to an encumbrance for the

obligation to expend funds is contingent upon his physical presence with the imperiled party. Consequently, an individual is proscribed from appropriating someone else's property in the owner's absence, even to save one's own life. However, according to a contemporary interpretation of *Tosafot* and Rosh,[37] R. Shalom Schwadron[38] and R. Shaul Yisraeli in the name of Rashba,[39] the owner's absence at the life-threatening situation does not affect his duty to aid. Hence, given the property owner's duty to expend funds, one can take or destroy his property, even in his absence, to save a life. In effect, the parameters of the duty of the owner encompass destroying his own property. Nevertheless, the imperiled party must provide appropriate compensation to the owner. Here again, we see that the permissibility or non-permissibility of appropriating property by the imperiled individual is contingent upon the applicability of a duty, namely, the obligation of the property owner to render assistance in cases of his own absence. Moreover, the endangered party's obligation of restitutionary liability is based upon the property owner's recovery of his disbursements as a rescuer fulfilling his duty to expend funds rather than as compensation for being a property owner.[40]

---

benefit of the imperiled party is subject to debate. See Goldberg, *supra* n. 7, p. 439; Jacobovits, *supra* n. 7, p. 405 and R. Shaul Yisraeli (Israel, 20th century), *Amud ha-Yemini, Sha'ar* 1 16, 12 subsection 1, p. 182.

[36] See R. Hayyim Pelaggi (Izmir, 19th century), *Teshuvot Nishmat Kol Hai* 2:48 and ensuing discussion in Bleich, *supra* n. 3, p.310. For the basis of this approach, see *Tosefta Pe'ah* 3:13 and Goldberg, *supra* n. 7, p. 384.

[37] Goldberg, *supra* n. 7, p.386. For an implicit acceptance of this posture, see *Piskei ha-Rosh, Sanhedrin* 8:2.

[38] Schwadron, *supra* n. 22.

[39] *Amud ha-Yemini, supra* n. 35, p. 183.

[40] *Piskei ha-Rosh, Sanhedrin* 8:2; *Sema HM* 426:1 and *Shakh HM* 426:1. Even though the property owner's duty of rescue is unenforceable (see Kirschenbaum, *supra*, n. 3, pp. 15-18), nevertheless, the endangered individual is permitted to appropriate the property. In effect, his appropriation is a fulfillment of the owner's unenforceable duty!

2. A Jurisprudential Perspective

The foregoing analysis of the defense of tortuous necessity as "a study in a conflict of duties" demonstrates how various decisors resolve this conflict. As we have seen, there are conflicting types of duties, such as between the imperiled party's duties of *pikuah nefesh* and proscription against theft and the property owner's individual duty of rescue. Each individual decisor's perception of the nature and parameters of the particular duty will determine the resolution of this conflict. As we have seen, a firm ranking of these duties cannot be offered, such that whenever there is a conflict between these duties one of them prevails over the other.[41] There is no meta-Jewish legal rule that may settle these conflicts by informing us which of the two conflicting duties overrides the other. In fact, even upon concluding that *pikuah nefesh* is the overriding norm, there remains much controversy whether the norm is to be defined generically[42] or intrinsically.[43]

Apart from our rabbinic understanding of this conflict of duties, it is helpful to introduce one of the avenues of "*madda*" that has been utilized to resolve conflicts of rights in right-based systems[44] as a mode of reasoning to resolve this conflict of duties.

---

[41] For an attempt in secular jurisprudence to determine which duty in a conflict prevails, see W.D. Ross, *The Right and the Good* (London, 1930), 16-47. I am indebted to Professors Martin Golding and Phillip Montague for this reference. For suggested solutions for establishing a hierarchy of *prima facie* rights, see J.L. Mackie, "Can There be a Right-Based Moral Theory?" in *Studies in Ethical Theory*, ed. Hacker and Wettstein (Minneapolis, 1978), pp. 350, 356; Bernard Rosen, *Strategies of Ethics* (Boston, 1978), pp. 127, 130-31; and Samuel Stoljar, *An Analysis of Rights* (New York, 1984), pp. 98-100. The balancing of *prima facie* rights in terms of their weight equally will apply to the ranking of *prima facie* duties.

[42] See text accompanying notes 11-15 and 23-25.

[43] See text accompanying notes 16-22.

[44] See literature cited in notes 5 and 51.

As Rabbi Dr. Aharon Lichtenstein observes:

> *Madda* enriches our understanding of Torah ... by pro-
> viding a basis for comparison ... The social sciences
> and humanities ... are directly concerned with many
> issues which are the woof and warp of Torah proper.
> The structure and substance of law ... fall within the
> purview of general as well as Torah thought. Knowledge
> of how such questions, legal and/or philosophic, have
> been treated in different traditions can frequently en-
> hance our understanding of Torah positions, as regards
> either broad outlines or specific detail.[45]

We can suggest a theory about the structure of the duties
and an explanation of the duties conflict. Our dilemma can be
summarized by four propositions, each of which appears to be
true, but all of which taken together entail a contradiction:

(1) Reuven (hereinafter: R) is the owner of a cabin.

(2) If Reuven is a property owner, Shimon (hereinafter: S)
has a duty not to use the property without R's permission.

(3) S may use R's property without his permission.

(4) S is obligated to pay compensation for the theft of R's
property.

There are three possible sources of inconsistencies.
There is, first of all, a tension between (1) and (3). If R is a
property owner, then how can it be true that S is permitted to
appropriate the property? The second difficulty regards the
inconsistency between the first two propositions and (3). If S
has an obligation to refrain from using R's property, how can
he be permitted to destroy it? The third difficulty concerns a
tension between (3) and (4). If S is permitted to destroy it, then
why does he owe compensation?

One viewpoint denies the necessity in resolving this
conflict. The permissibility of appropriating property in order to

---

[45] Aharon Lichtenstein, "Torah and General Culture: Confluence and
Conflict," in *Judaism's Encounter with Other Cultures*, ed. Jacob J.
Schacter (Northvale, NJ: Aronson, 1997), pp. 220, 230.

save one's own life stems from the duty of the property owner. As we have shown, according to certain decisors, given the property owner's obligation to expend funds to save his fellow's life, appropriation by the imperiled party is allowed even in the absence of the property owner. Consequently, there has been no violation of property ownership.[46]

However, the foregoing view has been regarded as unsatisfactory by various authorities who contend that the property owner's duty to expend funds is contingent upon his physical presence at the rescue operation. Hence, in our situation, the laws of rescue fail to mandate that the owner must destroy his property. Therefore, we are left with our dilemma: what happens to property ownership when it appears to be violated?

A promising line of thought to deal with this conflict of duties is to deploy the apparatus of *prima facie* duties.[47] As the name indicates, a theory of *prima facie* duties asserts that the duty exists "on the face of things" but may be overridden or outweighed by a competing duty in certain circumstances, i.e., defeasible.

One response, as we have discussed, accepts propositions (1), (3) and (4), and claims that the relevant duty (2), is merely *prima facie*.[48] Proponents of this view contend that the endangered individual's duty for self-preservation outweighs the duty against theft. Hence, the duty against theft (2) is characterized as *prima facie*. The striking feature of this position is that it posits the continued existence of the *prima facie* duty vs. theft

---

[46] Whereas Thomson concludes that any compensation claim in tortuous necessity situations must "pass through" the prism of the property owner's right that his property not be taken, this viewpoint predicated on a duty-based system introduces another prism. See Judith Thomson, *supra* n. 5, p. 15.

[47] The notion of *prima facie* duties was first introduced by Ross, *supra* n. 41. Though the employment of this terminology is culled from discussions of right-based systems, nevertheless, its application in the Jewish legal system, which is duty-based, enhances our conceptual understanding of the defense of necessity.

[48] See text accompanying notes 19-26.

despite a permissible infringement thereof. Accordingly, the duty against theft does not disappear when overridden; it persists. It has not been extinguished; property has been taken. If property had not been taken in the first place, one could hardly have a duty to compensate the owner![49] Consequently, the imperiled party owes a latent obligation of compensation.

If we reverse our substantive conclusion regarding our problem and claim that the imperiled party is proscribed from appropriating the property, we can explain the remaining two positions. One solution to the apparent duties conflict is to claim that (3) is a *prima facie* duty.[50] So, if on a particular occasion, my *prima facie* duty of theft comes into conflict with my *prima facie* duty for self- preservation, the latter assumes priority. The duty against theft isn't simply outweighed; it disappears. The imperiled party is permitted to appropriate the property without making restitution. In effect, affirming proposition (3), due to "the overriding nature" of the duty of self-preservation, the endangered individual is permitted to destroy the property without providing compensation. Thus we are abandoning proposition (4).[51]

---

[49] Characterizing the nature of rights, Joel Feinberg notes that rights "are not something that one has only at specific moments, only to lose, regain, and lose again as circumstances shift. Rights are themselves property, things we own and from which we may not even temporarily be dispossessed. Perhaps in some circumstances rights may be rightfully infringed, but that is quite different from being taken away and then returned ..." (Feinberg, *supra* n. 5, p.75). Though Feinberg is dealing with the nature of rights functioning in a right-based system, nonetheless, his observation, in certain respects, is analogous to our understanding of the operation of the *prima facie* obligation in a duty-based system. See *supra* notes 21-22. A nuanced analysis of the similarity and difference of the operation of a prima facie duty in a duty-based system and a *prima-facie* right in a right-based system is beyond the scope of this presentation.

[50] See text accompanying n. 18.

[51] Alternatively, this position can be framed in what has been termed "the specification view." Accordingly, there is no duty against theft, but rather a duty not to steal except in circumstances A, B, C, etc. According to this theory, the duty is always absolute and can never be overridden. Any

Conversely, pursuant to another approach, one must claim that the relevant duty of theft (2) is *prima facie*.[52] In other words, the *prima facie* duty against theft takes precedence over the imperiled party's *prima facie* duty for self-preservation. Moreover, the duty proscribing theft is neither extinguished nor infringed. Despite being driven by the unforeseeable necessity to take or damage the property of another in order to avoid a much greater harm to himself, he must refrain from committing an act of theft. Here again, we are abandoning proposition (4).[53]

In sum, though both the jurisprudential and rabbinic presentations invoke identical argumentation utilizing similar terminology (*prima facie* and defeasible vs. *hutrah* and *dehuyah*);

---

scenario that initially appears to entail infringement is to be subsumed under one of the exceptive clauses. In short, there ultimately is no conflict of duties. There is no conflict because the duty entails implicit "unless" clauses that indicate exceptions to the duty. Since this specificationist theory is predicated upon the absence of any duty infringement, consequently, it cannot adequately explain the need for compensation. Therefore, though this line of reasoning serves as an explanatory device for the approach that precludes compensation, it fails to be explanatory for another viewpoint that mandates compensation (see text accompanying notes 19-21, 23-25 and 33-39). For literature dealing with the specification model within the context of rights conflict, see Feinberg, *supra* n. 5, p. 75; Judith Thomson, "Self-Defense and Rights," in *Rights, Restitution and Risk: Essays in Moral Theory* (Cambridge, 1986), pp. 33-48; Judith Thomson, *The Realm of Rights* (Cambridge, 1990), pp. 88-92; and Phillip Montague, "When Rights are Permissibly Infringed," 53 *Philosophical Studies* (1988), pp. 347-66; Russ Shafer-Landau, "Specifying Absolute Rights," 37 *Arizona Law Review* (1995), pp. 209-26.

[52] See text accompanying notes 27-31.

[53] In our presentation, we have adopted a duty-based approach towards analyzing the defense of tortuous necessity in Jewish law. Some Western legal systems have attempted to explain the necessity defense utilizing principles of corrective justice, the "lesser of the two evils" theories and unjust enrichment. See for example, Jules Coleman, "Moral Theories of Torts: Their Scope and Limits: Part II," 2 *Law and Philosophy* (1983), pp. 5-30; George Fletcher, *Rethinking Criminal Law* (Boston, 1978), pp. 760-61, 777-79; and Howard Klepper, "Torts of Necessity: A Moral Theory of Compensation," 9 *Law and Philosophy* (1990), pp. 223-24. Whether these lines of thought would serve to illuminate the Jewish legal defense of necessity is beyond the scope of this presentation.

nevertheless, the emergence of identical contributions from two diverse thought systems is enriching.

3. Concluding Reflections

In light of our analysis, our study has implications for a contemporary proposal to interpret one of Israel's pieces of legislation from the perspective of Jewish law. On March 25, 1992, the Knesset passed legislation entitled *Basic Law: Human Dignity and Liberty*. According to section 3 of the law: "There shall be no impairment of an individual's acquisitive capacity."[54] Rabbi Avrahom Sherman, a contemporary decisor, attempts a critical conversation between classical Jewish legal sources, values and concepts and those regnant, on his view, in this legislation. Broadly speaking, pursuant to his understanding, one of the legislator's defining characteristics of personhood is a man's ability to acquire property. Though he readily admits God's overriding title to all possessions, nevertheless, R. Sherman notes that the Jewish legal system recognizes individual ownership of private property.[55]

Clearly, diverse areas of Jewish civil law such as the laws of *hazakah* (lit., taking possession), restoration of lost property, *ye'ush*, ownerless property, easements and theft presuppose recognition of individual property ownership.[56] Hence, there is

---

[54] *Hok Yesod: Kevod ha-Adam ve-Heiruto*, 1992, *Sefer Hukim* 150.

[55] Abraham Sherman, "The Fundamental Laws of Human Rights According to *Torat Yisrael* and His Laws," [Hebrew] *Torah she-Be'al Peh* (1984), pp. 79, 82-83.

[56] For the significance of an individual's ownership rights within the Jewish legal system, see R. Moshe Amiel (Israel, 20th century), *Middot le-Heker ha-Halakhah*, *Midah* 11, *Metzi'ut ve-Din* and the text accompanying notes 61-63.

The implications of this affirmation of rights within the duty-centered system of Jewish law are beyond the scope of this presentation. For an academic attempt to address this issue, albeit from a different concern than ours, see Daniel Gutenmacher, "Rights as Derivatives: A Note on Haim Cohn's Human Rights in Jewish Law," 17 *Dine Israel* (1993-94), p. 127.

an affinity between Jewish law and Israeli law, both systems affirming man's ownership of private property.[57]

However, as we noted at the outset of our presentation, in the Jewish legal system, once ownership is established the focus is upon the duty against theft rather than private ownership.[58] Moreover, our study has addressed the contours of the proscription against theft as it emerges in conflict with the duty of *pikuah nefesh*. In his examination, R. Sherman fails to focus upon this duty or upon its apparent conflicts with other duties such as the saving of life that define the parameters of the duty.

However, the significance of our study lies beyond the pale of R. Sherman's analysis. Trying to develop a common language and interface with the Israeli secular legal community, R. Sherman offers the fruits of his rabbinic scholarship. Can we move beyond the ivory tower of scholarship and suggest that the Jewish legal posture on the defense of necessity (in its entirety or in part) become integrated into Israeli law? One of the basic challenges to the incorporation of Jewish civil law into the Israeli legal system is the need to recognize that one is trying to integrate norms of a religious legal system into the fabric of a secular legal system. Throughout his thirty-year academic and judicial career, Professor Menachem Elon, an arch proponent of "*hakikah datit*" (the incorporation of Jewish law into Israeli legislation, and infusion of Jewish law into

---

[57] Whether the Jewish legal system's recognition of individual property rights allows for the incorporation of Jewish legal matters such as commercial and criminal law, contracts, torts, property and evidence into Israeli law has been a subject of much heated debate. See Izhak Englard, "The Problem of Jewish Law in a Jewish State," 3 *Israel Law Review* (1968), p. 254; Menachem Elon, "Jewish Law in the Legal System of the State: Reality and Ideal," [Hebrew] 25 *Ha-Praklit* (1968), pp. 27-53; and a subsequent exchange between Professors Elon and Englard initially published in *Mishpatim*, Hebrew University Faculty of Law's student law review which was subsequently translated into English and reprinted in *Modern Research in Jewish Law,* ed. Bernard Jackson (Leiden, Netherlands, 1980), 21-111.

[58] See text accompanying notes 1 and 61-62.

Israeli judicial opinions), responded to his plan being characterized as a threat to "the secularization of the *Halakhah*"[59] by
offering various counterarguments to legitimate his stance.[60]
One of the means to bridge this seemingly unbridgeable gap
between these two different legal systems was introduced by
Elon in the latter part of his career. In effect, Elon contends
that the Jewish legal recognition of individual property rights
may serve as the link, i.e., the *baree'ah ha-tikhon*, between
these two systems.[61]

For Elon, the contribution from the commentary of R.
Shimon Shkop, a twentieth century Talmudist, affirming
individual rights of property ownership, will facilitate the
interface between these seemingly diverse legal systems. In an
oft-cited quotation in rabbinic and academic circles, R. Shkop
observes:

---

[59] Moreover, reception of Jewish law by the state means transforming it
into the law of the state. In *Skornik v. Skornik* (1954) 8 *Piskei Din* 141, 179,
180, Justice Witkon of the Israeli Supreme Court observed:

> And if it be argued that Jewish law is universal, it must be replied
> that all religious law in so far as it has effect in this country is
> derived from the will of the secular legislator ... whose position
> is that of the basic norm of Kelsen's doctrine – and from which it
> draws its power.

For the legal ramifications of the secular legal reception of Jewish law, see
Izhak Englard, *Religious Law in the Israeli Legal System* (Jerusalem, 1975);
Bernard Jackson, "Secular Jurisprudence and the Philosophy of Jewish
Law: A Commentary on Some Recent Literature," 6 *The Jewish Law Annual*
(1987), 3; Bernard Jackson, "Mishpat Ivri, Halakhah and Legal Philosophy:
Agunah and The Theory of Legal Sources," 1 *Jewish Studies Internet
Journal* (2002), p. 69; Ruth Halperin-Kaddari, "Expressions of Legal
Pluralism in Israel: The Interaction Between the High Court of Justice and
Rabbinical Courts in Family Matters and Beyond," 13 *Jewish Law
Association Studies* (2002), p. 185 and literature cited in n. 57.

[60] See literature cited in n. 57.

[61] In the first edition (1973) and second edition (1978) of his work,
Menachem Elon, *Jewish Law* [Hebrew] (Jerusalem, 1973 and 1978), there
is no mention of this argument. It first appears in the third edition
published in 1988. See Menachem Elon, *Jewish Law* [Hebrew] (Jerusalem,
1988), 121ff., 184. It also appears in the English edition published in
1994. See Elon, *supra* n. 3, p. 137ff., 184.

Civil laws, which govern the relations among people, operate differently from the other commandments of the Torah. In respect to all other commandments ... our obligation to fulfill them rests on our duty to obey God's command. Matters of *mamon* [civil law] however, are different; there must be a legal duty before a religious obligation arises to pay damages or make restitution ...

When we deal with a legal right (*zekhut ve-kinyan*) in a chattel or with a lien, the focus of our concern is not the observance of a religious commandment but rather the objective circumstances determining who has the legal ownership of the object or is legally entitled to its possession.[62]

In a case of theft, one must determine who the owner of the object is. Once ownership has been determined, the owner has a legal right to this object.[63] In effect, the diverse norms of *hazakah*, lost property, easements, theft and the like will serve as the grounds for establishment of this legal right. With the emergence of this *legal right*, any subsequent infringement of this right such as theft will create a *legal duty* to return the stolen object. After the establishment of this legal duty, there

---

[62] *Sha'arei Yosher* 5:1.The translation is culled from Elon, *supra* n. 3, p. 136. For an earlier discussion, see Elon, *supra* n. 3, pp. 132-37. For contemporary rabbinic and scholarly academic attempts to elucidate R. Shkop's view, see Avraham Sherman, *supra* n. 55; Avi Sagi, "The Religious Commandment and Legal System: A Chapter in the Halakhic Thought of Rabbi Shimon Shkop," [Hebrew] *Da'at* 35 (1997), p. 99 and Shay Wosner, "Legal Thinking in Lithuanian Yeshivoth Within the Perspective of Rabbi Shimon Shkop" [Hebrew] (Jerusalem, 2005) (Hebrew University Unpublished Dissertation), pp. 247-321.

[63] "*Torah mishpatim*" or "*hukei mishpatim*" are the two terms utilized interchangeably by R. Shkop to identify the basis for establishing the legal right of ownership. Whether these terms refer to the realm of legal logic (*sevarah*) recognized by the Jewish legal system or some form of natural law is subject to rabbinic and scholarly academic debate. See Sherman, *supra* n. 54, pp. 82-83; Sagi, *supra* n. 62, pp. 103-106; Warhaftig, *supra* n. 3, p. 34; Shay Wosner, "The Meaning of Fidelity to Halakha," [Hebrew] *The Quest for Halakha*, ed. Amichai Berholz (Jerusalem, 5763), pp. 97-98 and Wosner, *supra* n. 62, at pp. 260-274, 311-321.

emerges a *religious duty* to return the stolen property or compensate the owner. Pursuant to R. Shkop's reasoning, Elon contends that the recognition of the legal right of ownership serves as the basis for demonstrating the halakhic compatibility of its religious legal system with a secular right-based system that affirms individual rights of property. In sum, the mutual recognition by the two legal systems of private ownership as reflected in the laws of property allows for the incorporation of Jewish law into Israeli law.

In fact, one contemporary authority suggests that R. Shkop's perspective has relevance to our issue at hand. Elucidating the rationale for the school of thought that proscribes property destruction in order to save human life, R. Ariel observes:

> The logical explanation is that the prohibition against theft stems from the monetary ownership of one's neighbor. Monetary ownership is a reality which predates the prohibition and causes it (i.e., the prohibition) to materialize. Therefore, there is no basis for arguing that the proscription against theft ought to nullify the saving of life. Since before the emergence of the prohibition there is a reality that the assets belong to the other and no one else possesses a right, neither legal nor moral to infringe it, it is as if it does not exist for anyone else except the owner.[64]

For R. Ariel, the teaching of R. Shkop serves as the underlying reason for prohibiting property destruction even in cases of saving human life.

Whether R. Shkop's "rights-talk" is a persuasive approach towards understanding the diverse spheres of *Hoshen Mishpat*, i.e., Jewish monetary relations, is an intriguing question. However, it is beyond the scope of our discussion. Clearly, our analysis of the varying positions regarding the defense of

---

[64] R. Yaakov Ariel, "Halakhic Perspectives Regarding Withdrawal from Portions of the Land of Israel," [Hebrew] 9 *Morashah* (5735), pp. 31, 35.

necessity is predicated upon private ownership. In effect, on a halakhic-legal level, Elon is correct. Both systems, Israeli and Jewish, recognize the notion of property rights. However, from a *halakhic-jurisprudential* perspective, the bridge between the two systems cannot be made. Aside from R. Ariel's observation and a passing comment of another contemporary decisor,[65] all other authorities, as we have seen, fail to engage in a discussion of *rights* emerging from the fact of ownership. In fact, one other decisor who incorporates R. Shkop's perspective readily admits that this right is ensconced within the context of a system of duties.[66] The system focuses upon the individual's obligation to protect his neighbor's rights and the individual's duty to waive one's rights in order to save human life. Hence, the absence of "rights-talk" within the framework of varying duties precludes bridging the gap between the Jewish law of necessity and the Israeli law of necessity.

Furthermore, our case study demonstrates that the Jewish legal system, at least with regard to the defense of necessity, is molded jurisprudentially by the presence of varying duties. In fact, pursuant to one school of thought,[67] the focus of the stranded backpacker is upon the *property owner's duty* to save another life even at the possible loss of his own property.[68] Given the absence of a legal obligation to save human life, most other legal systems would resolve that conflict much differently.[69] From the perspective of Jewish law, the law of necessity focuses upon the rescuer's duty and from the perspective of a secular legal system

---

[65] R. Ariel, ibid.; Eishon, *supra* n. 7, pp. 326-27; R. Joshua Ehrenberg, *supra* n. 27.

[66] See Eishon, *supra* n. 7, p. 338.

[67] See text accompanying notes 33-39.

[68] *Beit ha-Behirah, Kiddushin* 8b.

[69] James Ratcliffe, ed., *The Good Samaritan and the Law: The Morality and the Problems of Aiding Those in Peril* (New York, 1966).

the focus is upon the property owner's right. Consequently, there are no grounds for bridging the gap between these two diverse systems.

The Jewish legal system provides norms of behavior that establish property obligations resulting from violations of ownership as well the creation of norms that establish property ownership. Though the varying positions regarding the defense of necessity are premised upon the existence of ownership and its violation, nevertheless, there is a jurisprudential dimension of necessity that is molded by the presence of conflicting duties rather than conflicting rights. As noted by Eishon, in Israeli law, the defense of necessity is molded solely by a jurisprudence of rights built upon property ownership.[70] In short, R. Shkop's recognition of property ownership rights cannot serve as the medium for incorporating the Jewish law of necessity into the corpus of the Israeli law of necessity due to the presence of conflicting duties rather than the balancing of rights.

Our analysis reflects the instructive words penned by Professor Izhak Englard in 1980:

> The feature characterizing a legal system is the method of solving a problem by means of its standard rules. It is often the intellectual process involved in problem-solving and not the solution itself which constitutes the unique characteristic of any particular system ... The process of decision-making is a dogmatic one and the judge, therefore, must accept the binding authority of the sources in accordance with the internal interpretation of the system. If he does not do so, then he is deviating from the framework of the existing normative system and creating a new one.... The religious elements [of Jewish law] go to the essence of the normative

---

[70] See Eishon, *supra* n. 7, p. 338 and Gad Tedeschi, ed., *The Law of Civil Wrongs: The General Part* [Hebrew] (Jerusalem, 5736), pp. 295, 299, 301 n. 11.

order. Its validity lies ultimately in its *supra*-human activity; its ends are of a transcendent nature.[71]

Undoubtedly, an arbiter of the Jewish legal system, similar to a judge in a secular legal system, is bound to interpret its provisions affirming the integrity of its norms and the thought process of its decision making procedure.

As Professor Englard noted at the outset of his academic career:

> We still hold firm to our view that the religious character of Jewish law constitutes its soul and by losing it, the law loses its essence. We disagree with the assumption that the halakhic solutions to interpersonal human conflicts possess a specific Jewish character unheard of in other legal systems. We claim that the specific Jewish trait is to be found not in the continuity of a substantive legal principle, but in the continuity of legal tradition ... by the conscious acceptance of their binding force and metaphysical significance.[72]

---

[71] Izhak Englard, "Research in Jewish Law-Its Nature and Function," in *Modern Research in Jewish Law*, ed. B. Jackson (1980), pp. 21, 25. In effect, Englard's observation is a reflection of his recognition of the implausibility of using religious norms, halakhic or otherwise, as a source for Israeli law. See Englard's writings, *supra* n. 57.

For antecedents of this approach, see Yeshayahu Leibowitz, "Hebrew Law as a Law of the State?" [Hebrew] 3 *Sura* (1957-58), p. 495. Cf. with Leibowitz's earlier vision of the establishment of a "Torah state" in Israel; see Yeshayahu Leibowitz, *Torah and Mitzvot Today* [Hebrew] (Tel Aviv, 1954), pp. 101-30.

[72] Englard, *supra* n. 57, p. 274.

HEBREW
SECTION

מוחזקים שיש חרם הקהילות בדבר,[63] או תקנת רבינו גרשום ז"ל,[64]
ודבר זה פשט איסורו בכל ישראל, שלא שמענו ולא ראינו אשה
מתגרשת בעל כרחה, ואין אומרים לו לאדם לפרוץ גדרן של
ראשונים כדי לקיים שבועתו, שהרי אפילו איסורא דרבנן דוחה של
תורה בשב ואל תעשה.[65] וכיוון דלגרש אינו רשאי, אף להניחה
עגונה ולילך לארץ ישראל אינו רשאי,[66] ונמצא שקרוב הדבר
ששבועה זו אינה צריכה היתר חכם אלא בטלה היא מאליה.

63 ראה ראב"ן דפוס פראג (קכא:) שקורא לתקנה זו "תקנת הקהילות." וע' מאמרו של
הרב י. שצ'יפאנסקי, הדרום כב (תשרי תשכ"ו): 105.

64 שהובאה בסוף ש"ס כ"י מינכן ובכל בו סי' קטז ועוד.

65 יבמות צ, ע"ב.

66 מפני שהוא חייב בשאר כסות ועונה.

משם, וכיוון שכן לא כל הימנו להוציאה משם ולהוליכה בקצות
הארץ, וכדתנן בפרק "שני דייני גזירות": "שלוש ארצות לנישואין,
יהודה ועבר הירדן והגליל, אין מוציאין" וכו'.[56] וכי תימא הרי
שנינו: "הכל מעלין לירושלים,"[57] וזה הרי יכול לקיים שבועתו אם
ילך לירושלים – ליתא, שזה על מנת כן נשבע שיוכל לדור בדמשק
ובאלכסנדריאה או בשיפירי, וכיוון שאינו רשאי לצאת משם אלא
על מנת לעלות לירושלים – לא חיילא שבועה, שכל הנשבע על
דעת (אחר) [אחת] ונמצא אותו דעת בטל, אף השבועה בטלה ולא
חיילא כלל, וכדאמרינן בפרק "השולח": "כיוון דאמרי להו מארץ
רחוקה קאתינן ולא אתו מי חיילא שבועה כלל."[58] וכיוצא בו אמרו
לעניין דיני ממונות בפרק "האיש מקדש": "ההוא גברא דזבין נכסי
אדעתא למיסק לארץ ישראל, סליק ולא איתדר ליה; אמר רבא: כל
דסליק אדעתא דאיתדר הוא, והא לא איתדר,"[59] ופי' אדעתא
(למידר בארעא) [למיסק דאמר הכי בהדיא],[60] אלמא כיון דפריש
ואמר שעל דעת כן הוא עושה ולא נתקיימה מחשבתו – אין בדבריו
כלום, אף זה שפירש שנשבע לעבור הים כדי לדור באחד מן
המקומות שהזכיר, אותו שיבחר ונמצא שאינו רשאי לצאת אלא
כדי לעבור לארץ ישראל שבועתו בטלה. ולא עוד, אלא שאני אומר
שאף לעבור לארץ ישראל אינו רשאי, שאע"פ ששנינו: "הכל
מעלין לארץ ישראל," היינו לעניין שאם היא אינה רוצה לעלות
תצא שלא בכתובה וכדאיתא בברייתא בגמרא,[61] אבל כל שלא נתן
לה גט, כיון דמיחייב לה בשאר כסות ועונה לא כל הימנו לעקור
לאו זה בידים משום ישובו של ארץ ישראל. וכי תימא יתן לה גט,
שהרי האשה מתגרשת בעל כרחה,[62] ונמצא שיהא מותר ללכת בכל
אותן מקומות שירצה וחיילא שבועה, אף בזה אינו רשאי מפני
הקנס שיש בדבר מצד המלכות כאשר אמרתם, ולא עוד, אלא שאנו

---

[56] כתובות קי, ע"א.

[57] שם.

[58] גיטין מו, ע"א.

[59] קידושין נ, ע"א.

[60] כוונתו לדברי רש"י שם על פי הגמרא מט, ע"ב שדברים שבלב אינם דברים.

[61] כתובות קי, ע"ב.

[62] יבמות קיב, ע"ב.

מטה, נשבעו ראובן ושמעון ולוי שבועה חמורה בנקיטת חפץ ביד
בשם א-להי ישראל, על דעת המקום ועל דעת רבים, ועל דעת הרב
ר' יוסף ממרשיי״לא, ורבי חיים צרפתי אנשי ירושלים, ועל דעתינו
בלי שום פתח היתר וחרטה בעולם, שישתדלו ללכת וילכו ויעברו
עד שיפרי[51] בספינה זו אשר בברצלונה, העתידה ללכת שם במהלך
זה עכשיו בקרוב בחודש אוקטובר או נובינברי הבא ראשון, על
דעת לקבוע דירה זמן מה, הן רב הן מעט, בארץ ישראל או
בסביבותיה, בדמשק או באלכסנדריא של מצרים או בשיפרי או
באיזה מקום מעבר לים וכו', ועכשיו מתחרט שמעון על שבועתו
מפני שרואה אשתו מסרבת ללכת אחריו, כי הסיתוה קרוביה לבלתי
לכת אחרי אישה בשום פנים, וגם שלא לקבל גט ממנו, וקשה מאד
בעיני אישה לגרשה בעל כרחה, וגם כי יש קנס גוף וממון לפי
המקובל מצד המלכות, וקשין גרושין, וכ״ש להניחה עגונה, וגם כי
חושש עליה שמא היא מעוברת, לפיכך מתחרט חרטה גמורה
דמעיקרא על שבועתו ובא לישאל עליה ואומר שאילו היה יודע
שלא תרצה אשתו ללכת איתו לא היה נשבע כלל, וביקשת ממני
להעמידך על דעתי אם יש היתר לשבועה זו אם לאו, ואם יש לה
היתר, אם צריך שיסכימו [וירצו בזה ההיתר] ראובן ולוי כי
להנאתם ולצוות[52] להם נשבעו כל אחד ואחד לחבירו.

תשובה: אני מיראי הוראה אני, וכ״ש בהיתר שבועה חמורה כזו,
שראוי לכל בעל נפש לברוח מזה כבורח מן הנחש, אבל מה אעשה
ולפני שני דרכים כל אחד חמור מאד – חומר השבועה וחומר
עיגון האשה, ולפיכך אני מוכרח לכתוב לך דעתי. והוא, שקרוב אני
לומר ששבועה זו אינה צריכה היתר חכם, דהוה ליה נשבע לעבור
(את) [על] המצוה,[53] לפי שאין האיש רשאי להניח את אשתו וילילך
לו, דמחויב לה מדכתיב: "שארה כסותה ועֹנתה לא יגרע,"[54]
וכדאיתא בפרק "אע״פ."[55] וכי תימא תלך אשתו אחריו, כבר
חקרתי על שמעון זה ומצאתי שהוא מפרפינ״ייאן ונשא אשתו

---

[51] קפריסין.

[52] ר״ל: להתחבר עימהם.

[53] דקיי״ל בשבועות (כז.) שאינה חלה.

[54] שמות כא, י.

[55] כתובות סא, ע״ב.

כולם בלתי ה׳ יתברך לבד נוכרים בארץ ההיא. ולהיות ישראל יודעים זה, יהיו יותר קרובים לטעות בעבודה זרה בהיותם חוצה לארץ שמושלים שם האלוהות, כמו שאמרו: "קום עשה לנו אלהים אשר ילכו לפנינו,"[46] יותר ממה שיטעו בזה בארץ ישראל. מצורף,[47] שיותר ראוי שיהיו דבקים בשם הנכבד בארץ הקדושה מבחוצה לארץ. וגם כי ראוי לחוש פן ישיגם הכיליון בהמרותם דבר ה׳ יתברך יותר במדבר מבארץ ישראל, מצד היות המדבר מקום סכנה, נחש שרף ועקרב וצמאון אשר אין מים,[48] והמקום[49] עלול שם יותר לקבל הכיליון משאר המקומות. ולא כמו אותם שמתחסדים לומר כי יכולת ה׳ יתברך שוה בכל מקום להיטיב ולהרע, כי אין העניין כן, אבל ה׳ יתברך הטביע המציאות בעניין שיהיו מקומות הסכנה יותר קרובים להפסד משאר המקומות, מפני שאם לא יתמיד שם השגחתו על האיש המעיין ההוא ויעזבנו למקרה הזמן, ישיגנו הרע, ולא כן הדבר בשאר המציאות.[50] מכל זה אין ראוי לפחד שם עליהם כל כך.

הלכה למעשה

להשלמת הנושא, מן הראוי להביא כאן את דברי הר״ן באחת מתשובותיו (סי׳ לח) בה אנו למדים שעל אף המעלה הגדולה של ארץ ישראל, השתעבדות הבעל לאשתו גדולה יותר, ואין אדם רשאי לעזוב את אשתו בחוץ לארץ ולעלות לארץ ישראל. ואלו דבריו:

שאלת: ראובן ושמעון ולוי נתחברו והתעוררו לעבור הים ולהתקרב לארץ ישראל, ובאו לפני שם ועבר ונשבעו בנקיטת חפץ ביד על דעתם, ובזה הלשון העידו שם ועבר: בפנינו עדים חתומי

46 שמות לב, א.

47 מכאן שוב מובא ב"פירוש הר״י מסרגוסה" הנ״ל.

48 דברים ח, טו.

49 "והמקום ... אין ראוי לפחד שם עליהם כל כך" – ב"פירוש הר״י מסרגוסה": "וכמעט שיהיה מעלים עינו מהם ישיגם הרע ההוא, מה שלא יקרם כן בכל שאר המקומות, וכבר רמזו חז״ל באומרם: 'השטן מקטרג בשעת הסכנה.'"

50 "המציאות" – ב"פירוש הר״י מסרגוסה": "המקומות."

דעתי בכך, כי פני ילכו בקרבכם כאשר אניח לך ולהם, וזה כאשר
יהיו בארץ ישראל אשר שם מנוחתם עדי עד.[38]

לאור דברים אלה מתקשה הר"ן:

אמנם צריך ביאור: למה לא יחוש ה' יתברך למה שאמר: "כי לא
אעלה בקרבך כי עם קשה ע'רף אתה פן אכלך בדרך" אחרי היותם
בארץ ישראל כמו שיחוש בהיותם במדבר?

ומיישב הר"ן:

כי החטא שיחוש עליו ה' יתברך פן ישיג כיליון לישראל ממנו, הוא
חטא עבודה זרה דומה למעשה העגל, כי בשאר העבירות לא ייצא
הקצף מה' יתברך כל כך, אבל על עבודה זרה ראוי לחוש יותר, וזה
החטא ראוי לחוש ממנו במדבר יותר מבארץ ישראל, כי מצד
שישראל היו יודעים ששאר הארצות נמסרות להנהגת כוכבים
ומזלות, כמו שאמרו: "כל הדר בארץ ישראל דומה כמי שיש לו
אלוה, וכל הדר בחוץ לארץ דומה כמי שאין לו אלוה,"[39] וזה מצד
ששאר ארצות מסורות לשרי מעלה,[40] והנהגתם אי אפשר שתשתנה
אלא מצד[41] הפלא, כמו שפירש באומרם: "כי לא ישא לפשעכם,"[42]
ולפיכך, כל הדר בחוצה לארץ מצד היותו תחת כוכב או מזל – אין
תפילתו נשמעת כל כך כאילו היה בארץ ישראל שאינה תחת
ממשלת קצין שוטר ומושל[43] בלתי לה' יתברך,[44] כמו שאמר
הכתוב: "וזנה אחרי אלהי נכר הארץ."[45] הנה ביאר שהאלוהות

---

[38] ע"פ תהלים קלב, יד.

[39] כתובות קי, ע"א.

[40] ראה מכילתא בשלח, מסכתא דשירה פ"ב; ותנחומא בא ד, ובשלח יג.

[41] "מצד" – בשאר כ"י: "על דרך"; בנד': "על צד."

[42] שמות כג, כא.

[43] ע"פ משלי ו, ז.

[44] ראה פירושי ההגדות לרשב"א תענית י, ע"א (מהדורתי, עמ' סט-ע): "וכבר ידעת
שארץ ישראל נחלת ה' יתברך וכו', וע"כ ניתנה לעם בחר לנחלה לו, ואחר שהם נחלתו
יתברך לא מסר הארץ והעם למזל או לשר משרי מעלה וכו', ואין מעשיהם נעשים לא
ע"י מלאך ולא ע"י שליח, והוא שאמר משה ע"ה בבקשתו: 'ובמה יודע אפוא כי
מצאתי חן בעיניך אני ועמך הלוא בלכתך עימנו.'"

[45] דברים לא, טז.

אחר ששנה לו הקב"ה עוד: "גם את הדבר הזה אשר דברת
אעשה,"[31] איך שילש עוד ואמר: "אם נא מצאתי חן בעיניך ה' ילך
נא ה' בקרבנו,"[32] ונתן טעם לזה ואמר: "כי עם קשה עֹרף הוא."
וכללו של דבר, שפרשה זו צריכה ביאור רחב.

ומיישב הר"ן ואומר:

כי בתחילה קבל משה לפני הקב"ה, כי אמר: "ראה אתה אֹמר אלי
העל את העם הזה ואתה לא הודעתני את אשר תשלח עמי,"[33] והוא
כאומר: אחרי שבחרת לתועלתם של ישראל שתהיה הנהגתם על
ידי מלאך, אם נא מצאתי חן בעיניך, היה ראוי שתודיעני המלאך מי
יהיה, ושלא תדבר עימי ברמז ובמסתר פנים.[34] ואחר שאמר לו זה
כקובל עליו, לא רצה להתפלל ראשונה שילך ה' יתברך עימהם,
להיותו ירא למה שחשש ה' יתברך שלא יהיה זה סיבת כליונם, אבל
התפלל על העניין שמחמתו יתבטל החשש ההוא. ואמר: "ועתה
אם נא מצאתי חן בעיניך הודיעני נא את דרכך ואדעך למען אמצא
חן בעיניך וראה כי עמך הגוי הזה."[35] ופירושו כך: הודעני נא את
דרכיך, והם מידותיך, בעניין שאהיה מצד ידיעתי מוצא חן
בעיניך ומספיק להתפלל עליהם ולבטל כל צרה שתבוא עליהם
מצד עונש חטא מה, ובכן יסתלק מה שחששת ואמרת: "פן אכלך
בדרך."[36] וראה כי עמך הגוי הזה, כלומר: ראה כי הדרך הזה יותר
הגון, והוא: שיסתלק חשש כליונם בדרך זה ושלא תצטרך לעלות
מעליהם, יותר משתצטרך להיפרד מאיתם מפני חשש כליונם, כי
הם עמך, ואיננו נאה לאב החומל מעל בניו, וטוב יותר
להסיר מעליהם הרע על דרך זה. ואז השיבו ה' יתברך ואמר: "פני
ילכו והנחֹתי לך,"[37] והוא כאומר: איני צריך להודיע דרכי בשביל
זה, ומה שאמרת שאיני ראוי להיפרד מהם כי הם עמי, גם אני אין

31 שם, יז.

32 שם לד, ט.

33 שם לג, יב.

34 ע"פ ישעיה נג, ג.

35 שמות לג, יג.

36 שם, ג.

37 שם, יד.

יעקב שם המקום ההוא "מחנים"[22] – ירצה: כי המציאות על שלוש מדריגות – משכן מיוחס למחנה העליונים והוא השמים, ומשכן למחנה התחתונים והיא הארץ כולה מלבד ארץ ישראל, שהיא משכן למחנה התחתונים כי בני האדם שוכנים בו ומשכן למחנה העליונים כי פגעתי בו מחנה א-להים, ולכן היה ראוי להיקרא המקום ההוא[23] מחנים,[24] והוא אומרו: "ויאמר יעקב כאשר ראם מחנה א-להים זה ויקרא שם המקום ההוא מחנים."[25]

הדרוש הרביעי

המקום השני בו הרחיב הר"ן לבאר מעלתה של ארץ ישראל, הוא הדרוש הרביעי. חלק נכבד מדרוש זה מוקדש לביאור פרשה קשה וסתומה בפרשת כי תשא: פרשת "ראה אתה אֹמר אלי," ומתוך הדברים הוא מגיע לבאר את מעלתה הייחודית של ארץ ישראל. וזה לשונו:

וכן בקשר הפרשה ספיקות רבים צריכים שיותרו – הראשון: אחרי שאמר משה אל ה' יתברך: "ראה אתה אֹמר אלי העל את העם הזה ואתה לא הודעתני את אשר תשלח עמי,"[26] היה לו להתפלל מיד ולומר: "אם אין פניך הֹלכים אל תעלנו מזה." והוא לא עשה כן, אבל אמר: "ועתה אם נא מצאתי חן בעיניך הודעני נא את דרכיך,"[27] וזו באמת בקשה טובה וראויה, אבל מה שאינה מעניינו של דבר כלל. והשני: אחר שה' יתברך אמר לו: "פני ילכו והנחֹתי לך,"[28] איך השיב משה: "אם אין פניך הֹלכים אל תעלנו מזה,"[29] ולמה הטיל ספק במה שהודיע לו ה' יתברך בוודאי?[30] והשלישי:

---

22 שם, ג.

23 "ולכן היה ראוי להיקרא המקום ההוא" – בנד': "ולכן קרא שם המקום."

24 ראה רש"י ראב"ע ורמב"ן שם שפירשו באופן אחר.

25 בראשית לב, ג.

26 שמות לג, יב.

27 שם, יג.

28 שם, יד.

29 שם, טו.

30 ראה ראב"ע פסוק כא; ורמב"ן פסוק יד.

אשר הוא מלך המשיח,[16] שאז מתחייב יותר שלא תסור המלוכה
ממנו. וכן "כי לא אעזבך עד אשר אם עשיתי את אשר דיברתי לך"
הוא על זה הדרך, כי אי אפשר שיהיה פירושו: כי לא אעזבך עד
אשר אם עשיתי, אבל לאחר מכאן אעזבך, אבל פירושו: שהודיעו
שבהיות דביקות הצדיקים בה' יתברך בארץ הנבחרת יותר מבחוצה
לארץ, היה מתחייב מזה שיעזבנו, אך מאשר היתה הליכתו לקיים
מצות אביו כמו שציוהו ואמר לו: "לא תקח אשה מבנות כנען,"[17]
ישמרנו ה' יתברך ויהיה עימו, כי עם היות הליכתו מחייבת מצד
טבע המקומות שלא יהיה דבק בה' כאילו היה שוכן בארץ, הנה
היה זה מחויב וראוי יותר משיישאר בארץ ויקח אשה מבנות כנען
שהזהירו עליהן האבות, כי הנדבק בטובים גורם שיהיה מתקרב
זרעו[18] לעבודת ה' יתברך, ומי שאינו עושה כן גורם לזרעו הריחוק
ממנו.

ולקראת סוף דרשתו הנ"ל חוזר הר"ן על דבריו, שמראה הסולם בא
ללמדו שארץ ישראל היא מקום השכינה, ומוסיף לבאר על פי זה את
המסופר בסוף פרשת ויצא על פגישת יעקב את מלאכי א-להים. וכך הוא
מבאר:

ומפני שבמראה ההוא נתייחד אליו מקום אשר הוא "בית אל,"[19]
הראוהו[20] בהיפרדו מלבן ושובו לארץ ישראל כי יש לארץ ההיא
בכללה מעלה גדולה על הארצות האחרות, וכי שם הנפש מוכנת
להידבק באור העליון, והוא אומר: "ויעקב הלך לדרכו ויפגעו בו
מלאכי א-להים,"[21] והורה באומרו "ויפגעו בו" — כי המלאכים
מהלכים תמיד בארץ ההיא, ולכן הנכנס שם יפגע בהם, ולכן קרא

---

[16] סנהדרין צח, ע"א; ובראשית רבה צח, ח.

[17] בראשית כח, א.

[18] "שיהיה מתקרב זרעו" — בנד': "שיתקרב ליבו."

[19] בראשית כח, יט.

[20] הובא ב"פירוש הר"י מסרגוסה," סוף פר' ויצא (עמ' לז), ושם: "ותיכף שהגיע אל
תחילת הארץ מיד 'ויפגעו בו מלאכי א-להים,' כי הנה כמו שהראוהו בלכתו את מראה
הסולם אשר הוא מורה על מעלת הארץ כן בהיפרדו מלבן בשובו אל ארץ אבותיו
הראוהו כן, כי יש לארץ" וכו'.

[21] בראשית לב, ב.

עולים ויורדים בו." ואמנם הראה לו ה' יתברך להיות ארץ ישראל
יקרה בעיניו, ולהיות מגמתו אליה אחרי שיישא את נשיו.

על פי דברים אלה ממשיך הר"ן ומבאר גם את דבר ה' אליו באותו
מראה, "והנה אנכי עמך" וגו' (בראשית כח, טו). וזה לשונו:

והודיעו עוד,[10] כי בצאתו מארץ ישראל הוא צריך שמירה מיוחדת
יותר מבהיותו שם, והוא אומרו: "והנה אנכי עמך ושמרתיך בכל
אשר תלך והשיבֹתיך אל האדמה הזאת כי לא אעזבך עד אשר אם
עשיתי את אשר דברתי לך,"[11] וכל "עד" שהוא במקרא מורה על
אחד משני דברים:[12] אם שהדבר הקודם ייפסק כשיגיע זמן אותו
ה"עד," כאומרו: "ואל הזקנים אמר, שבו לנו בזה עד אשר נשוב
אליכם,"[13] שהוא מורה שאחרי שישובו אליהם לא יישבו עוד שם,
ועל זה הדרך הוא רוב "עד" שבמקרא. ואם שהדבר הקודם יתחייב
שיימשך יותר כשיגיע זמן אותו ה"עד," ואמר בכיוצא בזה
להורות[14] כי גם עד אותו זמן יהיה דבר הפלוני, וכל שכן מאותו
הזמן ואילך שהוא מתחייב יותר, ומזה המין הוא: "לא יסור שבט
מיהודה ומחֹקק מבין רגליו עד כי יבֹא שילה" וגו'.[15] שפירושו: כי
גם בהיות המלכות משוטטת בין השבטים ושיתחייב יהודה שלא
תהיה כל המלכות לשבטו, עם כל זה, כל עוד שיהיה מלך בישראל
לא יגיע עונשו שיסור ממנו שבט המלוכה לגמרי, עד כי יבא שילה

---

10 מכאן עד "ישמרנו ה' יתברך ויהיה עימו" הובא ב"פירוש הר"י מסרגוסה,"
פר' ויצא (עמ' כח).

11 בראשית שם.

12 השוה שו"ת הרשב"א ח"ד סי' קפז: "אמרתי: אין מלת 'עד' מורה להפסק העניין
מכאן ואילך, אלא פעמים מבטיח על ביאת העניין, וכל שכן שיימשך לאחריו.
והעד: 'כי לא אעזבך עד אשר אם עשיתי את אשר דברתי לך,' ואין לזה הפסק, שאם
כן, לא היתה הבטחת העזר, רק קללת העזיבה מכאן ואילך."

13 שמות כד, יד.

14 "ואמר בכיוצא בזה להורות" — בנד': "ויורה."

15 בראשית מט, י. ראה שו"ת הרשב"א הנ"ל שהנוצרים רצו להוכיח מזה שכביכול
המשיח כבר בא, שהרי נאמר שלא יסור השבט מיהודה עד שיבוא המשיח, משמע
שכשיבוא המשיח כבר סר שר השבט, וכיון שבזמננו סר השבט מיהודה בהכרח שמשיח
כבר בא, אך לפי פירושו במשמעות "עד" אין כמובן שום ראיה.

פירושים רבים נאמרו בפרשה זו, כל מפרש לפי דרכו. לר"ן דרך מקורית,
לפיה כוונת מראה החלום היתה ללמד את יעקב את מעלת ארץ ישראל,
שמכיוון שיוצא הוא עתה את הארץ במצוות אביו, הראה לו הקב"ה את
מעלתה, כדי שלאחר שיישא אשה ישוב אליה.

ואלו הם דבריו:

היה[2] זה המשל להודיעו מעלת ארץ ישראל על שאר הארצות,
שהיא הסולם[3] אשר ממנה יעלו אל השמים הצדיקים אשר הם
נקראים "מלאכי א-להים,"[4] כי אילו היה[5] להורותו כי כל אשר
נעשה בארץ הוא באמצעות המלאכים, ויהיה המשל שהמלאכים
יתהלכו בארץ וישיבו אל ה' יתברך דבר לומר: "התהלכנו בארץ
והנה היא בעניין הפלוני,"[6] היה לו לומר: "מלאכי א-להים יורדים
ועולים בו," כי הירידה קודם העלייה. אבל "מלאכי א-להים" בכאן
רמז לצדיקים, אשר הם עולים דרך במעלות ארץ ישראל.[7] ומפני זה
אמר "עולים ויורדים" — כי אי אפשר שתהיה העלייה לצדיקים
רצופה, כי נפש האדם כמו שאמרנו[8] יש לה שתי פניות — אל צד
המעלה ואל צד המטה, ואי אפשר כל עוד שתהיה בגוף שתהיה
פנייתה אל צד המעלה לבד, אבל תצטרך לפנות גם כן למטה
להנהגת גופה. והנה[9] המשל הנרמז באומרו: "והנה מלאכי א-להים

---

[2] עד "ולהיות מגמתו אליה" הובא ב"פירוש רבי יוסף בן דוד מסרגוסה על התורה," פר' ויצא (עמ' כו-כז).

[3] "שהיא הסולם" — בפירוש הנ"ל: "שבה הסולם."

[4] דה"ב לו, טז; ועי' שבת קיט, ע"ב; ו"מורה נבוכים" ח"א פט"ו.

[5] כפירוש הרמב"ן בראשית כח, יב.

[6] "בעניין הפלוני" — בדפוס ורשה: "כעניין השטן," ראה איוב א,ז. ב"פירוש הר"י מסרגוסה": "ואי אפשר לומר שיהיה הרצון במקום הזה כמו שנמצא שם בתחילת ספר איוב שבא להורות כי כל מה שנעשה בארץ שהוא באמצעות המלאכים, שיהיה המשל שהמלאכים יתהלכו בארץ וישיבו אל ה' דבר לאמר התהלכנו בארץ."

[7] "אשר הם עולים דרך במעלות ארץ ישראל" — בכ"י אסקוריאל: "אשר הם עולים במעלות דרך ארץ ישראל"; ב"פירוש הר"י מסרגוסה": "אשר הם עולים דרך במעלות השכליות בארץ ישראל."

[8] לעיל בדרשה זו.

[9] "והנה" — בנד': "והוא."

מעלת ארץ ישראל
במשנתו של רבינו ניסים גירונדי

אריה ליאון פלדמן

אחת היצירות החשובות ביותר בהגות המחשבתית הדתית המעמיקה, היא ללא ספק, ספר דרשותיו של רבינו ניסים גירונדי (הר״ן). כל דרשה ודרשה בספר זה היא בניין רב היקף, הכולל שורשים עמוקים ויסודות מוצקים של עיקרי תורה ואמונה.[1]

עשרות נושאים נתבארו בספר זה לעומקם ולרוחבם; אחד מהם הוא מעלתה של ארץ ישראל על שאר הארצות. בשתי דרשות מרחיב הר״ן בעניין זה מנקודות מבט שונות אך משלימות זו את זו. במאמר שלפנינו ננסה לצרף ולאחד את הדברים עד שייראו כמקשה אחת.

הדרוש החמישי

בדרוש החמישי, מקדיש הר״ן מקום נכבד לבאר את חלום יעקב הידוע, היינו: מראה הסולם והמלאכים העולים ויורדים בו (בראשית כח, יב).

---

[1] הספר יצא לאור על ידי בשנת תשל״ג על פי כתבי יד, ועם מקורות, ציונים והערות, ושוב בצירוף פירוש "בארות משה" מאת הרב מרדכי קצנלנבוגן בהוצאת מוסד הרב קוק בשנת תשס״ג.

ינון-פנטון חתם את מאמרו על מורשתם הספרותית של צאצאי הרמב"ם
במלים אלה:

[...] באיזה אור מאיר זה של חסידות מעין צופית את
כתבי הרמב"ם עצמו. אנו משוכנעים כי את תורת המוסר של
הרמב"ם וכן את תפיסות היסוד שלו שבפרקי הסיום המיסטיים של
המורה יש להבין על רקע קיומה של סביבה צופית. פרקים אלה
נכתבו אם כדי למתן פרקטיקות צופיות מסוימות תוך הצגתן באור
אינטלקטואלי, אם כתגובה לביטוייהן הקיצוניים יותר. ולבסוף,
שושלת מרשימה זו של חסידים צאצאי הרמב"ם, המשתרעת על
פני חמישה דורות – מר' אברהם ועד ר' דוד – מחייבת הרהור נוסף:
הייתכן כי בשושלת המימונית המפוארת היה הרמב"ם, גדול
הפילוסופים הרציונליסטיים, היוצא מן הכלל שהפך, בסופו של
דבר, לכלל?[66]

פנטון הדגיש כאן שני עניינים: האחד, שיש להבין לפחות חלק מדברי
הרמב"ם בהקשר צופי, ובייחוד את פרקי הסיום של 'מורה הנבוכים'; האחר,
הרמב"ם נותר לגבי דידו פילוסוף רציונליסטי, וגם אם בקרב צאצאיו בדורות
הבאים היה חריג, בסופו של תהליך דעכה תורתם עד שנשתכחה, ואילו
משנתו נותרה עומדת על איתנה. דומה שבנוגע לחתימת 'מורה הנבוכים' אין
בין בלומנטל לפנטון מחלוקת מהותית אלא ויכוח על מידת המובהקות של
ההשפעה הצופית. נראה אפוא שהגירויי הצופי ונוכחותו ב'מורה הנבוכים'
זוקקים בדיקה מקיפה בכל חיבוריו של הרמב"ם.

הספרות הצופית היהודית, ההולכת ונחשפת בתנופה מרשימה בדור
האחרון, מעוררת למחשבה מחודשת על מהות התופעה הדתית, על טיב
יחסי הגומלין בין ממסדים דתיים ובין קבוצות מחאה בתוך אותה דת, וכן
בין קבוצות רעיוניות בדתות השונות. ספרות זו מספקת עמדת התבוננות
חדשה ורעננה גם בספרות העיונית הפילוסופית שפרחה בתרבות היהודית
בעיקר מסוף האלף הראשון ואילך. ששת היעדים שהתוויתי לעיל משקפים
את ההישגי המחקר עד כה ובה בעת מסמנים גם אופק רחוק שאליו ראוי
לחתור במאמץ הבלתי מתפשר לפענוח התופעה הקרויה 'צופיות יהודית'.

ד׳, הניתוח הספרותי והרעיוני ישמש בסיס מוצק למחקר משווה בתחום
האמנות והדעות. מאלף יהיה לראות כיצד רעיונות נאופלטוניים או
אריסטוטליים נארגו במשנות פילוסופיות ומיסטיות כאחת. בחינה שכזו
יכולה לזרות אור חדש על ההגות היהודית בימי הביניים מבחינת גבולותיה,
שיטותיה וקווי התיחום הפנימיים בין השיטות.

ה׳, שיחזור הספרייה המוסלמית והיהודית של מחברי היצירות. זהו שלב
מחקרי נחוץ לגבי כל חיבור בפני עצמו. ערך מיוחד גלום בחקר הספרייה
הווירטואלית של המאגר כולו. בדרך זו יתבררו נתיבי ההשפעה העיקריים
והמשניים, הדרכים הישירות והעקיפות, והתהליכים הגלויים והסמויים. אחד
ממוצרי הלוואי של מחקר שכזה יהיה שיחזור תהליכי ההשפעה ההדדיים
בין מוסלמים ויהודים על ציר הזמן ובחתך גאוגרפי.

ו׳, חמשת השלבים שסימנתי עד כה יכולים לשמש קרקע פורייה
למחקר פנומנולוגי. ינון-פנטון הניח יסודות ראשונים גם למחקר הזה,
והשווה בין תופעות דומות בתרבות מוסלמית והיהודית ובהיקרויות
שונות בתוך התרבות היהודית עצמה.[64] במחקריו אלה הרחיק פנטון מעבר
לתופעה המוגדרת של צופיות יהודית ודן בתופעה החסידית בגילוייה
השונים ובטקסטים מיסטיים בהקשרים מגוונים. עוד רמז למחקר משווה
בין הצופיות והקבלה.[65] מחקר פנומנולוגי זהיר ומקצועי כרוך בשילוב
מושכל של תחומי דעת רבים ממדעי הרוח והחברה. ההתפתחות
הרבה בדיסציפלינות השונות בשני הדורות האחרונים מזמנת לחוקר
תשתית איתנה, ומזמינה לגבש מתודולוגיה שתהלום את המחקר המורכב
של הצופיות היהודית בזיקותיה הפנימיות והחיצוניות, הסינכרוניות
והדיאכרוניות.

---

[64] ראו: יוסף ינון-פנטון, הקבלה בצפת (הערה 4 לעיל); הנ״ל, יהדות וצופיות
(הערה 4 לעיל), עמ׳ 212-216; הנ״ל, ״על מערכת הצדיקים במיסטיקה היהודית
ובמיסטיקה המוסלמית״, דעת 39 (תשנ״ז), עמ׳ 5-22; הנ״ל, ״ראש בין הברכיים;
תרומה למחקר על תנוחת מדיטציה במיסטיקה היהודית והאיסלמית״, דעת 32-33
(תשנ״ד), עמ׳ 19-29; הנ״ל, ״שתי אסכולות חסידיות; חסידי אשכנז והיהודים הצופים
במצרים״, דעת 45 (תש״ס), עמ׳ 5-23.

[65] ראו: מקגהה (הערה 27 לעיל); פנטון, יהדות וצופיות (הערה 4 לעיל),
עמ׳ 212-216.

יעדי מחקר אפשריים ומתבקשים

לאור השגי המחקר עד כה

כאמור בראשית הדברים, הדור האחרון זכה לחשוף ולשחזר חלקים חשובים ומרתקים מן הספרייה הצופית היהודית, ומתברר שלבית הרמב״ם יש חלק מכריע בעיצוב הספרייה הזאת ובפיתוחה. בקרב החוקרים שמור מקום של כבוד לפרופ׳ יוסף (פול) ינון-פנטון, שתרומתו לחקר התחום ולהבנתו היא סגולית.

על רקע כל מה שנעשה עד כה מסתמנים ששת היעדים הבאים:

א׳, המשך הקיטלוג והמיפוי של הספרות הצופית היהודית, בעיקר זו שבערבית-יהודית. אגב התהליך הזה יתברר אם הספרות הזאת כולה נכתבה רק בערבית-יהודית או בשפות נוספות, והאם נעשו תרגומים לעברית – מתי, היכן, בידי מי ולאיזה צורך.

ב׳, הכנת מילון של הספרות הזאת, שהוא כלי חיוני להבנה מדויקת של לשון החיבורים הנוגעים בדבר ולזיהוי טקסטים נוספים בעתיד. אין צריך לומר שהתהליך אינו טורי אלא מקבילי – ככל שיימצאו עוד טקסטים ילך המילון ויתעשר, ומכוחו ישוייכו עוד טקסטים למאגר הספרות הצופית היהודית. ולחילופין, העשרת המאגר תביא להרחבת המילון, לליטוש הערכים בו ולהגדרות מדויקות יותר של המונחים הרווחים בחיבורים השונים.[63]

ג׳, ניתוח ספרותי ורעיוני של המאגר. כך אפשר יהיה ללמוד על מגוון הסוגות שנקטו המחברים השונים, מטבעות הלשון שבהן השתמשו, קהלי היעד שנזקקו לטקסטים הצופיים הללו, האירועים שבהם שימשו טקסטים צופיים למטרות ליטורגיות או ריטואליות, וטווח השיטות העיוניות שאותם מחברים אימצו (ואולי אפילו שעבדו) במהלך גיבוש משנתם הצופית. על בסיס הניתוח המוצע כאן אפשר יהיה לבדוק אם מחברי היצירות הצופיות היהודיות נקטו שיטת קריאה מסוימת דווקא בעת שהסתמכו על ספרות קודמת (המקרא, ספרות התנאים והאמוראים, חיבורים הגותיים שקדמו להם, קבצי הלכות), כלומר האם הייתה קריאה ״צופית״ ייחודית.

---

63 ראו בהקשר זה: אילן, סודות (הערה 38 לעיל), בסוף המאמר.

המחבר עלום השם בתחילת 'ראשית חכמה' (10א, שורות 13-18) על זיקתו
ל'חובות הלבבות' וטעם השם שקבע לחיבורו:

וגרית פיה עלי מדהב רבינו בחיי הדיין ז״ל צאחב כתאב אלהדאיא
פאנה תלכיץ כתאבה האדה וסמיתה ראשית חכמה אד קטבה אלדי
ידור עליה הו אלתרייץ' עלי תקוי אללה אלחקיקיה אלדי לא ריב
פיהא ולא מרייה.

(תרגום: נהגתי בו בשיטת רבינו בחיי הדיין ז״ל, בעל הספר 'חובות
הלבבות', שכן [ספרי] הוא תקציר[60] של ספרו זה. קראתיו ראשית
חכמה שכן הציר שעליו הוא נסוב הוא האילוף ליראת ה' האמיתית
אשר לגביה אין ספק ולא מחלוקת)

במקרים אחרים, שבהם אין עדות בעל דין, שומה על החוקר לנקוט זהירות
רבה ולבדוק היטב אם אמנם מדובר בהשפעה, היינו בזיקה מוכחת שאין
ספק לגביה, שכן אין דרך אחרת להסביר את הלשון, התוכן, המבנה,
הנסיבות וההקשר אלא באמצעותה. כל עוד אין אלה פני הדברים, מוטב
לדבר על השראה, וגם זה יחס נכבד הדורש הוכחה.[61]

דברי המחבר של 'ראשית חכמה' מורים, שאין לגזור באופן גורף
השפעה מוסלמית ישירה על חיבורים יהודיים המזוהים כ'צופיים'. מסקנה זו
יפה בעיקר לחיבורים מאוחרים באופן יחסי, אשר יכלו לספוג את האווירה
הצופית ממקורות יהודיים פנימיים בלא לדעת כלל שמקורה בתרבות
המוסלמית. תופעה זו מוכרת מהמקשרים נוספים, בלתי תלויים.[62] ההבחנה
בין 'השפעה' ל'השראה' מחייבת אפוא בדיקה כפולה: האמנם מדובר בזיקה
ישירה בין משפיע למושפע, ובכל מקרה, האם מקור ההשפעה או ההשראה
הוא פנים-יהודי או חיצוני.

---

60 במקור: ״תלכ'יץ״, והוראת מלה זו היא גם כתיבה מקוצרת בהשפעת או בהשראת
חיבור אחר. אני מודה לפרופ' חגי בן-שמאי על שהאיר את עיני בעניין זה.

61 דוגמה לזהירות הנחוצה בעת עריכת השוואה שכזו ראו: חוה לצרוס-יפה,
״האם הושפע הרמב״ם מאלגזאלי?״, תהלה למשה, מחקרים במקרא ובמדעי היהדות
מוגשים למשה גרינברג, בעריכת אליהו דב אייכלר, יעקב חיים טיגאי ומרדכי כוגן,
אייזנבראונס תשנ״ז, עמ' 163-169.

62 ראו, למשל: דוד צבי בנעט, ״חלוקא דרבנן, 'חיבור יפה מהישועה' ומסורת
איסלאמית״, תרביץ כה (תשט״ז), עמ' 331-336.

או הישיבה, בית הכנסת, הבית ופינת ההתבודדות. תכלית הקריאה
הייתה: (א) עיונית, כלומר לשם השכלה; (ב) יישומית, היינו לגזור
הנחיות כיצד לנהוג ומה לומר; או (ג) מעשית, זאת אומרת הטקסטים
שימשו בפועל לווידוי או לתחינות, ובאופן כללי יותר לעורר חוויה
רוחנית.

דעת לנבון נקל, שהתחום המוצע כאן הוא אפשרי בלבד, וגם אם הוא
קולע אל האמת, עדיין יש בו ממד מלאכותי, שהרי עיון לשם למידה יכול
להיעשות מדריך מעשי כיצד לממש את ההתבודדות או את התפילה
האינטימית, בסוד שיח (מֶנאגְ'אה) עובר לעשייתן. ממילא אין לייחס קריאה
מסוג מוגדר למקום מסוים דווקא.

טיב ההשפעה של התפיסות הצופיות המוסלמיות
על התרבות היהודית: בין השפעה להשראה

כאמור לעיל, על אף הדמיון המרשים בין הספרות הצופית המוסלמית לזו
היהודית יש לנקוט מידה רבה של זהירות בעת חשיפת מקורות ההשפעה
המוסלמיים ובמהלך שיחזור הספרייה המוסלמית שבה השתמשו המחברים
היהודים. עתה מתבקש להוסיף, שראוי להבחין בין השפעה להשראה.
במונח 'השפעה' כוונתי לזיקה ישירה, מודעת או בלתי מודעת, בין חיבור
מוסלמי לחיבור יהודי. זיקה שכזו ניכרת בראש ובראשונה במונחים
משותפים, שאין להסבירם אלא ביניקה מן המקור המוסלמי, כפי שהראו
כבר בנעט וגולדרייך.[59] הזיקה מתבטאת באופן עמוק יותר בתכנים משותפים
ומשתקפת גם בתבניות ספרותיות דומות או זהות. בהקשר רחב ומופשט
יותר הזיקה יכולה להימצא גם בדרכי מימוש דומות בזמן, במקום ובאופן
המימוש.

'השראה', לעומת 'השפעה', משמעה זיקה עמומה ועקיפה יותר. כיצד
אפשר אפוא לזהותה? לעתים המחבר מודיע על כך במפורש. כך הכריז

כאחת במגמה של זרמים אינטלקטואליים מגוונים, והיטשטשו ההבחנות
שהיו תקפות קודם לכן בין מזרח למערב.[58] אם אכן אלה פני הדברים,
נדרשת בדיקה כפולה: תחילה יש לברר אם הבחנה זו תקפה גם
ביחס לספרות הצופית היהודית, ואם לא, מדוע; על סמך ממצאי
הבדיקה הראשונה ראוי לבדוק כיצד השתמשו המלומדים היהודים
בחיבורים הצופיים המוסלמיים. קרוב לשער שלבד מן הזיקה הרעיונית עוד
הושפעו המחברים היהודים גם מנסיבות הזמן והמקום בקרב קהיליהם,
מהלכי רוח וממגמות עיוניות פנימיות, ואף אלה השאירו את רושמם
על העמדות העיוניות, המוסריות והחברתיות, שנקטו אותם מחברים.
בקצרה, שאלת הזיקה או הזיקות של הספרות הצופית היהודית אל
הספרות הצופית המוסלמית רחוקה עדיין ממיצוי.

קהלי היעד וזירות הפעולה

שכלול כלי המיון הסוגתיים יכול לסייע בזיהוי קהלי היעד המגוונים
שלמענם נכתבו החיבורים הצופיים שנמנו לעיל. אף שתמונת המקורות
אינה שלמה, כבר עתה מסתמנים שלושה קהלי יעד לפחות: א׳, עילית
למדנית, שלמענה נכתבו חיבורים דוגמת ׳חובות הלבבות׳, ׳המספיק
לעובדי ה׳׳, פירוש הראב״ם לבראשית ולשמות, וכן ׳מורה הפרישות׳.
ב׳, הציבור הרחב, שבעבורו נתחברו חיבורים דוגמת ׳מאמר הבריכה׳
ו׳ראשית חכמה׳. ג׳, נשים, שבשבילן נתגבשה התפילה בעת הדלקת הנר.
הנשים הן קהל היעד המסקרן מבין השלושה, שכן עד כה טרם נודעו
חיבורים מעין אלה שמיענו לנשים. יתכן אפוא שהממצא של לנגרמן
הוא שריד ראשון, יחיד לפי שעה, למגמה שעד כה הייתה סמויה מן העין
ומן התודעה.

היכן ובאילו נסיבות השתמשו הקוראים השונים בחיבור הצופי
שבידיהם? אפשר להעלות על הדעת ארבעה מקומות לפחות: בית המדרש

---

[58] בהרצאה שנשאה בחוג בנעט באוניברסיטה העברית בירושלים בחורף תשס״ה.
אני מקווה שלא ירחק היום ודבריה יתפרסמו בכתב.

מכל מקום כבר עתה ברור, שהיצירה היהודית הצופית אינה נתחמת
בתחום דעת מוגדר אחד ואינה מובעת בסוגה ספרותית אחת. הבחינות הללו,
שהן צורניות ותוכניות כאחת, מורות שבעיני המחברים נחשבה תפיסת
העולם הצופית כוללת דיה להכיל בקרבה את הסוגות השונות.

הזיקות לספרות הצופית המוסלמית

המושג 'זיקה' הוא רב משמעי בהקשר הנדון כאן. הזיקה יכולה להיות
לשונית, היינו שימוש באותם מונחים 'מקצועיים' ובאותם מטבעות לשון
ספרותית, כלומר שאילה ממקורות קודמים משותפים גם אם אין ציטוט
מדויק;[56] רעיונית, ואז הדמיון ניכר גם בתוכן גם אם אין זהות לשונית;
או תרבותית, זאת אומרת שילוב של ההיבטים שמניתי זה עתה ואחרים
ומזוגגם ביחד. הזיקה הלשונית והספרותית קלה לזיהוי ולאבחון יותר
מן הזיקה הרעיונית והתרבותית, ולעתים היא יכולה להטעות. שימוש
בלשונות זהים או קרובים אינו מעיד בהכרח על השפעה או על יניקה
ממקור משותף.[57]

שרה סבירי הציעה להבחין בין הצופיות המוסלמית במערב (ספרד
ומרוקו) לזו שבמזרח (מצרים וסוריה). לשיטתה, באנדלוס התפתחה
מיסטיקה בעלת גוון פילוסופי ואוקולטי, ואילו במזרח פותחו בעיקר
הכיוונים האתיים. ממילא כוונה הצופיות המוסלמית במערב לציבור קטן
ואליטיסטי. לעומתה, פנתה הצופיות המזרחית, בעיקר במאות השלוש
עשרה והארבע עשרה, לקהלים מגוונים ורבים יותר. מכל מקום, מן המאה
ה-13 ואילך, וביותר אחרי אבן ערבי, התפתחה הצופיות במערב ובמזרח

---

[56] כך, למשל, הביא בחיי אנקדוטות מספרות החדית' המוסלמית תוך ששינה את
שמות הדמויות והמיר אותם לכינוי הכללי 'אחד הצדיקים', 'אחד החסידים' וכדומה.
עוד עיינו: אלומה סולניק-דנקוביץ, "על דמותו והגותו של המיסטיקן חאתם אלאצם;
אנקדוטות צופיות במקורות יהודיים", ספונות ח [כג] (תשס"ג), עמ' 75‏-97.

[57] דוגמאות קולעות לאיתור השפעה כזו ראו: גולדרייך (הערה 16 לעיל); דוד צבי
בנעט, "מקור משותף לר' בחיי בר יוסף ולאלגזאלי", ספר מאגנס, ירושלים תרח"ץ,
עמ' 23‏-30. פנטון, יהדות וצופיות (הערה 4 לעיל), ציין מקורות מוסלמים רבים אגב
סקירתו הכללית. לצד אחר אחר עיינו במאמר הביקורת של סבירי (הערה 24 לעיל), הדנה
במגבלות הזהות המושגית.

שונים (ככל הנראה).[52] קרוב להניח שהמספר גדל במהלך הזמן שחלף
מאז. ג', פירושים מיסטיים לספרי המקרא. ד', כתבים שונים ובהם
מכתבים פרטיים. חלוקה זו יכולה להועיל במיון ראשוני של שפע
החומר שנזדמן לידיו של פנטון, אולם אין היא מְסַפֶּקֶת. יש בה עירוב
של שיקולים תוכניים (פרשנות או תאולוגיה, מכתבים פרטיים), צורניים
(אותיות ערביות או עבריות) והקשריים (אמנותו של המחבר – אסלאם
או יהדות).[53] ינון-פנטון עצמו נקט שיטה אחרת כשדן במורשת הספרותית
של צאצאי הרמב"ם,[54] ואף בה לא הקפיד על עקיבות: כשסקר את
מפעלו הספרותי של הראב"ם מיין אותו לשתי קבוצות: פרשנות, הלכה
ומוסר (עמ' 8-9); ואילו כשהגיע לר' דוד בן יהושע בחן את חיבוריו
על פי ארבע הסוגות הבאות: מוסר, פילוסופיה, פרשנות ודרש, הלכה
(עמ' 18-21).

כוחו וערכו של כל מיון סוגתי הוא מוגבל. יש יצירות שאפשר למיינן
על פי יותר משיקול אחד ועל פי יותר מאמת מידה אחת. התיחום בין מוסר
לפילוסופיה ובין מוסר לדרש הוא לעתים עמום ולא מובהק, ובהקשר הנדון
כאן אינו מספק. חלק מן החיבורים הצופים היהודיים הם תחינות, כלומר
טקסטים המשמשים לצרכים ליטורגיים.[55] זו קבוצה שראוי להבחינה גם
מצד שימושה ולא רק מצד תוכנה, כפי שעשה פנטון. הבחנה זו תהיה פורייה
גם בהמשך הדיון.

אני מציע אפוא לראות בקבוצות המשנה שהציע פנטון כלים אפשריים
ומועילים למיון כל עוד הם מסייעים למיפוי החומר, לניתוחו ולשיבוצו
בהקשר תרבותי. משעה שהחוקר חש שאין בהם לסייע בידו, עליו לשכלל
את אמות המידה ולפתח לעצמו אזמלים חדים ומדויקים יותר.

---

[52] פנטון, כתבים (הערה 12 לעיל), עמ' 93.

[53] על שיקולי המיון לסוגות ראו: עזריאל אוכמני, תכנים וצורות, ב, תל אביב תשל"ז,
עמ' 88-91; רנה וולק ואוסטין וורן, תורת הספרות, תל אביב 1967, עמ' 245-257
(פרק שבעה עשר: הסוגות הספרותיות); אברהם שאנן, מלון הספרות החדשה העברית
והכללית, תל אביב תשי"ט, טורים 961-965.

[54] ראו ינון-פנטון, מורשתם (הערה 43 לעיל).

[55] ראו: אילן, ראשית חכמה (הערה 5 לעיל); חובה"ל (הערה 12 לעיל), עמ'
תלב-תמא; לנגרמן, הדלקת הנר (הערה 25 לעיל); הנ"ל, כתר מלכות (הערה 25 לעיל).

אלה רומזים לכך שבקרב היהודים הצופים במזרח רווחו שיטות עיוניות
מגוונות, שטרם נחשפו במלואן. קרוב אפוא להניח שבשנים הבאות תתגלה
תמונה מורכבת ומסועפת מזו שנחשפה עד כה.

סקירת מצאי זו היא חלקית, אולם די בה להתרשם מן הגיוון התוכני
והסוגתי של הספרות הצופית היהודית. האוסף החשוב ביותר שבו נשמרו
חיבורים מעין אלה הוא האוסף השני של פירקוביץ', השמור בספרייה
העירונית בסנט פטרסבורג. מלאכת הקיטלוג של האוצר היקר הזה נמצאת
בעיצומה, ולפיכך סביר לצפות שיתגלו חיבורים נוספים ויזוהו קטעים
אנונימיים, אשר יעשירו את ידיעותינו על אודות הספרייה הצופייה היהודית.

הסוגות

לפני כעשרים שנה[49] הציע ינון-פנטון למיין את ממצאי הגניזות שיש
בהם השפעות צופיות לארבע סוגות עיקריות:[50] א', העתקות של טקסטים
מוסלמים מיסטיים.[51] פנטון מנה קרוב לעשרים חיבורים, חלקם באותיות
ערביות וחלקם באותיות עבריות. ב', חיבורים מוסריים ותאולוגיים
מקוריים. בעת כתיבת המאמר היו בידיי למעלה ממאה קטעים מחיבורים

---

[49] הדברים ראו אור ב-1997, אך בכותרת המשנה של הכרך נאמר "Proceedings of the
Founding Conference of the Society for Judaeo-Arabic Studies", והאירוע היה במאי 1984
בשיקגו. איני יודע מתי מסר פנטון את מאמרו לפרסום.

[50] פנטון, כתבים (הערה 12 לעיל), עמ' 91.

[51] על מה שהביא שם יש להוסיף את החיבורים שציין במאמריו הבאים: "קראים
וצופים: רישומי צופיות בכתבי יד קראיים", פעמים 90 (תשס"ב), עמ' 5-19 ; "רישומי
אלחלאג' – הרוג מלכות מוסלמי בספרות הערבית-יהודית", קבלה 10 (תשס"ד),
עמ' 159-180 ; "שני כתבי יד אַכְּבָּרִיִים בגלגולם בערבית-יהודית", בין עבר לערב ג
(תשס"ד), עמ' 82-94. הפריט האחרון מבטל את הערתו בגוף הדיון שם, שעד כה
(בעת כתיבת מאמרו הראשון) לא נמצאו העתקות מחיבורי מֶחְיִי אלדין אלערבִּי,
וממילא אין צורך בסברה שהציע לכך; Paul B. Fenton, "Karaism and Sufism", Karaite
Judaism, edited by Meira Polliack, Leiden 2003, pp. 199-212. פנטון, יהדות וצופיות
(הערה 4 לעיל), עמ' 207, ציין קבוצה זו כאחד משני הטיפוסים העיקריים של כתבי יד
צופים יהודיים. הטיפוס השני הוא חיבורים יהודיים מקוריים (סעיף ב' על פי המיון
שנדפס בשנת 1997).

פירוש צופי לשיר השירים.[44] חיבורים אלו הם מעט מהרבה המוכרים עתה,
שהרי פנטון ציין כבר לפני שנים אחדות שרשומים אצלו למעלה ממאה
חיבורים צופיים בערבית-יהודית.[45]

לאלה יש להוסיף את 'ראשית חכמה', שרק חלקים ממנו שרדו.[46]
חיבור זה נכתב בהשראת 'חובות הלבבות' של בחיי, כעדות המחבר
עצמו בהקדמתו. לפי שעה אין ביכולתי לקבוע את זמנו ומקומו של
החיבור. בחודשים האחרונים זיהה מר יונתן מרוז מן המפעל לחקר הספרות
הערבית-היהודית בימי הביניים, המתנהל במכון בן-צבי בירושלים, שני
קטעים מן החיבור; אחד מהם חופף בחלקו לכתב היד העיקרי שבו טיפלתי.
מתברר אפוא כי חיבור זה הועתק לפחות פעם אחת (אם אחד משני כתבי
היד הוא אוטוגרף, ודומני שאין זה המצב), ומשמעות הממצא הזה היא שלא
נותר גנוז בידי מחברו אלא נודע ברבים, ולו במעגל מצומצם.

עניין מיוחד יש בקטעי חיבור אנונימי, בעל צביון צופי מובהק, ובו
ביקורת על הרמב"ם. ינון-פנטון פרסם לפני חודשים ספורים קטעים אחדים
מן הטקסט הזה.[47] יונתן מרוז איתר בחודשים האחרונים עוד קטעים מן
החיבור הזה בשיעור העולה פי ארבעה ויותר על מה שפרסם פנטון.[48]
מתברר אפוא ש'מורה הנבוכים' ומחברו שימשו יעד להתייחסות בקרב
מלומדים יהודים בעלי נטייה צופית. היחס המורכב הזה אל הרמב"ם ואל
משנתו מלמד, כמדומה, על המעמד הסמכותי של תורת הרמב"ם אפילו
בקרב אנשים שהסתייגו ממנה, אך לא יכלו להתעלם ממנה. שברי טקסטים

---

44 יוסף ינון (פנטון), "פירוש מיסטי לשיר השירים בידו של ר' דוד בן יהושע מימוני",
תרביץ סט (תש"ס), עמ' 539-589, ובמיוחד דיונו בעמ' 546-548.

45 פנטון, כתבים (הערה 12 לעיל), עמ' 93. דוגמאות לחיבורים נוספים ראו שם,
עמ' 97-98.

46 אילן, ראשית חכמה (הערה 5 לעיל).

47 יוסף ינון-פנטון, "ביקורת על הרמב"ם בחיבור חסידי מן הגניזה", גנזי קדם א
(תשס"ה), עמ' 139-161.

48 מר מרוז הרצה על היבט אחד של חיבור זה בוועידה הבינלאומית האחת עשרה של
החברה לחקר התרבות הערבית היהודית בימי הביניים, שהתקיימה באוניברסיטת חיפה
בקיץ 2005. אני מקווה כי ממצאיו ומחקרו יראו אור בקרוב. אני מודה למר מרוז על
שהואיל להעמיד לרשותי את מחקרו טרם פרסומו.

ובפסיקותיו הלכה למעשה.[39] עובדיה, בנו של הרמב"ם, כתב את 'מַקַאלַה
אלחַוְץ'יַיַה' ('מאמר הבריכה'), חיבור עיוני ובו השפעות ברורות של אביו
ושל סבו (הרמב"ם), ובה בעת גם ביטוי להשקפותיו הצופיות המחמירות
יותר מאלה של אביו.[40] שניים מחיבורי דוד בן יהושע,[41] נכד הרמב"ם, נתגלו
במאה העשרים: 'אלמֻרְשַד אלי אלתַּפַרֻד וַאלמֻרְפַד אלי אלתַּגַ'רֻד' ('מורה
הפרישות ומדריך הפשיטות')[42] וּתַגְ'רִיד אלחַקַאיְק אלנַט'רִיַה וַתַלְכִ'יץ
אלמַקַאצֻד אלנַפְסַאנִיַה' ('חשיפת האמיתות העיוניות ותמצית הכוונות
המעשיות'); האחרון נמצא עדיין בכתבי יד.[43] עוד אפשר שדוד כתב גם

(בהכנה; להלן: אילן, סודות); אפרים יהודה ויזנברג (מהדיר), פירוש רבינו אברהם
בן הרמב"ם ז"ל על בראשית ושמות, לונדון תשי"ח; -Paul B. Fenton, "The Post
Maimonidean Schools of Exegesis in the East: Abraham Maimonides, the Pietists, Tanhûm
ha-Yerušalmi and the Yemenite School", *Hebrew Bible/Old Testament*, I/2, Göttingen
2000, pp. 433-55

[39] יעקב בלידשטיין, "ציבור ותפילה בציבור בכתבי ר' אברהם בן הרמב"ם", פעמים 78
(תשנ"ט), עמ' 148-163; נפתלי וידר, "השפעות איסלאמיות על הפולחן היהודי",
מלילה ב (תש"ו), עמ' 37-120 (ובהדפסה מיוחדת, אוקספורד תש"ז; נדפס מחדש עם
תוספות ותיקונים באסופת מאמריו: התגבשות נוסח התפילה במזרח ובמערב, ירושלים
תשנ"ח, ב, עמ' 659-777); מרדכי עקיבא פרידמן, "זעקת שבר על ביטול אמירת
הפיוטים – בקשה לפנות לסולטן", פעמים 78 (תשנ"ט), עמ' 128-147; הנ"ל,
"מחלוקת לשם שמים – עיונים בפולמוס התפילה של ר' אברהם בן הרמב"ם ובני
דורו", תעודה י (תשנ"ו), עמ' 245-298; ;Y. Tzvi Langermann, "From Private Devotion to
Communal Prayer: New Light on Abraham Maimonides' Synagogue Reforms", *Ginzei
Qedem* 1 (2005), pp. 31-49

[40] Paul B. Fenton, *The Treatise of the Pool; Al-Maqāla al-Hawdiyya by 'Obadyāh
Maimonides*, London 1981; Paul B. Fenton, *Deux Traités Mystiques: Le Traité du Puits
d'Obadyah Maïmonide et le Guide du Détachement de David Maïmonide*, Paris 1987
[ביקורת עליו: חוה לצרוס-יפה, "מקור חדש לתולדות 'הצופיות היהודית'", תרביץ נב
(תשמ"ג), עמ' 665-668]; פנטון, יהדות וצופיות (הערה 4 לעיל), עמ' 211.

[41] Paul B. Fenton, "The Literary Legacy of David ben Joshua, Last of the Maimonidean
'Negidim'", *JQR* 75 (1984), pp. 1-56

[42] Franz Rosenthal, "A Judaeo-Arabic Work under Sûfic Influence", *HUCA* 15 (1940), pp.
433-84. כעבור עשרות שנים זיהה פנטון את בעל החיבור והוציאו לאור בגרסה שלמה.
ראו: יוסף ינון (פנטון) (מהדיר), מורה הפרישות ומדריך הפשיטות לר' דוד בן יהושע
הנגיד, ירושלים תשמ"ז; פנטון, יהדות וצופיות (הערה 4 לעיל), עמ' 211-212.

[43] יוסף ינון-פנטון, "מורשתם הספרותית של צאצאי הרמב"ם", פעמים 97 (תשס"ד),
עמ' 19 (להלן: ינון-פנטון, מורשתם).

הראב"ם הוא דמות המפתח בחקר הצופיּוּת היהודית במזרח הן משום
שחיבוריו נפוצו יותר מחיבורי צאצאיו הן משום ייחוסו ומעמדו. יצירותיו
של הראב"ם נדונו במחקר הרבה יותר מחיבורי כל צאצאיו בחמשת הדורות
הבאים, ועדיין דומה שרב הפרוץ על העומד גם ביחס למפעלו הספרותי
וההגותי של הראב"ם ולהשפעתו הישירה והעקיפה – בימיו ולאחריהם,
במקומו ומחוצה לו.[36]

המימד הצופי בתפיסתו של הראב"ם התבטא בשני תחומי הבעה
עיקריים: ביצירותיו העיוניות והפרשניות – חיבורו הגדול 'כִּפַאיַת
אלְעַאבִּדִין' ('המספיק לעובדי ה'')[37] ופירושו לבראשית ולשמות;[38]

ערך מוגבל יותר יש לדבריו של תום בלוק על הרמב"ם כצופי, ראו: ,Tom Block, "Moses
Maimonides and the Sufis of Islam", *Sufi* 64 (2004-2005), pp. 26-31. מלבד האכסניה
המסקרנת *Sufi* הוא כתב עת באנגלית, היוצא לאור בלונדון מאז 1988 מטעם
Khaniqahi Nimatullahi Sufi Order, ומופץ במקביל גם בפרסית), עיון במאמר מלמד
שבלוק ביסס את טיעוניו על קריאה באנגלית בלבד – התרגום האנגלי של פרידלנדר
ל'מורה הנבוכים' וחיבורי מלומדים חשובים במדעי היהדות (אידל, אלטמן, בלומנטל,
גוייטיין, זפרני, לובל ופנטון), ולא על קריאת חיבורים צופיים במקורם בערבית.

36 Paul B. Fenton, "Abraham Maimonides (1186-1237): Founding a Mystical Dynasty", in:
Moshe Idel and Mortimer Ostow (eds.), *Jewish Mystical Leaders and Leadership in the*
13th Century, New Jersey 1998, pp. 127-54; פנטון, יהדות וצופיות (הערה 4 לעיל), עמ'
207-211.

37 יוסף דורי (מתרגם), פרקי מוסר ומדות מהספר הגדול הנקרא ספר המספיק
לעובדי ה' [כפאיה אלעאבדין] שחברו בערבית רבינו אברהם בן הרמב"ם זצ"ל,
ירושלים תשכ"ה; נסים דנה (מהדיר), ר' אברהם בן הרמב"ם, ספר המספיק לעובדי
השם, רמת גן תשמ"ט [ביקורת עליו: Paul B. Fenton, "Dana's Edition of Abraham
Maimuni's Kifāyat Al-ʿĀbidīn", *JQR* 82 (1991), pp. 194-206]; יוסף ינון (פנטון),
"תורת הדבקות במשנתו של ר' אברהם בן הרמב"ם; קטעים מתוך החלק האבוד של
'המספיק לעובדי השם'", *דעת* 50-52 (תשנ"ג), עמ' 107-119; אביבה שוסמן, "שאלת
המקורות המוסלמיים לחיבורו של ר' אברהם בן הרמב"ם 'כתאב כפאיה אלעאבדין'",
תרביץ נה (תשמ"ה), עמ' 229-251; Samuel Rosenblatt (ed.), *The High Ways to*
Perfection of Abraham Maimonides, 1-2, New York-Baltimore 1927-38. גישה מתונה יותר
כלפי צופיותו של הראב"ם נקט גרשון כהן. ראו: Gershon Cohen, "The Soteriology of
Abraham Maimuni", *PAAJR* 35 (1967), pp. 75-98; 36 (1969), pp. 33-56 [republished in:
idem, *Studies in the Variety of Rabbinic Cultures*, Philadelphia: JPS 1991, pp. 209-42]

38 נחם אילן, "הנחות תאולוגיות ועקרונות פרשניים בפירוש ר' אברהם בן הרמב"ם
לתורה", בתוך: דָּבָר דָּבֻר עַל אָפְנָיו, בעריכת מאיר מ' בר-אשר ואחרים,
ירושלים תשס"ז, עמ' 31-70; הנ"ל, "סודות ופשרם בפירוש התורה לראב"ם

השגחה ונבואה;[31] ומסכת על התפילה.[32] אבי רעייתו של הרמב"ם נמנה עם חבורת ה'חסידים' הללו.[33] לנתון זה יש חשיבות רבה, שכן משמעותו היא שר' אברהם בן הרמב"ם (הראב"ם) (1186-1237) ספג בבית הוריו לא רק את מוסר אביו אלא גם את תורת אמו.[34]

מה הייתה זיקתו של הרמב"ם לחבורת החסידים ולמשנתם? סוגיה זו טרם נתלבנה במחקר די הצורך. בדרך כלל מתואר הרמב"ם כרציונליסט מובהק, ולפי גישה זו אימץ בנו אברהם תפיסה שונה בתכלית משל אביו, כפי שיתברר להלן בסמוך. אולם בדור האחרון החלו מובעות עמדות המסתייגות מן ההצגה המנגדת את הבן לעומת אביו. בולט במגמה זו דוד בלומנטל, ודבריו על אודות 'המיסטיציזם האינטלקטואלי' של הרמב"ם מחייבים עיון מחודש במשנת הרמב"ם.[35]

---

[31] פנטון, כתבים (הערה 12 לעיל), עמ' 96; Paul B. Fenton, "A Mystical Treatise on Perfection, Providence and Prophecy from the Jewish Sufi Circle", *The Jews of Medieval Islam*, edited by Daniel Frank, Leiden 1995, pp. 301-34

[32] Paul B. Fenton, "A Mystical Treatise on Prayer and the Spiritual Quest from the Pietist Circle", *JSAI* 16 (1993), pp.137-75

[33] מרדכי עקיבא פרידמן, "משפחת אבן אלאמשאטי, בית מחותני הרמב"ם", ציון סט (תשס"ד), עמ' 271-297, ובייחוד דיונו בעמ' 291-295; פנטון, יהדות וצופיות (הערה 4 לעיל), עמ' 212.

[34] שלמה דב גויטיין, "רבנו אברהם בן הרמב"ם וחוגו החסידי", תרביץ לג (תשכ"ד), עמ' 181-197; דב מימון, "גבולות המפגש בין יהדות רבנית ומיסטיקה מוסלמית. חלק א': חוג חסידי מצרים והצופיות – רקע היסטורי ורעיוני", אקדמות ז (תשנ"ט), עמ' 9-29; "גבולות המפגש בין יהדות רבנית ומיסטיקה מוסלמית; חלק ב': רבי אברהם בן הרמב"ם וחוג חסידי מצרים", אקדמות ח (תש"ס), עמ' 43-72; גויטיין, חברה (הערה 30 לעיל), 5, עמ' 474-496; Shlomo Dov Goitein, "Abraham Maimonides and his Pietist Circle", *Jewish Medieval and Renaissance Studies*, edited by Alexander Altmann, Cambridge Mass. 1967, pp. 145-64; idem, "A Treatise in Defence of the Pietists by Abraham Maimonides", *Journal of Jewish Studies* XVI (1966), pp. 105-14

[35] ראו: David R. Blumenthal, "Maimonides' Intellectualist Mysticism and the Superiority of the Prophecy of Moses", *Studies in Medieval Culture* 10 (1975), pp. 51-67 [Reprinted in: *Approaches to Judaism in Medieval Times*, ed. David R. Blumenthal, 1, Chico 1984, pp.27-51] לפני זמן קצר ראה אור ספרו *Philosophic Mysticism: Studies in Rational Religion*, Ramat Gan 2006, ובו, מן הסתם, מלובנת גישתו בצורה מפורטת יותר. פנטון, יהדות וצופיות (הערה 4 לעיל), עמ' 213, ציין דיווח של הביוגרף המוסלמי אלכֻּתֻבֵּי, ולפיו יהודים בדמשק למדו במאה השלוש עשרה את 'מורה הנבוכים' בבית הצופי חסן אבן הוד ובפיקוחו.

הזירה העיקרית שבה ניכר החותם הצופי על היצירה היהודית הייתה
מצרים, מן המחצית השנייה של המאה השתים עשרה ועד ראשית המאה
החמש עשרה; זירת משנה שימשה סוריה, בעיקר במהלך המאה הארבע
עשרה. בתקופה זו נתמכו מוסדות צופיים בידי הממסד השלטוני במצרים,
בארץ ישראל ובסוריה, וברור שבתנאים כאלה קל היה להגביר את הפעילות
הצופית, הארגונית והחינוכית, ולהשפיע אף שלא במתכוון גם על המיעוט
היהודי בארצות אלו.[28]

לפחות בשנותיו האחרונות של הרמב״ם במצרים, לקראת סוף המאה
השתים עשרה, פעל בקהיר חוג של נכבדים יהודים שנתכנו 'חסידים',[29]
ומנהיגם היה ר' אברהם החסיד.[30] בשנים האחרונות פרסם יוסף ינון-פנטון
קטעים משני חיבורים של ר' אברהם החסיד: מסכת מיסטית על שלמות,

פנטון, יהדות וצופיות (הערה 4 לעיל), עמ' 204 (משפט כוללני אחד). לאור אמות
המידה החמורות שהנהיג שיינדלין ראוי לבדוק מחדש את ממצאיו של דנה. ראו:
יוסף דנה, ״השפעה ערבית וצופית על פיוטי ר' משה אבן עזרא״, קעמ״י 10, ג1
(תש״ן), עמ' 282-275.

Michael McGaha, "The *Sefer ha-Bahir* and Andalusian Sufism", *Medieval Encounters* [27]
3,1 (1997), pp. 20-57; Mustansir Mir, "Kabbalah and Sufism: A Comparative Look at
Jewish and Islamic Mysticism", *Jewish-Muslim Encounters: History, Philosophy, and
Culture*, edited by Charles Selengut, St. Paul, Minn. 2001, pp. 165-79

[28] דפנה אפרת, ״הפצת הצופיות וחותם האסלאם בארץ ישראל בימי הביניים״,
זמנים 92 (2005), עמ' 15-8; פ״ג' וטיקיוטיס, מצרים ממוחמד עלי עד סאדאת,
ירושלים תשמ״ג, עמ' 26; פנטון, יהדות וצופיות (הערה 4 לעיל), עמ' 206;
Michael Winter, "Saladin's Religious Personality, Policy, and Image", *Perspectives on
Maimonides*, ed. Joel L. Kraemer, Oxford 1991, pp. 309-22. רעיונות מעוררי השראה
בדבר יחסי הגומלין בין המיעוט היהודי לרוב המוסלמי במזרח יש בספרו של מרי, ראו:
Josef W. Meri, The Cult of Saints Among Muslims and Jews in Medieval Syria, Oxford
2002, בעיקר בדברי הסיכום שלו, עמ' 287-281. אני מודה לפרופ' שרה סבירי על
שהסבה את תשומת לבי למונוגרפיה של מרי.

[29] יוסף ינון-פנטון, ״עוד על ר' חננאל בן שמואל הדיין, גדול החסידים״, תרביץ נה
(תשמ״ו), עמ' 107-77.

Paul B. Fenton, "Some Judaeo-Arabic Fragments by Rabbi Abraham he-Hasid, the [30]
Jewish Sufi", *JSeS* 26 (1981), pp. 47-72; Shlomo Dov Goitein, *A Mediterranean Society*,
1-5, Berkeley-Los Angeles-London 1967-1988 (להלן: גויטיין, חברה), על פי המפתח
בערכו (Abraham the Pious); פנטון, יהדות וצופיות (הערה 4 לעיל), עמ' 212.

בשמו 'ספר הכוזרי'.[20] שרה סבירי הציגה תובנות חשובות על מגמתו
המיסטית של ריה"ל בחיבור זה ועל זיקתו האפשרית לצופים.[21] באחרונה
הראתה דיאנה לובל עד כמה ספוג חיבור זה מונחים צופיים.[22] בפסקת
הסיום של ספרה קבעה לובל, כי אף שריה"ל אימץ מונחים צופיים רבים
וניכר בעליל ששפתו משקפת היכרות קרובה עם ההגות הצופית, אין לראות
בו יהודי צופי. לשיטתה, הציג ריה"ל עמדה ייחודית המונעת מלשייכו
ל"משבצת" פשוטה ומוגדרת אחת.[23] מחקרה הלשוני המדוקדק ומסקנותיה
הזהירות מלמדים על עוצמת ההשפעה הצופית על ההנהגה היהודית במערב
(בספרד) במאה השתים עשרה.[24]

צבי לנגרמן הראה בשני מאמרים קצרים השפעות צופיות אפשריות
נוספות בספרד או בצפון אפריקה, כנראה מן המאה הארבע עשרה או מאוחר
יותר.[25] מִמְצָאָיו מעשירים את הידוע עד כה לא רק מבחינה כמותית, אלא
בעיקר מבחינת התפרוסת היישובית והסוגות הספרותיות (שיידונו להלן),
שבהן משתקפת השפעה צופית.

לעתים גדול הפיתוי לראות השפעה צופית אף במקום שבאמת איננה
מוכחת. תרומה חשובה לעניין זה מבחינה תוכנית ומתודולוגית כאחת הרים
לפני למעלה ממעשור פנחס שיינדלין, כשהראה שאין להוכיח השפעה צופית
מובהקת על שירת ר' שלמה אבן גבירול.[26] השפעה צופית אפשרית על
הקבלה המוקדמת בספרד נדונה אף היא במחקר בשנים האחרונות.[27]

---

20 יהודה הלוי, כתאב אלרד ואלדליל פי אלדין אלד'ליל (אלכתאב אלכ'זרי), מהדורת
דוד צבי בנעט וחגי בן-שמאי, ירושלים תשל"ז.

21 הערה 16 לעיל, עמ' 81-83; פנטון, יהדות וצופיות (הערה 4 לעיל), עמ' 204,
הסתפק במשפט כוללני בלבד.

22 Diana Lobel, *Between Mysticism and Philosophy*, New York 2000

23 שם, עמ' 177.

24 שרה סבירי הסתייגה מדרכי ההיסק שלה וממסקנותיה. ראו במאמר הביקורת שלה
בתוך: Journal of Jewish Studies 53 (2002), pp. 177-80

25 Tzvi Langermann, "A Judaeo-Arabic Candle-Lighting Prayer", *JQR* 92 (2001),
pp. 133-35 (להלן: לנגרמן, הדלקת הנר); idem, "A Judaeo-Arabic Paraphrase of Ibn
Gabirol's *Keter Malkhut*", *Zutot* 3 (2003), pp. 28-33 (להלן: לנגרמן, כתר מלכות).

26 Raymond P. Scheindlin, "Ibn Gabirol's Religious Poetry and Sufi Poetry", *Sefarad* 54
(1994), pp. 108-41; והשוו לנגרמן, כתר מלכות (הערה 25 לעיל), עמ' 32 הערה 11;

ו

הוא חיבור גדול, מגובש ושיטתי. אם אכן הוא החיבור היהודי הראשון
אשר נכתב בהשראה צופית, נראה שהשפעת הצופיּוּת על העילית
היהודית בספרד בתחילת המחצית השנייה של המאה האחת עשרה הייתה
כה ניכרת, עד שהניבה פרי ביכורים משוכלל בדמות 'חובות הלבבות'.[17] לצד
אחר אפשר שבעתיד יתגלו (או יזוהו) חיבורים וקטעי חיבורים
שקדמו ל'חובות הלבבות', ובאמצעותם אפשר יהיה לשחזר לפחות חלק
מן התהליך של קליטת הרעיונות הצופים והטמעתם ביצירה היהודית בת
הזמן בספרד.[18]

השפעה צופית ברורה התלבנה לאחרונה במחקר שייחדה חגית מיטלמן
(קיל) לפירוש לקהלת, אשר יצא יצא ככל הנראה מתחת ידיו של ר' יצחק אבן
גיאת', איש לוסינה שבספרד ובן המאה האחת עשרה.[19] עשרות שנים לאחר
בחיי כתב ר' יהודה הלוי (ריה"ל) את ספרו 'כתאב אלרד ואלדליל פי אלדין
אלד'ליל' ('ספר המענה והראיה על אודות הדת המושפלה'), המוכר יותר

Asceticism against its Rabbinic and Islamic Background", *JJS* 21 (1970), pp. 11-38;
Menachem Mansoor, "Arabic Sources of Ibn Pakuda's *Duties of the Heart*", *Proceedings of the Sixth World Congress of Jewish Studies*, III, Jerusalem 1977, pp. 81-90; Bezalel Safran, "Bahya ibn Paquda's Attitude towards the Courtier Class", in: Isadore Twersky (ed.), *Studies in Medieval Jewish History and Literature*, Cambridge Mass. and London 1979, pp. 154-96; Sara Sviri, "Spiritual Trends in Pre-Kabbalistic Judeo-Spanish Literature: The Cases of Bahya Ibn Paquda and Judah Halevi", *Donaire* 6 (Abril 1996), pp. 78-84; Raphael Jehuda Zwi Werblowsky, "Faith, Hope and Trust: A Study in the Concept of *Bittahon*", Papers of the Institute of Jewish Studies, London 1964 ; וּבְמַאֲמָרֵי :"Al-I'tidāl Al-Sharī'i Another Examination of the Perception of Asceticism in the *Duties of the Heart* of Bahya", *REJ* 164 (2005), pp. 149-61 ובספרות שהבאתי שם, בעיקר בהערות 3-5.

[17] ראו אצל: רקע מועיל על התרבות היהודית בספרד באותה עת Ross Brann, "The Arabizad Jews," in: Maria Rosa Menocal, Raymond P. Scheindlin and Michael Sells (eds.), *The Literature of al-Andalus*, Cambridge 2000, pp. 435-54; Joel L. Kraemer, "The Andalusian Mystic Ibn Hud and the Conversion of the Jews", *IOS* 12 (1992), pp. 59-73

[18] קריאה מדוקדקת בשער העשירי של אמו"ד מחד גיסא ובדברי בחיי (בהקדמתו) על רס"ג כמקור השראה וסמכות לחיבורו 'חובות הלבבות' מאידך גיסא מעוררת למחשבה שזיקתו של רס"ג לתפיסות צופיות ראויה לליבון נוסף, מעבר לדבריו השקולים של אפרת (הערה 10 לעיל).

[19] חגית מיטלמן (קיל), פירוש לספר 'קהלת' בערבית-יהודית המיוחס לר' יצחק אבן גיאת' — היבטים פילוסופיים ופרשניים, עבודת דוקטור, ירושלים תשנ"ט; הנ"ל, "תפיסת הפרישות ('אלזהד') בפירוש לקהלת המיוחס לאבן גיאת' והשוואתה למיסטיקה המוסלמית", דעת 48 (תשס"ב), עמ' 57-81.

מתחילת הפעילות הזאת. החיבור הצופי-היהודי הראשון המוכר הוא
'אלהדאיה אלי פראיץ' אלקלוב' מאת בחיי אבן יוסף אבן פקודה,[11] ונודע
בשמו העברי 'חובות הלבבות'.[12] ספר זה נכתב בסרגוסה שבספרד סביב שנת
1070 ותורגם לעברית בשלושה תרגומים עצמאיים כבר במחצית השנייה של
המאה השתים עשרה. הוא נפוץ בקהילות ישראל במזרח ובמערב,[13] הועתק
שוב ושוב בימי הביניים ונדפס למעלה ממאה פעמים מאז הופעת הדפוס.[14]
מאחר שנודע בעיקר בתרגומיו לעברית, הוא נתפס בעיקר כחיבור מוסרי,[15]
ורק חוקרים מעטים עמדו על אופן יחסו על טיבו הצופי.[16] 'חובות הלבבות'

---

[11] רב סעדיה גאון, ראו Israel Efros, "Saadia's General Ethical Theory and its Relation to Sufism", *JQRAV* (1967), pp. 166-77 (להלן: אפרת).

חיים שירמן, תולדות השירה העברית בספרד המוסלמית [ערך, השלים וליווה
בהערות עזרא פליישר], ירושלים תשנ"ו, עמ' 373-379.

[12] כך הציג אותו גם פנטון, יהדות וצופיות (הערה 4 לעיל), עמ' 204-205;
וכן במאמרו "Judaeo-Arabic Mystical Writings of the XIIIth-XIVth Centuries", in: Norman
Golb (ed.), *Judaeo-Arabic Studies*, Amsterdam 1997, pp. 87-101 (להלן: פנטון,
כתבים); יוסף קאפח (מהדיר ומתרגם), בחיי בן יוסף בן פקודה, ספר תורת חובות
הלבבות, ירושלים תשל"ג (להלן: חובה"ל); Menachem Mansoor (ed.), *The Book of
Direction to the Duties of the Heart*, London 1973; Avraham Shalom Yahuda, *Al-Hidāja
'ila Farā'id al-Qulūb des Bachja ibn Jōsef ibn Paqūda*, pp. 1-112, Leiden 1912

[13] אהרן מירסקי, מחובות הלבבות לשירת הלבבות, ירושלים תשנ"ב [ביקורת עליו:
יוסף טובי, פעמים 56 (תשנ"ג), עמ' 140-145]; George Vajda, *La théologie ascétique de
Bahya ibn Pakuda*, Paris 1947 (להלן: ויידה, בחיי).

[14] אברהם מאיר הברמן, "לחקר ספר 'חובות הלבבות' ונוסחאותיו העבריות", סיני כח
(תשי"א), עמ' שטו-שכט; כט (תשי"ב), עמ' נח-עט.

[15] ראו, כמבחר בלבד: יוסף דן, ספרות המוסר והדרוש, ירושלים 1975, עמ' 47-68;
יוסף דן, "על המוסר ועל ספרות המוסר", על הקדושה, ירושלים תשנ"ז, עמ'
322-354; אליעזר שביד, "דרך התשובה של היחיד המיטהר – פרקי מחקר בתורת
המוסר של חובות הלבבות", דעת 1 (תשל"ח), עמ' 17-42; הנ"ל, הפילוסופים
הגדולים שלנו, תל-אביב 1999, עמ' 59-79, 475, 476; דב שוורץ, "המתח בין המוסר
המתון למוסר הסגפני בפילוסופיה היהודית בימי הביניים", בתוך: דני סטטמן ואבי
שגיא (עורכים), בין דת למוסר, רמת-גן תשנ"ד, עמ' 185-208.

[16] עמוס גולדרייך, "המקורות הערביים האפשריים של ההבחנה בין 'חובות האיברים'
ו'חובות הלבבות'", תעודה ו (תשמ"ח), עמ' 179-208; ויידה, בחיי (הערה 13 לעיל);
שמעון שוקן, "רציונאליזם וספיריטואליזציה בספר חובות הלבבות", קעמ"י 11 בג
(תשנ"ד), עמ' 17-23; Howard Kreisel, "Asceticism in the Thought of R. Bahya Ibn
Paquda and Maimonides" דעת 21 (1988), עמ' v-xxii; Allan Lazaroff, "Bahya's

הצופים העמידו במרכז הגותם את הדרך, המאמץ, התהליך
וההשתדלות, וראו בהם ערך דתי.[7] אף כי מפתה לשמוע בדבריהם את קולם
של נביאי ישראל,[8] ראוי לתת את הדעת על כך שכבר בהגות הצופית
הקדומה התמזגו הלכי רוח שמקורם בתרבויות הסביבה, כלומר בדתות
הפרסיות, וייתכן שגם בתרבויות הודו, ועל כן יש להיזהר זהירות מרובה
בניסיון לזהות השפעות יהודיות עליה. ועוד מתבקש לומר, שהמתח בין דת
ממוסדת, המעצבת את הפרהסיה ומכילה בתוכה ציבורים גדולים, לבין דת
פרטית, המושתתת על הגיון לבו של היחיד ומלכתחילה אינה יכולה להכיל
ציבורים גדולים, הוא מתח המוכר היטב מתולדות הדתות, ודומה שאינו בר
התרה באופן מוחלט. עצם קיומו הוא ביטוי מורכב לחִיוּתָהּ של אותה דת,
גם אם הפתרונות אינם מספקים את המאמינים.[9]

המצאי

ראשית הפעילות הצופית הייתה במזרח, כנראה בעראק (בבל), וניכרת בה
השפעה יהודית.[10] עד כה טרם נתגלו חיבורים צופיים יהודיים מן המזרח

---

[7] על השורש ג'ה"ד בערבית ראו: Ella Landau-Tasseron, "Jihād", *Encyclopaedia of the Qur'ān*, 3, Leiden 2003, pp. 35-43; Edward W. Lane, *Arabic-English Lexicon*, London 1984, pp. 473-74; Joseph Schacht, "Idjtihād", *EI²*, Vol. 3, Leiden and London 1971, pp. 1026-27; E. Tyan, "Djihād", *EI²*, Vol. 2, Leiden and London 1965, pp. 538-40

[8] הנה דוגמאות אחדות מרבות מאוד: "הכזה יהיה צום אבחרהו יום ענות אדם נפשו
הלכף כאגמן ראשו ושק ואפר יציע הלזה תקרא צום ויום רצון לה'. הלוא זה
צום אבחרהו פתח חרצבות רשע התר אגדות מוטה ושלח רצוצים חפשים וכל מוטה
תנתקו ... ותפק לרעב נפשך ונפש נענה תשביע וזרח בחשך אורך ואפלתך כצהרים"
(ישעיה נח,ה,ה-י); "עקב הלב מכל ואנש הוא מי ידענו. אני ה' חקר לב בחן כליות ולתת
לאיש כדרכיו כפרי מעלליו" (ירמיה יז,ט-י); "ההפכים ללענה משפט וצדקה לארץ
הניחו.... שנאו בשער מוכיח ודבר תמים יתעבו" (עמוס ה,ז; ה,י); "הגיד לך אדם
מה טוב ומה ה' דורש ממך כי אם עשות משפט ואהבת חסד והצנע לכת עם א-להיך"
(מיכה ו,ח).

[9] ראו: אלומה סולניק-דנקוביץ, "היחסים בין המיסטיקנים לבין חכמי ההלכה במאות
הראשונות לאסלאם: חילוקי דעות בסוגיות מהות הקשר בין האדם לאל ואופן
ההתייחסות למצוות", מַגַ'לַّת אלמֻעַלֶّם — ביטאון המורים לערבית ולאסלאם 29-30
(2003), עמ' 21-33.

[10] על השפעות יהודיות אפשריות על הצופיות הקדומה ראו: פנטון, יהדות וצופיות
(הערה 4 לעיל), עמ' 203; ישראל אפרת הציע לראות נטיות צופיות בהגותו של

מאחר שכל דבריי אינם חורגים מגדר הערכה טנטטיבית, אחתום את
דבריי בהתווית יעדי מחקר אפשריים ומתבקשים לאור השגי המחקר
עד כה.

בתולדות הדתות מוכרת התופעה של התפתחות מגמות ביקורתיות
בתוך דת נתונה משעה שהחלה להתמסד. יעדי הביקורת יכולים להיות
מנגנונים ומוסדות בתוך אותה דת, בעלי תפקידים מוגדרים או דפוסי פעילות
שהתקבעו. כל אלה גורמים להיחלשות הלהט הדתי, למיסוד דרכי הפולחן
ולהיעלמות כמעט מוחלטת של החוויה הדתית האישית ושל אופני הביטוי
האישיים. נגד כל הגילויים הללו מופנית הביקורת, המבקשת להעמיד במוקד
המעשה הדתי את היחיד (ולא את הציבור) ואת עולמו הפנימי (כוונת
הלב וחוויות רגשיות ואינטלקטואליות ולא מחוות חיצוניות המושתתות
על שגרה).

סמוך לאחר התבססות השלטון המוסלמי במזרח החלו נשמעים בקרב
קהל המאמינים קולות המסתייגים מדרכי המיסוד של הפולחן החדש,
ובעיקר הקובלים על אבדן החיות מן המעשה הדתי. אחת מקבוצות המחאה
נקראה לימים הצופים, כנראה בשל בגדי חבריה, שהיו עשויים צמר,
ביטוי מוחצן לחוסר החשיבות שייחסו לחזותם. התנועה הצופית
פשטה צורה ולבשה צורה, והיא קיימת עד ימינו אלה. מדובר אפוא בתופעה
יציבה בתולדות האסלאם, גם אם נשתנו פניה, זירות פעולתה ומופעיה.[6]
הצופים העמידו במוקד ביקורתם את היחיד ואת עולמו הפנימי. הם תבעו מן
המאמינים לא להסתפק בקיום המצוות כמתחייב מן השריעה, אלא לחתור
לחוויה דתית פנימית שישיאה דבקות באל, ולשיטתם של צופים רדיקלים אף
התאחדות עמו. תחילה הם הטיפו לחוויה שבמוקדה נמצא היחיד והיא
מתחוללת בנפשו או בתודעתו. בהמשך התפתח מרכז כובד נוסף, לצד
התאולוגי, בתחום החברתי-המוסרי.

---

6 מיכאל וינטר, "צופיות", האנציקלופדיה העברית, כרך כח, ירושלים ותל אביב
תשל"ו, טורים 568-571; ח'אלד אלח'אלדי, "הדרווישים ועלם אלקין", דארנא 34
(2001), עמ' 157-171; הנ"ל, "הסגפנות והצופיות באסלאם", דארנא 33 (2000),
עמ' 127-141; Peter J. Awn, "Sufism", The Encyclopedia of Religion, Vol. 14, New York
and London 1987, pp. 104-23; L. Massignon and B. Radtke, "Tasawwuf", EI², Vol. 10,
Leiden 2000, pp. 313-40; Seyyed Hossein Nasr, Living Sufism, London 1980

עשרה במצרים ובסוריה.[3] יתכן שראוי למתוח את טווח הזמן עד לסוף המאה
השש עשרה,[4] ושמא אף לעומקי המאה השבע עשרה או ראשית המאה
השמונה עשרה.[5] מדובר אפוא בתופעה הפורצת גבולות של זמן ומקום,
הקשר תרבותי אחד ונסיבות חיים מוגדרות.

בדבריי להלן אסמן את היצירות העיקריות השייכות לספרות הצופית
היהודית, אאפיין אותן מבחינת הסוגה ומבחינת טיב הזיקות אל
הספרות הצופית המוסלמית, אדון בקהלי היעד השונים ובזירות הפעולה
המתגוונות, אברר את טיב ההשפעה של התפיסות הצופיות על התרבות
היהודית, וכמובן אנסה לסמן את קצה טווח ההשפעה. חלק מן היצירות
היהודיות נכתבו ממש בהשפעה צופית מוסלמית; חלק אחר נכתב
בהשראתה. בדבריי אעמוד גם על ההבדלים בין השפעה להשראה. לשון
אחר: אני מציע בחינה תרבותית של הספרות הצופית היהודית, שנדבכיה
העיקריים הם העיון הלשוני, הספרותי, הרעיוני, ההיסטורי והפנומנולוגי.

Medieval Times, 2, Chico 1985, pp. 149-67, esp. pp. 150-52; Shlomo Dov Goitein, "Islamic and Jewish Mysticism", *Jews and Arabs: Their Contacts through the Ages*, New York 1974, pp. 150-52 (להלן גויטיין, יהודים וערבים).

[3] בסקירתו הקצרה על המיסטיקה המוסלמית והיהודית ציין גויטיין לאחר בחיי רק את ר' אברהם בן הרמב"ם; ראו: גויטיין, יהודים וערבים (הערה 2 לעיל), עמ' 148-154.

[4] ר' יששכר בן סוסאן, שחי בצפת במחצית השנייה של המאה השש עשרה, ציין בהקדמתו ל'שרח' שחיבר, כי ה'כפאיה' של הראב"ם (על חיבור זה בהמשך) עדיין נקראת בזמנו ובמקומו בערבית-יהודית. (ראו: S. D. Sassoon, *Ohel David*, 1, London 159 § ,p. 65 ,1932.). לדיון כללי יותר ראו: יוסף ינון-פנטון, "השפעות צופיות על הקבלה בצפת", מחניים 6 (תשנ"ד), עמ' 170-179 (להלן: ינון-פנטון, הקבלה בצפת); Paul B. Fenton, "Judaism and Sufism", *The Cambridge Companion to Medieval Jewish Philosophy*, edited by Daniel H. Frank and Oliver Leaman, Cambridge 2003, pp. 201-17 (להלן: פנטון, יהדות וצופיות), בייחוד עמ' 214-216.

[5] נחם אילן, " 'ראשית חכמה' — שרידי חיבור צופי בערבית יהודית בהשראת 'חובות הלבבות' ", אשל באר שבע (תשס"ז) (בדפוס; להלן: אילן, ראשית חכמה). חיבור זה שרד בשני כתבי יד לפחות, והעיקרי שבהם הועתק, ככל הנראה, בראשית המאה השמונה עשרה. אני מניח אפוא שההעתקה מעידה על ביקוש ועל עניין מסוימים, ובמיוחד בערבית-יהודית. אכן, שני כתבי יד עדיין אינם ראיה מכרעת להיקפה של תפוצת חיבור כלשהו. לצד אחר, במאות ה-18 וה-19 החלה התעניינות מחדש בחיבורים בערבית-יהודית, במיוחד בצפון אפריקה, שעניינם תורת המידות וספרות המוסר היהודית לענפיה, ושמא יש לקשור בין הנתונים הללו.

הספרות הצופית היהודית:
בין השפעה להשראה*

נַחֵם אילן

הקדמה

בין חידושי המחקר המשמעותיים ביותר בדור האחרון בתחום היצירה
ההגותית היהודית בימי הביניים בולטת הספרות הצופית היהודית, שרובה
ככולה נכתבה בערבית-יהודית.[1] מאחר שמדובר בתחום חקר חדש, יחסית,
אף טווח הזמן והמקום, ובוודאי המצאי, הם משוערים בלבד. לפי שעה
גבולות הזמן והמקום הם בין המאה התשיעית בבבל[2] לשלהי המאה הארבע

---

* אני מודה לשרה סבירי, מאיר מ' בר-אשר, אורי מלמד ויונתן מרוז שקראו טיוטה
של המאמר. הערותיהם סייעו בידי לשפרו. עיקרי הדברים הוצגו בכנס הבינלאומי
על "הגשר בין יהדות לאיסלאם", שהתקיים באוניברסיטת בר-אילן בטבת תשס"ו
(ינואר 2006).

[1] המחקרים הראשונים בתחום זה הם: Ignaz Goldziher, "Ibn Hud, The Mohammedan
Mystic, and the Jews of Damascus", *JQR* (o.s.) 6 (1894), pp. 218-20; Moritz
Steinschneider, *Die Arabische Literatur der Juden*, Frankfurt a. M. 1902 [reprinted
(Hildesheim 1964), pp. 132-35 (§ 86), 221-25 (§§159-162b)]. מחקרים ראשונים וחשובים
נדפסו כבר במחצית הראשונה של המאה העשרים, וחלקם יוזכר בהערות הבאות.

[2] David S. Ariel, " 'The Eastern Dawn of Wisdom': The Problem of the Relation between
Islamic and Jewish Mysticism", in: David R. Blumenthal (ed.), *Approaches to Judaism in*

א

תוכן העניינים

חלק העברי

תוכן העניינים השלם מודפס בהקדמת הספר

טורים

מחקרים
בהיסטוריה ותרבות יהודית

מוגשים
לד"ר ברנרד לנדר

כרך ראשון

בעריכת
מיכאל שמידמן

טורו קולג'
ניו יורק
תשס"ז

טורים

מחקרים
בהיסטוריה ותרבות יהודית

מוגשים
לד"ר ברנרד לנדר

כרך ראשון